Crossing
Cultures

Crossing Cultures

Readings for Composition

THIRD EDITION

Henry Knepler
Illinois Institute of Technology

Myrna Knepler
Northeastern Illinois University

Macmillan Publishing Company
New York

Editor: Barbara A. Heinssen
Production Supervisors: Eric Newman and Elisabeth Fleshler
Production Manager: Nick Sklitsis
Cover Designer: Robert Freese
Cover Art: "Across the River" painted by Ralph Fasanella.
Courtesy of R. Mark Fasanella.
Photo Researcher: Chris Migdol

This book was set in ITC Garamond and Cochin by Digitype, Inc., and
printed and bound by Halliday Lithograph.
The cover was printed by Phoenix Color Corp.

PHOTO CREDITS: Peter Southwick/Stock, Boston (Part One); © 1981
Andy Levin (Part Two); © Harry Wilks/Stock, Boston (Part Three);
© 1989 Erica Berger/*Newsday* (Part Four); © Eugene Gordon 1987
(Part Five); Library of Congress (Part Six); © Robert A. Isaacs 1988
(Part Seven); © James R. Holland/Stock, Boston (Part Eight);
© Paul Conklin (Part Nine).

Macmillan Publishing Company
866 Third Avenue, New York, New York 10022

Collier Macmillan Canada, Inc.
1200 Eglinton Avenue East, Suite 200
Don Mills, Ontario M3C 3N1

LIBRARY OF CONGRESS CATALOGING-IN-PUBLICATION DATA

Crossing cultures : readings for composition / [compiled by] Henry
    Knepler, Myrna Knepler. — 3rd ed.
        p.   cm.
    ISBN 0-02-365231-4
    1. College readers.   2. English language — Rhetoric.   3. Cross-
cultural studies.   I. Knepler, Henry W.   II. Knepler, Myrna.
PE1417.C75 1991
808'.0427 — dc20   90-32641
                            CIP

Copyright acknowledgments begin on page 457, which constitutes an extension of the
copyright page.

Printing: 4 5 6 7   Year: 2 3 4 5 6 7

*For
Elizabeth,
Elinor, and
Anne*

PREFACE

The preparation of the third edition of our reader *Crossing Cultures* has made us, its editors, realize how far, and how fast, the world has advanced in its need for cross-cultural understanding. In the early 1980s, when we prepared the first edition, it still seemed necessary to justify the development of an anthology on such a theme. In the 1990s, entering freshmen can reasonably be expected to be aware of the significance to themselves of foreign places a student in the 1980s was unlikely to have heard of. They know that Peruvian farmers support "the habit" of Americans, that sweatshops in Singapore imply a loss of jobs in the United States, and that a "peace dividend" in the American budget may depend on what happens in places like Lithuania. Above all, the threat to the environment makes us conscious, more than the threat of war ever did, of the need to interact on a world scale — in fact, of the virtual impossibility not to interact.

Using Cross-Cultural Themes

The success of this book has established the fact that cross-cultural subjects, broadly construed, work well in a composition course. They have a strong impact on students: They challenge accepted beliefs by asking students to consider the lives, ideas, aspirations — and prejudices — of people who are very different from them. At the same time, reading, and having one's classmates read, selections related to one's own culture are likely to heighten self-assurance and stimulate ethnic or racial pride. Of course, *Crossing Cultures* addresses itself to a wider audience than that. It is safe to say that virtually all students will, in their lives and careers, encounter ethnic diversity. In a multiethnic society like that of the United States, they can expect to work with people of diverse backgrounds. Increasingly they are also likely to come in contact with other cultures by working abroad for a time, or with people who come from other parts of the world. For that reason, *Crossing Cultures* includes selections that address themselves to American issues as well as global ones.

vii

Moving to a Global Perspective

The nine parts into which the selections have been organized represent topics that seem to us important to cross-cultural understanding. At the same time we wanted to provide a systematic progression from the more familiar to the more distant. In the earlier parts, therefore, the concentration is on intra-American issues. From these the selections gradually move to global subjects.

Crossing Cultures as a Composition Text

Content that is thematically interesting and challenging is not enough, however, for a reader in composition. To be useful in the fullest sense, such a text has to go beyond ideas to meet the rhetorical requirements. *Crossing Cultures* is designed to meet these requirements. The selections represent the major patterns of organization; they vary widely in length and difficulty; some may be useful as models, others as challenges for argumentation.

It is in this last respect that the third edition has been strengthened in particular. More than before, selections can be used in conjunction for the development of argument. To give one example: We have retained, from the second edition, the essays by Richard Rodriguez and James Fallows that argue their differing views of bilingual education. To these we have added an essay by a major African writer, Ngugi wa Thiong'o, that brings yet another point of view to bear on that subject and at the same time raises an issue that may put yet another piece, "World Language: English," in a new and different light.

As noted previously, the nine parts of the book move thematically from the more to the less familiar, the simpler to the more complex. The same holds for the rhetorical aspect: Each of the earlier parts moves from narration to exposition; in the later parts the personal narratives diminish, and expository and argumentative selections increase both in number and intricacy.

Each selection, except for the poems, is followed by a set of exercises. "Words to Know" singles out words and terms with which students may not be familiar. "Some of the Issues" aids students in a careful reading of the selection. "The Way We Are Told" leads them to an examination of the author's strategies. Each exercise section concludes with "Some Subjects for Essays." Asterisks indicate questions or topics that combine more than one selection or relate to the part-opening photograph.

New in the Third Edition

Thirty percent of the selections are new to this edition. Among the writers included are Toni Morrison and Margaret Atwood, the latter also adding a country (Canada) not previously represented. More selections than previously cross the Pacific Ocean rather than the Atlantic. The increased interest in the "Pacific Rim," particularly China and Japan, led to the inclusion of several new selections. Three new pieces are by very young writers still in college or recently out of it. Two poems and one piece of fiction have been added. A wide range of personal narratives remains one of the strengths of the book.

Headnotes have been expanded, when it seemed appropriate, to include information on the country, the culture, or the history that forms the background of the selection. For the first time, photographs precede each of the nine parts and are tied into one or more selections through the exercises.

Acknowledgments

As was the case with the second edition, reviewers of the book have given much helpful advice on the choice of selections as well as other features. In particular we thank: Steve Adams, University of Minnesota — Duluth; Nancy K. Barry, University of Iowa; Vilma Chemers, California State University — Long Beach; T. Obinkaram Echewa, West Chester University; Susan Feinberg, Illinois Institute of Technology; R. Janie Isackson, DePaul University; Susan Dean Jacobs, DePaul University; Michelle M. Tokarczyk, Goucher College; Joan R. Vandergriff, University of Missouri — Kansas City; Victor Villanueva, Northern Arizona University; Winifred J. Wood, Wellesley College; and Mitsuye Yamada, Cypress College.

We give particular thanks to our editor at Macmillan, Barbara Heinssen. Her constant willingness to give time and thought to this edition has led to several changes that we believe improve the book. Peter A. Knapp, the assistant editor, has been very resourceful in helping us to solve a number of problems. Eric Newman has been an exemplary production supervisor, and Chris Migdol found us a group of remarkable photographs.

CONTENTS

RHETORICAL CONTENTS

Narration (Observation and reporting)

Definition

Classification and Division

Comparison and Contrast

Cause and Effect

Argument and Persuasion

Irony, Humor, and Satire

Fiction

Poetry

Crossing Cultures

PART ONE

Growing Up

As we grow up, our awareness of the world around us gradually expands. The learning process begins at birth and never stops. We get to know our physical surroundings—a crib, perhaps, then a room, a house. We become aware of a parent and learn that if we cry, that parent will do something for us. We also learn that others want things from us; much of the time these demands are designed to stop us from doing what we want at that moment. Communication, we find, works in both directions.

What we learn in those ways depends of course on our environment, though we do not know that in our early lives. Then we believe that our way of talking—our language—is the only one, and that the way things happen is the only way they can be done. For most of us the earliest experiences are confined to one culture. Sooner or later we learn, however, that we coexist with people whose experiences or upbringing differs from ours. The discovery of that fact may come as a shock, particularly when we find at the same time that our culture is in some way not welcomed or accepted, that there is a barrier between ours and "theirs," a barrier that we cannot readily cross.

Each author in Part One confronts that barrier while growing up. Maya Angelou, as a black student in a segregated elementary school in Arkansas in the 1940s, discovers the attitude of the mainstream culture at her graduation from the eighth grade. Maxine Hong Kingston, brought up in a Chinese environment in California, turns silent when she enters public school. Elizabeth Wong, on the other hand, wants to be an "all-American girl" and fights her mother's attempt to have her keep her Chinese background. Jack Agueros believes he is an all-American boy until he finds that there is another, different America across the hill, one where he is not welcome. Maria Muñiz feels deprived of part of her childhood and wants to find it by visiting, though not returning to, her native Cuba. Finally, Countee Cullen speaks simply but tellingly of his first confrontation, at age eight, with prejudice.

GRADUATION

Maya Angelou

Maya Angelou, born Marquerite Johnson in 1928, spent her childhood in Stamps, Arkansas, the small town in which her story is set.
The author of several books of prose and poetry, she has also acted
on stage and screen, hosted a television show, and appeared in the
popular television series "Roots." She has taught and served as
writer-in-residence at several universities and worked as the northern coordinator of the Southern Christian Leadership Conference
at the invitation of Dr. Martin Luther King, Jr.

   This selection is taken from *I Know Why the Caged Bird
Sings* (1970), the first volume in an autobiographical series that
includes *Gather Together in My Name* (1975), *Singin' and
Swingin' and Merry Like Christmas* (1976), and *The Heart of a
Woman* (1981).

   Angelou grew up in a rigidly segregated society. The Civil
War (1861–1865) had ended slavery but had not eliminated
segregation. In fact, several decisions of the United States Supreme
Court reaffirmed its legality. In the case of *Plessy* v. *Ferguson*
(1896) in particular, the Court gave its approval to segregation,
declaring it to be constitutional as long the affected facilities, such
as public schools, were "separate but equal." Schools were separate after that in large parts of the country, but not equal, as
Angelou's memory of the early 1940s demonstrates.

   In 1954 the Supreme Court reversed itself in *Brown* v.
Board of Education, declaring that segregation was "inherently
unequal" and therefore unconstitutional.

The children in Stamps trembled visibly with anticipation. Some adults
were excited too, but to be certain the whole young population had
come down with graduation epidemic. Large classes were graduating
from both the grammar school and the high school. Even those who
were years removed from their own day of glorious release were
anxious to help with preparations as a kind of dry run. The junior
students who were moving into the vacating classes' chairs were tradi-
tion-bound to show their talents for leadership and management. They
strutted through the school and around the campus exerting pressure
on the lower grades. Their authority was so new that occasionally if
they pressed a little too hard it had to be overlooked. After all, next
term was coming, and it never hurt a sixth grader to have a play sister
in the eighth grade, or a tenth-year student to be able to call a twelfth

3

grader Bubba. So all was endured in a spirit of shared understanding. But the graduating classes themselves were the nobility. Like travelers with exotic destinations on their minds, the graduates were remarkably forgetful. They came to school without their books, or tablets or even pencils. Volunteers fell over themselves to secure replacements for the missing equipment. When accepted, the willing workers might or might not be thanked, and it was of no importance to the pregraduation rites. Even teachers were respectful of the now quiet and aging seniors, and tended to speak to them, if not as equals, as beings only slightly lower than themselves. After tests were returned and grades given, the student body, which acted like an extended family, knew who did well, who excelled, and what piteous ones had failed.

Unlike the white high school, Lafayette County Training School   2 distinguished itself by having neither lawn, nor hedges, nor tennis court, nor climbing ivy. Its two buildings (main classrooms, the grade school and home economics) were set on a dirt hill with no fence to limit either its boundaries or those of bordering farms. There was a large expanse to the left of the school which was used alternately as a baseball diamond or a basketball court. Rusty hoops on the swaying poles represented the permanent recreational equipment, although bats and balls could be borrowed from the P.E. teacher if the borrower was qualified and if the diamond wasn't occupied.

Over this rocky area relieved by a few shady tall persimmon trees   3 the graduating class walked. The girls often held hands and no longer bothered to speak to the lower students. There was a sadness about them, as if this old world was not their home and they were bound for higher ground. The boys, on the other hand, had become more friendly, more outgoing. A decided change from the closed attitude they projected while studying for finals. Now they seemed not ready to give up the old school, the familiar paths and classrooms. Only a small percentage would be continuing on to college — one of the South's A & M (agricultural and mechanical) schools, which trained Negro youths to be carpenters, farmers, handymen, masons, maids, cooks and baby nurses. Their future rode heavily on their shoulders, and blinded them to the collective joy that had pervaded the lives of the boys and girls in the grammar school graduating class.

Parents who could afford it had ordered new shoes and ready-   4 made clothes for themselves from Sears and Roebuck or Montgomery Ward. They also engaged the best seamstresses to make the floating graduating dresses and to cut down secondhand pants which would be pressed to a military slickness for the important event.

Oh, it was important, all right. Whitefolks would attend the   5 ceremony, and two or three would speak of God and home, and the Southern way of life, and Mrs. Parsons, the principal's wife, would play the graduation march while the lower-grade graduates paraded down the aisles and took their seats below the platform. The high school seniors would wait in empty classrooms to make their dramatic entrance.

In the Store I was the person of the moment. The birthday girl. The center. Bailey had graduated the year before, although to do so he had to forfeit all pleasures to make up for his time lost in Baton Rouge.   6

My class was wearing butter-yellow piqué dresses, and Momma launched out on mine. She smocked the yoke into tiny crisscrossing puckers, then shirred the rest of the bodice. Her dark fingers ducked in and out of the lemony cloth as she embroidered raised daisies around the hem. Before she considered herself finished she had added a crocheted cuff on the puff sleeves, and a pointy crocheted collar.   7

I was going to be lovely. A walking model of all the various styles of fine hand sewing and it didn't worry me that I was only twelve years old and merely graduating from the eighth grade. Besides, many teachers in Arkansas Negro schools had only that diploma and were licensed to impart wisdom.   8

The days had become longer and more noticeable. The faded beige of former times had been replaced with strong and sure colors. I began to see my classmates' clothes, their skin tones, and the dust that waved off pussy willows. Clouds that lazed across the sky were objects of great concern to me. Their shiftier shapes might have held a message that in my new happiness and with a little bit of time I'd soon decipher. During that period I looked at the arch of heaven so religiously my neck kept a steady ache. I had taken to smiling more often, and my jaws hurt from the unaccustomed activity. Between the two physical sore spots, I suppose I could have been uncomfortable, but that was not the case. As a member of the winning team (the graduating class of 1940) I had outdistanced unpleasant sensations by miles. I was headed for the freedom of open fields.   9

Youth and social approval allied themselves with me and we trammeled memories of slights and insults. The wind of our swift passage remodeled my features. Lost tears were pounded to mud and then to dust. Years of withdrawal were brushed aside and left behind, as hanging ropes of parasitic moss.   10

My work alone had awarded me a top place and I was going to be one of the first called in the graduating ceremonies. On the classroom blackboard, as well as on the bulletin board in the auditorium, there were blue stars and white stars and red stars. No absences, no tardinesses, and my academic work was among the best of the year. I could say the preamble to the Constitution even faster than Bailey. We timed ourselves often: "WethepeopleoftheUnitedStatesinordertoformamore-   11 perfectunion . . ." I had memorized the Presidents of the United States from Washington to Roosevelt in chronological as well as alphabetical order.

My hair pleased me too. Gradually the black mass had lengthened   12
and thickened, so that it kept at last to its braided pattern, and I didn't have to yank my scalp off when I tried to comb it.

Louise and I had rehearsed the exercises until we tired out our-   13
selves. Henry Reed was class valedictorian. He was a small, very black boy with hooded eyes, a long, broad nose and an oddly shaped head. I had admired him for years because each term he and I vied for the best grades in our class. Most often he bested me, but instead of being disappointed I was pleased that we shared top places between us. Like many Southern Black children, he lived with his grandmother, who was as strict as Momma and as kind as she knew how to be. He was courteous, respectful and soft-spoken to elders, but on the playground he chose to play the roughest games. I admired him. Anyone, I reckoned, sufficiently afraid or sufficiently dull could be polite. But to be able to operate at a top level with both adults and children was admirable.

His valedictory speech was entitled "To Be or Not to Be." The   14
rigid tenth-grade teacher had helped him write it. He'd been working on the dramatic stresses for months.

The weeks until graduation were filled with heady activities. A   15
group of small children were to be presented in a play about buttercups and daisies and bunny rabbits. They could be heard throughout the building practicing their hops and their little songs that sounded like silver bells. The older girls (nongraduates, of course) were assigned the task of making refreshments for the night's festivities. A tangy scent of ginger, cinnamon, nutmeg and chocolate wafted around the home economics building as the budding cooks made samples for themselves and their teachers.

In every corner of the workshop, axes and saws split fresh timber   16
as the woodshop boys made sets and stage scenery. Only the graduates were left out of the general bustle. We were free to sit in the library at the back of the building or look in quite detachedly, naturally, on the measures being taken for our event.

Even the minister preached on graduation the Sunday before. His   17
subject was, "Let your light so shine that men will see your good works and praise your Father, Who is in Heaven." Although the sermon was purported to be addressed to us, he used the occasion to speak to backsliders, gamblers and general ne'er-do-wells. But since he had called our names at the beginning of the service we were mollified.

Among Negroes the tradition was to give presents to children   18
going only from one grade to another. How much more important this

was when the person was graduating at the top of the class. Uncle Willie and Momma had sent away for a Mickey Mouse watch like Bailey's. Louise gave me four embroidered handkerchiefs. (I gave her three crocheted doilies.) Mrs. Sneed, the minister's wife, made me an underskirt to wear for graduation, and nearly every customer gave me a nickel or maybe even a dime with the instruction "Keep on moving to higher ground," or some such encouragement.

Amazingly the great day finally dawned and I was out of bed before I knew it. I threw open the back door to see it more clearly, but Momma said, "Sister, come away from that door and put your robe on." 19

I hoped the memory of that morning would never leave me. Sunlight was itself still young, and the day had none of the insistence maturity would bring it in a few hours. In my robe and barefoot in the backyard, under cover of going to see about my new beans, I gave myself up to the gentle warmth and thanked God that no matter what evil I had done in my life He had allowed me to live to see this day. Somewhere in my fatalism I had expected to die, accidentally, and never have the chance to walk up the stairs in the auditorium and gracefully receive my hard-earned diploma. Out of God's merciful bosom I had won reprieve. 20

Bailey came out in his robe and gave me a box wrapped in Christmas paper. He said he had saved his money for months to pay for it. It felt like a box of chocolates, but I knew Bailey wouldn't save money to buy candy when we had all we could want under our noses. 21

He was as proud of the gift as I. It was a soft-leather-bound copy of a collection of poems by Edgar Allan Poe, or, as Bailey and I called him, "Eap." I turned to "Annabel Lee" and we walked up and down the garden rows, the cool dirt between our toes, reciting the beautifully sad lines. 22

Momma made a Sunday breakfast although it was only Friday. After we finished the blessing, I opened my eyes to find the watch on my plate. It was a dream of a day. Everything went smoothly and to my credit. I didn't have to be reminded or scolded for anything. Near evening I was too jittery to attend to chores, so Bailey volunteered to do all before his bath. 23

Days before, we had made a sign for the Store, and as we turned out the lights Momma hung the cardboard over the doorknob. It read clearly: CLOSED. GRADUATION. 24

My dress fitted perfectly and everyone said that I looked like a sunbeam in it. On the hill, going toward the school, Bailey walked behind with Uncle Willie, who muttered, "Go on, Ju." We wanted him to walk ahead with us because it embarrassed him to have to walk so slowly. Bailey said he'd let the ladies walk together, and the men would bring up the rear. We all laughed, nicely. 25

Little children dashed by out of the dark like fireflies. Their 26 crepe-paper dresses and butterfly wings were not made for running and we heard more than one rip, dryly, and the regretful "uh uh" that followed.

The school blazed without gaiety. The windows seemed cold and 27 unfriendly from the lower hill. A sense of ill-fated timing crept over me, and if Momma hadn't reached for my hand I would have drifted back to Bailey and Uncle Willie, and possibly beyond. She made a few slow jokes about my feet getting cold, and tugged me along to the now-strange building.

Around the front steps, assurance came back. There were my 28 fellow "greats," the graduating class. Hair brushed back, legs oiled, new dresses and pressed pleats, fresh pocket handkerchiefs and little handbags, all homesewn. Oh, we were up to snuff, all right. I joined my comrades and didn't even see my family go in to find seats in the crowded auditorium.

The school band struck up a march and all classes filed in as had 29 been rehearsed. We stood in front of our seats, as assigned, and on a signal from the choir director, we sat. No sooner had this been accomplished than the band started to play the national anthem. We rose again and sang the song, after which we recited the pledge of allegiance. We remained standing for a brief minute before the choir director and the principal signaled to us, rather desperately I thought, to take our seats. The command was so unusual that our carefully rehearsed and smooth-running machine was thrown off. For a full minute we fumbled for our chairs and bumped into each other awkwardly. Habits change or solidify under pressure, so in our state of nervous tension we had been ready to follow our usual assembly pattern: the American national anthem, then the pledge of allegiance, then the song every Black person I knew called the Negro National Anthem. All done in the same key, with the same passion and most often standing on the same foot.

Finding my seat at last, I was overcome with a presentiment of 30 worse things to come. Something unrehearsed, unplanned, was going to happen, and we were going to be made to look bad. I distinctly remember being explicit in the choice of pronoun. It was "we," the graduating class, the unit, that concerned me then.

The principal welcomed "parents and friends" and asked the 31 Baptist minister to lead us in prayer. His invocation was brief and punchy, and for a second I thought we were getting back on the high road to right action. When the principal came back to the dais, however, his voice had changed. Sounds always affected me profoundly and the principal's voice was one of my favorites. During assembly it melted and lowed weakly into the audience. It had not been in my plan to listen to him, but my curiosity was piqued and I straightened up to give him my attention.

He was talking about Booker T. Washington, our "late great   32 leader," who said we can be as close as the fingers on the hand, etc. . . . Then he said a few vague things about friendship and the friendship of kindly people to those less fortunate than themselves. With that his voice nearly faded, thin, away. Like a river diminishing to a stream and then to a trickle. But he cleared his throat and said, "Our speaker tonight, who is also our friend, came from Texarkana to deliver the commencement address, but due to the irregularity of the train schedule, he's going to, as they say, 'speak and run.' " He said that we understood and wanted the man to know that we were most grateful for the time he was able to give us and then something about how we were willing always to adjust to another's program, and without more ado — "I give you Mr. Edward Donleavy."

Not one but two white men came through the door offstage. The   33 shorter one walked to the speaker's platform, and the tall one moved over to the center seat and sat down. But that was our principal's seat, and already occupied. The dislodged gentleman bounced around for a long breath or two before the Baptist minister gave him his chair, then with more dignity than the situation deserved, the minister walked off the stage.

Donleavy looked at the audience once (on reflection, I'm sure   34 that he wanted only to reassure himself that we were really there), adjusted his glasses and began to read from a sheaf of papers.

He was glad "to be here and to see the work going on just as it   35 was in the other schools."

At the first "Amen" from the audience I willed the offender to   36 immediate death by choking on the word. But Amens and Yes, sir's began to fall around the room like rain through a ragged umbrella.

He told us of the wonderful changes we children in Stamps had in   37 store. The Central School (naturally, the white school was Central) had already been granted improvements that would be in use in the fall. A well-known artist was coming from Little Rock to teach art to them. They were going to have the newest microscopes and chemistry equipment for their laboratory. Mr. Donleavy didn't leave us long in the dark over who made these improvements available to Central High. Nor were we to be ignored in the general betterment scheme he had in mind.

He said that he had pointed out to people at a very high level that   38 one of the first-line football tacklers at Arkansas Agricultural and Mechanical College had graduated from good old Lafayette County Training School. Here fewer Amens were heard. Those few that did break through lay dully in the air with the heaviness of habit.

He went on to praise us. He went on to say how he had bragged   39
that "one of the best basketball players at Fisk sank his first ball right
here at Lafayette County Training School."

The white kids were going to have a chance to become Galileos   40
and Madame Curies and Edisons and Gauguins, and our boys (the girls
weren't even in on it) would try to be Jesse Owenses and Joe Louises.

Owens and the Brown Bomber were great heroes in our world,   41
but what school official in the white-goddom of Little Rock had the
right to decide that those two men must be our only heroes? Who
decided that for Henry Reed to become a scientist he had to work like
George Washington Carver, as a bootblack, to buy a lousy microscope?
Bailey was obviously always going to be too small to be an athlete, so
which concrete angel glued to what county seat had decided that if my
brother wanted to become a lawyer he had to first pay penance for his
skin by picking cotton and hoeing corn and studying correspondence
books at night for twenty years?

The man's dead words fell like bricks around the auditorium and   42
too many settled in my belly. Constrained by hard-learned manners I
couldn't look behind me, but to my left and right the proud graduating
class of 1940 had dropped their heads. Every girl in my row had found
something new to do with her handkerchief. Some folded the tiny
squares into love knots, some into triangles, but most were wadding
them, then pressing them flat on their yellow laps.

On the dais, the ancient tragedy was being replayed. Professor   43
Parsons sat, a sculptor's reject, rigid. His large, heavy body seemed
devoid of will or willingness, and his eyes said he was no longer with
us. The other teachers examined the flag (which was draped stage
right) or their notes, or the windows which opened on our now-
famous playing diamond.

Graduation, the hush-hush magic time of frills and gifts and   44
congratulations and diplomas, was finished for me before my name
was called. The accomplishment was nothing. The meticulous maps,
drawn in three colors of ink, learning and spelling decasyllabic words,
memorizing the whole of *The Rape of Lucrece*—it was for nothing.
Donleavy had exposed us.

We were maids and farmers, handymen and washerwomen, and   45
anything higher that we aspired to was farcical and presumptuous.

Then I wished that Gabriel Prosser and Nat Turner had killed all   46
whitefolks in their beds and that Abraham Lincoln had been assassinated before the signing of the Emancipation Proclamation, and that
Harriet Tubman had been killed by that blow on her head and Christopher Columbus had drowned in the *Santa María*.

It was awful to be Negro and have no control over my life. It was   47
brutal to be young and already trained to sit quietly and listen to
charges brought against my color with no chance of defense. We

should all be dead. I thought I should like to see us all dead, one on top of the other. A pyramid of flesh with the whitefolks on the bottom, as the broad base, then the Indians with their silly tomahawks and teepees and wigwams and treaties, the Negroes with their mops and recipes and cotton sacks and spirituals sticking out of their mouths. The Dutch children should all stumble in their wooden shoes and break their necks. The French should choke to death on the Louisiana Purchase (1803) while silkworms ate all the Chinese with their stupid pigtails. As a species, we were an abomination. All of us.

Donleavy was running for election, and assured our parents that **48** if he won we could count on having the only colored paved playing field in that part of Arkansas. Also — he never looked up to acknowledge the grunts of acceptance — also, we were bound to get some new equipment for the home economics building and the workshop.

He finished, and since there was no need to give any more than **49** the most perfunctory thank-you's, he nodded to the men on the stage, and the tall white man who was never introduced joined him at the door. They left with the attitude that now they were off to something really important. (The graduation ceremonies at Lafayette County Training School had been a mere preliminary.)

The ugliness they left was palpable. An uninvited guest who **50** wouldn't leave. The choir was summoned and sang a modern arrangement of "Onward, Christian Soldiers," with new words pertaining to graduates seeking their place in the world. But it didn't work. Elouise, the daughter of the Baptist minister, recited "Invictus," and I could have cried at the impertinence of "I am the master of my fate, I am the captain of my soul."

My name had lost its ring of familiarity and I had to be nudged to **51** go and receive my diploma. All my preparations had fled. I neither marched up to the stage like a conquering Amazon, nor did I look in the audience for Bailey's nod of approval. Marguerite Johnson, I heard the name again, my honors were read, there were noises in the audience of appreciation, and I took my place on the stage as rehearsed.

I thought about colors I hated: ecru, puce, lavender, beige and **52** black.

There was shuffling and rustling around me, then Henry Reed **53** was giving his valedictory address, "To Be or Not to Be." Hadn't he heard the whitefolks? We couldn't *be*, so the question was a waste of time. Henry's voice came out clear and strong. I feared to look at him. Hadn't he got the message? There was no "nobler in the mind" for Negroes because the world didn't think we had minds, and they let us know it. "Outrageous fortune"? Now, that was a joke. When the ceremony was over I had to tell Henry Reed some things. That is, if I still cared. Not "rub," Henry, "erase." "Ah, there's the erase." Us.

Henry had been a good student in elocution. His voice rose on **54**

tides of promise and fell on waves of warnings. The English teacher
had helped him to create a sermon winging through Hamlet's soliloquy. To be a man, a doer, a builder, a leader, or to be a tool, an
unfunny joke, a crusher of funky toadstools. I marveled that Henry
could go through with the speech as if we had a choice.

I had been listening and silently rebutting each sentence with my   55
eyes closed; then there was a hush, which in an audience warns that
something unplanned is happening. I looked up and saw Henry Reed,
the conservative, the proper, the A student, turn his back to the audience and turn to us (the proud graduating class of 1940) and sing,
nearly speaking,

> "Lift ev'ry voice and sing
> Till earth and heaven ring
> Ring with the harmonies of Liberty . . ."*

It was the poem written by James Weldon Johnson. It was the music
composed by J. Rosamond Johnson. It was the Negro national anthem.
Out of habit we were singing it.

Our mothers and fathers stood in the dark hall and joined the   56
hymn of encouragement. A kindergarten teacher led the small children
onto the stage and the buttercups and daisies and bunny rabbits
marked time and tried to follow:

> "Stony the road we trod
> Bitter the chastening rod
> Felt in the days when hope, unborn, had died.
> Yet with a steady beat
> Have not our weary feet
> Come to the place for which our fathers sighed?"

Every child I knew had learned that song with his ABC's and   57
along with "Jesus Loves Me This I Know." But I personally had never
heard it before. Never heard the words, despite the thousands of times
I had sung them. Never thought they had anything to do with me.

On the other hand, the words of Patrick Henry had made such an   58
impression on me that I had been able to stretch myself tall and
trembling and say, "I know not what course others may take, but as for
me, give me liberty or give me death."

And now I heard, really for the first time: 59

> "We have come over a way that with tears
> has been watered,
> We have come, treading our path through
> the blood of the slaughtered."

---

*Life Ev'ry Voice and Sing" — words by James Weldon Johnson and music by J. Rosa-
mond Johnson. Copyright by Edward B. Marks Music Corporation. Used by permission.

While echoes of the song shivered in the air, Henry Reed bowed   60
his head, said "Thank you," and returned to his place in the line. The
tears that slipped down many faces were not wiped away in shame.

We were on top again. As always, again. We survived. The depths   61
had been icy and dark, but now a bright sun spoke to our souls. I was
no longer simply a member of the proud graduating class of 1940; I
was a proud member of the wonderful, beautiful Negro race.

EXERCISES

Words to Know

strutted (paragraph 1), exotic (1), rites (1), extended family (1),
pervaded (3), forfeit (6), piqué (7), decipher (9), parasitic (10),
heady (15), fatalism (20), piqued (31), Booker T. Washington (32),
Galileo (40), Madame Curie (40), Edison (40), Gauguin (40), Jesse
Owens (40), Joe Louis (40), Brown Bomber (41), George Washington
Carver (41), *The Rape of Lucrece* (44), Gabriel Prosser (46), Nat
Turner (46), Harriet Tubman (46), abomination (47), perfunctory
(49), palpable (50), "Invictus" (50), ecru (52), puce (52), elocution (54), soliloquy (54), rebutting (55).

Some of the Issues

1. How does Angelou establish the importance of the graduation?
   How does she build it stage by stage?
2. Why does Angelou distinguish between the high school graduates
   (paragraph 3, end) and the eighth-graders like herself? How do
   their attitudes differ? Why is she happier?
3. How does Angelou describe her rising expectations for "the great
   day" in paragraphs 15 through 23?
4. At what point in the narrative do we first get the idea that things
   may be going wrong with the "dream of a day"? What are later
   indications that something is wrong?
5. In paragraph 29 the children are confronted with a change in the
   usual order of things. Why does Angelou make this seem important? Why does the principal "rather desperately" signal for the
   children to sit down?
6. How do the first words Mr. Donleavy says indicate what his
   attitude is?
7. In paragraphs 50 through 60 Angelou describes her shifting
   thoughts and emotions. Explain them in your own words and
   relate them to the conclusion reached in paragraph 61.

The Way We Are Told

8. Paragraph 1 talks about the graduates and their schoolmates. Paragraphs 2 and 3 describe the school. Why does Angelou write in that order? What distinguishes paragraph 1 from 2 and 3 in addition to the content?

9. Why does Angelou introduce Henry Reed so early (paragraphs 12 and 13)?

10. Explain the irony Angelou sees in Henry Reed's "To be or not to be" speech.

Some Subjects for Essays

11. Have you ever experienced an event — a dance, a party, a trip — that you looked forward to and that turned out to be a disaster? Or have you ever dreaded an event, such as an interview or a blind date, that turned out better than you had expected? Tell it, trying to make the reader feel the anticipation and the change through the specific, descriptive details you cite, rather than by direct statements. (You will find that the indirect way — making the reader feel or see the event — is more effective than simply saying, "I was bored" or "I found out it was a great evening after all.")

12. Describe a ceremony you have witnessed or participated in. Do it in two separate essays. In the first, describe the event simply in a neutral way. In the second, tell it from the point of view of a witness or participant.

*13. Read Grace Paley's "The Loudest Voice." Compare Mr. Donleavy's insensitivity to that shown by Shirley's teachers in the story. Cite specific instances to explain similarities and differences.

*14. Read Vine Deloria, Jr.'s "Custer Died for Your Sins." Deloria attacks the people who think they know what Indians want without consulting Indians. How does Angelou treat the same issue?

*15. Look at the photograph facing page 1. What feelings do you think the young woman's face expresses, and how do these feelings relate to the event that is taking place? How does her expression compare to the mood of the narrator in Angelou's "Graduation"? How does it compare to your own feelings about an important rite of passage you have experienced?

---

*Asterisks used in this context denote questions and essay topics that draw on more than one selection or that relate to the part-opening photographs.

GIRLHOOD AMONG GHOSTS

Maxine Hong Kingston

Maxine Hong Kingston's parents came to America from China in the 1930s. She was born in Stockton, California, in 1940 and was graduated from the University of California at Berkeley.

The following selection comes from *The Woman Warrior: Memories of a Girlhood Among Ghosts* (1976), for which Kingston received the National Book Critics Circle Award. The ghosts she refers to are of several kinds: the spirits and demons that Chinese peasants believed in, the ghosts of the dead, and, more significantly, the whole of non-Chinese America, peopled with strange creatures who seem very powerful but not quite human, and whose behavior is often inexplicable.

Kingston continued her autobiography with *China Men* (1981). Since then she has also written *Hawaii One Summer* (1981) and a novel, *Tripmaster Monkey* (1988).

1 Long ago in China, knot-makers tied string into buttons and frogs, and rope into bell pulls. There was one knot so complicated that it blinded the knot-maker. Finally an emperor outlawed this cruel knot, and the nobles could not order it anymore. If I had lived in China, I would have been an outlaw knot-maker.

2 Maybe that's why my mother cut my tongue. She pushed my tongue up and sliced the frenum. Or maybe she snipped it with a pair of nail scissors. I don't remember her doing it, only her telling me about it, but all during childhood I felt sorry for the baby whose mother waited with scissors or knife in hand for it to cry—and then, when its mouth was wide open like a baby bird's, cut. The Chinese say "a ready tongue is an evil."

3 I used to curl up my tongue in front of the mirror and tauten my frenum into a white line, itself as thin as a razor blade. I saw no scars in my mouth. I thought perhaps I had had two frena, and she had cut one. I made other children open their mouths so I could compare theirs to mine. I saw perfect pink membranes stretching into precise edges that looked easy enough to cut. Sometimes I felt very proud that my mother committed such a powerful act upon me. At other times I was terrified —the first thing my mother did when she saw me was to cut my tongue.

15

"Why did you do that to me, Mother?"   4

"I told you."   5

"Tell me again."   6

"I cut it so that you would not be tongue-tied. Your tongue   7
would be able to move in any language. You'll be able to speak
languages that are completely different from one another. You'll be
able to pronounce anything. Your frenum looked too tight to do those
things, so I cut it."

"But isn't 'a ready tongue an evil'?"   8

"Things are different in this ghost country."   9

"Did it hurt me? Did I cry and bleed?"   10

"I don't remember. Probaby."   11

She didn't cut the other children's. When I asked cousins and   12
other Chinese children whether their mothers had cut their tongues
loose, they said, "What?"

"Why didn't you cut my brothers' and sisters' tongues?"   13

"They didn't need it."   14

"Why not? Were theirs longer than mine?"   15

"Why don't you quit blabbering and get to work?"   16

If my mother was not lying she should have cut more, scraped   17
away the rest of the frenum skin, because I have a terrible time talking.
Or she should not have cut at all, tampering with my speech. When I
went to kindergarten and had to speak English for the first time, I
became silent. A dumbness — a shame — still cracks my voice in two,
even when I want to say "hello" casually, or ask an easy question in
front of the check-out counter, or ask directions of a bus driver. I stand
frozen, or I hold up the line with the complete, grammatical sentence
that comes squeaking out at impossible length. "What did you say?"
says the cab driver, or "Speak up," so I have to perform again, only
weaker the second time. A telephone call makes my throat bleed and
takes up that day's courage. It spoils my day with self-disgust when I
hear my broken voice come skittering out into the open. It makes
people wince to hear it. I'm getting better, though. Recently I asked
the postman for special-issue stamps; I've waited since childhood for
postmen to give me some of their own accord. I am making progress,
a little every day.

My silence was thickest — total — during the three years that I   18
covered my school paintings with black paint. I painted layers of black
over houses and flowers and suns, and when I drew on the blackboard,
I put a layer of chalk on top. I was making a stage curtain, and it was
the moment before the curtain parted or rose. The teachers called my
parents to school, and I saw they had been saving my pictures, curling
and cracking, all alike and black. The teachers pointed to the pictures
and looked serious, talked seriously too, but my parents did not under-

stand English. ("The parents and teachers of criminals were executed," said my father.) My parents took the pictures home. I spread them out (so black and full of possibilities) and pretended the curtains were swinging open, flying up, one after another, sunlight underneath, mighty operas.

During the first silent year I spoke to no one at school, did not ask before going to the lavatory, and flunked kindergarten. My sister also said nothing for three years, silent in the playground and silent at lunch. There were other quiet Chinese girls not of our family, but most of them got over it sooner than we did. I enjoyed the silence. At first it did not occur to me I was supposed to talk or to pass kindergarten. I talked at home and to one or two of the Chinese kids in class. I made motions and even made some jokes. I drank out of a toy saucer when the water spilled out of the cup, and everybody laughed, pointing at me, so I did it some more. I didn't know that Americans don't drink out of saucers.

I liked the Negro students (Black Ghosts) best because they laughed the loudest and talked to me as if I were a daring talker too. One of the Negro girls had her mother coil braids over her ears Shanghai-style like mine; we were Shanghai twins except that she was covered with black like my paintings. Two Negro kids enrolled in Chinese school, and the teachers gave them Chinese names. Some Negro kids walked me to school and home, protecting me from the Japanese kids, who hit me and chased me and stuck gum in my ears. The Japanese kids were noisy and tough. They appeared one day in kindergarten, released from concentration camp, which was a tic-tac-toe mark, like barbed wire, on the map.

It was when I found out I had to talk that school became a misery, that the silence became a misery. I did not speak and felt bad each time that I did not speak. I read aloud in first grade, though, and heard the barest whisper with little squeaks come out of my throat. "Louder," said the teacher, who scared the voice away again. The other Chinese girls did not talk either, so I knew the silence had to do with being a Chinese girl.

Reading out loud was easier than speaking because we did not have to make up what to say, but I stopped often, and the teacher would think I'd gone quiet again. I could not understand "I." The Chinese "I" had seven strokes, intricacies. How could the American "I," assuredly wearing a hat like the Chinese, have only three strokes, the middle so straight? Was it out of politeness that this writer left off strokes the way a Chinese has to write her own name small and crooked? No, it was not politeness; "I" is a capital and "you" is lowercase. I stared at the middle line and waited so long for its black center to resolve into tight strokes and dots that I forgot to pronounce it. The other troublesome word was "here," no strong consonant to hang on to, and so flat, when "here" is two mountainous ideographs. The teacher, who had already told me every day how to read "I" and "here" put me in the low corner under the stairs again, where the noisy boys usually sat.

When my second grade class did a play, the whole class went to the auditorium except the Chinese girls. The teacher, lovely and Hawaiian, should have understood about us, but instead left us behind in the classroom. Our voices were too soft or nonexistent, and our parents never signed the permission slips anyway. They never signed anything unnecessary. We opened the door a crack and peeked out, but closed it again quickly. One of us (not me) won every spelling bee, though. 23

I remember telling the Hawaiian teacher, "We Chinese can't sing 'land where our fathers died.'" She argued with me about politics, while I meant because of curses. But how can I have that memory when I couldn't talk? My mother says that we, like the ghosts, have no memories. 24

After American school, we picked up our cigar boxes, in which we had arranged books, brushes, and an inkbox neatly, and went to Chinese school, from 5:00 to 7:30 P.M. There we chanted together, voices rising and falling, loud and soft, some boys shouting, everybody reading together, reciting together and not alone with one voice. When we had a memorization test, the teacher let each of us come to his desk and say the lesson to him privately, while the rest of the class practiced copying or tracing. Most of the teachers were men. The boys who were so well behaved in the American school played tricks on them and talked back to them. The girls were not mute. They screamed and yelled during recess, when there were no rules; they had fistfights. Nobody was afraid of children hurting themselves or of children hurting school property. The glass doors to the red and green balconies with the gold joy symbols were left wide open so that we could run out and climb the fire escapes. We played capture-the-flag in the auditorium, where Sun Yat-sen and Chiang Kai-shek's pictures hung at the back of the stage, the Chinese flag on their left and the American flag on their right. We climbed the teak ceremonial chairs and made flying leaps off the stage. One flag headquarters was behind the glass door and the other on stage right. Our feet drummed on the hollow stage. During recess the teachers locked themselves up in their office with the shelves of books, copybooks, inks from China. They drank tea and warmed their hands at a stove. There was no play supervision. At recess we had the school to ourselves, and also we could roam as far as we could go — downtown, Chinatown stores, home — as long as we returned before the bell rang. 25

At exactly 7:30 the teacher again picked up the brass bell that sat on his desk and swung it over our heads, while we charged down the stairs, our cheering magnified in the stairwell. Nobody had to line up.

Not all of the children who were silent at American school found voice at Chinese school. One new teacher said each of us had to get up and recite in front of the class, who was to listen. My sister and I had memorized the lesson perfectly. We said it to each other at home, one chanting, one listening. The teacher called on my sister to recite first. It was the first time a teacher had called on the second-born to go first. My sister was scared. She glanced at me and looked away; I looked down at my desk. I hoped that she could do it because if she could, then I would have to. She opened her mouth and a voice came out that wasn't a whisper, but it wasn't a proper voice either. I hoped that she would not cry, fear breaking up her voice like twigs underfoot. She sounded as if she were trying to sing though weeping and strangling. She did not pause or stop to end the embarrassment. She kept going until she said the last word, and then she sat down. When it was my turn, the same voice came out, a crippled animal running on broken legs. You could hear splinters in my voice, bones rubbing jagged against one another. I was loud, though. I was glad I didn't whisper. There was one little girl who whispered.

EXERCISES

Words to Know

frenum (paragraph 2), tauten (3), tampering (17), skittering (17), wince (17), intricacies (22), ideographs (22), mute (25), Sun Yat-sen (25), Chiang Kai-shek (25).

Some of the Issues

1. After reading the selection explain why Kingston says in the first paragraph, "In China, I would have been an outlaw knot-maker." Why does she call herself an outlaw? And, considering the legend she tells, why would she have been a knot-maker?
2. "Maybe that's why my mother cut my tongue." That startling sentence introduces a remembered conversation with her mother. Is it possible that the tongue-cutting never took place? What evidence do you find either way?
3. Kingston is silent in some situations but not in others. When is she the one and when the other?
4. How did the American and the Chinese schools differ in the way they were run? In the way they affected the children?

The Way We Are Told

5. Kingston uses several symbols: the knot, the tongue, the Chinese word for *I*. Explain their meaning and use.
6. What is the effect of the first sentence of paragraph 2?
7. Kingston departs from strict chronological order in telling her story. What is the effect?

Some Subjects for Essays

8. Kingston describes times when she was embarrassed or "tongue-tied." Describe a time when you were afraid to speak. Include descriptions of your feelings before, during, and after the incident.
9. Kingston suggests that in Chinese-American culture girls are brought up very differently from boys. In your own experience of the culture in which you were raised does gender make an important difference in upbringing? Give examples in your answer.
*10. Read Richard Rodriguez's "Public and Private Language." Both he and Kingston describe the experience of attending school for the first time with children different from themselves. Compare and contrast their reactions.

THE STRUGGLE
TO BE AN
ALL-AMERICAN GIRL

Elizabeth Wong

Elizabeth Wong's mother insisted that she learn Chinese and be aware of her cultural background. In her essay, which first appeared in the *Los Angeles Times*, Wong vividly portrays her childhood resistance to her mother's wishes and the anger and embarrassment she felt. Chinese school interfered with her being, as she puts it, "an all-American girl." Here, writing as a young adult, she recognizes in herself a sense of the loss.

    Born in 1958, Elizabeth Wong has worked as a reporter for the *Hartford Courant* and the *San Diego Tribune*. She is attending the Tisch School of the Arts at New York University and hopes to become a playwright.

1   It's still there, the Chinese school on Yale Street where my brother and I used to go. Despite the new coat of paint and the high wire fence, the school I knew 10 years ago remains remarkably, stoically the same.

2   Every day at 5 P.M., instead of playing with our fourth- and fifth-grade friends or sneaking out to the empty lot to hunt ghosts and animal bones, my brother and I had to go to Chinese school. No amount of kicking, screaming, or pleading could dissuade my mother, who was solidly determined to have us learn the language of our heritage.

3   Forcibly, she walked us the seven long, hilly blocks from our home to school, depositing our defiant tearful faces before the stern principal. My only memory of him is that he swayed on his heels like a palm tree, and he always clasped his impatient twitching hands behind his back. I recognized him as a repressed maniacal child killer, and knew that it ever saw his hands we'd be in big trouble.

4   We all sat in little chairs in an empty auditorium. The room smelled like Chinese medicine, an imported faraway mustiness. Like ancient mothballs or dirty closets. I hated that smell. I favored crisp new scents. Like the soft French perfume that my American teacher wore in public school.

5   There was a stage far to the right, flanked by an American flag and

the flag of the Nationalist Republic of China, which was also red, white and blue but not as pretty.

Although the emphasis at the school was mainly language — speaking, reading, writing — the lessons always began with an exercise in politeness. With the entrance of the teacher, the best student would tap a bell and everyone would get up, kowtow, and chant, "Sing san ho," the phonetic for "How are you, teacher?"   6

Being ten years old, I had better things to learn than ideographs copied painstakingly in lines that ran right to left from the tip of a *moc but*, a real ink pen that had to be held in an awkward way if blotches were to be avoided. After all, I could do the multiplication tables, name the satellites of Mars, and write reports on "Little Women" and "Black Beauty." Nancy Drew, my favorite book heroine, never spoke Chinese.   7

The language was a source of embarrassment. More times than not, I had tried to disassociate myself from the nagging loud voice that followed me wherever I wandered in the nearby American supermarket outside Chinatown. The voice belonged to my grandmother, a fragile woman in her seventies who could outshout the best of the street vendors. Her humor was raunchy, her Chinese rhythmless, patternless. It was quick, it was loud, it was unbeautiful. It was not like the quiet, lilting romance of French or the gentle refinement of the American South. Chinese sounded pedestrian. Public.   8

In Chinatown, the comings and goings of hundreds of Chinese on their daily tasks sounded chaotic and frenzied. I did not want to be thought of as mad, as talking gibberish. When I spoke English, people nodded at me, smiled sweetly, said encouraging words. Even the people in my culture would cluck and say that I'd do well in life. "My, doesn't she move her lips fast," they would say, meaning that I'd be able to keep up with the world outside Chinatown.   9

My brother was even more fanatical than I about speaking English. He was especially hard on my mother, criticizing her, often cruelly, for her pidgin speech — smatterings of Chinese scattered like chop suey in her conversation. "It's not 'What it is,' Mom," he'd say in exasperation. "It's 'What *is* it, what *is* it, what *is* it!'" Sometimes Mom might leave out an occasional "the" or "a," or perhaps a verb of being. He would stop her in mid-sentence: "Say it again, Mom. Say it right." When he tripped over his own tongue, he'd blame it on her: "See, Mom, it's all your fault. You set a bad example."   10

What infuriated my mother most was when my brother cornered her on her consonants, especially "r." My father had played a cruel joke on Mom by assigning her an American name that her tongue wouldn't allow her to say. No matter how hard she tried, "Ruth" always ended up "Luth" or "Roof."   11

After two years of writing with a *moc but* and reciting words with   12
multiples of meanings, I finally was granted a cultural divorce. I was
permitted to stop Chinese school.

I thought of myself as multicultural. I preferred tacos to egg rolls;   13
I enjoyed Cinco de Mayo more than Chinese New Year.

At last, I was one of you; I wasn't one of them.   14

Sadly, I still am.   15

EXERCISES

Words to Know

stoically (paragraph 1), dissuade (2), defiant (3), stern (3), maniacal
(3), mustiness (4), kowtow (6), phonetic (6), ideographs (7), disassociate (8), raunchy (8), pedestrian (8), chaotic (9), frenzied (9),
gibberish (9), fanatical (10), pidgin (10), smatterings (10), exasperation (10), infuriated (11), multicultural (13), *Cinco de Mayo*—fifth
of May: a Mexican national holiday (13).

Some of the Issues

1. Cite some of the characteristics of the Chinese school as Wong
   describes it; how does it differ from her American school?
2. Why was the Chinese language "a source of embarrassment" to
   Wong? What are her feelings about speaking English?
3. Consider the last sentence: "Sadly, I still am." Why "sadly"?
*4. Read Maxine Hong Kingston's "Girlhood Among Ghosts." Com-
   pare Kingston's attitude toward Chinese school with Wong's.
*5. Read Maria Muñiz's "Back, but Not Home." What similarities do
   you notice in her experiences and Wong's? What differences?

The Way We Are Told

6. Consider the title. To what extent does Wong succeed in becoming the "all-American Girl" she wanted to be? Explain why the
   title could be considered ironic.
7. What details does Wong give about her experience in Chinese
   school to make her feelings explicit? What senses does she appeal
   to?
8. How does the description of the principal in paragraph 3 reflect
   the fact that Wong sees him through the eyes of a child?
9. In paragraph 14 whom do "you" and "them" refer to? What is
   their effect?

10. Wong does not state a thesis directly. Nevertheless a thesis statement that sums up the essay could be constructed. What might the thesis be? What do you think the author would gain or lose by stating it directly?

Some Subjects for Essays

11. Describe an experience you disliked. Try like Wong to build your case by the way you describe the details.
*12. Read Maria Muñiz's "Back, but Not Home." Compare Wong's and Muñiz's attitudes toward their respective cultures. How does each woman's experience explain her attitude?

HALFWAY TO DICK AND JANE: A PUERTO RICAN PILGRIMAGE

Jack Agueros

Dick and Jane are no longer with us, but generations of American children learned to read with them. In Agueros's childhood they were the central characters in the most popular first-grade reader: two children with their dog Spot, their aproned mother keeping house, and their pipe-smoking father going out to earn the money that would keep the family firmly anchored to the middle class. They were a kindly, friendly family living the American Dream in an immaculate house with a white picket fence. Agueros speaks not only for himself but for many others when he says that he never got more than halfway toward that dreamland. In fact, it receded further as he was growing up.

Jack Agueros was born in New York City in 1934 of parents who had recently migrated from the island of Puerto Rico. He grew up in Spanish Harlem, was graduated from Brooklyn College, and has served in the administration of New York City. The following selection was his first published work.

Puerto Rico, conquered by Spain in the early sixteenth century, became part of the United States as a result of the Spanish–American War (1898). Since 1917, Puerto Ricans have been U.S. citizens. They elect their governor and legislature but cannot vote for president. A resident commissioner (without vote) represents them in the U.S. Congress. Many Puerto Ricans have come to the mainland either to settle or to work for a time.

I was born in Harlem in 1934. We lived on 111th Street off Fifth   1
Avenue. It was a block of mainly three-story buildings—with brick fronts, or brownstone, or limestone imitations of brownstone. Our apartment was a three-room first-floor walk-up. It faced north and had three windows on the street, none in back. There was a master bedroom, a living room, a kitchen-dining room, a foyer with a short hall, and a bathroom. In the kitchen there was an air shaft to evacuate cooking odors and grease—we converted it to a chimney for Santa Claus.

The kitchen was dominated by a large Victorian china closet, and   2

25

the built-in wall shelves were lined with oilcloth, trimmed with ruffle, both decorated by brilliant and miniature fruits. Prominent on a wall of the kitchen was a large reproduction of a still life, a harvest table full of produce, framed and under glass. From it, I learned to identify apples, pumpkins, bananas, pears, grapes, and melons, and "peaches without worms." A joke between my mother and me. (A peach we had bought in the city market, under the New Haven's elevated tracks, bore, like the trains above, passengers.)

On one shelf of the kitchen, over the stove, there was a lineup of   3
ceramic canisters that carried words like "nutmeg," "ginger," and "basil." I did not know what those words meant and I don't know if my mother did either. "Spices," she would say, and that was that. They were of a yellow color that was not unlike the yellow of the stove. The kitchen was itself painted yellow, I think, very pale. But I am sure of one thing, it was not "Mickey Moused." "Mickey Mousing" was a technique used by house painters to decorate the areas of the walls that were contained by wood molding. Outside the molding they might paint a solid green. Inside the wood mold, the same solid green. Then with a twisted-up rag dipped in a lighter green they would trace random patterns.

We never used wallpaper or rugs. Our floors were covered with   4
linoleum in every room. My father painted the apartment every year before Christmas, and in addition, he did all the maintenance, doing his own plastering and plumbing. No sooner would we move into an apartment than my father would repair holes or cracks, and if there were bulges in the plaster, he would break them open and redo the area—sometimes a whole wall. He would immediately modify the bathrooms to add a shower with separate valves, and usually as a routine matter, he cleaned out all the elbow traps, and changed all the washers on faucets. This was true of the other families in the buildings where I lived. Not a December came without a painting of the apartment.

We had Louis XIV furniture in the living room, reflected in the   5
curved glass door and curved glass sides of the china closet. On the walls of the living room hung two prints that I loved. I would spend hours playing games with my mother based on the pictures, making up stories, etc. One day at Brooklyn College, a slide projector slammed, and I awoke after having dozed off during a dull lecture to see Van Gogh's "The Gleaners" on the screen. I almost cried. Another time I came across the other print in a book. A scene of Venice by Canaletto.

The important pieces of the living room, for me, were a Detrola   6
radio with magic-eye tuning and the nightingale, Keero. The nightingale and the radio went back before my recollection. The bird could not stop singing, and people listened on the sidewalk below and came upstairs offering to buy Keero.

The Detrola, shaped like a Gothic arch with inlaid woodwork, was a great source of entertainment for the family. I memorized all the hit songs sung by Libertad Lamarque and Carlos Gardel. Sundays I listened to the Canary Hour presented by Hartz Mountain Seed Company. Puppy, a white Spitz, was my constant companion. Puppy slept at the foot of my bed from the first day he came to our house till the day he died, when I was eleven or twelve and he was seven or eight. 7

I am an only child. My parents and I always talked about my becoming a doctor. The law and politics were not highly regarded in my house. Lawyers, my mother would explain, had to defend people whether they were guilty or not, while politicians, my father would say, were all crooks. A doctor helped everybody, rich and poor, white and black. If I became a doctor, I could study hay fever and find a cure for it, my godmother would say. Also, I could take care of my parents when they were old. I liked the idea of helping, and for nineteen years my sole ambition was to study medicine. 8

My house had books, not many, but my parents encouraged me to read. As I became a good reader they bought books for me and never refused me money for their purchase. My father once built a bookcase for me. It was an important moment, for I had always believed that my father was not too happy about my being a bookworm. The atmosphere at home was always warm. We seemed to be a popular family. We entertained frequently, with two standing parties a year — at Christmas and for my birthday. Parties were always large. My father would dismantle the beds and move all the furniture so that the full two rooms could be used for dancing. My mother would cook up a storm, particularly at Christmas. *Pasteles*, *lechon asado*, *arroz con gandules*, and a lot of *coquito* to drink (meat-stuffed plantain, roast pork, rice with pigeon peas, and coconut nog). My father always brought in a band. They played without compensation and were guests at the party. They ate and drank and danced while a victrola covered the intermissions. One year my father brought home a whole pig and hung it in the foyer doorway. He and my mother prepared it by rubbing it down with oil, oregano, and garlic. After preparation, the pig was taken down and carried over to a local bakery where it was cooked and returned home. Parties always went on till daybreak, and in addition to the band, there were always volunteers to sing and declaim poetry. 9

My mother kept an immaculate household. Bedspreads (chenille seemed to be very in) and lace curtains, washed at home like everything else, were hung up on huge racks with rows of tight nails. The racks were assembled in the living room, and the moisture from the wet bedspreads would fill the apartment. In a sense, that seems to be the lasting image of that period of my life. The house was clean. The neighbors were clean. The streets, with few cars, were clean. The buildings were clean and uncluttered with people on the stoops. 10

The park was clean. The visitors to my house were clean, and the relationships that my family had with other Puerto Rican families, and the Italian families that my father had met through baseball and my mother through the garment center, were clean. Second Avenue was clean and most of the apartment windows had awnings. There was always music, there seemed to be no rain, and snow did not become slush. School was fun, we wrote essays about how grand America was, we put up hunchbacked cats at Halloween, we believed Santa Claus visited everyone. I believed everyone was Catholic. I grew up with dogs, nightingales, my godmother's guitar, rocking chair, cat, guppies, my father's occasional roosters, kept in a cage on the fire escape. Laundry delivered and collected by horse and wagon, fruits and vegetables sold the same way, windowsill refrigeration in winter, iceman and box in summer. The police my friends, likewise the teachers.

In short, the first seven or so years of my life were not too great a   11
variation on Dick and Jane, the school book figures who, if my memory serves me correctly, were blond Anglo-Saxons, not immigrants, not migrants like the Puerto Ricans, and not the children of either immigrants or migrants.

My family moved in 1941 to Lexington Avenue into a larger   12
apartment where I could have my own room. It was a light, sunny, railroad flat on the top floor of a well-kept building. I transferred to a new school, and whereas before my classmates had been mostly black, the new school had few blacks. The classes were made up of Italians, Irish, Jews, and a sprinkling of Puerto Ricans. My block was populated by Jews, Italians, and Puerto Ricans.

And then a whole series of different events began. I went to   13
junior high school. We played in the backyards, where we tore down fences to build fires to cook stolen potatoes. We tore up whole hedges, because the green tender limbs would not burn when they were peeled, and thus made perfect skewers for our stolen "mickies." We played tag in the abandoned buildings, tearing the plaster off the walls, tearing the wire lath off the wooden slats, tearing the wooden slats themselves, good for fires, for kites, for sword fighting. We ran up and down the fire escapes playing tag and over and across many rooftops. The war ended and the heavy Puerto Rican migration began. The Irish and the Jews disappeared from the neighborhood. The Italians tried to consolidate east of Third Avenue.

What caused the clean and open world to end? Many things. Into   14
an ancient neighborhood came pouring four to five times more people than it had been designed to hold. Men who came running at the promise of jobs were jobless as the war ended. They were confused. They could not see the economic forces that ruled their lives as they drank beer on the corners, reassuring themselves of good times to

come while they were hell-bent toward alcoholism. The sudden surge in numbers caused new resentments, and prejudice was intensified. Some were forced to live in cellars, and were then characterized as cave dwellers. Kids came who were confused by the new surroundings; their Puerto Ricanness forced us against a mirror asking, "If they are Puerto Ricans, what are we?" and thus they confused us. In our confusion we were sometimes pathetically reaching out, sometimes pathologically striking out. Gangs. Drugs. Wine. Smoking. Girls. Dances and slow-drag music. Mambo. Spics, Spooks, and Wops. Territories, brother gangs, and war councils establishing rules for right of way on blocks and avenues and for seating in the local theater. Pegged pants and zip guns. Slang.

Dick and Jane were dead, man. Education collapsed. Every 15 classroom had ten kids who spoke no English. Black, Italian, Puerto Rican relations in the classroom were good, but we all knew we couldn't visit one another's neighborhoods. Sometimes we could not move too freely within our own blocks. On 109th, from the lamp post west, the Latin Aces, and from the lamp post east, the Senecas, the "club" I belonged to. The kids who spoke no English became known as Marine Tigers, picked up from a popular Spanish song. (The *Marine Tiger* and the *Marine Shark* were two ships that sailed from San Juan to New York and brought over many, many migrants from the island.)

The neighborhood had its boundaries. Third Avenue and east, 16 Italian. Fifth Avenue and west, black. South, there was a hill on 103rd Street known locally as Cooney's Hill. When you got to the top of the hill, something strange happened: America began, because from the hill south was where the "Americans" lived. Dick and Jane were not dead; they were alive and well in a better neighborhood.

When, as a group of Puerto Rican kids, we decided to go swim- 17 ming to Jefferson Park Pool, we knew we risked a fight and a beating from the Italians. And when we went to La Milagrosa Church in Harlem, we knew we risked a fight and a beating from the blacks. But when we went over Cooney's Hill, we risked dirty looks, disapproving looks, and questions from the police like, "What are you doing in this neighborhood?" and "Why don't you kids go back where you belong?"

Where we belonged! Man, I had written compositions about 18 America. Didn't I belong on the Central Park tennis courts, even if I didn't know how to play? Couldn't I watch Dick play? Weren't these policemen working for me too?

Junior high school was a waste. I can say with 90 per cent 19 accuracy that I learned nothing. The woodshop was used to manufacture stocks for "home-mades" after Macy's stopped selling zipguns. We went from classroom to classroom answering "here," and trying to be "good." The math class was generally permitted to go to the gym after roll call. English was still a good class. Partly because of a damn good, tough teacher named Miss Beck, and partly because of the grade-number system (7-1 the smartest seventh grade and 7-12, the dumbest). Books were left in school, there was little or no homework, and the whole thing seemed to be a holding operation until high school. Somehow or other, I passed the entrance exam to Brooklyn Technical High School. But I couldn't cut the mustard, either academically or with the "American" kids. After one semester, I came back to PS 83, waited a semester, and went on to Benjamin Franklin High School.

I still wanted to study medicine and excelled in biology. English was always an interesting subject, and I still enjoyed writing compositions and reading. In the neighborhood it was becoming a problem being categorized as a bookworm and as one who used "Sunday words," or "big words." I dug school, but I wanted to be one of the boys more. I think the boys respected my intelligence, despite their ribbing. Besides which, I belonged to a club with a number of members who were interested in going to college, and so I wasn't so far out.   20

My introduction to marijuana was in junior high school in 1948. A kid named Dixie from 124th street brought a pack of joints to school and taught about twelve guys to smoke. He told us we could buy joints at a quarter each or five for a dollar. Bombers, or thicker cigarettes, were thirty-five cents each or three for a dollar. There were a lot of experimenters, but not too many buyers. Actually, among the boys there was a strong taboo on drugs, and the Spanish word "*motto*" was a term of disparagement. Many clubs would kick out members who were known to use drugs. Heroin was easily available, and in those days came packaged in capsules or "caps" which sold for fifty cents each. Method of use was inhalation through the nose, or "sniffing," or "snorting."   21

I still remember vividly the first kid I ever saw who was mainlining. Prior to this encounter, I had known of "skin-popping," or subcutaneous injection, but not of mainlining. Most of the sniffers were afraid of skin-popping because they knew of the danger of addiction. They seemed to think that you could not become addicted by sniffing.   22

I went over to 108th Street and Madison where we played softball on an empty lot. This kid came over who was maybe sixteen or seventeen and asked us if we wanted to buy Horse. He started telling us about shooting up and showed me his arms. He had tracks, big black marks on the inside of his arm from the inner joint of the elbow down to his wrist and then over onto the back of his hand. I was stunned. Then he said, "That's nothing, man. I ain't hooked, and I ain't no junky. I can stop anytime I want to." I believe that he believed what he was saying. Invariably the kids talking about their drug experiences would say over and over, "I ain't hooked. I can stop anytime."   23

But they didn't stop; and the drug traffic grew greater and more   24
open. Kids were smoking on the corners and on the stoops. Deals were
made on the street, and you knew fifteen places within a block radius
where you could buy anything you wanted. Cocaine never seemed to
catch on although it was readily available. In the beginning, the kids
seemed to be able to get money for stuff easily. As the number of
shooters grew and the prices went up, the kids got more desperate and
apartment robbing became a real problem.

More of the boys began to leave school. We didn't use the term   25
drop out; rather, a guy would say one day, after forty-three truancies,
"I'm quitting school." And so he would. It was an irony, for what was
really happening was that after many years of being rejected, ignored,
and shuffled around by the school, the kid wanted to quit. Only you
can't quit something you were never a part of, nor can you drop out if
you were never in.

Some kids lied about their age and joined the army. Most just   26
hung around. Not drifting to drugs or crime or to work either. They
used to talk about going back at night and getting the diploma. I
believe that they did not believe they could get their diplomas. They
knew that the schools had abandoned them a long time ago — that to
get the diploma meant starting all over again and that was impossible.
Besides, day or night, it was the same school, the same staff, the same
shit. But what do you say when you are powerless to get what you
want, and what do you say when the other side has all the cards and
writes all the rules? You say, "Tennis is for fags," and "School is for
fags."

My mother leads me by the hand and carries a plain brown   27
shopping bag. We enter an immense airplane hangar. Structural steel
crisscrosses on the ceiling and walls; large round and square rivets
look like buttons or bubbles of air trapped in the girders. There are
long metallic counters with people bustling behind them. It smells of
C.N. disinfectant. Many people stand on many lines up to these
counters; there are many conversations going on simultaneously. The
huge space plays tricks with voices and a very eerie combination of
sounds results. A white cabbage is rolled down a counter at us. We
retaliate by throwing down stamps.

For years I thought that sequence happened in a dream. The   28
rolling cabbage rolled in my head, and little unrelated incidents
seemed to bring it to the surface of my mind. I could not understand
why I remembered a once-dreamt dream so vividly. I was sixteen when
I picked up and read Freud's *The Interpretation of Dreams*. One part
I understood immediately and well, sex and symbolism. In no time, I
had hung my shingle; Streetcorner Analyst. My friends would tell me
their dreams and with the most outrageous sexual explanations we

laughed whole evenings away. But the rolling cabbage could not be stopped and neither quack analysis nor serious thought could explain it away. One day I asked my mother if she knew anything about it.

"That was home relief, 1937 or 1938. You were no more than   29
four years old then. Your farther had been working at a restaurant and I had a job downtown. I used to take you every morning to Dona Eduvije who cared for you all day. She loved you very much, and she was very clean and neat, but I used to cry on my way to work, wishing I could stay home with my son and bring him up like a proper mother would. But I guess I was fated to be a workhorse. When I was pregnant, I would get on the crowded subway and go to work. I would get on a crowded elevator up. Then down. Then back on the subway. Every day I was afraid that the crowd would hurt me, that I would lose my baby. But I had to work. I worked for the WPA right into my ninth month."

My mother was telling it "like it was," and I sat stupefied, for I   30
could not believe that what she said applied to the time I thought of as open and clean. I had been existing in my life like a small plant in a bell jar, my parents defining my awareness. There were things all around me I could not see.

"When you were born we had been living as boarders. It was hard   31
to find an apartment, even in Harlem. You saw signs that said 'No Renting to Colored or Spanish.' That meant Puerto Ricans. We used to say, 'This is supposed to be such a great country? But with a new baby we were determined not to be boarders and we took an apartment on 111th Street. Soon after we moved, I lost my job because my factory closed down. Your father was making seven or eight dollars a week in a terrible job in a carpet factory. They used to clean rugs, and your father's hands were always in strong chemicals. You know how funny some of his fingernails are? It was from that factory. He came home one night and he was looking at his fingers, and he started saying that he didn't come to this country to lose his hands. He wanted to hold a bat and play ball and he wanted to work — but he didn't want to lose his hands. So he quit the job and went to a restaurant for less pay. With me out of work, a new apartment and therefore higher rent, we couldn't manage. Your father was furious when I mentioned home relief. He said he would rather starve than go on relief. But I went and filled out the papers and answered all the questions and swallowed my pride when they treated me like an intruder. I used to say to them, 'Find me a job — get my husband a better job — we don't want home relief.' But we had to take it. And all that mess with the stamps in exchange for food. And they used to have weekly 'specials' sort of — but a lot of things were useless — because they were American food. I don't re-member if we went once a week or once every two weeks. You were so small I don't know how you remember that place and the long lines. It

didn't last long because your father had everybody trying to find him a better job and finally somebody did. Pretty soon I went into the WPA and thank God, we never had to deal with those people again. I don't know how you remember that place, but I wish you didn't. I wish I could forget that home relief thing myself. It was the worst time for your father and me. He still hates it.

(He still hates it and so do many people. The expressions, "I'd   32 rather starve than go on welfare" is common in the Puerto Rican community. This characteristic pride is well chronicled throughout Spanish literature. For example, one episode of *Lazarillo de Tormes*, the sixteenth-century picaresque novel, tells of a squire who struts around all day with his shiny sword and pressed cape. At night the squire takes food from the boy, Lazarillo — who has begged or stolen it — explaining that it is not proper for a squire to beg or steal, or even to work! Without Lazarillo to feed him, the squire would probably starve.)

"You don't know how hard it was being married to your father   33 then. He was young and very strong and very active and he wanted to work. Welfare deeply disturbed him, and I was afraid that he would actually get very violent if an investigator came to the house. They had a terrible way with people, like throwing that cabbage, that was the way they gave you everything, the way we used to throw the kitchen slop to the pigs in Puerto Rico. Some giving! Your father was, is, *muy macho,* and I used to worry if anybody says anything or gives him that why-do-you-people-come-here-to-ruin-things look he'll be in jail for thirty years. He almost got arrested once when you were just a baby. We went to a hospital clinic — I don't remember now if it was Sydenham or Harlem Hospital — you had a swelling around your throat — and the doctor told me, 'Put on cold compresses.' I said I did that and it didn't help. The doctor said, 'Then put hot compresses.' Your father blew up. In his broken English, he asked the doctor to do that to his mother, and then invited him to transfer over to the stable on 104th Street. 'You do better with horses — maybe they don't care what kind of compresses they get.'

"One morning your father tells me, 'I got a new job. I start today   34 driving a truck delivering soft drinks.' That night I ask him about the job — he says, 'I quit — bunch of Mafia — I went to the first four places on my list and each storeowner said, "I didn't order any soda." So I got the idea real fast. The Mafia was going to leave soda in each place and then make the guys buy from them only. As soon as I figured it out, I took the truck back, left it parked where I got it, and didn't even say good-bye.' The restaurant took him back. They liked him. The chef used to give him eggs and meats; it was very important to us. Your father never could keep still (still can't), so he was loved wherever he worked. I feel sorry for people on welfare — forget about the cabbage — I never should have taken you there.''

My father and I are walking through East Harlem, south down Lexington from 112th toward 110th, in 1952. Saturday in late spring, I am eighteen years old, sun brilliant on the streets, people running back and forth on household errands. My father is telling me a story about how back in nineteen thirty something, we were very poor and Con Ed light meters were in every apartment. ''The Puerto Ricans, maybe everybody else, would hook up a shunt wire around the meter, specially in the evenings when the use was heavy — that way you didn't pay for all the electric you used. We called it '*pillo*' (thief).'' 35

We arrive at 110th Street and all the cart vendors are there peddling plantains, avocados, yams, various subtropical roots. I make a casual remark about how foolish it all seemed, and my father catches that I am looking down on them. ''Are they stealing?'' he asks. ''Are they selling people colored water? Aren't they working honestly? Are they any different from a bank president? Aren't they hung like you and me? They are *machos*, and to be respected. Don't let college go to your head. You think a Ph.D. is automatically better than a peddler? Remember where you come from — poor people. I mopped floors for people and I wasn't ashamed, but I never let them look down on me. Don't you look down on anybody.'' 36

We walk for a way in silence, I am mortified, but he is not angry. ''One day I decide to play a joke on your mother. I come home a little early and knock. When she says 'Who?' I say 'Edison man.' Well, there is this long silence and then a scream. I open the door and run in. Your mother's on a chair, in tears, her right arm black from pinky to elbow. She ran to take the *pillo* out, but in her nervousness she got a very slight shock, the black from the spark. She never has forgiven me. After that, I always thought through my jokes.'' 37

We walk some more and he says, ''I'll tell you another story. This one on me. I was twenty-five years old and was married to your mother. I took her down to Puerto Rico to meet Papa and Mama. We were sitting in the living room, and I remember it like it happened this morning. The room had rattan furniture very popular in that time. Papa had climbed in rank back to captain and had a new house. The living room had double doors which opened onto a large *balcón*. At the other end of the room you could see the dining table with a beautiful white handmade needlework cloth. We were sitting and talking and I took out a cigarette. I was smoking Chesterfields then. No sooner had I lit up than Papa got up, came over, and smacked me in the face. 'You haven't received my permission to smoke,' he said. Can you imagine how I felt?'' So my father dealt with his love for me through lateral 38

actions: building bookcases, and through tales of how he got his wounds, he anointed mine.

What is a migration? What does it happen to? Why are the Eskimos still dark after living in that snow all these centuries? Why don't they have a word for snow? What things are around me with such high saturation that I have not named them? What is a migration? If you rob my purse, are you really a fool? Can a poor boy really be president? In America? Of anything? If he is not white? Should one man's achievement fulfill one million people? Will you let us come near your new machine: after all, there is no more ditch digging? What is a migration? What does it happen to? 39

The most closely watched migrants of this world are birds. Birds migrate because they get bored singing in the same place to the same people. And they see that the environment gets hostile. Men move for the same reasons. When a Puerto Rican comes to America, he comes looking for a job. He takes the cold as one of a negative series of givens. The mad hustle, the filthy city, filthy air, filthy housing, sardine transportation, are in the series. He knows life will be tough and dangerous. But he thinks he can make a buck. And in his mind, there is only one tableau: himself retired, owner of his home in Puerto Rico, chickens cackling in the back yard. 40

It startles me still, though it has been five years since my parents went back to the island. I never believed them. My father, driving around New York for the Housing Authority, knowing more streets in more boroughs than I do, and my mother, curious in her later years about museums and theaters, and reading my books as fast as I would put them down, then giving me cryptic reviews. Salinger is really silly (*Catcher in the Rye*), but entertaining. That evil man deserved to die (*Moby Dick*). He's too much (Dostoevski in *Crime and Punishment*). I read this when I was a little girl in school (*Hamlet* and *Macbeth*). It's too sad for me (*Cry, the Beloved Country*). 41

My father, intrigued by the thought of passing the foreman's exam, sitting down with a couple of arithmetic books, and teaching himself at age fifty-five to do work problems and mixture problems and fractions and decimals, and going into the civil service exam and scoring a seventy-four and waiting up one night for me to show me three poems he had written. These two cosmopolites, gladiators without skills or language, battling hostile environments and prejudiced people and systems, had graduated from Harlem to the Bronx, had risen into America's dream-cherished lower middle class, and then put it down for Puerto Rico after thirty plus years. 42

What is a migration, when is it not just a long visit? 43

I was born in Harlem, and I live downtown. And I am a migrant, 44 for if a migration is anything, it is a state of mind. I have known those Eskimos who lived in America twenty and thirty years and never voted, never attended a community meeting, never filed a complaint against a landlord, never informed the police when they were robbed or swindled, or when their daughters were molested. Never appeared at the State or City Commission on Human Rights, never reported a business fraud, never, in other words, saw the snow.

And I am very much a migrant because I am still not quite at   45
home in America. Always there are hills; on the other side — people inclined to throwing cabbages. I cannot "earn and return" — there is no position for me in my father's tableau.

However, I approach the future with optimism. Fewer Puerto   46
Ricans like Eskimos, a larger number of leaders like myself, trained in the university, tempered in the ghetto, and with a vision of America moving from its unexecuted policy to a society open and clean, accessible to anyone.

Dick and Jane? They, too, were tripped by the society, and in our   47
several ways, we are all still migrating.

EXERCISES

Words to Know

Harlem (paragraph 1), evacuate (1), Victorian (2), Louis XIV furniture (5), Van Gogh (5), Canaletto (5), compensation (9), foyer (9), immaculate (10), Anglo-Saxon (11), railroad flat (12), pathologically (14), disparagement (21), subcutaneous (22), immense (27), stupefied (30), mortified (37), lateral (38), anointed (38), migration (39), saturation (39), tableau (40), cryptic (41), cosmopolites (42), gladiators (42).

Some of the Issues

1. The first seven paragraphs describe Agueros's first house: its layout, its furnishings, and decorations. What impression does Agueros's description give you? Cite details that contribute to this impression.
2. In paragraph 4 Agueros lists the activities of his father in the home. In paragraph 10 he does the same for his mother's work. How do their roles differ? Are these differences similar to those in homes you know?

3. What is the key word in paragraph 10? How does it contribute to the impression the author gives of his childhood?

4. In paragraph 11 Agueros sums up his feelings about his childhood. How do the preceding paragraphs, and paragraph 10 in particular, justify that conclusion?

5. Compare the early experiences of Agueros, as he remembers them, with his experiences in junior high. "What caused the clean and open world to end?"

6. Explain what Agueros means when he says, "Their Puerto Ricanness forced us against a mirror, asking, 'If they are Puerto Rican, what are we?'"

7. Paragraphs 13 through 26 describe the author's progression through junior high and high school. What changes does he record? What are the way stations?

8. During the Great Depression of the 1930s Agueros's family went on relief. Much later he finds out about that time from his mother when he learns that the story of the cabbage (27) was not a dream. Compare that adult experience with his recollection of childhood in paragraph 10. Which is the real dream world?

9. In paragraphs 35 through 38 Agueros describes a talk with his father. What do we learn from their conversation?

10. In the last part of the essay Agueros repeatedly asks, "What is a migration?" What does he mean by that question? In what ways has he remained a migrant? What is he trying to tell the reader about migration?

*11. Which family is more distant, in your opinion, from "mainstream" America: Agueros's or Kingston's as described in "Girlhood Among Ghosts"? Explain.

The Way We Are Told

12. Find the various references to Dick and Jane in the text. How does the author use them to express his theme? What does the essay's title mean?

13. How does paragraph 13 serve as a transition?

14. Note the last few lines of paragraph 14 and the opening sentence of paragraph 15. What is their effect? How has the language changed since paragraph 10?

15. Why does Agueros change to the present tense for paragraph 27? (He reverts to the past tense in paragraph 28.)

16. Agueros tells of the talk with his father (paragraphs 35 through 38) in the present tense as well. Are his reasons for doing so the same as in the cabbage story? Look at paragraphs 39 through 46 before you answer.

Some Subjects for Essays

17. Compare two schools you have attended and explain the differences between them. To what do you attribute these differences: your classmates, your teachers, the administration, different locations, or changes in you?

18. Agueros describes several objects that were important to him as a child. Describe an object that was important to you and explain its meaning. How would it affect you now?

19. "I am a migrant, for if migration is anything, it is a state of mind." (44) Describe yourself as a migrant; consider in what ways you have "moved," not necessarily physically, but mentally or emotionally.

BACK, BUT NOT HOME

Maria L. Muñiz

Maria L. Muñiz was born in Cuba in 1958. A few months later, on
January 1, 1959, after years of fighting, Fidel Castro led his followers into Havana, Cuba's capital, forcing the dictator Batista to
flee the country. Many of Batista's followers left at that time. Later,
others disillusioned with the new government joined them.

Muñiz arrived in the United States with her parents when she
was five years old, leaving behind, as she explains in this essay,
many members of her extended family — grandparents, aunts and
uncles, and cousins. As she grew older she felt more keenly a
wider sense of cultural loss, which led her to the views expressed
in this essay.

In 1978 Muñiz was graduated from New York University and
began to work for Catalyst, an organization devoted to expanding
career possibilities for women in business and the professions. She
has written or edited a number of books on careers for women and
published articles in magazines such as *Family Circle* and
Seventeen.

The essay included here was written when the author was
only 20 and first appeared in the *New York Times* on July 13,
1979.

With all the talk about resuming diplomatic relations with Cuba, and 1
with the increasing number of Cuban exiles returning to visit friends
and relatives, I am constantly being asked, "Would you ever go back?"
In turn, I have asked myself, "Is there any reason for me to go?" I have
had to think long and hard before finding my answer. Yes.

I came to the United States with my parents when I was almost 2
five years old. We left behind grandparents, aunts, uncles and several
cousins. I grew up in a very middle-class neighborhood in Brooklyn.
With one exception, all my friends were Americans. Outside of my
family, I do not know many Cubans. I often feel awkward visiting
relatives in Miami because it is such a different world. The way of life
in Cuban Miami seems very strange to me and I am accused of being
too "Americanized." Yet, although I am now an American citizen,
whenever anyone has asked me my nationality, I have always and
unhesitatingly replied, "Cuban."

Outside American, inside Cuban. 3

I recently had a conversation with a man who generally sympa- 4 thizes with the Castro regime. We talked of Cuban politics and although the discussion was very casual, I felt an old anger welling inside. After 16 years of living an "American" life, I am still unable to view the revolution with detachment or objectivity. I cannot interpret its results in social, political or economic terms. Too many memories stand in my way.

And as I listened to this man talk of the Cuban situation, I began   5
to remember how as a little girl I would wake up crying because I had dreamed of my aunts and grandmothers and I missed them. I remembered my mother's trembling voice and the sad look on her face whenever she spoke to her mother over the phone. I thought of the many letters and photographs that somehow were always lost in transit. And as the conversation continued, I began to remember how difficult it often was to grow up Latina in an American world.

It meant going to kindergarten knowing little English. I'd been in   6
this country only a few months and although I understood a good deal of what was said to me, I could not express myself very well. On the first day of school I remember one little girl's saying to the teacher: "But how can we play with her? She's so stupid she can't even talk!" I felt so helpless because inside I was crying, "Don't you know I can understand everything you're saying?" But I did not have words for my thoughts and my inability to communicate terrified me.

As I grew a little older, Latina meant being automatically rele-   7
gated to the slowest reading classes in school. By now my English was fluent, but the teachers would always assume I was somewhat illiterate or slow. I recall one teacher's amazement at discovering I could read and write just as well as her American pupils. Her incredulity astounded me. As a child, I began to realize that Latina would always mean proving I was as good as the others. As I grew older, it became a matter of pride to prove I was better than the others.

As an adult I have come to terms with these memories and they   8
don't hurt as much. I don't look or sound very Cuban. I don't speak with an accent and my English is far better than my Spanish. I am beginning my career and look forward to the many possibilities ahead of me.

But a persistent little voice is constantly saying, "There's some-   9
thing missing. It's not enough." And this is why when I am now asked, "Do you want to go back?" I say "yes" with conviction.

I do not say to Cubans, "It is time to lay aside the hurt and forgive   10
and forget." It is impossible to forget an event that has altered and scarred all our lives so profoundly. But I find I am beginning to care less and less about politics. And I am beginning to remember and care more about the child (and how many others like her) who left her

grandma behind. I have to return to Cuba one day because I want to know that little girl better.

When I try to review my life during the past 16 years, I almost 11 feel as if I've walked into a theater right in the middle of a movie. And I'm afraid I won't fully understand or enjoy the rest of the movie unless I can see and understand the beginning. And for me, the beginning is Cuba. I don't want to go "home" again; the life and home we all left behind are long gone. My home is here and I am happy. But I need to talk to my family still in Cuba.

Like all immigrants, my family and I have had to build a new life 12 from almost nothing. It was often difficult, but I believe the struggle made us strong. Most of my memories are good ones.

But I want to preserve and renew my cultural heritage. I want to 13 keep "la Cubana" within me alive. I want to return because the journey back will also mean a journey within. Only then will I see the missing piece.

EXERCISES

Words to Know

exile (paragraph 1), Latina (5), relegated (7), illiterate (7), incredulity (7).

Some of the Issues

1. In paragraph 1 Muñiz says "yes" when she asks herself if there is any reason to go back to Cuba. What does she say in paragraphs 2–5 that helps us to understand her response?
2. What were the difficulties Muñiz encountered in school (paragraphs 6–7)? What bearing do these experiences have on her wish to visit Cuba?
3. In paragraph 8, Muñiz, at 20, states that she has "come to terms" with her memories. How does she describe herself?
4. What does "the persistent little voice" (paragraph 9) tell Muñiz? What is missing? Why is it not enough?
5. What does Muñiz mean by saying in the final paragraph that "the journey back will also mean a journey within"?
*6. Read Elizabeth Wong's "The Struggle to Be an All-American Girl"; then consider Muñiz's characterization of herself as: "Outside American, inside Cuban." Would a similar statement ("Outside American, inside Chinese") apply to Wong? Why or why not?

*7. Read Jack Agueros's "Halfway to Dick and Jane." Both he and Muñiz see themselves as half in one culture, half out of it. Compare and contrast their experiences.

The Way We Are Told

8. Muñiz uses a common introductory technique: a question whose answer will be the focus of her essay. What are the advantages of this technique?
9. In paragraphs 1, 4, and 10 Muñiz interrupts her personal story with references to more general political issues. What does she gain by doing so?
10. Paragraph 3 consists of one striking statement. How does it sum up what Muñiz has said in the preceding paragraphs? How does it anticipate what she will say later?

Some Subjects for Essays

11. Muñiz was underestimated by teachers and later proved her ability. Recall a time when you or someone else doubted your ability. Describe the circumstances and the outcome.
12. Have you had the experience of returning to a place you knew as a young child? If so, describe that experience telling what you saw and what you felt.
13. Do you believe it is possible or advisable for a person exposed to two cultures to maintain the customs and language of both? You may want to examine other essays that refer to the bicultural experience, such as those by Kingston, Agueros, Wong, and Rodriguez. You may also want to interview someone who has had that experience.

INCIDENT

Countee Cullen

Countee Cullen (1903–1946) gained recognition for his poetry while still in high school and published his first volume of poetry at the age of 22. He attended New York University and Harvard and continued to publish poetry and fiction. "Incident" is included in *On These I Stand* (1947).

Once riding in old Baltimore
    Heart-filled head-filled with glee,
I saw a Baltimorean
    Keep looking straight at me.

Now I was eight and very small,
    And he was no whit bigger,
And so I smiled, but he poked out
    His tongue, and called me, "Nigger."

I saw the whole of Baltimore
    From May until December;
Of all the things that happened there
    That's all that I remember.

PART TWO

Heritage

All of us inherit something: in some cases it may be money, property or some object — a family heirloom such as a grandmother's wedding dress or a father's set of tools. But beyond that all of us inherit something else, something much less concrete and tangible, something we may not even be fully aware of. It may be a way of doing a daily task, or the way we solve a particular problem or decide a moral issue for ourselves. It may be a special way of keeping a holiday or a tradition to have a picnic on a certain date. It may be something important or central to our thinking, or something minor that we have long accepted quite casually.

Some of us may be proudly aware of something we think of as "our heritage." In the opening selection of Part Two, Barba Nikos, the old grocer in the story by Harry Mark Petrakis, speaks movingly about the ancient heritage of Greek culture. On the other hand, our heritage may be a source of conflict or a burden. Lillian Smith, in the second selection, feels such a burden. She cannot forget a childhood experience that undermined, perhaps destroyed, her feelings for her parents.

For Americans, largely descended from immigrants, that heritage often includes more than one culture. Sometimes that may be a source of embarrassment, as it was for the narrator in "Barba Nikos," at least until the old grocer's stories changed his view. Often such a cross-cultural heritage gives rise to mixed feelings, especially in the children of immigrants. A sense of pride in a distant land where a father or a mother came from may be mingled with a sense of embarrassment when that parent tries to be — and does not quite succeed in being — part of the son's or daughter's new lifestyle. John Tarkov, son of a Russian father, reveals such mingled sentiments. Toni Morrison, granddaughter of a slave, describes how her parents and grandparents strove to overcome a set of obstacles, very different from those which faced immigrants like John Tarkov's father or the narrator in "Barba Nikos." In her essay "A Slow Walk of Trees," she records the effect of segregation and discrimination against blacks over three generations.

The first four selections in Part Two are concerned with the heritage individuals carry with them. The next three are general discussions and comments on the subject. Michael Novak's essay "In Ethnic America" is a defense of the people from Eastern and Southern Europe, millions of whom immigrated to the United States in the early twentieth century. Mostly of peasant origin, they have a strong heritage of hard work — and silence, including a silent acceptance of the disregard for them, as Novak asserts, by mainstream America. Next, in "Anglo vs. Chicano: Why?" Arthur Campa attributes the strains between the English-speaking and Spanish-speaking people in the Southeastern states to several elements in their different heritages.

One general trait that is part of the American heritage is a belief in the importance of individual rights and in the need to protect the individual against being overpowered by the group. For that reason the loner, such as the cowboy and the gritty, hard-boiled detective, is popular in American myth and story. In "American Individualism," Robert N. Bellah and his colleagues explain the significance of these two figures.

Part Two concludes with Nikki Giovanni's poem "They Clapped," a search for heritage in which expectations are not fulfilled.

BARBA NIKOS

Harry Mark Petrakis

Harry Mark Petrakis was born in St. Louis in 1923 but has spent most of his life in and around Chicago. A novelist and short story writer, his books include *Pericles on 31st Street* (1965), *A Dream of Kings* (1966), and *Stelmark: A Family Recollection* (1970), from which the following selection is an excerpt.

In more recent years he has written *Reflections on a Writer's Life and Work* (1983) and published his *Collected Stories* (1983). Petrakis, himself of Greek descent, often sets the scene of his writing among Greek Americans and immigrants.

The story Petrakis tells describes the strains that can come between first- and second-generation immigrants, when the ways of the Old Country—and their parents' accented English—become a source of embarrassment. Young people, trying to conform with their peers, may find this situation particularly trying.

Located in the eastern Mediterranean, Greece has some ten million inhabitants. It gained its independence in the nineteenth century after centuries of rule by the Turkish empire. It is a relatively poor country, many of whose people have sought their fortunes elsewhere, often in the United States, which has a large population of Greek descent.

Ancient Greece, the Greece Barba Nikos talks about so proudly, has often been called "the cradle of Western civilization." Among its many small city states, Athens stands out as the first representative democracy. Of the earliest philosophers, poets, historians, and scientists whose works have been preserved, most are Athenians. Achilles, whom Barba Nikos mentions, is a mythical warrior who plays a central role in Homer's *Iliad*, the epic poem about the war between the Greek city states and Troy. Alexander the Great, King of Macedonia, conquered the Middle East as far as India some 2,300 years ago. Marathon was not a race but a city in Greece where, in 490 B.C., the Athenians won a major battle against the invading Persians. According to legend, a Greek soldier ran from Marathon to Athens to carry the news of victory —before collapsing dead from the strain. He ran the same distance as the thousands who now run in marathons all over the world, except he ran it in full armor.

There was one storekeeper I remember above all others in my youth. It was shortly before I became ill, spending a good portion of my time

47

with a motley group of varied ethnic ancestry. We contended with one another to deride the customs of the old country. On our Saturday forays into neighborhoods beyond our own, to prove we were really Americans, we ate hot dogs and drank Cokes. If a boy didn't have ten cents for this repast he went hungry, for he dared not bring a sandwich from home made of the spiced meats our families ate.

One of our untamed games was to seek out the owner of a pushcart or a store, unmistakably an immigrant, and bedevil him with a chorus of insults and jeers. To prove allegiance to the gang it was necessary to reserve our fiercest malevolence for a storekeeper or peddler belonging to our own ethnic background. 2

For that reason I led a raid on the small, shabby grocery of old Barba Nikos, a short, sinewy Greek who walked with a slight limp and sported a flaring, handlebar mustache. 3

We stood outside his store and dared him to come out. When he emerged to do battle, we plucked a few plums and peaches from the baskets on the sidewalk and retreated across the street to eat them while he watched. He waved a fist and hurled epithets at us in ornamental Greek. 4

Aware that my mettle was being tested, I raised my arm and threw my half-eaten plum at the old man. My aim was accurate and the plum struck him on the cheek. He shuddered and put his hand to the stain. He stared at me across the street, and although I could not see his eyes, I felt them sear my flesh. He turned and walked silently back into the store. The boys slapped my shoulders in admiration, but it was a hollow victory that rested like a stone in the pit of my stomach. 5

At twilight when we disbanded, I passed the grocery alone on my way home. There was a small light burning in the store and the shadow of the old man's body outlined against the glass. Goaded by remorse, I walked to the door and entered. 6

The old man moved from behind the narrow wooden counter and stared at me. I wanted to turn and flee, but by then it was too late. As he motioned for me to come closer, I braced myself for a curse or a blow. 7

"You were the one," he said, finally, in a harsh voice. 8

I nodded mutely. 9

"Why did you come back?" 10

I stood there unable to answer. 11

"What's your name?" 12

"Haralambos," I said, speaking to him in Greek. 13

He looked at me in shock. "You are Greek!" he cried. "A Greek boy attacking a Greek grocer!" He stood appalled at the immensity of my crime. "All right," he said coldly. "You are here because you wish to make amends." His great mustache bristled in concentration. "Four 14 plums, two peaches," he said. "That makes a total of 78 cents. Call it 75. Do you have 75 cents, boy?"

I shook my head.   15

"Then you will work it off," he said. "Fifteen cents an hour into   16
75 cents makes" — he paused — "five hours of work. Can you come here Saturday morning?"

"Yes," I said.   17

"Yes, Barba Nikos," he said sternly. "Show respect."   18

"Yes, Barba Nikos," I said.   19

"Saturday morning at eight o'clock," he said. "Now go home and   20
say thanks in your prayers that I did not loosen your impudent head with a solid smack on the ear." I needed no further urging and fled.

Saturday morning, still apprehensive, I returned to the store. I   21
began by sweeping, raising clouds of dust in dark and hidden corners. I washed the windows, whipping the squeegee swiftly up and down the glass in a fever of fear that some member of the gang would see me. When I finished I hurried back inside.

For the balance of the morning I stacked cans, washed the   22
counter, and dusted bottles of yellow wine. A few customers entered, and Barba Nikos served them. A little after twelve o'clock he locked the door so he could eat lunch. He cut himself a few slices of sausage, tore a large chunk from a loaf of crisp-crusted bread, and filled a small cup with a dozen black shiny olives floating in brine. He offered me the cup. I could not help myself and grimaced.

"You are a stupid boy," the old man said. "You are not really   23
Greek, are you?"

"Yes, I am."   24

"You might be," he admitted grudgingly. "But you do not act   25
Greek. Wrinkling your nose at these fine olives. Look around this store for a minute. What do you see?"

"Fruits and vegetables," I said. "Cheese and olives and things   26
like that."

He stared at me with a massive scorn. "That's what I mean," he   27
said. "You are a bonehead. You don't understand that a whole nation and a people are in this store."

I looked uneasily toward the storeroom in the rear, almost ex-   28
pecting someone to emerge.

"What about olives?" he cut the air with a sweep of his arm.   29
"There are olives of many shapes and colors. Pointed black ones from Kalamata, oval ones from Amphissa, pickled green olives and sharp tangy yellow ones. Achilles carried black olives to Troy and after a day of savage battle leading his Myrmidons, he'd rest and eat cheese and

ripe black olives such as these right here. You have heard of Achilles, boy, haven't you?"

"Yes," I said.   30

"Yes, Barba Nikos."   31

"Yes, Barba Nikos," I said.   32

He motioned at the row of jars filled with varied spices. "There is   33
origanon there and basilikon and daphne and sesame and miantanos, all the marvelous flavorings that we have used in our food for thousands of years. The men of Marathon carried small packets of these spices into battle, and the scents reminded them of their homes, their families, and their children."

He rose and tugged his napkin free from around his throat.   34
"Cheese, you said. Cheese! Come closer, boy, and I educate your abysmal ignorance." He motioned toward a wooden container on the counter. "That glistening white delight is feta, made from goat's milk, packed in wooden buckets to retain the flavor. Alexander the Great demanded it on his table with his casks of wine when he planned his campaigns."

He walked limping from the counter to the window where the   35
piles of tomatoes, celery, and green peppers clustered. "I suppose all you see here are some random vegetables?" He did not wait for me to answer. "You are dumb again. These are some of the ingredients that go to make up a Greek salad. Do you know what a Greek salad really is? A meal in itself, an experience, an emotional involvement. It is created deftly and with grace. First, you place large lettuce leaves in a big, deep bowl." He spread his fingers and moved them slowly, carefully, as if he were arranging the leaves. "The remainder of the lettuce is shredded and piled in a small mound," he said. "Then comes celery, cucumbers, tomatoes sliced lengthwise, green peppers, origanon, green olives, feta, avocado and anchovies. At the end you dress it with lemon, vinegar, and pure olive oil, glinting golden in the light."

He finished with a heartfelt sigh and for a moment closed his   36
eyes. Then he opened one eye to mark me with a baleful intensity. "The story goes that Zeus himself created the recipe and assembled and mixed the ingredients on Mount Olympus one night when he had invited some of the other gods to dinner."

He turned his back on me and walked slowly again across the   37
store, dragging one foot slightly behind him. I looked uneasily at the clock, which showed that it was a few minutes past one. He turned quickly and startled me. "And everything else in here," he said loudly. "White beans, lentils, garlic, crisp bread, kokoretsi, meat balls, mussels and clams." He paused and drew a deep, long breath. "And the wine," he went on, "wine from Samos, Santorini, and Crete, retsina and mavrodaphne, a taste almost as old as water . . . and then the

fragrant melons, the pastries, yellow diples and golden loukoumades, the honey custard galatobouriko. Everything a part of our history, as much a part as the exquisite sculpture in marble, the bearded warriors, Pan and the oracles at Delphi, and the nymphs dancing in the shadowed groves under Homer's glittering moon." He paused, out of breath again, and coughed harshly. "Do you understand now, boy?"

He watched my face for some response and then grunted. We 38 stood silent for a moment until he cocked his head and stared at the clock. "It is time for you to leave," he motioned brusquely toward the door. "We are square now. Keep it that way."

I decided the old man was crazy and reached behind the counter 39 for my jacket and cap and started for the door. He called me back. From a box he drew out several soft, yellow figs that he placed in a piece of paper. "A bonus because you worked well," he said. "Take them. When you taste them, maybe you will understand what I have been talking about."

I took the figs and he unlocked the door and I hurried from the 40 store. I looked back once and saw him standing in the doorway, watching me, the swirling tendrils of food curling like mist about his head.

I ate the figs late that night. I forgot about them until I was in 41 bed, and then I rose and took the package from my jacket. I nibbled at one, then ate them all. They broke apart between my teeth with a tangy nectar, a thick sweetness running like honey across my tongue and into the pockets of my cheeks. In the morning when I woke, I could still taste and inhale their fragrance.

I never again entered Barba Nikos's store. My spell of illness, 42 which began some months later, lasted two years. When I returned to the streets I had forgotten the old man and the grocery. Shortly afterwards my family moved from the neighborhood.

Some twelve years later, after the war, I drove through the old 43 neighborhood and passed the grocery. I stopped the car and for a moment stood before the store. The windows were stained with dust and grime, the interior bare and desolate, a store in a decrepit group of stores marked for razing so new structures could be built.

I have been in many Greek groceries since then and have often 44 bought the feta and Kalamata olives. I have eaten countless Greek salads and have indeed found them a meal for the gods. On the holidays in our house, my wife and sons and I sit down to a dinner of steaming, buttered pilaf like my mother used to make and lemon-egg avgolemono and roast lamb richly seasoned with cloves of garlic. I drink the red and yellow wines, and for dessert I have come to relish the delicate pastries coated with honey and powdered sugar. Old Barba Nikos would have been pleased.

But I have never been able to recapture the halcyon flavor of 45
those figs he gave me on that day so long ago, although I have bought
figs many times. I have found them pleasant to my tongue, but there is
something missing. And to this day I am not sure whether it was the
figs or the vision and passion of the old grocer that coated the fruit so
sweetly I can still recall their savor and fragrance after almost thirty
years.

EXERCISES

Words to Know

motley (paragraph 1), deride (1), foray (1), repast (1), bedevil (2),
allegiance (2), appalled (14), immensity (14), Achilles (29), Troy
(29), Myrmidons (29), Marathon (33), Alexander the Great (34),
Zeus (36), Mount Olympus (36), Pan (37), Delphi (37), Homer (37),
halcyon (45).

Some of the Issues

1. Why do the gang members attack immigrants of their own ethnic
   groups?
2. What is the first sign that the narrator will change his mind about
   his deed?
3. What is the boy's first reaction to the olives? How does it set the
   scene for later reactions?
4. What does Barba Nikos mean when he says, "a whole nation and a
   people are in this store"?

The Way We Are Told

5. In the first four paragraphs the author uses a number of rather
   unusual words and phrases for simple events: motley, repast,
   untamed, bedevil, malevolence, to do battle. What effect is
   achieved by this choice?
6. Contrast the tone of the narrative frame at the beginning and end
   of the selection with the telling of the story through dialog in the
   middle. What is the effect?
7. Examine the various references to Barba Nikos throughout the
   selection. What impression do we have of him in the beginning?
   How does it change?
8. List the various references linking food and drink to mythology.
   What is their purpose?

9. In what way do the last two paragraphs sum up the theme of the essay?

Some Subjects for Essays

10. Describe a time when you did something against your better judgment, perhaps under pressure from friends. What exactly was the pressure that led you to it, and how did you feel afterwards?

*11. Read Michael Novak's "In Ethnic America." Novak asserts that ethnics—Greeks among them—have subtly been made to feel inferior in America. In an essay examine why and how Novak's view accounts for the attitude Petrakis's narrator initially displays.

*12. Consider the photograph on page 44. What kind of store does it show, and in what kind of neighborhood is such a store likely to be located? Compare this store to the one described in "Barba Nikos," and to the store where you or your family do much of your grocery shopping. What does each of these stores suggest about their patrons' heritage?

WHEN I WAS A CHILD

Lillian Smith

Lillian Smith was born in 1897, in Jasper, Florida—the small town in which her story is set. Her novel *Strange Fruit* (1944) was, in its day, a daring treatment of race relations, dealing with the love of a black woman and a white man. It sold three million copies and was translated into 15 languages. The autobiographical *Killers of the Dream* (1949), from which the following selection is taken, explores the psychology of prejudice. Lillian Smith died in 1966.

In turn-of-the-century Florida, Smith grew up a privileged child carefully raised according to strict ethical and religious standards. Her family was affluent; her father, a mill owner, clearly considered himself not only an upright, principled man, but a progressive, open-minded, God-fearing Christian. All this Smith describes—the strict but nevertheless sunny and fun-filled child-hood, her parents' eminent fairness—or so it seemed. The story she tells is of the discovery that the world she believed in was an illusion.

I was born and reared in a small Deep South town whose population   1
was about equally Negro and white. There were nine of us who grew up freely in a rambling house of many rooms, surrounded by big lawn, back yard, gardens, fields, and barn. It was the kind of home that gathers memories like dust, a place filled with laughter and play and pain and hurt and ghosts and games. We were given such advantages of schooling, music, and art as were available in the South, and our world was not limited to the South, for travel to far places seemed a natural thing to us, and usually one of the family was in a remote part of the earth.

We knew we were a respected and important family in this small   2
town but beyond this we gave little thought to status. Our father made money in lumber and naval stores for the excitement of making and losing it—not for what money can buy nor the security which it sometimes gives. I do not remember at any time wanting "to be rich" nor do I remember that thrift and saving were ideals which our parents considered important enough to urge upon us. In the family there was acceptance of risk, a mild delight in burning bridges, an expectant "what next?" We were not irresponsible; living according to the plea-

sure principle was by no means our way of life. On the contrary we were trained to think that each of us should do something of genuine usefulness, and the family thought it right to make sacrifices, if necessary, to give each child preparation for such work. We were also trained to think learning important, and books; but "bad" books our mother burned. We valued music and art and craftsmanship but it was people and their welfare and religion that were the foci around which our lives seemed naturally to move. Above all else, the important thing was what we "planned to do." That each of us must do something was as inevitable as breathing for we owed a "debt to society which must be paid." This was a family commandment.

While many neighbors spent their energies in counting limbs on   3 the family tree and grafting some on now and then to give symmetry to it, or in licking scars to cure their vague malaise, or in fighting each battle and turn of battle of that Civil War which has haunted the southern conscience so long, my father was pushing his nine children straight into the future. "You have your heritage," he used to say, "some of it good, some not so good; and as far as I know you had the usual number of grandmothers and grandfathers. Yes, there were slaves, too many of them in the family, but that was your grandfather's mistake, not yours. The past has been lived. It is gone. The future is yours. What are you going to do with it?" He asked this question often and sometimes one knew it was but an echo of a question he had spent his life trying to answer for himself. For the future held my father's dreams; always there, not in the past, did he expect to find what he had spent his life searching for.

We lived the same segregated life as did other southerners but   4 our parents talked in excessively Christian and democratic terms. We were told ten thousand times that status and money are unimportant (though we were well supplied with both); we were told that "all men are brothers," that we are a part of a democracy and must act like democrats. We were told that the teachings of Jesus are important and could be practiced if we tried. We were told that to be "radical" is bad, silly too; and that one must always conform to the "best behavior" of one's community and make it better if one can. We were taught that we were superior to hate and resentment, and that no member of the Smith family could stoop so low as to have an enemy. No matter what injury was done us, we must not injure ourselves further by retaliating. That was a family commandment.

We had family prayers once each day. All of us as children read   5 the Bible in its entirety each year. We memorized hundreds of Bible verses and repeated them at breakfast, and said "sentence prayers" around the family table. God was not someone we met on Sunday but a permanent member of our household. It never occurred to me until I was fourteen or fifteen years old that He did not chalk up the daily score on eternity's tablets.

Despite the strain of living so intimately with God, the nine of us were strong, healthy, energetic youngsters who filled days with play and sports and music and books and managed to live most of the time on the careless level at which young lives should be lived. We had our times of anxiety of course, for there were hard lessons to be learned about the soul and "bad things" to be learned about sex. Sometimes I have wondered how we learned them with a mother so shy with words.   6

She was a wistful creature who loved beautiful things like lace and sunsets and flowers in a vague inarticulate way, and took good care of her children. We always knew this was not her world but one she accepted under duress. Her private world we rarely entered, though the shadow of it lay heavily on our hearts.   7

Our father owned large business interests, employed hundreds of colored and white laborers, paid them the prevailing low wages, worked them the prevailing long hours, built for them mill towns (Negro and white), built for each group a church, saw to it that religion was supplied free, saw to it that a commissary supplied commodities at a high price, and in general managed his affairs much as ten thousand other southern businessmen managed theirs.   8

Even now, I can hear him chuckling as he told my mother how he won his fight for Prohibition. The high point of the campaign was election afternoon, when he lined up the mill force of several hundred (white and black), passed out a shining silver dollar to each one, marched them in and voted liquor out of our county. It was a great day. He had won the Big Game, a game he was always playing against all kinds of evil. It did not occur to him to scrutinize the methods he used. Evil was a word written in capitals; the devil was smart; if you wanted to win you outsmarted him. It was as simple as that.   9

He was a hardheaded, warmhearted, high-spirited man born during the Civil War, earning his living at twelve, struggling through decades of Reconstruction and post-Reconstruction, through populist movement, through the panic of 1893, the panic of 1907, on into the twentieth century accepting his region as he found it, accepting its morals and its mores as he accepted its climate, with only scorn for those who held grudges against the North or pitied themselves or the South; scheming, dreaming, expanding his business, making and losing money, making friends whom he did not lose, with never a doubt that God was by his side whispering hunches as to how to pull off successful deals. When he lost, it was his own fault. When he won, God had helped him.   10

Once while we were kneeling at family prayers the fire siren at   11 the mill sounded the alarm that the mill was on fire. My father did not falter. The alarm sounded again and again—which signified the fire was big. With dignity he continued his talk with God while his children sweated and wriggled and hearts beat out of their chests in excitement. He was talking to God—how could he hurry out to save his mills! When he finished his prayer, he quietly stood up, laid the Bible carefully on the table. Then, and only then, did he show an interest in what was happening in Mill Town. . . . When the telegram was placed in his hands telling of the death of his beloved favorite son, he gathered his children together, knelt down, and in a steady voice which contained no hint of his shattered heart, loyally repeated, "God is our refuge and strength, a very present help in trouble. Therefore will we not fear, though the earth be removed, and though the mountains to be carried into the midst of the sea." On his deathbed, he whispered to his old Business Partner in Heaven: "I have fought a good fight . . . I have kept the faith."

Against this backdrop the drama of the South was played out one day in my life: 12

A little white girl was found in the colored section of our town, living with a Negro family in a broken-down shack. This family had moved in a few weeks before and little was known of them. One of the ladies in my mother's club, while driving over to her washerwoman's, saw the child swinging on a gate. The shack, as she said, was hardly more than a pigsty and this white child was living with dirty and sick-looking colored folks. "They must have kidnapped her," she told her friends. Genuinely shocked, the clubwomen busied themselves in an attempt to do something, for the child was very white indeed. The strange Negroes were subjected to a grueling questioning and finally grew evasive and refused to talk at all. This only increased the suspicion of the white group. The next day the clubwomen, escorted by the town marshal, took the child from her adopted family despite their tears. 13

She was brought to our home. I do not know why my mother consented to this plan. Perhaps because she loved children and always showed concern for them. It was easy for one more to fit into our ample household and Janie was soon at home there. She roomed with me, sat next to me at the table; I found Bible verses for her to say at breakfast; she wore my clothes, played with my dolls and followed me around from morning to night. She was dazed by her new comforts and by the interesting activities of this big lively family; and I was as happily dazed, for her adoration was a new thing to me; and as time passed a quick, childish, and deeply felt bond grew up between us. 14

But a day came when a telephone message was received from a 15 colored orphanage. There was a meeting at our home. Many whispers. All afternoon the ladies went in and out of our house talking to Mother in tones too low for children to hear. As they passed us at play, they looked at Janie and quickly looked away again, though a few stopped and stared at her as if they could not tear their eyes from her face. When my father came home Mother closed her door against our young ears and talked a long time with him. I heard him laugh, heard Mother say, "But Papa, this is no laughing matter!" And then they were back in the living room with us and my mother was pale and my father was saying, "Well, work it out, Mama, as best you can. After all, now that you know, it is pretty simple."

In a little while my mother called my sister and me into her bedroom and told us that in the morning Janie would return to Colored Town. She said Janie was to have the dresses the ladies had given her and a few of my own, and the toys we had shared with her. She asked me if I would like to give Janie one of my dolls. She seemed hurried, though Janie was not to leave until next day. She said, "Why not select it now?" And in dreamlike stiffness I brought in my dolls and chose one for Janie. And then I found it possible to say, "Why is she leaving? She likes us, she hardly knows them. She told me she had been with them only a month." 16

"Because," Mother said gently, "Janie is a little colored girl." 17
"But she's white!" 18
"We were mistaken. She is colored." 19
"But she looks —" 20
"She is colored. Please don't argue!" 21
"What does it mean?" I whispered. 22
"It means," Mother said slowly, "that she has to live in Colored Town with colored people." 23
"But why? She lived here three weeks and she doesn't belong to them, she told me so." 24
"She is a little colored girl." 25
"But you said yourself she has nice manners. You said that," I persisted. 26
"Yes, she is a nice child. But a colored child cannot live in our home." 27
"Why?" 28
"You know, dear! You have always known that white and colored people do not live together." 29
"Can she come to play?" 30
"No." 31
"I don't understand." 32
"I don't either," my young sister quavered. 33

"You're too young to understand. And don't ask me again, ever   34
again, about this!''

Mother's voice was sharp but her face was sad and there was no   35
certainty left there. She hurried out and busied herself in the kitchen
and I wandered through that room where I had been born, touching
the old familiar things in it, looking at them, trying to find the answer
to a question that moaned like a hurt thing. . . .

And then I went out to Janie, who was waiting, knowing things   36
were happening that concerned her but waiting until they were spoken aloud.

I do not know quite how the words were said but I told her she   37
was to return in the morning to the little place where she had lived
because she was colored and colored children could not live with
white children.

"Are you white?" she said.   38

"I'm white," I replied, "and my sister is white. And you're   39
colored. And white and colored can't live together because my mother
says so."

"Why?" Janie whispered.   40

"Because they can't," I said. But I knew, though I said it firmly,   41
that something was wrong. I knew my father and mother whom I
passionately admired had betrayed something which they held dear.
And they could not help doing it. And I was shamed by their failure and
frightened, for I felt they were no longer as powerful as I had thought.
There was something Out There that was stronger than they and I
could not bear to believe it. I could not confess that my father, who
always solved the family dilemmas easily and with laughter, could not
solve this. I knew that my mother who was so good to children did not
believe in her heart that she was being good to this child. There was
not a word in my mind that said it but my body knew and my glands,
and I was filled with anxiety.

But I felt compelled to believe they were right. It was the only   42
way my world could be held together. And, slowly, it began to seep
through me: *I was white. She was colored. We must not be together.
It was bad to be together. Though you ate with your nurse when you
were little, it was bad to eat with any colored person after that. It
was bad just as other things were bad that your mother had told
you. It was bad that she was to sleep in the room with me that night.
It was bad. . . .*

I was overcome with guilt. For three weeks I had done things that   43
white children were not supposed to do. And now I knew these things
had been wrong.

I went to the piano and began to play, as I had always done when   44

I was in trouble. I tried to play my next lesson and as I stumbled through it, the little girl came over and sat on the bench with me. Feeling lost in the deep currents sweeping through our house that night, she crept closer and put her arms around me and I shrank away as if my body had been uncovered. I had not said a word, I did not say one, but she knew, and tears slowly rolled down her little white face. . . .

　　And then I forgot it. For more than thirty years the experience was wiped out of my memory. But that night, and the weeks it was tied to, worked its way like a splinter, bit by bit, down to the hurt places in my memory and festered there. And as I grew older, as more experiences collected around that faithless time, as memories of earlier, more profound hurts crept closer, drawn to that night as if to a magnet, I began to know that people who talked of love and children did not mean it. That is a hard thing for a child to learn. I still admired my parents, there was so much that was strong and vital and sane and good about them and I never forgot this; I stubbornly believed in their sincerity, as I do to this day, and I loved them. Yet in my heart they were under suspicion. Something was wrong. 45

EXERCISES

Words to Know

rambling (paragraph 1), expectant (2), foci (2), grafting (3), symmetry (3), malaise (3), retaliating (4), wistful (7), duress (7), prevailing (8), scrutinize (9), Reconstruction (10), populist (10), grueling (13), evasive (13), dazed (14), dilemmas (41).

Some of the Issues

1. Paragraphs 2 and 3 describe the lives and attitudes of Smith's family, contrasting them to other families in their environment. What was her and her family's attitude toward their neighbors? Cite some words and phrases that make the comparison explicit.
2. Paragraphs 4, 5, and 6 describe the religious life of the family. What is the significance of their religious beliefs in relation to the rest of the story Smith tells?
3. How do the three anecdotes in paragraphs 9 and 11 add to our understanding of the values of Smith's father?
4. The values of Smith's parents are in some sense in conflict with their actions. Could Smith's parents be called hypocrites? What evidence can you cite that Smith would object to such a label?

The Way We Are Told

5. Smith spends more time setting the background than telling the story of Janie. What effect does that lengthy introduction have on the narrative?
6. Cite elements in paragraph 4 that will be important to the way Smith sees the story of Janie.
7. How does paragraph 15 prepare the reader for what is to follow? How does Smith create suspense?
8. Compare the final few paragraphs, which return the narrative to Smith and her family, to the opening section (before the discovery of Janie). How do these last paragraphs differ in tone and attitude from the earlier ones?

Some Subjects for Essays

9. One factor in the story changes everything: Janie is black. Do you know, or have you experienced, a case when finding out something new about a person fundamentally changed your or someone else's attitude toward that person? After describing the circumstances, examine any justification for the change.
10. Are there parts of your family's or community's value system that you have come to question? If so, examine the changes and your reason for change. If not, explain how the values you grew up with have served you.
11. We generally believe that our actions should be in accord with our value systems; otherwise, we are guilty of hypocrisy. In an essay, try to argue the opposite: try to show, by means of logic and examples, that it is not always possible to live up to this ideal.

FITTING IN

John Tarkov

John Tarkov is a writer and editor who lives in Queens, New York. "This newspaper" (paragraph 12) refers to the *New York Times*, in whose *Sunday Magazine* the following selection was published on July 7, 1985. In this autobiographical essay, Tarkov speaks about the question of identity from the point of view of a second-generation American. He loves his Russian immigrant father and yet is exasperated by him — as much by his attempts to be American as by his foreignness.

Russian Americans of John Tarkov's father's generation often encountered an added difficulty in integrating themselves into mainstream America. Deeply attached to their homeland, they were out of sympathy with the communist government under Josef Stalin — a government, moreover, disliked and often feared by a majority of Americans.

1   Not quite two miles and 30 years from the church where these thoughts came to me, is a small, graveled parking lot cut out of the New Jersey pines, behind a restaurant and a dance hall. On road signs, the town is called Cassville. But to the several generations of Russian-Americans whose center of gravity tipped to the Old World, it was known as Roova Farms. I think the acronym stands for Russian Orthodox Outing and Vacation Association. In the summers, the place might as well have been on the Black Sea.

2   One day during one of those summers, my old man showed up from a job, just off a cargo ship. He made his living that way, in the merchant marine. With him, he had a brittle new baseball glove and a baseball as yet unmarked by human error. We went out to that parking lot and started tossing the ball back and forth; me even at the age of 8 at ease with the motions of this American game, him grabbing at the ball with his bare hands then sending it back with an unpolished stiff-armed heave. It was a very hot day. I remember that clearly. What I can't remember is who put the first scuff mark on the ball. Either I missed it, or he tossed it out of my reach.

3   I chased it down, I'm sure with American-kid peevishness. I wonder if I said anything. Probably I mouthed off about it.

4   Last winter, the phone call comes on a Saturday morning. The old man's heart had stopped. They had started it beating again. When I get

to the hospital, he's not conscious. They let me in to see him briefly. Then comes an afternoon of drinking coffee and leaning on walls. Around 4 o'clock, two doctors come out of coronary care. One of them puts his hand on my arm and tells me. A nurse takes me behind the closed door.

Two fragments of thought surface. One is primitive and it reso- 5 nates from somewhere deep: *This all began in Russia long ago.* The other is sentimental: *He died near the sea.*

I joined the tips of the first three fingers of my right hand and 6 touch them to his forehead, then his stomach, then one side of his chest, then the other. It's what I believe. I pause just briefly, then give him a couple of quick cuffs on the side of his face, the way men do when they want to express affection but something stops them from embracing. The nurse takes me downstairs to sign some forms.

He never did quite get the hang of this country. He never went to 7 the movies. Didn't watch television on his own. Didn't listen to the radio. Ate a lot of kielbasa. Read a lot. Read the paper almost cover to cover every day. He read English well, but when he talked about what he'd read, he'd mispronounce some words and put a heavy accent on them all. The paper was the window through which he examined a landscape and a people that were nearly as impenetrable to him as they were known and manageable to me. For a touch of home, he'd pick up *Soviet Life.* "I'm not a Communist," he used to tell me. "I'm a Russian." Then he'd catch me up about some new hydroelectric project on the Dnieper.

And so he vaguely embarrassed me. Who knows how many times, 8 over the years, this story has repeated itself: the immigrant father and the uneasy son. This Melting Pot of ours absorbs the second generation over a flame so high that the first is left encrusted on the rim. In college, I read the literature — Lenski on the three-generation hypothesis, stuff like that — but I read it to make my grades, not particularly to understand that I was living it.

When he finally retired from the ocean, he took his first real 9 apartment, on the Lower East Side, and we saw each other more regularly. We'd sit there on Saturday or Sunday afternoons, drinking beer and eating Chinese food. He bought a television set for our diversion, and, depending on the season, the voices of Keith Jackson and Ara Parseghian or Ralph Kiner and Lindsey Nelson would overlap with, and sometimes submerge, our own.

After the game, he'd get us a couple more beers, and we would 10 become emissaries: from land and sea, America and ports of destination. We were never strangers — never that — but we dealt, for the most part, in small talk. It was a son trying — or maybe trying to try — to share what little he knew with his father, and flinching privately at his father's foreignness. And it was a father outspokenly proud of his son, beyond basis in reason, yet at times openly frustrated that the kid had grown up unlike himself.

Every father has a vision of what he'd like his son to be. Every son   11
has a vision in kind of his father. Eventually, one of them goes, and the one remaining has little choice but to extinguish the ideal and confront the man of flesh and blood who was. Time and again it happens: The vision shed, the son, once vaguely embarrassed by the father, begins to wear the old man's name and story with pride.

Though he read it daily, the old man hated this newspaper.   12
Sometimes I think he bought it just to make himself angry. He felt the sports editor was trying to suppress the growth of soccer in America. So naturally, I would egg him on. I'd say things like: "Yeah, you're right. It's a conspiracy. The sports editor plus 200 million other Americans." Then we'd start yelling.

But when it came time to put the obituary announcements in the   13
press, after I phoned one in to the Russian-language paper, I started to dial The Times. And I remembered. And I put the phone down. And started laughing. "O.K.," I said. "O.K. They won't get any of our business."

So he went out Russian, like he came in. Up on the hill, the   14
church is topped by weathered gold onion domes — sort of like back in the Old Country, but in fact just down the road from his attempt to sneak us both into America through a side door in New Jersey, by tossing a baseball back and forth on a hot, still, bake-in-the-bleachers kind of summer day.

I believe he threw the thing over my head, actually. It *was* a   15
throwing error, the more I think about it. No way I could have caught it. But it was only a baseball, and he was my father, so it's no big deal. I bounced a few off his shins that day myself. Next time, the baseball doesn't touch the ground.

EXERCISES

Words to Know

acronym (paragraph 1), Black Sea (1), merchant marine (2), brittle (2), heave (2), peevishness (3), resonates (5), sentimental (5), kielbasa (7), impenetrable (7), hydroelectric (7), Melting Pot (8), encrusted (8), hypothesis (8), diversion (9), submerge (9), emissaries (10), flinching (10), extinguish (11), conspiracy (12), obituary (13), onion domes (14).

Some of the Issues

1. Tarkov begins his reminiscence with a description of a summer day. Describe the location and the event.
2. Paragraphs 4 through 6 abruptly change the time and location. What are Tarkov's thoughts and actions on that day?
3. Tarkov says of his father: "He never did quite get the hang of this country." What examples does he give?
4. What does the father say after reading *Soviet Life*, and what does he mean by it?
5. Explain the sentence in paragraph 8: "This Melting Pot of ours absorbs the second generation over a flame so high that the first is encrusted on the rim."
6. Tarkov cites several incidents when his father's behavior embarrassed him. What are they? In your opinion, is Tarkov embarrassed because his father was an immigrant, or does Tarkov feel what many children feel about their parents from time to time?
7. In several instances the roles of father and son seem to be reversed: the son is more knowledgeable than the father and at one point speaks in the father's voice. Cite some examples of this reversal of roles.
8. In paragraph 8 Tarkov mentions reading a book as a student, without realizing that it might have personal relevance to him. Why did he not understand it at that time?
9. What does paragraph 10 tell you about the relationship between father and son? Why are they "emissaries from land and sea"?
10. In paragraph 12 Tarkov describes an argument with his father. What is its significance?
11. Why did Tarkov refuse to put an obituary in the *New York Times*?
12. Examine the final paragraph. Why is it important to Tarkov to determine who was responsible for an error in a baseball game long ago?

The Way We Are Told

13. The essay begins with the description of a place — Roova Farms —and an activity — baseball. Why would Tarkov choose to describe this particular place and activity?
14. Tarkov looks at the relationship between himself and his father at several different points in their lives. How would the character of the essay be changed if he had put his account in chronological order?
15. Tarkov uses colloquial language or slang several times, such as "my old man" (paragraphs 2 and 4) and "mouthed off" (para-

graph 3). Find some additional examples. Are such expressions appropriate in an otherwise serious essay?

16. Paragraph 7 contains several intentional sentence fragments. Identify them. What effect do they have?

17. Cite other examples of the use of informal and formal language. Is the combination effective for Tarkov's purposes?

Some Subjects for Essays

18. In his essay Tarkov explains the ways in which he is both a part of and separate from his heritage. Write an essay in which you describe some specific aspect of your own heritage. Examine the ways in which you have departed from it, or have accepted it.

19. Tarkov writes about a relationship with one person that changes, yet in some ways stays the same over a long period of time. In an essay, describe your own relationship with someone whom you have known over a long period of time, perhaps your own parents, perhaps another relative or a friend of long standing. Give "snapshots" of at least three different periods in the relationship and explain how it has changed over time.

*20. Read Harry Mark Petrakis's "Barba Nikos." Tarkov and the character created by Petrakis both are children of immigrants to America, and both reflect on what their heritage meant to them in their youth, and later on. In your essay first describe and then compare their experiences and attitudes.

A SLOW WALK
OF
TREES

Toni Morrison

Toni Morrison was born in 1931 in Lorrain, a small town near Cleveland, Ohio. She received a B.A. degree from Howard University and an M.A. from Cornell. Since 1964 she has lived in New York, where she is an editor for Random House. In that capacity she has worked on the autobiographies of Angela Davis, an activist in the Civil Rights Movement, and Muhammad Ali, among other books.

Morrison is the author of five novels, among them *Song of Solomon* (1977), which received the National Book Critics Circle Award for fiction. Her most recent works are *Tar Baby* (1981) and *Beloved* (1986), for which she won the Pulitzer Prize.

The article included here was first published in *The New York Times Magazine* on July 4, 1976, the date of the American bicentennial. Morrison describes as well as contrasts the attitudes of her grandparents and parents toward the discrimination that was a central factor in their lives. In each of the two generations, she explains, the male had an essentially pessimistic outlook that nothing could be done; the female, on the other hand, set out to cope with whatever particular adversity was likely to befall her family. At the same time, Morrison sees a generational difference between the views of her grandparents and her parents which indicates some progress: an increased belief in the possibility of assuming control of their lives.

His name was John Solomon Willis, and when at age 5 he heard from   1
the old folks that "the Emancipation Proclamation was coming," he crawled under the bed. It was his earliest recollection of what was to be his habitual response to the promise of white people: horror and an instinctive yearning for safety. He was my grandfather, a musician who managed to hold on to his violin but not his land. He lost all 88 acres of his Indian mother's inheritance to legal predators who built their fortunes on the likes of him. He was an unreconstructed black pessimist who, in spite of or because of emancipation, was convinced for 85 years that there was no hope whatever for black people in this

country. His rancor was legitimate, for he, John Solomon, was not only an artist but a first-rate carpenter and farmer, reduced to sending home to his family money he had made playing the violin because he was not able to find work. And this during the years when almost half the black male population were skilled craftsmen who lost their jobs to white ex-convicts and immigrant farmers.

His wife, however, was of a quite different frame of mind and believed that all things could be improved by faith in Jesus and an effort of the will. So it was she, Ardelia Willis, who sneaked her seven children out of the back window into the darkness, rather than permit the patron of their sharecropper's existence to become their executioner as well, and headed north in 1912, when 99.2 percent of all black people in the U.S. were native-born and only 60 percent of white Americans were. And it was Ardelia who told her husband that they could not stay in the Kentucky town they ended up in because the teacher didn't know long division.   2

They have been dead now for 30 years and more and I still don't know which of them came closer to the truth about the possibilities of life for black people in this country. One of their grandchildren is a tenured professor at Princeton. Another, who suffered from what the Peruvian poet called "anger that breaks a man into children," was picked up just as he entered his teens and emotionally lobotomized by the reformatories and mental institutions specifically designed to serve him. Neither John Solomon nor Ardelia lived long enough to despair over one or swell with pride over the other. But if they were alive today each would have selected and collected enough evidence to support the accuracy of the other's original point of view. And it would be difficult to convince either one that the other was right.   3

Some of the monstrous events that took place in John Solomon's America have been duplicated in alarming detail in my own America. There was the public murder of a President in a theater in 1865 and the public murder of another President on television in 1963. The Civil War of 1861 had its encore as the civil-rights movement of 1960. The torture and mutilation of a black West Point Cadet (Cadet Johnson Whittaker) in 1880 had its rerun with the 1970's murders of students at Jackson State College, Texas Southern and Southern University in Baton Rouge. And in 1976 we watch for what must be the thousandth time a pitched battle between the children of slaves and the children of immigrants — only this time, it is not the New York draft riots of 1863, but the busing turmoil in Paul Revere's home town, Boston.   4

Hopeless, he'd said. Hopeless. For he was certain that white people of every political, religious, geographical and economic background would band together against black people everywhere when they felt the threat of our progress. And a hundred years after he sought   5 safety from the white man's "promise," somebody put a bullet in Martin Luther King's brain. And not long before that some excellent samples of the master race demonstrated their courage and virility by dynamiting some little black girls to death. If he were here now, my grandfather, he would shake his head, close his eyes and pull out his violin — too polite to say, "I told you so." And his wife would pay attention to the music but not to the sadness in her husband's eyes, for she would see what she expected to see — not the occasional historical repetition, but, *like the slow walk of certain species of trees from the flatlands up into the mountains*, she would see the signs of irrevocable and permanent change. She, who pulled her girls out of an inadequate school in the Cumberland Mountains, knew all along that the gentlemen from Alabama who had killed the little girls would be rounded up. And it wouldn't surprise her in the least to know that the number of black college graduates jumped 12 percent in the last three years: 47 percent in 20 years. That there are 140 black mayors in this country; 14 black judges in the District Circuit, 4 in the Courts of Appeals and one on the Supreme Court. That there are 17 blacks in Congress, one in the Senate; 276 in state legislatures — 223 in state houses, 53 in state senates. That there are 112 elected black police chiefs and sheriffs, 1 Pulitzer Prize winner; 1 winner of the Prix de Rome; a dozen or so winners of the Guggenheim; 4 deans of predominantly white colleges. . . . Oh, her list would go on and on. But so would John Solomon's sweet sad music.

While my grandparents held opposite views on whether the fortunes of black people were improving, my own parents struck similarly opposed postures, but from another slant. They differed about whether the moral fiber of white people would ever improve. Quite a different argument. The old folks argued about how and if black people could improve themselves, who could be counted on to help us, who would hinder us and so on. My parents took issue over the question of whether it was possible for white people to improve. They assumed that black people were the humans of the globe, but had serious doubts about the quality and existence of white humanity. Thus my father, distrusting every word and every gesture of every white man on earth, assumed that the white man who crept up the stairs one afternoon had come to molest his daughters and threw him down the stairs and then our tricycle after him. (I think my father was wrong, but considering what I have seen since, it may have been very healthy for me to have witnessed that as my first black-white encounter.) My mother, however, *believed* in them — their possibilities. So when the meal we got on relief was bug-ridden, she wrote a long letter to Franklin Delano Roosevelt. And when white bill collectors came to our door, it was she who received them civilly and explained in a sweet voice that we were people of honor and that the debt would be taken care of. Her message to Roosevelt got through — our meal improved. Her message to the bill collectors did not always get through and there was occasional violence when my father (self-exiled to the bedroom for fear he could not hold his temper) would hear that her reasonableness had failed. My mother was always wounded by these scenes, for she thought the bill collector knew that she loved good credit more than life and that being in arrears on a payment horrified her probably more than it did him. So she thought he was rude because he was white. For years she walked to utility companies and department stores to pay bills in person and even now she does not seem convinced that checks are legal tender. My father loved excellence, worked hard (he held three jobs at once for 17 years) and was so outraged by the suggestion of personal slackness that he could explain it to himself only in terms of racism. He was a fastidious worker who was frightened of one thing: unemployment. I can remember now the dooms day-cum-graveyard sound of "laid off" and how the minute school was out he asked us, "Where you workin'?" Both my parents believed that all succor and aid came from themselves and their neighborhood, since "they" — white people in charge and those not in charge but in obstructionist positions — were in some way fundamentally, genetically corrupt.

So I grew up in a basically racist household with more than a child's share of contempt for white people. And for each white friend I acquired who made a small crack in that contempt, there was another who repaired it. For each one who related to me as a person, there was one who in my presence at least, became actively "white." And like most black people of my generation, I suffer from racial vertigo that can be cured only by taking what one needs from one's ancestors. John Solomon's cynicism and his deployment of his art as both weapon and solace, Ardelia's faith in the magic that can be wrought by sheer effort of the will; my mother's open-mindedness in each new encounter and her habit of trying reasonableness first; my father's temper, his impatience and his efforts to keep "them" (throw them) out of his life. And it is out of these learned and selected attitudes that I look at the quality of life for my people in this country now. These widely disparate and sometimes conflicting views, I suspect, were held not only by me, but by most black people. Some I know are clearer in their positions, have not sullied their anger with optimism or dirtied their hope with despair. But most of us are plagued by a sense of being worn shell-thin by constant repression and hostility as well as the impression of being buoyed by visible testimony of tremendous strides. There *is* repetition of the grotesque in our history. And there *is* the miraculous walk of

trees. The question is whether our walk is progress or merely movement. O.J. Simpson leaning on a Hertz car *is* better than the Gold Dust
Twins on the back of a soap box. But is "Good Times" better than
Stepin Fetchit? Has the first order of business been taken care of? Does
the law of the land work for us?

EXERCISES

Words to Know

Emancipation Proclamation (paragraph 1), predators (1), unreconstructed (1), rancor (1), sharecropper (2), tenured (3), lobotomized
(3), turmoil (4), Paul Revere (4), Martin Luther King (5), master race
(5), virility (5), irrevocable (5), moral fiber (6), Franklin Delano
Roosevelt (6), civilly (6), self-exiled (6), in arrears (6), legal tender
(6), fastidious (6), doomsday (6), succor (6), obstructionist (6),
genetically (6), vertigo (7), cynicism (7), deployment (7), solace
(7), disparate (7), sullied (7), buoyed (7), grotesque (7).

Some of the Issues

1. Toni Morrison describes her grandfather as a pessimist and says
   that "his rancor was legitimate." Why does she call it legitimate?
   Toward whom was it directed?
2. What was the difference in basic outlook between Morrison's
   grandfather and grandmother? What did the grandmother believe?
   How does the author show that she lived up to her beliefs?
3. Why does Morrison cite the lives of their two grandchildren in
   paragraph 3? How do these lives relate to their grandparents'
   beliefs? In what way does Morrison think these lives would have
   affected her grandparents' beliefs?
4. Reread paragraph 4. What bearing does what Morrison tells here
   have on the grandparents' views?
5. After rereading paragraph 5, explain the title of the essay. Whose
   beliefs does Morrison reflect in this paragraph?
6. Explain the distinction Morrison makes between the views of her
   grandparents and her parents. What is the difference between the
   views of her father and mother?
7. Morrison says: "So I grew up in a basically racist household." How
   does Morrison trace her views back to the influence of her parents
   and grandparents?

The Way We Are Told

8. Morrison uses a mix of personal anecdotes and more general observations, including statistics, to support her thesis. How are these used to support the idea of black progress or the lack of it?
9. As Morrison tells it, one each of her parents and grandparents was an optimist, the other a pessimist. Try to determine Morrison's own stand. Whose side is she on?

Some Subjects for Essays

10. How would you characterize your own family's outlook on life? Is it more on the optimistic or pessimistic side? How have your family's attitudes influenced you?
11. With which of her grandparents or parents does Morrison identify most? Support your argument with specific references drawn from the essay.

IN ETHNIC AMERICA

Michael Novak

Michael Novak, an American of Slovak descent, was born in Johnstown, Pennsylvania, in 1933 and has been a resident scholar at the American Enterprise Institute, a conservative think-tank, since 1978. He holds honorary degrees from several universities. A prolific author, Novak's books include *The American Vision* (1978), *The Spirit of Democratic Capitalism* (1982), *Moral Clarity in the Nuclear Age* (1983), *Freedom and Justice* (1984), *Character and Crime* (1986), and *The Consensus on Family and Welfare* (1987).

The selection included here is an excerpt from one of his earlier books, *The Rise of the Unmeltable Ethnics* (1972). It is a spirited defense of the cultural roles of southern and eastern European immigrants to America. These immigrants, often referred to collectively as "ethnics," arrived in large numbers in the late nineteenth and early twentieth centuries. Mostly of peasant origin, they have been, Novak asserts, discriminated against in many ways. Yet, Novak claims, whereas other minorities who suffer from discrimination have aroused the sympathy and concern of many mainstream Americans, ethnics have been treated with neglect and often with scorn.

To learn more about the conditions under which immigrants like Novak's ancestors came to the United States, read Alistair Cooke's "The Huddled Masses."

1   Growing up in America has been an assault upon my sense of worthiness. It has also been a kind of liberation and delight.

2   There must be countless women in America who have known for years that something is peculiarly unfair, yet who only recently have found it possible, because of Women's Liberation, to give tongue to their pain. In recent months I have experienced a similar inner thaw, a gradual relaxation, a willingness to think about feelings heretofore shepherded out of sight.

3   I am born of PIGS—those Poles, Italians, Greeks, and Slavs, those non-English-speaking immigrants numbered so heavily among the workingmen of this nation. Not particularly liberal or radical; born into a history not white Anglo-Saxon and not Jewish; born outside what, in America, is considered the intellectual mainstream—and thus privy to neither power nor status nor intellectual voice.

Those Poles of Buffalo and Milwaukee — so notoriously taciturn, 4
sullen, nearly speechless. Who has ever understood them? It is not that
Poles do not feel emotion — what is their history if not dark passion,
romanticism, betrayal, courage, blood? But where in America is there
anywhere a language for voicing what a Christian Pole in this nation
feels? He has no Polish culture left him, no Polish tongue. Yet Polish
feelings do not go easily into the idiom of happy America, the America
of the Anglo-Saxons and yes, in the arts, the Jews. (The Jews have long
been a culture of the word, accustomed to exile, skilled in scholarship
and in reflection. The Christian Poles are largely of peasant origin, free
men for hardly more than a hundred years.) Of what shall the young
man of Lackawanna think on his way to work in the mills, departing his
relatively dreary home and street? What roots does he have? What
language of the heart is available to him?

The PIGS are not silent willingly. The silence burns like hidden 5
coals in the chest.

All four of my grandparents, unknown to one another, arrived in 6
America from the same county in Slovakia. My grandfather had a small
farm in Pennsylvania; his wife died in a wagon accident. Meanwhile,
Johanna, fifteen, arrived on Ellis Island, dizzy from witnessing births
and deaths and illnesses aboard the crowded ship. She had a sign
around her neck lettered PASSAIC. There an aunt told her of a man who
had lost his wife in Pennsylvania. She went. They were married. She
inherited his three children.

Each year for five years Grandma had a child of her own. She was 7
among the lucky; only one died. When she was twenty-two and the
mother of seven (my father was the last), her husband died. "Grandma
Novak," as I came to know her many years later, resumed the work she
had begun in Slovakia at the town home of a man known to my father
only as "the Professor"; she housecleaned and she laundered.

I heard this story only weeks ago. Strange that I had not asked 8
insistently before. Odd that I should have such shallow knowledge of
my roots. Amazing to me that I do not know what my family suffered,
endured, learned, and hoped these last six or seven generations. It is as
if there were no project in which we all have been involved, as if
history in some way began with my father and with me.

The estrangement I have come to feel derives not only from 9
lack of family history. Early in life, I was made to feel a slight uneasi-
ness when I said my name. When I was very young, the "American"
kids still made something out of names unlike their own, and their
earnest, ambitious mothers thought long thoughts when I introduced
myself.

Under challenge in grammar school concerning my nationality, I 10
had been instructed by my father to announce proudly: "American."
When my family moved from the Slovak ghetto of Johnstown to the

WASP suburb on the hill, my mother impressed upon us how well we must be dressed, and show good manners, and behave — people think of us as "different" and we mustn't give them any cause. "Whatever you do, marry a Slovak girl," was other advice to a similar end: "They cook. They clean. They take good care of you. For your own good." I was taught to be proud of being Slovak, but to recognize that others wouldn't know what it meant, or care.

Nowhere in my schooling do I recall any attempt to put me in touch with my own history. The strategy was clearly to make an American of me. English literature, American literature, and even the history books, as I recall them, were peopled mainly by Anglo-Saxons from Boston (where most historians seemed to live). Not even my native Pennsylvania, let alone my Slovak forebears, counted for very many paragraphs. (We did have something called "Pennsylvania History" somewhere; I seem to remember its puffs for industry. It could have been written by a Mellon.) I don't remember feeling envy or regret: a feeling, perhaps, of unimportance, of remoteness, of not having heft enough to count. 11

The fact that I was born a Catholic also complicated life. What is a Catholic but what everybody else is in reaction against? Protestants reformed "the whore of Babylon." Others were "enlightened" from it, and Jews had reason to help Catholicism and the social structure it was rooted in fall apart. The history books and the whole of education hummed in upon that point (for during crucial years I attended a public school): to be modern is decidedly not to be medieval; to be reasonable is not to be dogmatic; to be free is clearly not to live under ecclesiastical authority; to be scientific is not to attend ancient rituals, cherish irrational symbols, indulge in mythic practices. It is hard to grow up Catholic in America without becoming defensive, perhaps a little paranoid, feeling forced to divide the world between "us" and "them." 12

We had a special language all our own, our own pronunciation for words we shared in common with others (Augústine, contémplative), sights and sounds and smells in which few others participated (incense at Benediction of the Most Blessed Sacrament, Forty Hours, wakes, and altar bells at the silent consecration of the Host); and we had our own politics and slant on world affairs. Since earliest childhood, I have known about a "power elite" that runs America: the boys from the Ivy League in the State Department as opposed to the Catholic boys in Hoover's FBI who (as Daniel Moynihan once put it), keep watch on them. And on a whole host of issues, my people have been, though largely Democratic, conservative: on censorship, on communism, on abortion, on religious schools, etc. "Harvard" and "Yale" long meant "them" to us. 13

We did not feel this country belonged to us. We felt fierce pride   14
in it, more loyalty than anyone could know. But we felt blocked at
every turn. There were not many intellectuals among us, not even very
many professional men. Laborers mostly. Small businessmen, agents
for corporations perhaps. Content with a little, yes, modest in expectation, and content. But somehow feeling cheated. For a thousand
years the Slovaks survived Hungarian hegemony and our strategy here
remained the same: endurance and steady work. Slowly, one day, we
would overcome.

A special word is required about a complicated symbol: sex. To   15
this day my mother finds it hard to spell the word intact, preferring to
write "s--." Not that much was made of sex in our environment. And
that's the point: silence. Demonstrative affection, emotive dances, an
exuberance Anglo-Saxons seldom seem to share; but on the realities of
sex, discretion. Reverence, perhaps; seriousness, surely. On intima-
cies, it was as though our tongues had been stolen, as though in
peasant life for a thousand years — as in the novels of Tolstoi, Sholokhov, and even Kosinski — the context had been otherwise. Passion,
certainly; romance, yes; family and children, certainly; but sex rather a
minor if explosive part of life.

Imagine, then, the conflict in the generation of my brothers,   16
sister, and myself. Suddenly, what for a thousand years was minor
becomes an all-absorbing investigation. Some view it as a drama of
"liberation" when the ruling classes (subscribers to the *New Yorker*, I
suppose) move progressively, generation by generation since Sigmund
Freud, toward concentration upon genital stimulation, and latterly
toward consciousness-raising sessions in Clit. Lib. But it is rather a
different drama when we stumble suddenly upon mores staggering any
expectation our grandparents ever cherished.

Yet more significant in the ethnic experience in America is the   17
intellectual world one meets: the definition of values, ideas, and purposes emanating from universities, books, magazines, radio, and television. One hears one's own voice echoed back neither by spokesmen of
"middle America" (so complacent, smug, nativist, and Protestant),
nor by the "intellectuals." Almost unavoidably, perhaps, education in
America leads the student who entrusts his soul to it in a direction
which, lacking a better word, we might call liberal: respect for individual conscience, a sense of social responsibility, trust in the free
exchange of ideas and procedures of dissent, a certain confidence in
the ability of men to "reason together" and adjudicate their differences, a frank recognition of the vitality of the unconscious, a willingness to protect workers and the poor against the vast economic power
of industrial corporations, and the like.

On the other hand, the liberal imagination has appeared to be   18
astonishingly universalist and relentlessly missionary. Perhaps the
metaphor "enlightenment" offers a key. One is *initiated into light*.
Liberal education tends to separate children from their parents, from
their roots, from their history, in the cause of a universal and superior
religion.

In particular, I have regretted and keenly felt the absence of that   19
sympathy for PIGS which simple human feeling might have prodded
intelligence to muster, that same sympathy which the educated find so
easy to conjure up for black culture, Chicano culture, Indian culture,
and other cultures of the poor. In such cases one finds the universalist
pretensions of liberal culture suspended; some groups, at least, are
entitled to be both different and respected. Why do the educated
classes find it so difficult to want to understand the man who drives a
beer truck, or the fellow with a helmet working on a site across the
street with plumbers and electricians, while their sensitivities race
easily to Mississippi or even Bedford-Stuyvesant?

There are deep secrets here, no doubt, unvoiced fantasies and   20
scarcely admitted historical resentments. Few persons in describing
"middle Americans," "the silent majority," or Scammon and Watten-
berg's "typical American voter" distinguish clearly enough between
the nativist American and the ethnic American. The first is likely to be
Protestant, the second Catholic. Both may be, in various ways, conservative, loyalist, and unenlightened. Each has his own agonies, fears,
betrayed expectations. Neither is ready, quite, to become an ally of
the other. Neither has the same history behind him here. Neither
has the same hopes. Neither lives out the same psychic voyage, shares
the same symbols, has the same sense of reality. The rhetoric and
metaphors proper to each differ from those of the other.

There is overlap, of course. But country music is not a polka; a   21
successful politician in a Chicago ward needs a very different "common touch" from the one needed by the county clerk in Normal. The
urban experience of immigration lacks that mellifluous, optimistic,
biblical vision of the good America which springs naturally to the lips
of politicians from the Bible Belt. The nativist tends to believe with
Richard Nixon that he "knows America, and the American heart is
good." The ethnic tends to believe that every American who preceded
him has an angle, and that he, by God, will some day find one, too.
(Often, ethnics complain that by working hard, obeying the law,
trusting their political leaders, and relying upon the American dream,
they now have only their own naiveté to blame for rising no higher
than they have.)

Unfortunately, it seems, the ethnics erred in attempting to Ameri-   22 canize themselves before clearing the project with the educated classes. They learned to wave the flag and to send their sons to war. They learned to support their President—an easy task, after all, for those accustomed to obeying authority. And where would they have been if Franklin Roosevelt had not sided with them against established interests? They knew a little about communism—the radicals among them in one way, and by far the larger number of conservatives in another. To this day not a few exchange letters with cousins and uncles who did not leave for America when they might have, whose lot is demonstrably harder than their own and less than free.

Finally, the ethnics do not like, or trust, or even understand the   23
intellectuals. It is not easy to feel uncomplicated affection for those who call you "pig," "fascist," "racist." One had not yet grown accustomed to not hearing "hunkie," "Polack," "spic," "mick," "dago," and the rest.

At no little sacrifice, one had apologized for foods that smelled   24
too strong for Anglo-Saxon noses; moderated the wide swings of Slavic and Italian emotion; learned decorum; given oneself to education, American style; tried to learn tolerance and assimilation. Each generation criticized the earlier for its authoritarian and European and old-fashioned ways. "Up-to-date" was a moral lever. And now when the process nears completion, when a generation appears that speaks without accent and goes to college, still you are considered "pigs," "fascists," and "racists." Racists? Our ancestors owned no slaves. Most of us ceased being serfs only in the last two hundred years—the Russians in 1861. . . .

Whereas the Anglo-Saxon model appears to be a system of atomic   25
individuals and high mobility, our model has tended to stress communities of our own, attachment to family and relatives, stability, and roots. Ethnics tend to have a fierce sense of attachment to their homes, having been homeowners for less than three generations: a home is almost fulfillment enough for one man's life. Some groups save arduously in a passion to *own*; others rent. We have most ambivalent feelings about suburban assimilation and mobility. The melting pot is a kind of homogenized soup, and its mores only partly appeal to ethnics: to some, yes, and to others, no.

It must be said that ethnics think they are better people than the   26
blacks. Smarter, tougher, harder working, stronger in their families. But maybe many are not sure. Maybe many are uneasy. Emotions here are delicate; one can understand the immensely more difficult circumstances under which the blacks have suffered; and one is not unaware of peculiar forms of fear, envy, and suspicion across color lines. How much of this we learned in America by being made conscious of our olive skin, brawny backs, accents, names, and cultural quirks is not

plain to us. Racism is not our invention; we did not bring it with us; we had prejudices enough and would gladly have been spared new ones. Especially regarding people who suffer more than we.

EXERCISES

Words to Know

assault (paragraph 1), privy (3), taciturn (4), WASP (10), Mellon (11), ecclesiastical (12), ritual (12), mythic (12), Augústine (13), contemplative (13), hegemony (14), Tolstoi (15), Sholokhov (15), Kosinski (15), nativist (17), adjudicate (17), unconscious (17), Bedford-Stuyvesant (19), mellifluous (21), authoritarian (24).

Some of the Issues

1. Explain the meaning of the first paragraph after you have read the third. What aspects of his own background does Novak single out? How do they relate to his opening statement?
2. Novak refers to his background in paragraph 3 and returns to his family history in paragraphs 6 through 8. What is his reason for inserting paragraphs 4 and 5 in between?
3. How does Novak's family history reflect the silence of the ethnics to which he refers?
4. In paragraph 14 Novak says, "We did not feel this country belonged to us." What has he said in the preceding part of the essay to substantiate that assertion?
5. Explain the anger Novak reflects in discussing sex (paragraphs 15 and 16).
6. Show the points Novak makes to contrast the ethnic and liberal outlook on life in America.
7. What reasons does Novak give for the liberal, intellectual sympathy for blacks, Chicanos, or Indians, but not for ethnics?

The Way We Are Told

8. Why does Novak make the analogy between Women's Liberation and his own "inner thaw" (paragraph 2)?
9. In paragraphs 4 and 5 Novak uses emotional terms to characterize ethnics. Find some of them, and then contrast them to the language of paragraphs 6 and 7. Can you explain the reasons for the difference between the two sets of paragraphs?

10. In paragraph 10 Novak refers to his people as "different." Different from whom? How does he show that difference? What do his comments imply about Americans?
11. On a few occasions Novak uses sarcasm, or satirizes the people he considers anti-ethnic, the "them" at the end of paragraph 12. Find some examples of satiric statements.
12. Look at the last sentence of paragraph 14. Do you hear any echoes?

Some Subject for Essays

13. In paragraph 1 Novak refers to growing up in America as "an assault upon my sense of worthiness" as well as "a kind of liberation and delight." In an essay explain how Novak's experience could be both of these.
14. In an essay determine Novak's intended audience. Is it PIGS, for example? Liberals? Argue from the contents of the essay and the way it is written.

ANGLO VS. CHICANO: WHY?

Arthur L. Campa

Arthur L. Campa (1905–1978) was born to American missionary parents in Mexico. He attended the University of New Mexico and Columbia, and was professor and chairman of the Department of Modern Languages at the University of Denver. He also served as cultural attaché at several United States embassies. The following selection appeared in the *Western Review*.

In his essay Campa discusses the differences between the two main cultures that meet in the southwestern United States: He contrasts the Anglo culture derived from English sources and the Chicano, whose cultural sources are Hispanic. He uses history, geography, and language to show how and why these two cultures living side by side find it hard to overcome the differences between them.

The cultural differences between Hispanic and Anglo-American people 1 have been dwelt upon by so many writers that we should all be well informed about the values of both. But audiences are usually of the same persuasion as the speakers, and those who consult published works are for the most part specialists looking for affirmation of what they believe. So, let us consider the same subject, exploring briefly some of the basic cultural differences that cause conflict in the Southwest, where Hispanic and Anglo-American cultures meet.

Cultural differences are implicit in the conceptual content of the 2 languages of these two civilizations, and their value systems stem from a long series of historical circumstances. Therefore, it may be well to consider some of the English and Spanish cultural configurations before these Europeans set foot on American soil. English culture was basically insular, geographically and ideologically; was more integrated on the whole, except for some strong theological differences; and was particularly zealous of its racial purity. Spanish culture was peninsular, a geographical circumstance that made it a catchall of Mediterranean, central European and north African peoples. The composite nature of the population produced a marked regionalism that prevented close integration, except for religion, and led to a strong sense of individualism. These differences were reflected in the colonizing enterprise of the two cultures. The English isolated themselves from the Indians physically and culturally; the Spanish, who had strong notions about *pureza de sangre* [purity of blood] among the nobility, were not collectively averse to adding one more strain to their racial cocktail. Cortés led the way by siring the first *mestizo* in North America, and the rest of the conquistadores followed suit. The ultimate products of these two orientations meet today in the Southwest.

Anglo-American culture was absolutist at the onset; that is, all the   3
dominant values were considered identical for all, regardless of time and place. Such values as justice, charity, honesty were considered the superior social order for all men and were later embodied in the American Constitution. The Spaniard brought with him a relativistic viewpoint and saw fewer moral implications in man's actions. Values were looked upon as the result of social and economic conditions.

The motives that brought Spaniards and Englishmen to America   4
also differed. The former came on an enterprise of discovery, searching for a new route to India initially, and later for new lands to conquer, the fountain of youth, minerals, the Seven Cities of Cíbola and, in the case of the missionaries, new souls to win for the Kingdom of Heaven. The English came to escape religious persecution, and once having found a haven, they settled down to cultivate the soil and establish their homes. Since the Spaniards were not seeking a refuge or running away from anything, they continued their explorations and circled the globe 25 years after the discovery of the New World.

This peripatetic tendency of the Spaniard may be accounted for   5
in part by the fact that he was the product of an equestrian culture. Men on foot do not venture far into the unknown. It was almost a century after the landing on Plymouth Rock that Governor Alexander Spotswood of Virginia crossed the Blue Ridge Mountains, and it was not until the nineteenth century that the Anglo-Americans began to move west of the Mississippi.

The Spaniard's equestrian role meant that he was not close to the   6
soil, as was the Anglo-American pioneer, who tilled the land and built the greatest agricultural industry in history. The Spaniard cultivated the land only when he had Indians available to do it for him. The uses to which the horse was put also varied. The Spanish horse was essentially a mount, while the more robust English horse was used in cultivating the soil. It is therefore not surprising that the viewpoints of these two cultures should differ when we consider that the pioneer is looking at the world at the level of his eyes while the *caballero* [horseman] is looking beyond and down at the rest of the world.

One of the most commonly quoted, and often misinterpreted,   7
characteristics of Hispanic peoples is the deeply ingrained individual-

ism in all walks of life. Hispanic individualism is a revolt against the incursion of collectivity, strongly asserted when it is felt that the ego is being fenced in. This attitude leads to a deficiency in those social qualities based on collective standards, an attitude that Hispanos do not consider negative because it manifests a measure of resistance to standardization in order to achieve a measure of individual freedom. Naturally, such an attitude has no *reglas fijas* [fixed rules].

Anglo-Americans who achieve a measure of success and security   8 through institutional guidance not only do not mind a few fixed rules but demand them. The lack of a concerted plan of action, whether in business or in politics, appears unreasonable to Anglo-Americans. They have a sense of individualism, but they achieve it through action and self-determination. Spanish individualism is based on feeling, on something that is the result not of rules and collective standards but of a person's momentary, emotional reaction. And it is subject to change when the mood changes. In contrast to Spanish emotional individualism, the Anglo-American strives for objectivity when choosing a course of action or making a decision.

The Southwestern Hispanos voiced strong objections to the lack   9 of courtesy of the Anglo-Americans when they first met them in the early days of the Santa Fe trade. The same accusation is leveled at the *Americanos* today in many quarters of the Hispanic world. Some of this results from their different conceptions of polite behavior. Here too one can say that the Spanish have no *reglas fijas* because for them courtesy is simply an expression of the way one person feels toward another. To some they extend the hand, to some they bow and for the more *íntimos* there is the well-known *abrazo*. The concepts of "good or bad" or "right and wrong" in polite behavior are moral considerations of an absolutist culture.

Another cultural contrast appears in the way both cultures share   10 part of their material substance with others. The pragmatic Anglo-American contributes regularly to such institutions as the Red Cross, the United Fund and a myriad of associations. He also establishes foundations and quite often leaves millions to such institutions. The Hispano prefers to give his contribution directly to the recipient so he can see the person he is helping.

A century of association has inevitably acculturated both His-   11 panos and Anglo-Americans to some extent, but there still persist a number of culture traits that neither group has relinquished altogether. Nothing is more disquieting to an Anglo-American who believes that time is money than the time perspective of Hispanos. They usually refer to this attitude as the *"mañana* psychology." Actually, it is more of a "today psychology," because Hispanos cultivate the present to the exclusion of the future; because the latter has not arrived yet, it is not a reality. They are reluctant to relinquish the present, so they hold on to it until it becomes the past. To an Hispano, nine is nine until it is ten, so when he arrives at nine-thirty, he jubilantly exclaims: "*¡Justo!*" [right on time]. This may be why the clock is slowed down to a walk in Spanish while in English it runs. In the United States, our future-oriented civilization plans our lives so far in advance that the present loses its meaning. January magazine issues are out in December; 1973 cars have been out since October; cemetery plots and even funeral arrangements are bought on the installment plan. To a person engrossed in living today the very idea of planning his funeral sounds like the tolling of the bells.

It is a natural corollary that a person who is present oriented   12
should be compensated by being good at improvising. An Anglo-American is told in advance to prepare for an "impromptu speech," but an Hispano usually can improvise a speech because "*Nosotros lo improvisamos todo*" [we improvise everything].

Another source of cultural conflict arises from the difference   13
between *being* and *doing*. Even when trying to be individualistic, the Anglo-American achieves it by what he does. Today's young generation decided to be themselves, to get away from standardization, so they let their hair grow, wore ragged clothes and even went barefoot in order to be different from the Establishment. As a result they all ended up doing the same things and created another stereotype. The freedom enjoyed by the individuality of *being* makes it unnecessary for Hispanos to strive to be different.

In 1963 a team of psychologists from the University of Guadala-   14
jara in Mexico and the University of Michigan compared 74 upper-middle-class students from each university. Individualism and personalism were found to be central values for the Mexican students. This was explained by saying that a Mexican's value as a person lies in his *being* rather than, as is the case of the Anglo-Americans, in concrete accomplishments. Efficiency and accomplishments are derived characteristics that do not affect worthiness in the Mexican, whereas in the American it is equated with success, a value of highest priority in the American culture. Hispanic people disassociate themselves from material things or from actions that may impugn a person's sense of being, but the Anglo-American shows great concern for material things and assumes responsibility for his actions. This is expressed in the language of each culture. In Spanish one says, "*Se me cayó la taza*" [the cup fell away from me] instead of "I dropped the cup."

In English, one speaks of money, cash and all related transactions   15
with frankness because material things of this high order do not trouble Anglo-Americans. In Spanish such materialistic concepts are circumvented by referring to cash as *efectivo* [effective] and when buying

or selling as something *al contado* [counted out], and when without it by saying *No tengo fondos* [I have no funds]. This disassociation from material things is what produces *sobriedad* [sobriety] in the Spaniard according to Miguel de Unamuno, but in the Southwest the disassociation from materialism leads to *dejadez* [lassitude] and *desprendimiento* [disinterestedness]. A man may lose his life defending his honor but is unconcerned about the lack of material things. *Desprendimiento* causes a man to spend his last cent on a friend, which when added to lack of concern for the future may mean that tomorrow he will eat beans as a result of today's binge.

The implicit differences in words that appear to be identical in 16
meaning are astonishing. Versatile is a compliment in English and an insult in Spanish. An Hispano student who is told to apologize cannot do it, because the word doesn't exist in Spanish. *Apología* means words in praise of a person. The Anglo-American either apologizes, which is a form of retraction abhorrent in Spanish, or compromises, another concept foreign to Hispanic culture. *Compromiso* means a date, not a compromise. In colonial Mexico City, two hidalgos once entered a narrow street from opposite sides, and when they could not go around, they sat in their coaches for three days until the viceroy ordered them to back out. All this because they could not work out a compromise.

It was that way then and to some extent now. Many of today's 17
conflicts in the Southwest have their roots in polarized cultural differences, which need not be irreconcilable when approached with mutual respect and understanding.

EXERCISES

Words to Know

implicit (paragraph 2), conceptual (2), configuration (2), zealous (2), *mestizo*—mixed blood (2), conquistadores (2), absolutist (3), relativistic (3), peripatetic (5), equestrian (5), incursion (7), collectivity (7), *abrazo*—embrace, greeting (9), circumvented (15), versatile (16), *hidalgo*—gentleman, nobleman (16).

Some of the Issues

1. Find the sentence that most precisely states the thesis of the essay.
2. It is relatively easy to find thesis statements for the various paragraphs. Find them for paragraphs 3, 7, and 10. What is the arrangement of supporting evidence in each case?

3. Campa makes a number of assertions throughout the essay. Examine the evidence he presents for each. Which ones do you find to be strongly supported? Which are less well sustained?
4. According to Campa, individuality is a virtue in both Anglo and Hispanic cultures. How do the notions of individuality differ in the two cultures?

The Way We Are Told

5. Make an outline of the essay, showing its organizational pattern.
6. Each paragraph (or small group of paragraphs) deals with a particular contrast between Anglos and Chicanos. In your view, would the essay be more or less effective if the author had used a different pattern, that is, if he had developed the Anglo and Hispanic characteristics in two major, separate sections? Support your opinion.
7. How objective do you find Campa's article? Does the author favor one side? If you think he does, what evidence can you cite for your view?

Some Subjects for Essays

8. Write an essay comparing and contrasting two related subjects you know well: high school and college; an old home and your present one; two jobs.
*9. Read Robert N. Bellah and others' "American Individualism." Compare and contrast their characterization of American individualism with Campa's description of Anglo individualism and its causes.

AMERICAN INDIVIDUALISM

Robert N. Bellah, Richard Madsen, William M. Sullivan, Ann Swidler, and Steven M. Tipton

This selection is taken from *Habits of the Heart: Individualism and Commitment in American Life* (1985). Highly praised as a penetrating study of contemporary American values, it became a best seller.

The lead author of the book, Robert Bellah, born in 1927, is Elliott Professor of Sociology at the University of California, Berkeley. He has taught at Harvard and McGill University and has written several books, including *The New Religious Consciousness*. Bellah's coauthors are professors at various American colleges and universities.

The authors describe two of the most widely used character types in American fiction, movies, and TV serials—the hard-boiled detective and the cowboy—attributing their popularity to the American faith in individualism. That same faith, the authors say, has also turned Abraham Lincoln into a mythical figure larger than life.

Individualism lies at the very core of American culture. We believe in the dignity, indeed the sacredness, of the individual. Anything that would violate our right to think for ourselves, judge for ourselves, make our own decisions, live our lives as we see fit, is not only morally wrong, it is sacrilegious. Our highest and noblest aspirations, not only for ourselves, but for those we care about, for our society and for the world, are closely linked to our individualism. Yet, some of our deepest problems both as individuals and as a society are also closely linked to our individualism. We do not argue that Americans should abandon individualism—that would mean for us to abandon our deepest identity. But individualism has come to mean so many things and to contain such contradictions and paradoxes that even to defend it requires that

87

we analyze it critically, that we consider especially those tendencies that would destroy it from within.

America is the inventor of that most mythic individual hero, the   2
cowboy, who again and again saves a society he can never completely fit into. The cowboy has a special talent — he can shoot straighter and faster than other men — and a special sense of justice. But these characteristics make him so unique that he can never fully belong to society. His destiny is to defend society without ever really joining it. He rides off alone into the sunset like Shane, or like the Lone Ranger moves on accompanied only by his Indian companion. But the cowboy's importance is not that he is isolated or antisocial. Rather, his significance lies in his unique, individual virtue and special skill and it is because of those qualities that society needs and welcomes him. Shane, after all, starts as a real outsider, but ends up with the gratitude of the community and the love of a woman and a boy. And while the Lone Ranger never settles down and marries the local schoolteacher, he always leaves with the affection and gratitude of the people he has helped. It is as if the myth says you can be a truly good person, worthy of admiration and love, only if you resist fully joining the group. But sometimes the tension leads to an irreparable break. Will Kane, the hero of *High Noon*, abandoned by the cowardly townspeople, saves them from an unrestrained killer, but then throws his sheriff's badge in the dust and goes off into the desert with his bride. One is left wondering where they will go, for there is no longer any link with any town.

The connection of moral courage and lonely individualism is   3
even tighter for that other, more modern American hero, the hard-boiled detective. From Sam Spade to Serpico, the detective is a loner. He is often unsuccessful in conventional terms, working out of a shabby office where the phone never rings. Wily, tough, smart, he is nonetheless unappreciated. But his marginality is also his strength. When a bit of business finally comes their way, Philip Marlowe, Lew Archer, and Travis McGee are tenacious. They pursue justice and help the unprotected even when it threatens to unravel the fabric of society itself. Indeed, what is remarkable about the American detective story is less its hero than its image of crime. When the detective begins his quest, it appears to be an isolated incident. But as it develops, the case turns out to be linked to the powerful and privileged of the community. Society, particularly "high society," is corrupt to the core. It is this boring into the center of society to find it rotten that constitutes the fundamental drama of the American detective story. It is not a personal but a social mystery that the detective must unravel.

To seek justice in a corrupt society, the American detective must   4
be tough, and above all, he must be a loner. He lives outside the

normal bourgeois pattern of career and family. As his investigations begin to lead him beyond the initial crime to the glamorous and powerful center of the society, its leaders make attempts to buy off the detective, to corrupt him with money, power, or sex. This counterpoint to the gradual unraveling of the crime is the battle the detective wages for his own integrity, in the end rejecting the money of the powerful and spurning (sometimes jailing or killing) the beautiful woman who has tried to seduce him. The hard-boiled detective, who may long for love and success, for a place in society, is finally driven to stand alone, resisting the blandishments of society, to pursue a lonely crusade for justice. Sometimes, as in the film *Chinatown*, corruption is so powerful and so total that the honest detective no longer has a place to stand and the message is one of unrelieved cynicism.

Both the cowboy and the hard-boiled detective tell us something   5 important about American individualism. The cowboy, like the detective, can be valuable to society only because he is a completely autonomous individual who stands outside it. To serve society, one must be able to stand alone, not needing others, not depending on their judgment, and not submitting to their wishes. Yet this individualism is not selfishness. Indeed, it is a kind of heroic selflessness. One accepts the necessity of remaining alone in order to serve the values of the group. And this obligation to aloneness is an important key to the American moral imagination. Yet it is part of the profound ambiguity of the mythology of American individualism that its moral heroism is always just a step away from despair. For an Ahab, and occasionally for a cowboy or a detective, there is no return to society, no moral redemption. The hero's lonely quest for moral excellence ends in absolute nihilism.

If we may turn from the mythical heroes of fiction to a mythic,   6 but historically real, hero, Abraham Lincoln, we may begin to see what is necessary if the nihilistic alternative is to be avoided. In many respects, Lincoln conforms perfectly to the archetype of the lonely, individualistic hero. He was a self-made man, never comfortable with the eastern upper classes. His dual moral commitment to the preservation of the Union and the belief that "all men are created equal" roused the hostility of abolitionists and Southern sympathizers alike. In the war years, he was more and more isolated, misunderstood by Congress and cabinet, and unhappy at home. In the fact of almost universal mistrust, he nonetheless completed his self-appointed task of bringing the nation through its most devastating war, preaching reconciliation as he did so, only to be brought down by an assassin's bullet. What saved Lincoln from nihilism was the larger whole for which he felt it was important to live and worthwhile to die. No one understood better the meaning of the Republic and of the freedom and equality that it only very imperfectly embodies. But it was not only civic republicanism that gave his life value. Reinhold Niebuhr has said that Lincoln's biblical understanding of the Civil War was deeper than that of any contemporary theologian. The great symbols of death and rebirth that Lincoln invoked to give meaning to the sacrifice of those who died at Gettysburg, in a war he knew to be senseless and evil, came to redeem his own senseless death at the hand of an assassin. It is through his identification with a community and a tradition that Lincoln became the deeply and typically American individual that he was.

EXERCISES

Words to Know

sacrilegious (paragraph 1), Shane (2), Lone Ranger (2), mythic (2), antisocial (2), irreparable (2), loner (3), hard-boiled (3), marginality (3), Sam Spade (3), Serpico (3), tenacious (3), quest (3), bourgeois (4), counterpoint (4), unraveling (4), integrity (4), spurning (4), blandishments (4), cynicism (4), autonomous (5), selflessness (5), profound (5), ambiguity (5), mythology (5), Ahab (5), moral redemption (5), nihilism (5), archetype (6), hostility (6), abolitionists (6), devastating (6), reconciliation (6), embody (6), invoke (6), redeem (6).

Some of the Issues

1. What claims do the authors make about American individualism? Why do they believe that American attitudes must be examined critically?
2. What are the characteristics of the cowboy that make him representative of American individualism? Why can he never fully be part of society?
3. The hard-boiled detective (paragraphs 3 and 4) is even more a loner than the cowboy. How is he characterized? What temptations must he struggle with? How does his mission transcend the solution of a particular crime?
4. What are the sources of the cowboy's and the detective's strength (paragraph 5)? What dangers does their aloneness expose them to?
5. What links Abraham Lincoln, a historic figure, to the mythic heroes? What saved Lincoln from nihilism?

The Way We Are Told

6. Where do the authors state their thesis?
7. The authors explain the concept of the mythic individual hero before examining the life of a real hero, Lincoln. What do they gain by doing so? How does it contribute to our understanding?

Some Subjects for Essays

8. Examine in an essay if — or how — your upbringing has stressed "the dignity, indeed the sacredness, of the individual."
9. Reread paragraphs 2 and 3. The authors here develop the arguments for their thesis that the cowboy and the detective are fictional characters that represent the American ideal of individualism. In doing so, what kind of picture of American society do they present?

THEY CLAPPED

Nikki Giovanni

Nikki Giovanni (1943–) is a graduate of Fisk College. She has published a number of volumes of poetry, including *Black Feeling/Black Talk/Black Judgment* (1970), *The Women and the Men* (1975), and *My House* (1972), from which the following poem is taken. She has also written an autobiography, *Gemini* (1971).

      Giovanni's poem is a comment on a people's search for their roots, in this case the search of black Americans traveling to Africa, excited at the prospect and confident of finding the meaning they were searching for. Giovanni's wry humor only partly hides the hurt and disappointment, summed up in the line: "when they finally realized they were strangers all over." Yet, as the final lines indicate, there may be hope.

they clapped when we landed
thinking africa was just an extension
of the black world
they smiled as we taxied home to be met
black to black face not understanding africans lack
color prejudice
they rushed to declare
cigarettes, money, allegiance to the mother land
not knowing despite having read fanon and davenport
hearing all of j.h. clarke's lectures, supporting
nkrumah in ghana and nigeria in the war that there was once
a tribe called afro-americans that populated the whole
of africa
they stopped running when they learned the packages
on the women's heads were heavy and that babies didn't
cry and disease is uncomfortable and that villages are fun
only because you knew the feel of good leather on good
pavement
they cried when they saw mercedes benz were as common
in lagos as volkswagens are in berlin
they shook their heads when they understood there was no
difference between the french and the english and the americans
and the afro-americans or the tribe next door or the country
across the border

they were exasperated when they heard sly and the family stone
in francophone africa and they finally smiled when little boys
who spoke no western tongue said "james brown" with reverence
they brought out their cameras and bought out africa's drums
when they finally realized they are strangers all over
and love is only and always about the lover not the beloved
they marveled at the beauty of the people and the richness
of the land knowing they could never possess either

they clapped when they took off
for home despite the dead
dream they saw a free future

PART THREE

Families

As we approach the twenty-first century, we are aware that the family we used to consider the norm is now in a minority. The family in which the father went off to work and the mother kept house and raised the children has been replaced by a whole array of new families: one-parent families headed by the mother or, less frequently, by the father; families in which children from previous marriages are combined into a new unit; or families like the ones Jane Howard talks about in the first selection, those that may not be the result of blood relationships but of other commitments.

Recent statistics confirm the scope of these changes. The divorce rate has doubled since 1965. Half of all first marriages, and more than half of all second marriages, are likely to end in divorce. Single parents are raising a quarter of all children today. Approximately one-third of children born in the 1980s will live in a step-family before they are old enough to go off to college. In two-parent families the majority of women are part of the work force. The need for day care for children of families in which both parents work continues to be largely unmet. Many people view these changes away from what they think of as "the norm" of the family structure with considerable alarm.

However, if we consider the family in the light of its historical development, we come to a somewhat different view, as

Arlene Skolnick explains in her essay "The Paradox of Perfection," at the end of Part Three: the family we used to think of as "the family" — the one in which the father is the breadwinner and the mother keeps house and children — has actually not been a norm for society except in fairly recent times, and then only in some places. It developed largely as a result of industrialization. In an agricultural society, a way of life that still prevails in large parts of the world, men and women, as well as their children, work side by side. Only in relatively recent times have most fathers and, to a lesser extent, mothers gone off to work away from home.

In spite of all the changes in its makeup, the family remains the basic unit on which any society is built. Jane Howard, in her essay "Families," sets down some ground rules for any kind of family, the ones we are born into as well as the ones we pick. Alfred Kazin's family of immigrants from Eastern Europe, living in a tenement in early twentieth century New York, is held together by the ceaseless work and worry of the mother. The kitchen, in which most of the family's life takes place, becomes a symbol of its unity. Carolina Maria de Jesus, living in extreme poverty in Brazil, heads a one-parent household. She valiantly fights to provide not only food and clothing but a halfway decent moral environment for her children. Part Three concludes with a poem by Theodore Roethke, a brief glimpse of a child's memory of its father.

FAMILIES

Jane Howard

Jane Howard, born in Springfield, Illinois, in 1935, is a reporter, editor, and writer. Among her books are *Please Touch: A Guided Tour of the Human Potential Movement* (1970), the autobiographical *A Different Woman* (1973), and *Families* (1978). Her latest book is *Margaret Mead: A Life* (1984). She has taught at several universities.

Howard explains ten characteristics good families should have. Her definition of a family includes not only the one you are born into but also those that we may develop through close friendships.

Each of us is born into one family not of our choosing. If we're going to go around devising new ones, we might as well have the luxury of picking their members ourselves. Clever picking might result in new families whose benefits would surpass or at least equal those of the old. The new ones by definition cannot spawn us — as soon as they do that, they stop being new — but there is plenty they can do. I have seen them work wonders. As a member in reasonable standing of six or seven tribes in addition to the one I was born to, I have been trying to figure which earmarks are common to both kinds of families.

(1) Good families have a chief, or a heroine, or a founder — someone around whom others cluster, whose achievements as the Yiddish word has it, let them *kvell*, and whose example spurs them on to like feats. Some blood dynasties produce such figures regularly; others languish for as many as five generations between demigods, wondering with each new pregnancy whether this, at last, might be the messianic baby who will redeem us. Look, is there not something gubernatorial about her footstep, or musical about the way he bangs with his spoon on his cup? All clans, of all kinds, need such a figure now and then. Sometimes clans based on water rather than blood harbor several such personages at one time. The Bloomsbury Group in London six decades ago was not much hampered by its lack of a temporal history.

(2) Good families have a switchboard operator — someone like my mother who cannot help but keep track of what all the others are up to, who plays Houston Mission Control to everyone else's Apollo. This role, like the foregoing one, is assumed rather than assigned.

97

Someone always volunteers for it. That person often also has the instincts of an archivist, and feels driven to keep scrapbooks and photograph albums up to date, so that the clan can see proof of its own continuity.

(3) Good families are much to all their members, but everything ⁴ to none. Good families are fortresses with many windows and doors to the outer world. The blood clans I feel most drawn to were founded by parents who are nearly as devoted to whatever it is they do outside as they are to each other and their children. Their curiosity and passion are contagious. Everybody, where they live, is busy. Paint is spattered on eyeglasses. Mud lurks under fingernails. Person-to-person calls come in the middle of the night from Tokyo and Brussels. Catchers' mitts, ballet slippers, overdue library books and other signs of extra-familial concerns are everywhere.

(4) Good families are hospitable. Knowing that hosts need guests ⁵ as much as guests need hosts, they are generous with honorary memberships for friends, whom they urge to come early and often and to stay late. Such clans exude a vivid sense of surrounding rings of relatives, neighbors, teachers, students and godparents, any of whom at any time might break or slide into the inner circle. Inside that circle a wholesome, tacit emotional feudalism develops: you give me protection, I'll give you fealty. Such treaties begin with, but soon go far beyond, the jolly exchange of pie at Thanksgiving for cake on birthdays. It means you can ask me to supervise your children for the fortnight you will be in the hospital, and that however inconvenient this might be for me, I shall manage to. It means I can phone you on what for me is a dreary, wretched Sunday afternoon and for you is the eve of a deadline, knowing you will tell me to come right over, if only to watch you type. It means we need not dissemble. ("To yield to seeming," as Buber wrote, "is man's essential cowardice, to resist it is his essential courage . . . one must at times pay dearly for life lived from the being, but it is never too dear.")

(5) Good families deal squarely with direness. Pity the tribe that ⁶ doesn't have, and cherish, at least one flamboyant eccentric. Pity too the one that supposes it can avoid for long the woes to which all flesh is heir. Lunacy, bankruptcy, suicide and other unthinkable fates sooner or later afflict the noblest of clans with an undertow of gloom. Family life is a set of givens, someone once told me, and it takes courage to see certain givens as blessings rather than as curses. Contradictions and inconsistencies are givens, too. So is the war against what the Oregon patriarch Kenneth Babbs calls malarkey. "There's always malarkey lurking, bubbles in the cesspool, fetid bubbles that pop and smell. But I don't put up with malarkey, between my stepkids and my natural ones or anywhere else in the family."

(6) Good families prize their rituals. Nothing welds a family   7
more than these. Rituals are vital especially for clans without histories,
because they evoke a past, imply a future, and hint at continuity. No
line in the Seder service at Passover reassures more than the last: "Next
year in Jerusalem!" A clan becomes more of a clan each time it gathers
to observe a fixed ritual (Christmas, birthdays, Thanksgiving, and so
on), grieve at a funeral (anyone may come to most funerals; those who
do declare their tribalness), and devises a new rite of its own. Equinox
breakfasts and all-white dinners can be at least as welding as Memorial
Day parades. Several of us in the old *Life* magazine years used to meet
for lunch every Pearl Harbor Day, preferably to eat some politically
neutral fare like smorgasbord, to "forgive" our only ancestrally Japanese colleague Irene Kubota Neves. For that and other reasons we
became, and remain, a sort of family.

"Rituals," a California friend of mine said, "aren't just externals   8
and holidays. They are the performances of our lives. They are a kind
of shorthand. They can't be decreed. My mother used to try to decree
them. She'd make such a goddamn fuss over what we talked about at
dinner, aiming at Topics of Common Interest, topics that celebrated
our cohesion as a family. These performances were always hollow,
because the phenomenology of the moment got sacrificed for the *idea*
of the moment. Real rituals are discovered in retrospect. They emerge
around constitutive moments, moments that only happen once, around
whose memory meanings cluster. You don't choose those moments.
They choose themselves." A lucky clan includes a born mythologizer,
like my blood sister, who has the gift of apprehending such a moment
when she sees it, and who cannot help but invent new rituals every
where she goes.

(7) Good families are affectionate. This is of course a matter of   9
style. I know clans whose members greet each other with gingerly
handshakes or, in what pass for kisses, with hurried brushes of side
jawbones, as if the object were to touch not the lips but the ears. I
don't see how such people manage. "The tribe that does not hug," as
someone who has been part of many *ad hoc* families recently wrote to
me, "is no tribe at all. More and more I realize that everybody, regardless of age, needs to be hugged and comforted in a brotherly or sisterly
way now and then. Preferably now."

(8) Good families have a sense of place, which these days is not   10
achieved easily. As Susanne Langer wrote in 1957, "Most people have
no home that is a symbol of their childhood, not even a definite
memory of one place to serve that purpose . . . all the old symbols
are gone." Once I asked a roomful of supper guests who, if anyone,
felt any strong pull to any certain spot on the face of the earth.
Everyone was silent, except for a visitor from Bavaria. The rest of us

seemed to know all too well what Walker Percy means in *The Movie-goer* when he tells of the "genie-soul of the place which every place has or else is not a place [and which] wherever you go, you must meet and master or else be met and mastered." All that meeting and mastering saps plenty of strength. It also underscores our need for tribal bases of the sort which soaring real estate taxes and splintering families have made all but obsolete.

So what are we to do, those of us whose habit and pleasure and   11
doom is our tendency, as a Georgia lady put it, to "fly off at every other whipstitch?" Think in terms of movable feasts, for a start. Live here, wherever here may be, as if we were going to belong here for the rest of our lives. Learn to hallow whatever ground we happen to stand on or land on. Like medieval knights who took their tapestries along on Crusades, like modern Afghanis with their yurts, we must pack such totems and icons as we can to make short-term quarters feel like home. Pillows, small rugs, watercolors can dispel much of the chilling anonymity of a sublet apartment or motel room. When we can, we should live in rooms with stoves or fireplaces or anyway candlelight. The ancient saying still is true: Extinguished hearth, extinguished family. Round tables help, too, and as a friend of mine once put it, so do "too many comfortable chairs, with surfaces to put feet on, arranged so as to encourage a maximum of eye contact." Such rooms inspire good talk, of which good clans can never have enough.

(9) Good families, not just the blood kind, find some way to   12
connect with posterity. "To forge a link in the humble chain of being, encircling heirs to ancestors," as Michael Novak has written, "is to walk within a circle of magic as primitive as humans knew in caves." He is talking of course about babies, feeling them leap in wombs, giving them suck. Parenthood, however, is a state which some miss by chance and others by design, and a vocation to which not all are called. Some of us, like the novelist Richard P. Brickner, "look on as others name their children who in turn name their own lives, devising their own flags from their parents' cloth." What are we who lack children to do? Build houses? Plant trees? Write books or symphonies or laws? Perhaps, but even if we do these things, there still should be children on the sidelines, if not at the center, of our lives. It is a sadly impoverished tribe that does not allow access to, and make much of, some children. Not too much, of course: it has truly been said that never in history have so many educated people devoted so much attention to so few children. Attention, in excess, can turn to fawning, which isn't much better than neglect. Still, if we don't regularly see and talk to and laugh with people who can expect to outlive us by twenty years or so, we had better get busy and find some.

(10) Good families also honor their elders. The wider the age   13

range, the stronger the tribe. Jean-Paul Sartre and Margaret Mead, to name two spectacularly confident former children, have both remarked on the central importance of grandparents in their own early lives. Grandparents now are in much more abundant supply than they were a generation or two ago when old age was more rare. If actual grandparents are not at hand, no family should have too hard a time finding substitute ones to whom to give unfeigned homage. The Soviet Union's enchantment with day care centers, I have heard, stems at least in part from the state's eagerness to keep children away from their presumably subversive grandparents. Let that be a lesson to clans based on interest as well as to those based on genes.

EXERCISES

Words to Know

messianic (paragraph 2), Bloomsbury Group (2), temporal (2), exude (5), feudalism (5), fortnight (5), direness (6), flamboyant (6), inconsistencies (6), Passover (7), Equinox (7), smorgasbord (7), decreed (8), constitutive (8), whipstitch (11), Crusades (11), anonymity (11), posterity (12), fawning (12), Jean-Paul Sartre (13), Margaret Mead (13).

Some of the Issues

1. In paragraph 1, and elsewhere in her book *Families*, Howard suggests that people should build their own families, "devising new ones" with friends, supplementing (or replacing?) natural families. What do you think of her idea?
2. In offering her ten "earmarks . . . common to both kinds of families" does she distinguish at any time between "natural" and "new" families? If so, in what way?
3. Look at each of the ten points, and consider if each one is convincing. If you agree, try to add evidence from your own experience. If you disagree, try to develop counterarguments.
*4. Read Alfred Kazin's "The Kitchen." Which of the ten points fit that family and why?

The Way We Are Told

5. Each of the ten points begins in exactly the same way. What is the effect of this repetition?

6. Describe how each of the points is constructed. How is the content arranged? How consistent is the arrangement?
7. Howard frequently uses what one can call "the part for the whole"; examples are the last two sentences of point 3; or, in point 4, "you can ask me to supervise your children for the fortnight you will be in the hospital." Find other examples. What is their effect?

Some Subjects for Essays

8. Select a topic similar to Howard's, for example, "The good citizen," or "An educated person," or "An effective teacher." Then treat it as Howard might, developing the points one by one that together constitute a series of definitions of the subject.
9. Are gangs families? Argue for or against that proposition.
10. Howard's definitions are implicitly based on mainstream American culture. On the basis of your experience or reading, would you say that her definitions hold for families in another culture?

THE KITCHEN

Alfred Kazin

Alfred Kazin, born in New York in 1915, has taught at several
universities, most recently at the City University of New York. He
has held several distinguished fellowships and is a member of the
American Academy of Arts and Sciences. His books include *On
Native Grounds* (1942), *The Inmost Leaf* (1955), *Starting Out
in the Thirties* (1965), *New York Jew* (1978), and *An American
Procession* (1984).

In this selection from *A Walker in the City* (1957) Kazin
describes the setting in which he grew up. It was not unusual for
its time and place: a tenement district in a large American city,
peopled with immigrants from eastern Europe, working hard,
struggling for a life for themselves and more importantly for their
children.

The large-scale immigration that brought as many as one
million new inhabitants annually from Europe to America lasted
from the 1880s to the First World War. The majority of the immigrants in those years came from eastern, southern, and central
Europe. They included large numbers of Jewish families like
Kazin's, escaping not only the stifling poverty of their regions but
also the outright persecution, the pogroms, to which they were
subjected in Czarist Russia.

In Brownsville tenements the kitchen is always the largest room and   1
the center of the household. As a child I felt we lived in a kitchen to
which four other rooms were annexed. My mother, a "home" dress-
maker, had her workshop in the kitchen. She told me once that she had
begun dressmaking in Poland at thirteen; as far back as I can remember, she was always making dresses for the local women. She had
an innate sense of design, a quick eye for all the subtleties in the latest
fashions, even when she despised them, and great boldness. For three
or four dollars she would study the fashion magazines with a customer,
go with the customer to the remnants store on Belmont Avenue to pick
out the material, argue the owner down — all remnants stores, for

some reason, were supposed to be shady, as if the owners dealt in stolen goods — and then for days would patiently fit and baste and sew and fit again. Our apartment was always full of women in their house-dresses sitting around the kitchen table waiting for a fitting. My little bedroom next to the kitchen was the fitting room. The sewing machine, an old nut-brown Singer with golden scrolls painted along the black arm and engraved along the two tiers of little drawers massed with needles and thread on each side of the treadle, stood next to the window and the great coal-black stove which up to my last year in college was our main source of heat. By December the two outer bedrooms were closed off, and used to chill bottles of milk and cream, cold borscht and jellied calves' feet.

The kitchen held our lives together. My mother worked in it all 2 day long, we ate in it almost all meals except the Passover *seder*, I did my homework and first writing at the kitchen table, and in winter I often had a bed made up for me on three kitchen chairs near the stove. On the wall just over the table hung a long horizontal mirror that sloped to a ship's prow at each end and was lined in cherry wood. It took up the whole wall, and drew every object in the kitchen to itself. The walls were a fiercely stippled whitewash, so often rewhitened by my father in slack seasons that the paint looked as if it had been squeezed and cracked into the walls. A large electric bulb hung down the center of the kitchen at the end of a chain that had been hooked into the ceiling; the old gas ring and key still jutted out of the wall like antlers. In the corner next to the toilet was the sink at which we washed, and the square tub in which my mother did our clothes. Above it, tacked to the shelf on which were pleasantly ranged square, blue bordered white sugar and spice jars, hung calendars from the Public National Bank on Pitkin Avenue and the Minsker Progressive Branch of the Workman's Circle; receipts for the payment of insurance premiums, and household bills on a spindle; two little boxes engraved with Hebrew letters. One of these was for the poor, the other to buy back the Land of Israel. Each spring a bearded little man would suddenly appear in our kitchen, salute us with a hurried Hebrew blessing, empty the boxes (sometimes with a sidelong look of disdain if they were not full), hurriedly bless us again for remembering our less fortunate Jewish brothers and sisters, and so take his departure until the next spring, after vainly trying to persuade my mother to take still another box. We did occasionally remember to drop coins in the boxes, but this was usually only on the dreaded morning of "mid-terms" and final examinations, because my mother thought it would bring me luck. She was extremely superstitious, but embarrassed about it, and always laughed at herself whenever, on the morning of an examination, she counseled me to leave the house on my right foot. "I know it's silly," her smile seemed to say, "but what harm can it do? It may calm God down."

The kitchen gave a special character to our lives; my mother's character. All my memories of that kitchen are dominated by the nearness of my mother sitting all day long at her sewing machine, by the clacking of the treadle against the linoleum floor, by the patient twist of her right shoulder as she automatically pushed at the wheel with one hand or lifted the foot to free the needle where it had got stuck in a thick piece of material. The kitchen was her life. Year by year, as I began to take in her fantastic capacity for labor and her anxious zeal, I realized it was ourselves she kept stitched together. I can never remember a time when she was not working. She worked because the law of her life was work, work and anxiety; she worked because she would have found life meaningless without work. She read almost no English; she could read the Yiddish paper, but never felt she had time to. We were always talking of a time when I would teach her how to read, but somehow there was never time. When I awoke in the morning she was already at her machine, or in the great morning crowd of housewives at the grocery getting fresh rolls for breakfast. When I returned from school she was at her machine, or conferring over *McCall's* with some neighborhood woman who had come in pointing hopefully to an illustration — "Mrs. Kazin! Mrs. Kazin! Make me a dress like it shows here in the picture!" When my father came home from work she had somehow mysteriously interrupted herself to make supper for us, and the dishes cleared and washed, was back at her machine. When I went to bed at night, often she was still there, pounding away at the treadle, hunched over the wheel, her hands steering a piece of gauze under the needle with a finesse that always contrasted sharply with her swollen hands and broken nails. Her left hand had been pierced through when as a girl she had worked in the infamous Triangle Shirtwaist Factory on the East Side. A needle had gone straight through the palm, severing a large vein. They had sewn it up for her so clumsily that a tuft of flesh always lay folded over the palm.

The kitchen was the great machine that set our lives running; it whirred down a little only on Saturdays and holy days. From my mother's kitchen I gained my first picture of life as a white, overheated, starkly lit workshop redolent with Jewish cooking, crowded with women in housedresses, strewn with fashion magazines, patterns, dress material, spools of thread — and at whose center, so lashed to her machine that bolts of energy seemed to dance out of her hands and feet as she worked, my mother stamped the treadle hard against the floor, hard, hard, and silently, grimly at war, beat out the first rhythm of the world for me.

EXERCISES

Words to Know

tenement (paragraph 1), innate (1), Passover *seder* (2), stippled (2), Triangle Shirtwaist Factory (3).

Some of the Issues

1. Kazin writes about the kitchen in his childhood home. Is he writing from the point of view of a child or an adult? What indications do you have of one or the other?
2. In speaking of his mother, Kazin says, "The law of her life was work, work and anxiety." In an age in which many people's goal is self-fulfillment this does not seem to be a happy life. Can you find any evidence as to whether Mrs. Kazin was happy or unhappy? What pleasures did she have?
3. What is the meaning of the first sentence in paragraph 4? Why does Kazin call the kitchen "the great machine"?

The Way We Are Told

4. The same two words are repeated in the first sentence of each paragraph. What purpose does that repetition serve?
5. Compare the first two paragraphs. How do they differ from each other in content and in the way they are written?
6. Kazin talks about the kitchen of his childhood home but does not describe it until the second paragraph. What would be the effect if he had started with that description?
7. Reread the second paragraph. What details does Kazin give? How are they arranged—in which kind of order? Could an artist draw a picture on the basis of Kazin's description? Could an architect draw a plan from it?
8. Kazin describes several items in detail—the sewing machine, aspects of the kitchen itself, and his mother's work. Find some adjectives that stand out because they are unusual or that add precision or feeling to his descriptions.

Some Subjects for Essays

9. Write a paragraph about a place of significance for you, using Kazin's second paragraph as your model. Try to show its significance by the way you describe it.
10. Consider the role of work in the life of Kazin's mother. If you

know someone whose life seems completely tied up with some specific activity, describe that person through his or her activity.

11. More and more women are joining the work force in America in the 1980's. Many of them are married and have children. Write an essay in which you discuss the causes for this major social change and argue either for or against it.

*12. Read Arlene Skolnick's "The Paradox of Perfection." Examine the extent to which Kazin's family represents the kind of family Skolnick describes, particularly in paragraphs 23 to 27.

*13. Look at the photograph on page 94. The lighted candles on the coffee table indicate that the scene depicts a Jewish home on an evening of Hanukkah. Consider the atmosphere created in the picture and compare it to the atmosphere Kazin describes in his essay. In what respects do you think a Hanukkah evening in the Kazin household would have differed from the one in the picture?

DIARY

Carolina Maria de Jesus

Carolina Maria de Jesus, the child of illiterate Brazilian farm workers, was born in 1913. She learned to read in the space of three months but had altogether no more than two years of schooling. In her youth she worked at various jobs until her first pregnancy forced her to give up regular work and, like thousands of other penniless people, built her own shack of boards and tin cans in one of Brazil's *favelas*, or slums. She bore seven children, only three of whom survived infancy. She kept a diary which a news reporter discovered and persuaded her to publish. It appeared in book form in 1960, became Brazil's all-time best-seller, and was instrumental in promoting some reforms in the slums that surround Brazil's major cities.

To learn more about Brazil, read the headnote for Conrad Phillip Kottak's "Swimming in Cross-Cultural Currents."

July 15, 1955   The birthday of my daughter Vera Eunice. I wanted to buy a pair of shoes for her, but the price of food keeps us from realizing our desires. Actually we are slaves to the cost of living. I found a pair of shoes in the garbage, washed them, and patched them for her to wear.

I didn't have one cent to buy bread. So I washed three bottles and traded them to Arnaldo. He kept the bottles and gave me bread. Then I went to sell my paper. I received 65 cruzeiros. I spent 20 cruzeiros for meat. I got one kilo of ham and one kilo of sugar and spent six cruzeiros on cheese. And the money was gone.

I was ill all day. I thought I had a cold. At night my chest pained me. I started to cough. I decided not to go out at night to look for paper. I searched for my son João. He was at Felisberto de Carvalho Street near the market. A bus had knocked a boy into the sidewalk and a crowd gathered. João was in the middle of it all. I poked him a couple of times and within five minutes he was home.

I washed the children, put them to bed, then washed myself and went to bed. I waited until 11:00 for a certain someone. He didn't come. I took an aspirin and laid down again. When I awoke the sun was sliding in space. My daughter Vera Eunice said: "Go get some water, Mother!"

108

July 16 I got up and obeyed Vera Eunice. I went to get the   5
water. I made coffee. I told the children that I didn't have any bread,
that they would have to drink their coffee plain and eat meat with
farinha. I was feeling ill and decided to cure myself. I stuck my finger
down my throat twice, vomited, and knew I was under the evil eye.
The upset feeling left and I went to Senhor Manuel, carrying some cans
to sell. Everything that I find in the garbage I sell. He gave me 13
cruzeiros. I kept thinking that I had to buy bread, soap, and milk for
Vera Eunice. The 13 cruzeiros wouldn't make it. I returned home, or
rather to my shack, nervous and exhausted. I thought of the worrisome
life that I led. Carrying paper, washing clothes for the children, staying
in the street all day long. Yet I'm always lacking things, Vera doesn't
have shoes and she doesn't like to go barefoot. For at least two years
I've wanted to buy a meat grinder. And a sewing machine.

I came home and made lunch for the two boys. Rice, beans, and   6
meat, and I'm going out to look for paper. I left the children, told them
to play in the yard and not go into the street, because the terrible
neighbors I have won't leave my children alone. I was feeling ill and
wished I could lie down. But the poor don't rest nor are they permitted
the pleasure of relaxation. I was nervous inside, cursing my luck, I
collected two sacks full of paper. Afterward I went back and gathered
up some scrap metal, some cans, and some kindling wood. As I walked
I thought — when I return to the favela there is going to be something
new. Maybe Dona Rosa or the insolent Angel Mary fought with my
children. I found Vera Eunice sleeping and the boys playing in the
street. I thought: it's 2:00. Maybe I'm going to get through this day
without anything happening. João told me that the truck that gives out
money was here to give out food. I took a sack and hurried out. It was
the leader of the Spiritist Center at 103 Vergueiro Street. I got two
kilos of rice, two of beans, and two kilos of macaroni. I was happy. The
truck went away. The nervousness that I had inside left me. I took
advantage of my calmness to read. I picked up a magazine and sat on
the grass, letting the rays of the sun warm me as I read a story. I wrote a
note and gave it to my boy João to take to Senhor Arnaldo to buy soap,
two aspirins, and some bread. Then I put water on the stove to make
coffee. João came back saying he had lost the aspirins. I went back with
him to look. We didn't find them.

When I came home there was a crowd at my door. Children and   7
women claiming José Carlos had thrown stones at their houses. They
wanted me to punish him.

July 17 Sunday A marvelous day. The sky was blue without one   8
cloud. The sun was warm. I got out of bed at 6:30 and went to get
water. I only had one piece of bread and three cruzeiros. I gave a small

piece to each child and put the beans, that I got yesterday from the Spiritist Center, on the fire. Then I went to wash clothes. When I returned from the river the beans were cooked. The children asked for bread. I gave the three cruzeiros to João to go and buy some. Today it was Nair Mathias who started an argument with my children. Silvia and her husband have begun an open-air spectacle. He is hitting her and I'm disgusted because the children are present. They heard words of the lowest kind. Oh, if I could move from here to a more decent neighborhood!

I went to Dona Florela to ask for a piece of garlic. I went to Dona   9
Analia and got exactly what I expected:

"I don't have any!"   10

I went to collect my clothes. Dona Aparecida asked me: 11

"Are you pregnant?"   12

"No, Senhora," I replied gently.   13

I cursed her under my breath. If I am pregnant it's not your   14
business. I can't stand these favela women, they want to know everything. Their tongues are like chicken feet. Scratching at everything.
The rumor is circulating that I am pregnant! If I am, I don't know about
it!

I went out at night to look for paper. When I was passing the São   15
Paulo football stadium many people were coming out. All of them
were white and only one black. And the black started to insult me:

"Are you looking for paper, auntie? Watch your step, auntie   16
dear!"

I was ill and wanted to lie down, but I went on. I met several   17
friends and stopped to talk to them. When I was going up Tiradentes
Avenue I met some women. One of them asked me:

"Are your legs healed?"   18

After I was operated on, I got better, thanks to God. I could even   19
dance at Carnival in my feather costume. Dr. José Torres Netto was
who operated on me. A good doctor. And we spoke of politics. When a
woman asked me what I thought of Carlos Lacerda [President of Brazil
from 1956 to 1961], I replied truthfully:

"He is very intelligent, but he doesn't have an education. He is a   20
slum politician. He likes intrigues, to agitate."

One woman said it was a pity, that the bullet that got the major   21
didn't get Carlos Lacerda.

"But his day . . . it's coming," commented another.   22

Many people had gathered and I was the center of attention. I was   23
embarrassed because I was looking for paper and dressed in rags. I
didn't want to talk to anyone, because I had to collect paper. I needed
the money. There was none in the house to buy bread. I worked until
11:30. When I returned home it was midnight. I warmed up some

food, gave some to Vera Eunice, ate and laid down. When I awoke the rays of the sun were coming through the gaps of the shack.

EXERCISES

Words to Know

cruzeiro—unit of Brazilian currency (paragraph 2), kilo (2), *farinha*—coarse wheat flour (5).

Some of the Issues

1. Carolina Maria de Jesus records events of her daily existence. What makes them interesting?
2. Occasionally de Jesus interrupts her record of events for a comment. Find several of these and try to show how they relate to the details she gives.
3. How does de Jesus separate herself from the other women in the *favela*?

The Way We Are Told

4. Some of the reasons for the effectiveness of the de Jesus diary are the absence of self-pity and her way of understating the hardships of her existence. Find and analyze two or three examples of each.
5. The usual account we read of slum life is written by a social scientist or journalist—an outsider. De Jesus's account differs in telling the story from the inside. Find several elements in the diary that indicate that difference.

Some Subjects for Essays

6. Keep a diary for one week, with daily entries, in which you record what happens to you and your immediate reactions to the events.

THE PARADOX
OF PERFECTION

Arlene Skolnick

Arlene Skolnick is a research psychologist at the Institute of Human Development, University of California at Berkeley. Born in 1933, she received her undergraduate education at Queens College and her Ph.D. in psychology from Yale in 1962. She is the author of *The Intimate Environment* (1973) and *The Psychology of Human Development* (1986). The article reprinted here first appeared in the *Wilson Quarterly*. In examining the development of the family from colonial times to the present, Skolnick finds that in recent times we have come to look upon the ideal as if it were the norm, making every state less than perfection seem like failure.

In examining the myth of perfection, Skolnick makes reference to *Brigadoon* (paragraph 8), a Broadway musical and Hollywood film. Brigadoon was an imaginary town that came to life every one hundred years, never changing from its idealized state. Dr. Benjamin Spock's (paragraph 31) advice to new parents, especially his best-selling book *Baby and Child Care*, has shaped family life for a generation. Alexis de Tocqueville (1805–1859), mentioned in paragraph 24, was a French aristocrat who traveled throughout America. Deeply impressed with what he saw as a new society, he published his observations and reflections in *Democracy in America*.

The American Family, as even readers of *Popular Mechanics* must know by now, is in what Sean O'Casey would have called "a terrible state of chassis." Yet, there are certain ironies about the much-publicized crisis that give one pause.

True, the statistics seem alarming. The U.S. divorce rate, though it has reached something of a plateau in recent years, remains the highest in American history. The number of births out-of-wedlock among all races and ethnic groups continues to climb. The plight of many elderly Americans subsisting on low fixed incomes is well known.

What puzzles me is an ambiguity, not in the facts, but in what we are asked to make of them. A series of opinion polls conducted in 1978 by Yankelovich, Skelley, and White, for example, found that 38 percent of those surveyed had recently witnessed one or more "destructive activities" (e.g., a divorce, a separation, a custody battle) within their own families or those of their parents or siblings. At the same time, 92 percent of the respondents said the family was highly important to them as a "personal value."

Can the family be at once a cherished "value" and a troubled   4
institution? I am inclined to think, in fact, that they go hand in hand. A recent "Talk of the Town" report in *The New Yorker* illustrates what I mean:

> A few months ago word was heard from Billy Gray, who used to play brother Bud in "Father Knows Best," the 1950s television show about the nice Anderson family who lived in the white frame house on a side street in some mythical Springfield — the house at which the father arrived each night swinging open the front door and singing out "Margaret, I'm home!" Gray said he felt "ashamed" that he had ever had anything to do with the show. It was all "totally false," he said, and had caused many Americans to feel inadequate, because they thought that was the way life was supposed to be and that their own lives failed to measure up.

As Susan Sontag has noted in *On Photography*, mass-produced   5
images have "extraordinary powers to determine our demands upon reality." The family is especially vulnerable to confusion between truth and illusion. What, after all, is "normal"? All of us have a backstairs view of our own families, but we know The Family, in the aggregate, only vicariously.

Like politics or athletics, the family has become a media event.   6
Television offers nightly portrayals of lump-in-the-throat family "normalcy" ("The Waltons," "Little House on the Prairie") and, nowadays, even humorous "deviance" ("One Day at a Time," "The Odd Couple"). Family advisers sally forth in syndicated newspaper columns to uphold standards, mend relationships, suggest counseling, and otherwise lead their readers back to the True Path. For commercial purposes, advertisers spend millions of dollars to create stirring vignettes of glamorous-but-ordinary families, the kind of family most 11-year-olds wish they had.

All Americans do not, of course, live in such a family, but most   7
share an intuitive sense of what the "ideal" family should be — reflected in the precepts of religion, the conventions of etiquette, and the assumptions of law. And, characteristically, Americans tend to project the ideal back into the past, the time when virtues of all sorts are thought to have flourished.

We do not come off well by comparison with that golden age, nor   8
could we, for it is as elusive and mythical as Brigadoon. If Billy Gray

shames too easily, he has a valid point: While Americans view the family as the proper context for their own lives — 9 out of 10 people live in one — they have no realistic context in which to view the family. Family history, until recently, was as neglected in academe as it still is in the press. The familiar, depressing charts of "leading family indicators" — marriage, divorce, illegitimacy — in newspapers and newsmagazines rarely survey the trends before World War II. The discussion, in short, lacks ballast.

Let us go back to before the American Revolution.   9

Perhaps what distinguishes the modern family most from its colo-   10
nial counterpart is its newfound privacy. Throughout the 17th and 18th centuries, well over 90 percent of the American population lived in small rural communities. Unusual behavior rarely went unnoticed, and neighbors often intervened directly in a family's affairs, to help or to chastise.

The most dramatic example was the rural "charivari," prevalent   11
in both Europe and the United States until the early 19th century. The purpose of these noisy gatherings was to censure community members for familial transgressions — unusual sexual behavior, marriages between persons of grossly discrepant ages, or "household disorder," to name but a few. As historian Edward Shorter describes it in *The Making of the Modern Family*:

> Sometimes the demonstration would consist of masked individuals circling somebody's house at night, screaming, beating on pans, and blowing cow horns . . . on other occasions, the offender would be seized and marched through the streets, seated perhaps backwards on a donkey or forced to wear a placard describing his sins.

The state itself had no qualms about intruding into a family's   12
affairs by statute, if necessary. Consider 17th-century New England's "stubborn child" laws that, though never actually enforced, sanctioned the death penalty for chronic disobedience to one's parents.

If the boundaries between home and society seem blurred during   13
the colonial era, it is because they were. People were neither very emotional nor very self-conscious about family life, and, as historian John Demos points out, family and community were "joined in a relation of profound reciprocity." In his *Of Domesticall Duties*, William Gouge, a 17th-century Puritan preacher, called the family "a little community." The home, like the larger community, was as much an economic as a social unit; all members of the family worked, be it on the farm, or in a shop, or in the home.

There was not much to idealize. Love was not considered the   14
basis for marriage but one possible result of it. According to historian
Carl Degler, it was easier to obtain a divorce in colonial New England
than anywhere else in the Western world, and the divorce rate climbed
steadily throughout the 18th century, though it remained low by
contemporary standards. Romantic images to the contrary, it was rare
for more than two generations (parents and children) to share a household, for the simple reason that very few people lived beyond the age
of 60. It is ironic that our nostalgia for the extended family —
including grandparents and grandchildren — comes at a time when,
thanks to improvements in health care, its existence is less threatened
than ever before.

Infant mortality was high in colonial days, though not as high as   15
we are accustomed to believe, since food was plentiful and epidemics,
owing to generally low population density, were few. In the
mid-1700s, the average age of marriage was about 24 for men, 21 for
women — not much different from what it is now. Households, on
average, were larger, but not startlingly so: A typical household in
1790 included about 5.6 members, versus about 3.5 today. Illegitimacy was widespread. Premarital pregnancies reached a high in 18th-
century America (10 percent of all first births) that was not equalled
until the 1950s.

In simple demographic terms, then, the differences between the   16
American family in colonial times and today are not all that stark; the
similarities are sometimes striking.

The chief contrast is psychological. While Western societies have   17
always idealized the family to some degree, the *most vivid* literary
portrayals of family life before the 19th century were negative or, at
best, ambivalent. In what might be called the "high tragic" tradition
— including Sophocles, Shakespeare, and the Bible, as well as fairy
tales and novels — the family was portrayed as a high-voltage emotional setting, laden with dark passions, sibling rivalries, and violence.
There was also the "low comic" tradition — the world of hen-pecked
husbands and tyrannical mothers-in-law.

It is unlikely that our 18th-century ancestors ever left the book of   18
Genesis or *Tom Jones* with the feeling that their own family lives were
seriously flawed.

By the time of the Civil War, however, American attitudes toward   19
the family had changed profoundly. The early decades of the 19th
century marked the beginnings of America's gradual transformation
into an urban, industrial society. In 1820, less than 8 percent of the
U.S. population lived in cities; by 1860, the urban concentration
approached 20 percent, and by 1900 that proportion had doubled.

Structurally, the American family did not immediately undergo a   20
comparable transformation. Despite the large families of many immigrants and farmers, the size of the *average* family declined — slowly
but steadily — as it had been doing since the 17th century. Infant
mortality remained about the same, and may even have increased
somewhat, owing to poor sanitation in crowded cities. Legal divorces
were easier to obtain than they had been in colonial times. Indeed, the
rise in the divorce rate was a matter of some concern during the 19th
century, though death, not divorce, was the prime cause of one-parent
families, as it was up to 1965.

Functionally, however, America's industrial revolution had a   21
lasting effect on the family. No longer was the household typically a
group of interdependent workers. Now, men went to offices and factories and became breadwinners; wives stayed home to mind the hearth;
children went off to the new public schools. The home was set apart
from the dog-eat-dog arena of economic life; it came to be viewed as a
utopian retreat or, in historian Christopher Lasch's phrase, a "haven in
a heartless world." Marriage was now valued primarily for its emotional attractions. Above all, the family became something to worry
about.

The earliest and most saccharine "sentimental model" of the   22
family appeared in the new mass media that proliferated during the
second quarter of the 19th century. Novels, tracts, newspaper articles,
and ladies' magazines — there were variations for each class of society
— elaborated a "Cult of True Womanhood" in which piety, submissiveness, and domesticity dominated the pantheon of desirable feminine qualities. This quotation from *The Ladies Book* (1830) is typical:

> See, she sits, she walks, she speaks, she looks — unutterable things!
> Inspiration springs up in her very paths — it follows her footsteps. A
> halo of glory encircles her, and illuminates her whole orbit. With her,
> man not only feels safe, but actually renovated.

In the late 1800s, science came into the picture. The "profes-   23
sionalization" of the housewife took two different forms. One involved motherhood and childrearing, according to the latest scientific
understanding of children's special physical and emotional needs. (It
is no accident that the publishing of children's books became a major
industry during this period.) The other was the domestic science
movement — "home economics," basically — which focused on the
woman as full-time homemaker, applying "scientific" and "industrial" rationality to shopping, making meals, and housework.

The new ideal of the family prompted a cultural split that has   24 endured, one that Tocqueville had glimpsed (and rather liked) in 1835. Society was divided more sharply into man's sphere and woman's sphere. Toughness, competition, and practicality were the masculine values that ruled the outside world. The softer values — affection, tranquility, piety — were worshiped in the home and the church. In contrast to the colonial view, the ideology of the "modern" family implied a critique of everything beyond the front door.

What is striking as one looks at the writings of the 19th-century   25
"experts" — the physicians, clergymen, phrenologists, and "scrib- bling ladies" — is how little their essential message differs from that of the sociologists, psychiatrists, pediatricians, and women's magazine writers of the 20th century, particularly since World War II.

Instead of men's and women's spheres, of course, sociologists   26
speak of "instrumental" and "expressive" roles. The notion of the family as a retreat from the harsh realities of the outside world crops up as "functional differentiation." And, like the 19th-century utopians who believed society could be regenerated through the perfection of family life, 20th-century social scientists have looked at the failed family as the source of most American social problems.

None of those who promoted the sentimental model of the   27
family — neither the popular writers nor the academics — considered the paradox of perfectionism: the ironic possibility that it would lead to trouble. Yet it has. The image of the perfect, happy family makes ordinary families seem like failures. Small problems loom as big prob- lems if the "normal" family is thought to be one where there are no real problems at all.

One sees this phenomenon at work on the generation of Ameri-   28
cans born and reared during the late 19th century, the first generation reared on the mother's milk of sentimental imagery. Between 1900 and 1920, the U.S. divorce rate doubled, from four to eight divorces annually per 1,000 married couples. The jump — comparable to the 100 percent increase in the divorce rate between 1960 and 1980 — is not attributable to changes in divorce laws, which were not greatly liberalized. Rather, it would appear that, as historian Thomas O'Neill believes, Americans were simply more willing to dissolve marriages that did not conform to their ideal of domestic bliss — and perhaps try again.

If anything, family standards became even more demanding as   29
the 20th century progressed. The new fields of psychology and sociol- ogy opened up whole new definitions of familial perfection. "Feelings" — fun, love, warmth, good orgasm — acquired heightened popular significance as the invisible glue of successful families.

Psychologist Martha Wolfenstein, in an analysis of several de-   30 cades of government-sponsored infant care manuals, has documented the emergence of a "fun morality." In former days, being a good parent meant carrying out certain tasks with punctilio; if your child was clean and reasonably obedient, you had no cause to probe his psyche. Now, we are told, parents must commune with their own feelings and those of their children — an edict which has seeped into the ethos of education as well. The distinction is rather like that between religions of deed and religions of faith. It is one thing to make your child brush his teeth; it is quite another to transform the whole process into a joyous "learning experience."

The task of 20th-century parents has been further complicated by the advice offered them. The experts disagree with each other and often contradict themselves. The kindly Dr. Benjamin Spock, for example, is full of contradictions. In a detailed analysis of *Baby and Child Care*, historian Michael Zuckerman observes that Spock tells mothers to relax ("trust yourself") yet warns them that they have an "ominous power" to destroy their children's innocence and make them discontented "for years" or even "forever."   31

Since the mid-1960s, there has been a youth rebellion of sorts, a new "sexual revolution," a revival of feminism, and the emergence of the two-worker family. The huge postwar Baby-Boom generation is pairing off, accounting in part for the upsurge in the divorce rate (half of all divorces occur within seven years of a first marriage). Media images of the family have become more "realistic," reflecting new patterns of family life that are emerging (and old patterns that are re-emerging).   32

Among social scientists, "realism" is becoming something of an ideal in itself. For some of them, realism translates as pluralism: All forms of the family, by virtue of the fact that they happen to exist, are equally acceptable — from communes and cohabitation to one-parent households, homosexual marriages, and, come to think of it, the nuclear family. What was once labeled "deviant" is now merely "variant." In some college texts, "the family" has been replaced by "family systems." Yet, this new approach does not seem to have squelched perfectionist standards. Indeed, a palpable strain of perfectionism runs through the pop literature on "alternative" family lifestyles.   33

For the majority of scholars, realism means a more down-to-earth view of the American household. Rather than seeing the family as a haven of peace and tranquility, they have begun to recognize that even "normal" families are less than ideal, that intimate relations of any sort inevitably involve antagonism as well as love. Conflict and change are inherent in social life. If the family is now in a state of flux, such is the nature of resilient institutions; if it is beset by problems, so is life. The family will survive.   34

EXERCISES

Words to Know

paradox (title), plateau (2), plight (2), subsisting (2), ambiguity (3), custody (3), mythical (4), vulnerable (5), vicariously (5), deviance (6), syndicated (6), vignettes (6), intuitive (7), elusive (8), academe (8), ballast (8), chastise (10), prevalent (11), qualms (12), chronic (13), nostalgia (14), demographic (16), ambivalent (17), Sophocles (17), sibling (17), henpecked (17), utopian (21), haven (21), saccharine (22), proliferated (22), tracts (22), submissiveness (22), phrenologists (25), regenerated (26), ironic (27), phenomenon (28), imagery (28), punctilio (29), psyche (30), ethos (30), nostrums (32), pluralism (33), palpable (33), resilient (34).

Some of the Issues

1. Skolnik begins her analysis by saying that just about everyone knows that the family is in crisis. How does she support that assertion in the first three paragraphs?
2. Why is the family, according to Skolnik, "particularly vulnerable to the confusion between truth and illusion"? How have the media increased that confusion?
3. In paragraph 8 Skolnik says: "While Americans view the family as the proper context for their own lives . . . they have no realistic context in which to view the family." What does she mean? How do Billy Gray's attitude (paragraph 4) and the examples drawn from the media (paragraphs 5–7) support her statement?
4. What reasons does Skolnik give for her decision to go back to before the American revolution in tracing the history of the American family (paragraph 8)? What is the chief distinction she sees between the modern family and the family of 200 years ago? On the other hand, in what respects is the difference not very great?
5. What was the gradual effect on the family of the change from a predominantly rural society to an industrial, urban one (paragraphs 19–21)?
6. What were the causes for the increasing division of family roles into a man's sphere and the woman's sphere, according to Skolnik? How do the two spheres differ?
7. In paragraph 27, Skolnik turns to the "paradox" she has referred to in her title. What is it? What is the irony in seeking perfectionism for the family?

8. What are the more demanding standards that modern social science has imposed on the family according to Skolnick (paragraphs 29–31)?
9. In the last two paragraphs (33–34) Skolnik speaks of "a new realism." What does she mean?
*10. Compare and contrast the "realism" Skolnick talks about in the last two paragraphs to Jane Howard's view of what constitutes a good family in her essay "Families."

The Way We Are Told

11. In paragraph 1 Skolnick first states the commonly held view that the family is in a sorry state. In what way does the second sentence foreshadow the argument she will make?
12. Consider paragraph 8; how does Skolnick make a transition from her analysis of the contemporary family to the topic she introduces with her one-line paragraph 9?
13. Skolnick puts words or sentences in quotation marks, but these "quotes" are of two kinds. One is the regular kind, as for example those in paragraph 3. The other is used for some specific effect, such as "normalcy" (paragraph 6) or "ideal" (paragraph 7). Find further examples of the second kind and explain their effect.

Some Subjects for Essays

14. In her final paragraph Skolnick gives the reader a rather optimistic view of the future of the family. Examine if her arguments based on history justify that conclusion, and why (or why not).
15. Skolnick claims that in 1980, when this essay was written, TV programs presenting family situations were becoming more realistic. Examine a current show that deals with family life. How realistic is the picture of family life, in terms of the situations, attitudes, and relationships presented?

MY PAPA'S WALTZ

Theodore Roethke

Theodore Roethke (1908–1963), a widely published and much-honored American poet, received a Pulitzer Prize in 1953 and a Bollingen Prize in 1958, among other awards. Two of his collections of poems, *Words for the Wind* (1958) and *The Far Field* (1964), received National Book Awards. His *Collected Poems* appeared in 1966. He taught at several universities, last as Poet in Residence at the University of Washington.

    This brief poem is like a snapshot—a recollection of a moment that sums up the relationship of father and son.

The whiskey on your breath
Could make a small boy dizzy;
But I hung on like death:
Such waltzing was not easy.

We romped until the pans
Slid from the kitchen shelf;
My mother's countenance
Could not unfrown itself.

The hand that held my wrist
Was battered on one knuckle;
At every step you missed
My right ear scraped a buckle.

You beat time on my head
With a palm caked hard by dirt,
Then waltzed me off to bed
Still clinging to your shirt.

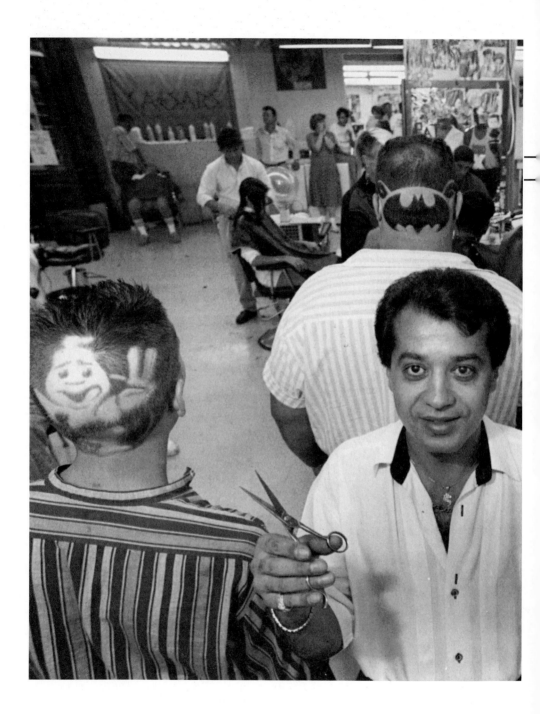

PART FOUR

Identities

Each of us carries a number of identities. We are identified as a son or daughter, as a parent, as a student; as a member of a club or team, a profession or union, a religious denomination, or a social class. In some cases our particular identity will not only associate us with a specific group of people, it will also type us. In American society, as multiethnic, multiracial as it is, this attribution of identity is particularly complex and often carries with it, rightly or wrongly, certain notions about the members of a group.

To compound this complexity, Americans are also a very mobile people. They move, not only physically from one part of the country to another, but socially as well. A young man or woman who, having finished high school, goes away from home to college, may be moving not only a hundred or a thousand miles, but also away from friends, associations, ideas about life. These changes may reshape their identity, the concept that they as well as others have of them.

The first two selections are concerned with education as a cause of such changes of identity. Marcus Mabry, while still an undergraduate, writes about the gap, the chasm between his earlier and present lives. He moved from the poverty in which he grew up in New Jersey to the affluence of Stanford University in California. He finds himself with two identities that are hard to reconcile. But the shift from one to the other has, as he may not have realized himself, already occurred: when he goes home on vacation he gets the one good bedroom in the house. He is already different. Norman Podhoretz, in the next selection, looks back on his high school years when he fought the relentless effort of a teacher to transform him from a "slum child" into a member of the educated middle class. Now a member of that class, he recognizes that his gains also meant some losses.

Two different concerns with questions of identity follow. Malcolm X describes how, as a boy, he sought to identify with whites by straightening his hair, not realizing until much later the extent to which he was degrading himself by that attempt. Jack G. Shaheen complains that the American media convey a consistently unfavorable image of Arabs, ignoring their positive sides. He is concerned that this will eventually undermine the feeling of identity of his children.

Grace Paley's short story concerns an attempt to ignore the culture of a group. Paley tells about a school administration that, with great unconcern, imposes a Christmas pageant on children whose culture does not include Christmas at all. Gwendolyn Brooks's poem at the end characterizes, in a very few lines, the identities of some who build a wall around themselves — or have others build one around them.

LIVING IN
TWO WORLDS

Marcus Mabry

Marcus Mabry was a junior at Stanford University when he wrote
this essay for the April 1988 issue of *Newsweek on Campus,* a
supplement to the popular newsmagazine distributed on college
campuses. As he himself tells it, he comes from a poor family in
New Jersey whose lives seem far removed from the life at Stanford,
one of the most affluent universities in the United States. It is this
wide gap between home — black, poor — and college — white,
mainstream, and affluent — that Mabry discusses. His double identity attests to both the mobility in American society and the tensions that it may create. In 1990 Mabry joined *Newsweek* as an
associate editor.

A round, green cardboard sign hangs from a string proclaiming, "We 1
built a proud new feeling," the slogan of a local supermarket. It is a
souvenir from one of my brother's last jobs. In addition to being a
bagger, he's worked at a fast-food restaurant, a gas station, a garage and
a textile factory. Now, in the icy clutches of the Northeastern winter,
he is unemployed. He will soon be a father. He is 19 years old.

In mid-December I was at Stanford, among the palm trees and 2
weighty chores of academe. And all I wanted to do was get out. I joined
the rest of the undergrads in a chorus of excitement, singing the
praises of Christmas break. No classes, no midterms, no finals . . .
and no freshmen! (I'm a resident assistant.) Awesome! I was looking
forward to escaping. I never gave a thought to what I was escaping to.

Once I got home to New Jersey, reality returned. My dreaded 3
freshmen had been replaced by unemployed relatives; badgering professors had been replaced by hard-working single mothers, and cold
classrooms by dilapidated bedrooms and kitchens. The room in which
the "proud new feeling" sign hung contained the belongings of myself, my mom and my brother. But for these two weeks it was mine.
They slept downstairs on couches.

Most students who travel between the universes of poverty and 4
affluence during breaks experience similar conditions, as well as the
guilt, the helplessness and, sometimes, the embarrassment associated
with them. Our friends are willing to listen, but most of them are
unable to imagine the pain of the impoverished lives that we see every

125

six months. Each time I return home I feel further away from the realities of poverty in America and more ashamed that they are allowed to persist. What frightens me most is not that the American socioeconomic system permits poverty to continue, but that by participating in that system I share some of the blame.

Last year I lived in an on-campus apartment, with a (relatively) modern bathroom, kitchen and two bedrooms. Using summer earnings, I added some expensive prints, a potted palm and some other plants, making the place look like the more-than-humble abode of a New York City Yuppie. I gave dinner parties, even a *soirée française*.

For my roommate, a doctor's son, this kind of life was nothing extraordinary. But my mom was struggling to provide a life for herself and my brother. In addition to working 24-hour-a-day cases as a practical nurse, she was trying to ensure that my brother would graduate from high school and have a decent life. She knew that she had to compete for his attention with drugs and other potentially dangerous things that can look attractive to a young man when he sees no better future.

Living in my grandmother's house this Christmas break restored all the forgotten, and the never acknowledged, guilt. I had gone to boarding school on a full scholarship since the ninth grade, so being away from poverty was not new. But my own growing affluence has increased my distance. My friends say that I should not feel guilty: what could I do substantially for my family at this age, they ask. Even though I know that education is the right thing to do, I can't help but feel, sometimes, that I have it too good. There is no reason that I deserve security and warmth, while my brother has to cope with potential unemployment and prejudice. I, too, encounter prejudice, but it is softened by my status as a student in an affluent and intellectual community.

More than my sense of guilt, my sense of helplessness increases each time I return home. As my success leads me further away for longer periods of time, poverty becomes harder to conceptualize and feels that much more oppressive when I visit with it. The first night of break, I lay in our bedroom, on a couch that let out into a bed that took up the whole room, except for a space heater. It was a little hard to sleep because the springs from the couch stuck through at inconvenient spots. But it would have been impossible to sleep anyway because of the groans coming from my grandmother's room next door. Only in her early 60s, she suffers from many chronic diseases and couldn't help but moan, then pray aloud, then moan, then pray aloud.

This wrenching of my heart was interrupted by the 3 A.M. entry of a relative who had been allowed to stay at the house despite rowdy behavior and threats toward the family in the past. As he came into the house, he slammed the door, and his heavy steps shook the second floor as he stomped into my grandmother's room to take his place, at the foot of her bed. There he slept, without blankets on a bare mattress. This was the first night. Later in the vacation, a Christmas turkey and a Christmas ham were stolen from my aunt's refrigerator on Christmas Eve. We think the thief was a relative. My mom and I decided not to exchange gifts that year because it just didn't seem festive.

A few days after New Year's I returned to California. The Northeast was soon hit by a blizzard. They were there, and I was here. That was the way it had to be, for now. I haven't forgotten; the ache of knowing their suffering is always there. It has to be kept deep down, or I can't find the logic in studying and partying while people, my people, are being killed by poverty. Ironically, success drives me away from those I most want to help by getting an education.   10

Somewhere in the midst of all that misery, my family has built, within me, "a proud feeling." As I travel between the two worlds it becomes harder to remember just how proud I should be — not just because of where I have come from and where I am going, but because of where they are. The fact that they survive in the world in which they live is something to be very proud of, indeed. It inspires within me a sense of tenacity and accomplishment that I hope every college graduate will someday possess.   11

EXERCISES

Words to Know

academe (paragraph 2), badgering (3), dilapidated (3), affluence (3), socioeconomic (4), abode (5), Yuppie (5), *soirée française* — elegant party in the French style (5), conceptualize (8), wrenching (9), ironically (10), tenacity (11).

Some of the Issues

1. Describe the two worlds Mabry lives in.
2. Mabry looks forward to "escaping" from school (paragraph 2), not an unusual sentiment at the end of a semester. What is he escaping to? Considering the rest of what he tells the reader, what is the real direction of escape?
3. "Once I got home to New Jersey, reality returned" (paragraph 3). Why does Mabry refer to life in New Jersey as "reality"? Is life at Stanford not real?

4. In paragraph 8 Mabry says "More than my sense of guilt, my sense of helplessness increases each time I return home." What events does he describe that contribute to this feeling?
5. Why does Mabry say in paragraph 11 that his family built "a proud feeling" within him?

The Way We Are Told

6. Consider the order of the first two paragraphs. Why does Mabry start with his brother rather than himself? Is the reader likely to be more familiar with the brother's world or Mabry's?
7. In the opening and concluding paragraphs and again in paragraph 3, Mabry refers to the supermarket sign about a "proud new feeling." How does the reference change each time he uses it? How does the repetition of the phrase help him to unify the essay? Try to define the kind of pride he is talking about.
8. Account for Mabry's use of expressions like "weighty chores of academe," "awesome!" "more-than-humble abode," "soirée française." From which of Mabry's two worlds do these phrases come? What does he gain by including them?

Some Subjects for Essays

9. Many people have had the experience of living in two different worlds — perhaps not the same two as Mabry's. If you have had such an experience — in family life, as a result of a job, a vacation, or some other cause — discuss your worlds and your relation to them.
*10. Read Norman Podhoretz's "The Brutal Bargain." Both he and Mabry originate in an environment of poverty, but they look upon it, and their relations to it, in different ways. Compare their attitudes.

THE BRUTAL BARGAIN

Norman Podhoretz

As the editor-in-chief of *Commentary*, Norman Podhoretz today is
a member of the New York literary establishment. He received a
B.A. degree from Columbia University in 1950 at the age of
twenty, and a further B.A. from Cambridge University in England
two years later. He has written a number of books. including
Breaking Ranks (1979), *The Present Danger* (1980), *Why We
Were in Viet Nam* (1982), *The Bloody Crossroads* (1986), and
Making It (1964), from which the following selection is taken.

   Like Alfred Kazin (see "The Kitchen"), Podhoretz is a child
of Jewish immigrants from eastern Europe. He grew up in Brooklyn where, as he tells it, he wanted as a teenager to conform to the
ways of his peers, children of poor immigrant origin whose sights
were definitely not set on an intellectual career. Podhoretz describes his early, fierce resistance to one of his high school
teachers who was determined to turn the "dirty slum child" into a
Harvard swan. He wins some of his battles with her, but in the end
he loses the war. Looking back he sees the "brutal bargain" he
struck. Getting his new identity was a wrenching process of gain
and loss.

One of the longest journeys in the world is the journey from Brooklyn   1
to Manhattan — or at least from certain neighborhoods in Brooklyn to
certain parts of Manhattan. I have made that journey, but it is not from
the experience of having made it that I know how very great the
distance is, for I started on the road many years before I realized what I
was doing, and by the time I did realize it I was for all practical
purposes already there. At so imperceptible a pace did I travel, and
with so little awareness, that I never felt footsore or out of breath or
weary at the thought of how far I still had to go. Yet whenever anyone
who has remained back there where I started — remained not physically but socially and culturally, for the neighborhood is now a Negro
ghetto and the Jews who have "remained" in it mostly reside in the
less affluent areas of Long Island — whenever anyone like that happens
into the world in which I now live with such perfect ease. I can see
that in his eyes I have become a fully acculturated citizen of a country
as foreign to him as China and infinitely more frightening.

   That country is sometimes called the upper middle class; and   2
indeed I am a member of that class, less by virtue of my income than by

virtue of the way my speech is accented, the way I dress, the way I furnish my home, the way I entertain and am entertained, the way I educate my children—the way, quite simply, I look and I live. It appalls me to think what an immense transformation I had to work on myself in order to become what I have become: if I had known what I was doing I would surely not have been able to do it, I would surely not have wanted to. No wonder the choice had to be blind; there was a kind of treason in it: treason toward my family, treason toward my friends. In choosing the road I chose, I was pronouncing a judgment upon them, and the fact that they themselves concurred in the judgment makes the whole thing sadder but no less cruel.

When I say that the choice was blind, I mean that I was never   3
aware—obviously not as a small child, certainly not as an adolescent, and not even as a young man already writing for publication and working on the staff of an important intellectual magazine in New York—how inextricably my "noblest" ambitions were tied to the vulgar desire to rise above the class into which I was born; nor did I understand to what an astonishing extent these ambitions were shaped and defined by the standards and values and tastes of the class into which I did not know I wanted to move. It is not that I was or am a social climber as that term is commonly used. High society interests me, if at all, only as a curiosity; I do not wish to be a member of it; and in any case, it is not, as I have learned from a small experience of contact with the very rich and fashionable, my "scene." Yet precisely because social climbing is not one of my vices (unless what might be called celebrity climbing, which very definitely *is* one of my vices, can be considered the contemporary variant of social climbing), I think there may be more than a merely personal significance in the fact that class has played so large a part both in my life and in my career.

But whether or not the significance is there, I feel certain that my   4
longtime blindness to the part class was playing in my life was not altogether idiosyncratic. "Privilege," Robert L. Heilbroner has shrewdly observed in *The Limits of American Capitalism*, "is not an attribute we are accustomed to stress when we consider the construction of *our* social order." For a variety of reasons, says Heilbroner, "privilege under capitalism is much less 'visible,' especially to the favored groups, than privilege under other systems" like feudalism. This "invisibility" extends in America to class as well.

No one, of course, is so naïve as to believe that America is a   5
classless society or that the force of egalitarianism, powerful as it has been in some respects, has ever been powerful enough to wipe out class distinctions altogether. There was a moment during the 1950's, to be sure, when social thought hovered on the brink of saying that the country had to all intents and purposes become a wholly middle-class

society. But the emergence of the civil-rights movements in the 1960's and the concomitant discovery of the poor — to whom, in helping to discover them, Michael Harrington interestingly enough applied, in *The Other America*, the very word ("invisible") that Heilbroner later used with reference to the rich — has put at least a temporary end to that kind of talk. And yet if class has become visible again, it is only in its grossest outlines — mainly, that is, in terms of income levels — and to the degree that manners and style of life are perceived as relevant at all, it is generally in the crudest of terms. There is something in us, it would seem, which resists the idea of class. Even our novelists, working in a genre for which class has traditionally been a supreme reality, are largely indifferent to it — which is to say, blind to its importance as a factor in the life of the individual.

In my own case, the blindness to class always expressed itself in 6 an outright and very often belligerent refusal to believe that it had anything to do with me at all. I no longer remember when or in what form I first discovered that there was such a thing as class, but whenever it was and whatever form the discovery took, it could only have coincided with the recognition that criteria existed by which I and everyone I knew were stamped as inferior: we were in the *lower* class. This was not a proposition I was willing to accept, and my way of not accepting it was to dismiss the whole idea of class as a prissy triviality.

Given the fact that I had literary ambitions even as a small boy, it 7 was inevitable that the issue of class would sooner or later arise for me with a sharpness it would never acquire for most of my friends. But given the fact also that I was on the whole very happy to be growing up where I was, that I was fiercely patriotic about Brownsville (the spawning-ground of so many famous athletes and gangsters), and that I felt genuinely patronizing toward other neighborhoods, especially the "better" ones like Crown Heights and East Flatbush which seemed by comparison colorless and unexciting — given the fact, in other words, that I was not, for all that I wrote poetry and read books, an "alienated" boy dreaming of escape — my confrontation with the issue of class would probably have come later rather than sooner if not for an English teacher in high school who decided that I was a gem in the rough and who took it upon herself to polish me to as high a sheen as she could manage and I would permit.

I resisted — far less effectively, I can see now, than I then 8 thought, though even then I knew that she was wearing me down far more than I would ever give her the satisfaction of admitting. Famous throughout the school for her altogether outspoken snobbery, which stopped short by only a hair, and sometimes did not shop short at all, of an old-fashioned kind of patrician anti-Semitism, Mrs. K. was also famous for being an extremely good teacher; indeed, I am sure that she saw no distinction between the hopeless task of teaching the proper use of English to the young Jewish barbarians whom fate had so unkindly deposited into her charge and the equally hopeless task of teaching them the proper "manners." (There were as many young Negro barbarians in her charge as Jewish ones, but I doubt that she could ever bring herself to pay very much attention to them. As she never hesitated to make clear, it was punishment enough for a woman of her background — her family was old-Brooklyn and, she would have us understand, extremely distinguished — to have fallen among the sons of East European immigrant Jews.)

For three years, from the age of thirteen to the age of sixteen, I 9 was her special pet, though that word is scarcely adequate to suggest the intensity of the relationship which developed between us. It was a relationship right out of *The Corn Is Green*, which may, for all I know, have served as her model; at any rate, her objective was much the same as the Welsh teacher's in that play: she was determined that I should win a scholarship to Harvard. But whereas (an irony much to the point here) the problem the teacher had in *The Corn Is Green* with her coal-miner pupil in the traditional class society of Edwardian England was strictly academic, Mrs. K.'s problem with me in the putatively egalitarian society of New Deal America was strictly social. My grades were very high and would obviously remain so, but what would they avail me if I continued to go about looking and sounding like a "filthy little slum child" (the epithet she would invariably hurl at me whenever we had an argument about "manners")?

Childless herself, she worked on me like a dementedly ambitious 10 mother with a somewhat recalcitrant son; married to a solemn and elderly man (she was then in her early forties or thereabouts), she treated me like a callous, ungrateful adolescent lover on whom she had humiliatingly bestowed her favors. She flirted with me and flattered me, she scolded me and insulted me. Slum child, filthy little slum child, so beautiful a mind and so vulgar a personality, so exquisite in sensibility and so coarse in manner. What would she do with me, what would become of me if I persisted out of stubbornness and perversity in the disgusting ways they had taught me at home and on the streets?

To her the most offensive of these ways was the style in which I 11 dressed: a tee shirt, tightly pegged pants, and a red satin jacket with the legend "Cherokees, S.A.C." (social-athletic club) stitched in large white letters across the back. This was bad enough, but when on certain days I would appear in school wearing, as a particular ceremonial occasion required, a suit and tie, the sight of those immense padded shoulders and my white-on-white shirt would drive her to even greater heights of contempt and even lower depths of loving despair than usual. *Slum child, filthy little slum child.* I was beyond saving; I deserved no better than to wind up with all the other horrible little Jewboys in the gutter (by which she meant Brooklyn College). If only I would listen to her, the whole world could be mine: I could win a scholarship to Harvard, I could get to know the best people, I could grow up into a life of elegance and refinement and taste. Why was I so stupid as not to understand?

In those days it was very unusual, and possibly even against the rules, for teachers in public high schools to associate with their students after hours. Nevertheless, Mrs. K. sometime invited me to her home, a beautiful old brownstone located in what was perhaps the only section in the whole of Brooklyn fashionable enough to be intimidating. I would read her my poems and she would tell me about her family, about the schools she had gone to, about Vassar, about writers she had met, while her husband, of whom I was frightened to death and who to my utter astonishment turned out to be Jewish (but not, as Mrs. K. quite unnecessarily hastened to inform me, *my* kind of Jewish), sat stiffly and silently in an armchair across the room, squinting at his newspaper through the first *pince-nez* I had ever seen outside the movies. He spoke to me but once, and that was after I had read Mrs. K. my tearful editorial for the school newspaper on the death of Roosevelt—an effusion which provoked him into a full five-minute harangue whose blasphemous contents would certainly have shocked me into insensibility if I had not been even more shocked to discover that he actually had a voice.

But Mrs. K. not only had me to her house; she also—what was even more unusual—took me out a few times, to the Frick Gallery and the Metropolitan Museum, and once to the theater, where we saw a dramatization of *The Late George Apley*, a play I imagine she deliberately chose with the not wholly mistaken idea that it would impress upon me the glories of aristocratic Boston.

One of our excursions into Manhattan I remember with particular vividness because she used it to bring the struggle between us to rather a dramatic head. The familiar argument began this time on the subway. Why, knowing that we would be spending the afternoon together "in public," had I come to school that morning improperly dressed? (I was, as usual, wearing my red satin club jacket over a white tee shirt.) She realized, of course, that I owned only one suit (this said not in compassion but in derision) and that my poor parents had, God only knew where, picked up the idea that it was too precious to be worn except at one of those bar mitzvahs I was always going to. Though why, if my parents were so worried about clothes, they had permitted me to buy a suit which made me look like a young hoodlum she found it very difficult to imagine. Still, much as she would have been embarrassed to be seen in public with a boy whose parents allowed him to wear a zoot suit, she would have been somewhat less embarrassed than she was now by the ridiculous costume I had on. Had I no consideration for her? Had I no consideration for myself? Did I want everyone who laid eyes on me to think that I was nothing but an ill-bred little slum child?

My standard ploy in these arguments was to take the position that   15 such things were of no concern to me: I was a poet and I had more important matters to think about than clothes. Besides, I would feel silly coming to school on an ordinary day dressed in a suit. Did Mrs. K. want me to look like one of those "creeps" from Crown Heights who were all going to become doctors? This was usually an effective counter, since Mrs. K. despised her middle-class Jewish students even more than she did the "slum children," but probably because she was growing desperate at the thought of how I would strike a Harvard interviewer (it was my senior year), she did not respond according to form on that particular occasion. "At least," she snapped, "they reflect well on their parents."

I was accustomed to her bantering gibes at my parents, and   16 sensing, probably, that they arose out of jealousy, I was rarely troubled by them. But this one bothered me; it went beyond banter and I did not know how to deal with it. I remember flushing, but I cannot remember what if anything I said in protest. It was the beginning of a very bad afternoon for both of us.

We had been heading for the Museum of Modern Art, but as we   17 got off the subway, Mrs. K. announced that she had changed her mind about the museum. She was going to show me something else instead, just down the street on Fifth Avenue. This mysterious "something else" to which we proceeded in silence turned out to be the college department of an expensive clothing store, de Pinna. I do not exaggerate when I say that an actual physical dread seized me as I followed her into the store. I had never been inside such a store; it was not a store, it was enemy territory, every inch of it mined with humiliations. "I am," Mrs. K. declared in the coldest human voice I hope I shall ever hear, "going to buy you a suit that you will be able to wear at your Harvard interview." I had guessed, of course, that this was what she had in mind, and even at fifteen I understood what a fantastic act of aggression she was planning to commit against my parents and asking me to participate in. Oh no, I said in a panic (suddenly realizing that I *wanted* her to buy me that suit), I can't, my mother wouldn't like it. "You can tell her it's a birthday present. Or else I will tell her. If I tell her, I'm sure she won't object." The idea of Mrs. K. meeting my mother was more than I could bear: my mother, who spoke with a

Yiddish accent and of whom, until that sickening moment, I had never known I was ashamed and so ready to betray.

To my immense relief and my equally immense disappointment, we left the store, finally, without buying a suit, but it was not to be the end of clothing or "manners" for me that day — not yet. There was still the ordeal of a restaurant to go through. Where I came from, people rarely ate in restaurants, not so much because most of them were too poor to afford such a luxury — although most of them certainly were — as because eating in restaurants was not regarded as a luxury at all; it was, rather, a necessity to which bachelors were pitiably condemned. A home-cooked meal was assumed to be better than anything one could possibly get in a restaurant, and considering the class of restaurants in question (they were really diners or luncheonettes), the assumption was probably correct. In the case of my own family, myself included until my late teens, the business of going to restaurants was complicated by the fact that we observed the Jewish-dietary laws, and except in certain neighborhoods, few places could be found which served kosher food; in midtown Manhattan in the 1940's, I believe there were only two and both were relatively expensive. All this is by way of explaining why I had had so little experience of restaurants up to the age of fifteen and why I grew apprehensive once more when Mrs. K. decided after we left de Pinna that we should have something to eat. 18

The restaurant she chose was not at all an elegant one — I have, like a criminal, revisited it since — but it seemed very elegant indeed to me: enemy territory again, and this time a mine exploded in my face the minute I set foot through the door. The hostess was very sorry, but she could not seat the young gentleman without a coat and tie. If the lady wished, however, something could be arranged. The lady (visibly pleased by this unexpected — or was it expected? — object lesson) did wish, and the so recently defiant but by now utterly docile young gentleman was forthwith divested of his so recently beloved but by now thoroughly loathsome red satin jacket and provided with a much oversized white waiter's coat and a tie — which, there being no collar to a tee shirt, had to be worn around his bare neck. Thus attired, and with his face supplying the touch of red which had moments earlier been supplied by his jacket, he was led into the dining room, there to be taught the importance of proper table manners through the same pedagogic instrumentality that had worked so well in impressing him with the importance of proper dress. 19

Like any other pedagogic technique, however, humiliation has its limits, and Mrs. K. was to make no further progress with it that day. For I had had enough, and I was not about to risk stepping on another 20 mine. Knowing she would subject me to still more ridicule if I made a point of my revulsion at the prospect of eating nonkosher food, I resolved to let her order for me and then to feign lack of appetite or possibly even illness when the meal was served. She did order — duck for both of us, undoubtedly because it would be a hard dish for me to manage without using my fingers.

The two portions came in deep oval-shaped dishes, swimming in a brown sauce and each with a sprig of parsley sitting on top. I had not the faintest idea of what to do — should the food be eaten directly from the oval dish or not? — nor which of the many implements on the table to do it with. But remembering that Mrs. K. herself had once advised me to watch my hostess in such a situation and then to do exactly as she did, I sat perfectly still and waited for her to make the first move. Unfortunately, Mrs. K. also remembered having taught me that trick, and determined as she was that I should be given a lesson that would force me to mend my ways, she waited too. And so we both waited, chatting amiably, pretending not to notice the food while it sat there getting colder and colder by the minute. Thanks partly to the fact that I would probably have gagged on the duck if I had tried to eat it — dietary taboos are very powerful if one has been conditioned to them — I was prepared to wait forever. And in fact it was Mrs. K. who broke first. 21

"Why aren't you eating?" she suddenly said after something like fifteen minutes had passed. "Aren't you hungry?" Not very, I answered. "Well," she said, "I think we'd better eat. The food is getting cold." Whereupon, as I watched with great fascination, she deftly captured the sprig of parsley between the prongs of her serving fork, set it aside, took up her serving spoon and delicately used those two esoteric implements to transfer a piece of duck from the oval dish to her plate. I imitated the whole operation as best I could, but not well enough to avoid splattering some partly congealed sauce onto my borrowed coat in the process. Still, things could have been worse, and having more or less successfully negotiated my way around that particular mine, I now had to cope with the problem of how to get out of eating the duck. But I need not have worried. Mrs. K. took one bite, pronounced it inedible (it must have been frozen by then), and called in quiet fury for the check. 22

Several months later, wearing an altered but respectably conservative suit which had been handed down to me in good condition by a bachelor uncle, I presented myself on two different occasions before interviewers from Harvard and from the Pulitzer Scholarship Committee. Some months after that, Mrs. K. had her triumph: I won the Harvard scholarship on which her heart had been so passionately set. It was not, however, large enough to cover all expenses, and since my 23 parents could not afford to make up the difference, I was unable to accept it. My parents felt wretched but not, I think, quite as wretched as Mrs. K. For a while it looked as though I would wind up in the "gutter" of Brooklyn College after all, but then the news arrived that I had also won a Pulitzer Scholarship which paid full tuition if used at Columbia and a small stipend besides. Everyone was consoled, even Mrs. K.: Columbia was at least in the Ivy League.

The last time I saw her was shortly before my graduation from   24
Columbia and just after a story had appeared in the *Times* announcing that I had been awarded a fellowship which was to send me to Cambridge University. Mrs. K. had passionately wanted to see me in Cambridge, Massachusetts, but Cambridge, England was even better. We met somewhere near Columbia for a drink, and her happiness over my fellowship, it seemed to me, was if anything exceeded by her delight at discovering that I now knew enough to know that the right thing to order in a cocktail lounge was a very dry martini with lemon peel, please.

EXERCISES

Words to Know

imperceptible (paragraph 1), acculturated (1), idiosyncratic (4), attribute (4), egalitarianism (5), genre (5), triviality (6), alienated (7), patrician (8), dementedly (10), recalcitrant (10), intimidating (12), *pince-nez* (12), effusion (12), harangue (12), blasphemous (12), insensibility (12), derision (14), zoot suit (14), bantering (16), gibes (16), pitiably (18), divested (19), pedagogic (19), instrumentality (19).

Some of the Issues

1. Explain what kind of "journey" Podhoretz refers to in paragraph 1.
2. In paragraph 2 Podhoretz refers to his journey as "a kind of treason." What does he mean?
3. In Podhoretz's view, America is not a classless society (paragraph 5), but seems so at times because both the poor and the rich seem invisible. (See Harrington's "The Invisible Poor.") What would you say is the meaning of class in America? On what grounds do you place people in this class structure?
4. Reread the first sentence of paragraph 7; why is a link between class and literary ambition "inevitable"?

5. Where and how does Podhoretz make the transition from his general observations to the particular story he wants to tell?
6. Beginning with paragraph 14, Podhoretz focuses on one particular day he spent with Mrs. K. How exactly do these episodes show what Mrs. K. wants to change in Podhoretz?
7. Consider the title of the selection: "The Brutal Bargain." How does Podhoretz's story relate to that title?
8. In the struggle between Podhoretz and Mrs. K., who wins the battle? Who wins the war?

The Way We Are Told

9. Podhoretz opens his essay with the image of a journey. Examine how he uses the analogy in paragraphs 1 and 2.
10. When Podhoretz introduces Mrs. K., he widens the analogy of the journey; it becomes a journey into battle. Paragraphs 8 through 11 contain words and phrases that introduce the idea of combat. Find them.
11. In paragraph 14 Podhoretz begins his climactic, detailed story about the store and the restaurant. Show how he continues to develop his analogy of the journey here, both the journey into a new class and the journey into battle.

Some Subjects for Essays

12. Try to describe some basic change in your life, using a controlling image such as one of those Podhoretz uses: a journey, a series of battles, or a treasonable activity, or another image appropriate to your story. Subjects might be the changing or dropping of friends, going off to college, leaving a job.
13. Education can take many forms. School and college are not the only places where it occurs. In an essay describe and analyze three or four situations in which significant nonformal education takes place.
*14. John Tarkov ("Fitting In"), Harry Mark Petrakis ("Barba Nikos"), and Podhoretz all look back to their youth and to the tensions inherent in cultural change. All three react somewhat differently. Compare and contrast their reactions in an essay.

HAIR

Malcolm X

Malcolm X, born in Omaha, Nebraska, in 1925, changed his name from Malcolm Little when he joined Elijah Muhammad's Black Muslims, in which he eventually moved up to become second in command. He broke with the Muslims because of major differences in policy and established an organization of his own. Soon after that he was assassinated at a public meeting, on February 21, 1965. *The Autobiography of Malcolm X*, written with the help of Alex Haley (later more widely known as the author of *Roots*), was published in 1964. The selection reprinted here is from one of the early parts of the book and records an experience during his junior high school years in Michigan, in 1941. Malcolm X gives the reader what amounts to a recipe, but a recipe on two levels: he describes in detail the painful process of "conking," straightening hair, that he as a boy subjected himself to. On a more fundamental level it was, as he says, a "big step toward self-degradation."

Shorty soon decided that my hair was finally long enough to be conked. He had promised to school me in how to beat the barbershop's three- and four-dollar price by making up congolene, and then conking ourselves. 1

I took the little list of ingredients he had printed out for me, and went to a grocery store, where I got a can of Red Devil lye, two eggs, and two medium-sized white potatoes. Then at a drugstore near the poolroom, I asked for a large jar of vaseline, a large bar of soap, a large-toothed comb and a fine-toothed comb, one of those rubber hoses with a metal spray-head, a rubber apron and a pair of gloves. 2

"Going to lay on that first conk?" the drugstore man asked me. I proudly told him, grinning, "Right!" 3

Shorty paid six dollars a week for a room in his cousin's shabby apartment. His cousin wasn't at home. "It's like the pad's mine, he spends so much time with his woman," Shorty said, "Now, you watch me — " 4

He peeled the potatoes and thin-sliced them into a quart-sized Mason fruit jar, then started stirring them with a wooden spoon as he gradually poured in a little over half the can of lye. "Never use a metal spoon; the lye will turn it black," he told me. 5

A jelly-like, starchy-looking glop resulted from the lye and pota- 6

139

toes, and Shorty broke in the two eggs, stirring real fast — his own conk and dark face bent down close. The congolene turned pale-yellowish. "Feel the jar," Shorty said. I cupped my hand against the outside, and snatched it away. "Damn right, it's hot, that's the lye," he said. "So you know it's going to burn when I comb it in — it burns *bad*. But the longer you can stand it, the straighter the hair."

He made me sit down, and he tied the string of the new rubber   7
apron tightly around my neck, and combed up my bush of hair. Then, from the big vaseline jar, he took a handful and massaged it hard all through my hair and into the scalp. He also thickly vaselined my neck, ears and forehead. "When I get to washing out your head, be sure to tell me anywhere you feel any little stinging," Shorty warned me, washing his hands, then pulling on the rubber gloves, and tying on his own rubber apron. "You always got to remember that any congolene left in burns a sore into your head."

The congolene just felt warm when Shorty started combing it in.   8
But then my head caught fire.

I gritted my teeth and tried to pull the sides of the kitchen table   9
together. The comb felt as if it was raking my skin off.

My eyes watered, my nose was running. I couldn't stand it any   10
longer; I bolted to the washbasin. I was cursing Shorty with every name I could think of when he got the spray going and started soap-lathering my head.

He lathered and spray-rinsed, lathered and spray-rinsed, maybe   11
ten or twelve times, each time gradually closing the hot-water faucet, until the rinse was cold, and that helped some.

"You feel any stinging spots?"   12

"No," I managed to say. My knees were trembling.   13

"Sit back down, then. I think we got it all out okay."   14

The flame came back as Shorty, with a thick towel, started drying   15
my head, rubbing hard. *"Easy, man, easy"* I kept shouting.

"The first time's always worst. You get used to it better before   16
long. You took it real good, homeboy. You got a good conk."

When Shorty let me stand up and see in the mirror, my hair hung   17
down in limp, damp strings. My scalp still flamed, but not as badly; I could bear it. He draped the towel around my shoulders, over my rubber apron, and began again vaselining my hair.

I could feel him combing, straight back, first the big comb, then   18
the fine-tooth one.

Then, he was using a razor, very delicately, on the back of my   19
neck. Then, finally, shaping the sideburns.

My first view in the mirror blotted out the hurting. I'd seen some   20
pretty conks, but when it's the first time, on your *own* head, the transformation, after the lifetime of kinks, is staggering.

The mirror reflected Shorty behind me. We both were grinning 21
and sweating. And on top of my head was this thick, smooth sheen of
shining red hair — real red — as straight as any white man's.

How ridiculous I was! Stupid enough to stand there simply lost in 22
admiration of my hair now looking "white," reflected in the mirror in
Shorty's room. I vowed that I'd never again be without a conk, and I
never was for many years.

This was my first really big step toward self-degradation: when I 23
endured all of that pain, literally burning my flesh to have it look like a
white man's hair. I had joined that multitude of Negro men and women
in America who are brainwashed into believing that the black people
are "inferior" — and white people "superior" — that they will even
violate and mutilate their God-created bodies to try to look "pretty"
by white standards.

EXERCISES

Some of the Issues

1. What is a conk and why did Malcolm X want it?
2. Why does Malcolm X describe the process of buying the ingredients
   and of applying them in such detail?
3. What is the thesis of this short selection? With what arguments,
   information, or assertions does Malcolm X support his thesis?

The Way We Are Told

4. The selection divides into two very different parts. What are they?
   How do they differ?
5. The main part of the selection is a description of a process. How is
   it arranged? What qualities of instruction, even of a recipe, has it?
   How and where does it differ from a recipe?

Some Subjects for Essays

6. Malcolm X describes a process that shows, among other things, that
   people will go to great lengths to conform. Develop a short essay
   describing, in a straightforward, neutral manner, some example of
   how people will subject themselves to pain, inconvenience, and
   embarrassment to conform to some fashion or idea.

7. Rewrite your previous essay, but take a strong stand indicating approval or disapproval of the process.

*8. Write an essay examining the rewards American society offers for conforming, or the penalties for not conforming. In addition to Malcolm X, you might read Podhoretz's "The Brutal Bargain."

*9. The photograph on page 122 shows a proud barber surrounded by some of his creations. Describe one of them, indicating its location in the photo and interpret what, in your view, it says about its owner. What kind of identity is the owner of the haircut trying to project, and how does it compare to the identity Malcolm X tries to achieve in "Hair"? Compare the motivations behind these haircuts.

THE MEDIA'S IMAGE
OF ARABS

Jack G. Shaheen

Jack G. Shaheen, born in 1935, teaches mass communications at
Southern Illinois University in Edwardsville. He has also taught at
the American University in Beirut and the University of Jordan in
Amman. He is the author of *The TV Arab* (1984).

Lebanon, where Shaheen's family came from, is a small
country at the eastern end of the Mediterranean, bordering on
Israel to the south and Syria to the east and north. Its capital,
Beirut, was once known as the Paris of the Middle East, a lively,
sophisticated city that was also the financial center of the region.
In recent years Lebanon has been in a state of civil war that has
ravaged much of the country and led at times to the occupation of
parts of it by its two neighbors.

The following selection first appeared in the "My Turn"
section of *Newsweek* on February 29, 1988. The media's image of
Arabs, Shaheen asserts, is almost invariably hostile and one-sided.
It contributes to, perhaps is even responsible for, the negative
stereotype Americans have of Arabs.

America's bogyman is the Arab. Until the nightly news brought us TV 1
pictures of Palestinian boys being punched and beaten, almost all
portraits of Arabs seen in America were dangerously threatening. Arabs
were either billionaires or bombers — rarely victims. They were hardly
ever seen as ordinary people practicing law, driving taxis, singing
lullabies or healing the sick. Though TV news may portray them more
sympathetically now, the absence of positive media images nurtures
suspicion and stereotype. As an Arab-American, I have found that ugly
caricatures have had an enduring impact on my family.

I was sheltered from prejudicial portraits at first. My parents 2
came from Lebanon in the 1920s; they met and married in America.
Our home in the steel city of Clairton, Pa., was a center for ethnic
sharing — black, white, Jew and gentile. There was only one major
source of media images then, at the State movie theater where I was
lucky enough to get a part-time job as an usher. But in the late 1940s,
Westerns and war movies were popular, not Middle Eastern dramas.
Memories of World War II were fresh, and the screen heavies were the

Japanese and the Germans. True to the cliché of the times, the only good Indian was a dead Indian. But when I mimicked or mocked the bad guys, my mother cautioned me. She explained that stereotypes blur our vision and corrupt the imagination. "Have compassion for all people, Jackie," she said. "This way, you'll learn to experience the joy of accepting people as they are, and not as they appear in films. Stereotypes hurt."

Mother was right. I can remember the Saturday afternoon when   3
my son, Michael, who was seven, and my daughter, Michele, six, suddenly called out: "Daddy, Daddy, they've got some bad Arabs on TV." They were watching that great American morality play, TV wrestling. Akbar the Great, who liked to hear the cracking of bones, and Abdullah the Butcher, a dirty fighter who liked to inflict pain, were pinning their foes with "camel locks." From that day on, I knew I had to try to neutralize the media caricatures.

It hasn't been easy. With my children, I have watched animated   4
heroes Heckle and Jeckle pull the rug from under "Ali Boo-Boo, the Desert Rat," and Laverne and Shirley stop "Sheik Ha-Mean-Ie" from conquering "the U.S. and the world." I have read comic books like the "Fantastic Four" and "G.I. Combat" whose characters have sketched Arabs as "lowlifes" and "human hyenas." Negative stereotypes were everywhere. A dictionary informed my youngsters that an Arab is a "vagabond, drifter, hobo and vagrant." Whatever happened, my wife wondered, to Aladdin's good genie?

To a child, the world is simple: good versus evil. But my children   5
and others with Arab roots grew up without ever having seen a humane Arab on the silver screen, someone to pattern their lives after. Is it easier for a camel to go through the eye of a needle than for a screen Arab to appear as a genuine human being?

Hollywood producers must have an instant Ali Baba kit that con-   6
tains scimitars, veils, sunglasses and such Arab clothing as *chadors* and *kufiyahs*. In the mythical "Ay-rabland," oil wells, tents, mosques, goats and shepherds prevail. Between the sand dunes, the camera focuses on a mock-up of a palace from "Arabian Nights" — or a military air base. Recent movies suggest that Americans are at war with Arabs, forgetting the fact that out of 21 Arab nations, America is friendly with 19 of them. And in "Wanted Dead or Alive," a movie that starred Gene Simmons, the leader of the rock group Kiss, the war comes home when an Arab terrorist comes to the United States dressed as a rabbi and, among other things, conspires with Arab-Americans to poison the people of Los Angeles. The movie was released last year.

The Arab remains American culture's favorite whipping boy. In   7
his memoirs, Terrel Bell, Ronald Reagan's first secretary of education,

writes about an "apparent bias among mid-level, right-wing staffers at the White House" who dismissed Arabs as "sand niggers." Sadly, the racial slurs continue. At a recent reacher's conference, I met a woman from Sioux Falls, S.D., who told me about the persistence of discrimination. She was in the process of adopting a baby when an agency staffer warned her that the infant had a problem. When she asked whether the child was mentally ill, or physically handicapped, there was silence. Finally, the worker said: "The baby is Jordanian."

To me, the Arab demon of today is much like the Jewish demon of   8
yesterday. We deplore the false portrait of Jews as a swarthy menace. Yet a similar portrait has been accepted and transferred to another group of Semites—the Arabs. Print and broadcast journalists have started to challenge this stereotype. They are now revealing more humane images of Palestinian Arabs, a people who traditionally suffered from the myth that Palestinian equals terrorist. Others could follow that lead and retire the stereotypical Arab to a media Valhalla.

It would be a step in the right direction if movie and TV pro-   9
ducers developed characters modeled after real-life Arab-Americans. We could then see a White House correspondent like Helen Thomas, whose father came from Lebanon, in "The Golden Girls," a heart surgeon patterned after Dr. Michael DeBakey on "St. Elsewhere," or a Syrian-American playing tournament chess like Yasser Seirawan, the Seattle grandmaster.

Politicians, too should speak out against the cardboard carica-   10
tures. They should refer to Arabs as friends, not just as moderates. And religious leaders could state that Islam like Christianity and Judaism maintains that all mankind is one family in the care of God. When all imagemakers rightfully begin to treat Arabs and all other minorities with respect and dignity, we may begin to unlearn our prejudices.

EXERCISES

Words to Know

bogeyman (paragraph 1), positive media images (1), stereotype (1), enduring (1), prejudicial (2), ethnic (2), gentile (2), heavies (2), cliché (2), morality play (3), neutralize (3), caricatures (3), animated (4), vagabond (4), drifter (4), hobo (4), vagrant (4), Aladdin's genie (4), humane (5), scimitars (6), *chadors* (6), *kufiyahs* (6), mythical (6), prevail (6), mock-up (6), bias (7), slurs (7), demon (8), swarthy (8), Semite (8), Valhalla (8), moderates (10).

Some of the Issues

1. What, according to the author, is the standard image of the Arab in the American media? Why is he concerned that Arabs are hardly ever portrayed as ordinary people?
2. When did Shaheen first become aware of stereotypes? Why was he not conscious of them earlier?
3. Shaheen is especially concerned about the influence of the media on his children. Why does he believe that children are particularly vulnerable to stereotypes?
4. Shaheen states that the image of Arabs in the media is changing somewhat (paragraphs 8 and 9). To what does he attribute that shift? What further changes does he advocate?

The Way We Are Told

5. Cite several instances in which Shaheen supports a general assertion with specific examples drawn from his own experience.
6. Shaheen's essay concentrates on the media's treatment of Arabs, yet he mentions unfair treatment of other groups as well. What does his argument gain from this expansion?

Some Subjects for Essays

7. If you have encountered stereotyping, describe the circumstances in an essay.
*8. Read Maya Angelou's "Graduation." Analyze the event she describes as an example of stereotyping.
9. Describe a character in a film or a TV program who is represented as a stereotype, either negatively or positively.

THE LOUDEST VOICE

Grace Paley

Grace Paley grew up in the Bronx, New York, where she was born in 1922. Her first published collection of short stories, *The Little Disturbances of Man*, which appeared in 1959, contained the story included here. Since then she has published additional collections of short stories, *Enormous Changes at the Last Minute* (1974), *Later the Same Day* (1985), and *Leaning Forward* (1985). Three of the stories in *Enormous Changes at the Last Minute* have been made into a movie by the same name. Most of Paley's stories are set in New York and treat the lives of a great range of people of different backgrounds, Jews, blacks, Italians, Puerto Ricans, and Irish. She is noted particularly for her ability to catch the flavor of urban American speech.

In her short story "The Loudest Voice" Grace Paley tells how an unthinking school administration dealt with the children under its authority. There are almost no Christian children in Shirley Abramovitz's grade school, but the teachers find it natural to foist a Christmas pageant on them. The results are hilarious as well as thought-provoking.

There is a certain place where dumb-waiters boom, doors slam, dishes 1 crash; every window is a mother's mouth bidding the street shut up, go skate somewhere else, come home. My voice is the loudest.

There, my own mother is still as full of breathing as me and the 2 grocer stands up to speak to her. "Mrs. Abramowitz," he says, "people should not be afraid of their children."

"Ah, Mr. Bialik," my mother replies, "if you say to her or her 3 father 'Ssh,' they say, 'In the grave it will be quiet.'"

"From Coney Island to the cemetery," says my papa. "It's the 4 same subway; it's the same fare."

I am right next to the pickle barrel. My pinky is making tiny 5 whirlpools in the brine. I stop a moment to announce: "Campbell's Tomato Soup. Campbell's Vegetable Beef Soup. Campbell's S-c-otch Broth . . ."

"Be quiet," the grocer says, "the labels are coming off." 6

"Please, Shirley, be a little quiet," my mother begs me. 7

In that place the whole street groans: Be quiet! Be quiet! but 8 steals from the happy chorus of my inside self not a tittle or a jot.

There, too, but just around the corner, is a red brick building that 9

147

has been old for many years. Every morning the children stand before it in double lines which must be straight. They are not insulted. They are waiting anyway.

I am usually among them. I am, in fact, the first, since I begin   10
with "A."

One cold morning the monitor tapped me on the shoulder. "Go   11
to Room 409, Shirley Abramowitz," he said. I did as I was told. I went in a hurry up a down staircase to Room 409, which contained sixth-graders. I had to wait at the desk without wiggling until Mr. Hilton, their teacher, had time to speak.

After five minutes he said, "Shirley?"   12

"What?" I whispered.   13

He said, "My! My! Shirley Abramowitz! They told me you had a   14
particularly loud, clear voice and read with lots of expression. Could that be true?"

"Oh yes," I whispered.   15

"In that case, don't be silly; I might very well be your teacher   16
someday. Speak up, speak up."

"Yes," I shouted.   17

"More like it," he said. "Now, Shirley, can you put a ribbon in   18
your hair or a bobby pin? It's too messy."

"Yes!" I bawled.   19

"Now, now, calm down." He turned to the class. "Children, not   20
a sound. Open at page 39. Read till 52. When you finish, start again."
He looked me over once more. "Now, Shirley, you know, I suppose, that Christmas is coming. We are preparing a beautiful play. Most of the parts have been given out. But I still need a child with a strong voice, lots of stamina. Do you know what stamina is? You do? Smart kid. You know, I heard you read 'The Lord is my shepherd' in Assembly yesterday. I was very impressed. Wonderful delivery. Mrs. Jordan, your teacher, speaks highly of you. Now listen to me, Shirley Abramowitz, if you want to take the part and be in the play, repeat after me, 'I swear to work harder than I ever did before.'"

I looked to heaven and said at once, "Oh, I swear." I kissed my   21
pinky and looked at God.

"That is an actor's life, my dear," he explained. "Like a soldier's,   22
never tardy or disobedient to his general, the director. Everything," he said, "absolutely everything will depend on you."

That afternoon, all over the building, children scraped and   23
scrubbed the turkeys and the sheaves of corn off the schoolroom windows. Goodbye Thanksgiving. The next morning a monitor brought red paper and green paper from the office. We made new shapes and hung them on the walls and glued them to the doors.

The teachers became happier and happier. Their heads were   24

ringing like the bells of childhood. My best friend Evie was prone to
evil, but she did not get a single demerit for whispering. We learned
"Holy Night" without an error. "How wonderful!" said Miss Glacé,
the student teacher. "To think that some of you don't even speak the
language!" We learned "Deck the Halls" and "Hark! The Herald
Angels". . . . They weren't ashamed and we weren't embarrassed.

Oh, but when my mother heard about it all, she said to my father: 25
"Misha, you don't know what's going on there. Cramer is the head of
the Tickets Committee."

"Who?" asked my father. "Cramer? Oh yes, an active woman."   26

"Active? Active has to have a reason. Listen," she said sadly, "I'm   27
surprised to see my neighbors making tra-la-la for Christmas."

My father couldn't think of what to say to that. Then he decided: 28
"You're in America! Clara, you wanted to come here. In Palestine the
Arabs would be eating you alive. Europe you had pogroms. Argentina is
full of Indians. Here you got Christmas. . . . Some joke, ha?"

"Very funny, Misha. What is becoming of you? If we came to a   29
new country a long time ago to run away from tyrants, and instead we
fall into a creeping pogrom, that our children learn a lot of lies, so
what's the joke? Ach, Misha, your idealism is going away."

"So is your sense of humor."   30

"That I never had, but idealism you had a lot of."   31

"I'm the same Misha Abramovitch, I didn't change an iota. Ask   32
anyone."

"Only ask me," says my mama, may she rest in peace. "I got the   33
answer."

Meanwhile the neighbors had to think of what to say too.   34

Marty's father said: "You know, he has a very important part, my   35
boy."

"Mine also," said Mr. Sauerfeld.   36

"Not my boy!" said Mrs. Klieg. "I said to him no. The answer is   37
no. When I say no! I mean no!"

The rabbi's wife said. "It's disgusting!" But no one listened to   38
her. Under the narrow sky of God's great wisdom she wore a straw-
berry-blond wig.

Every day was noisy and full of experience. I was Right-hand Man.   39
Mr. Hilton said: "How could I get along without you, Shirley?"

He said: "Your mother and father ought to get down on their   40
knees every night and thank God for giving them a child like you."

He also said: "You're absolutely a pleasure to work with, my   41
dear, dear child."

Sometimes he said: "For God's sakes, what did I do with the   42
script? Shirley! Shirley! Find it."

Then I answered quietly: "Here it is, Mr. Hilton."   43

Once in a while, when he was very tired, he would cry out: 44
"Shirley, I'm just tired of screaming at those kids. Will you tell Ira
Pushkov not to come in till Lester points to that star the second time?"

Then I roared: "Ira Pushkov, what's the matter with you? Dope!   45
Mr. Hilton told you five times already, don't come in till Lester points
to that star the second time."

"Ach, Clara," my father asked, "what does she do there till six   46
o'clock she can't even put the plates on the table?"

"Christmas," said my mother coldly.   47

"Ho! Ho!" my father said. "Christmas. What's the harm? After all,   48
history teaches everyone. We learn from reading this is a holiday from
pagan times also, candles, lights, even Chanukah. So we learn it's not
altogether Christian. So if they think it's a private holiday, they're only
ignorant, not patriotic. What belongs to history, belongs to all men.
You want to go back to the Middle Ages? Is it better to shave your head
with a secondhand razor? Does it hurt Shirley to learn to speak up? It
does not. So maybe someday she won't live between the kitchen and
the shop. She's not a fool."

I thank you, Papa, for your kindness. It is true about me to this   49
day. I am foolish but I am not a fool.

That night my father kissed me and said with great interest in my   50
career, "Shirley, tomorrow's your big day. Congrats."

"Save it," my mother said. Then she shut all the windows in   51
order to prevent tonsillitis.

In the morning it snowed. On the street corner a tree had been   52
decorated for us by a kind city administration. In order to miss its
chilly shadow our neighbors walked three blocks east to buy a loaf of
bread. The butcher pulled down black window shades to keep the
colored lights from shining on his chickens. Oh, not me. On the way to
school, with both my hands I tossed it a kiss of tolerance. Poor thing, it
was a stranger in Egypt.

I walked straight into the auditorium past the staring children.   53
"Go ahead, Shirley!" said the monitors. Four boys, big for their age,
had already started work as propmen and stagehands.

Mr. Hilton was very nervous. He was not even happy. Whatever   54
he started to say ended in a sideward look of sadness. He sat slumped in
the middle of the first row and asked me to help Miss Glacé. I did this,
although she thought my voice too resonant and said, "Show-off!"

Parents began to arrive long before we were ready. They wanted   55
to make a good impression. From among the yards of drapes I peeked
out at the audience. I saw my embarrassed mother.

Ira, Lester, and Meyer were pasted to their beards by Miss Glacé.   56
She almost forgot to thread the star on its wire, but I reminded her. I
coughed a few times to clear my throat. Miss Glacé looked around and

saw that everyone was in costume and on line waiting to play his part. She whispered, "All right . . ." Then:

Jackie Sauerfeld, the prettiest boy in first grade, parted the cur- 57
tains with his skinny elbow and in a high voice sang out:

"Parents dear
We are here
To make a Christmas play in time.
It we give
In narrative
And illustrate with pantomime."

He disappeared.   58

My voice burst immediately from the wings to the great shock of 59
Ira, Lester, and Meyer, who were waiting for it but were surprised all
the same.

"I remember, I remember, the house where I was born . . ."   60

Miss Glacé yanked the curtain open and there it was, the house 61
—an old hayloft, where Celia Kornbluh lay in the straw with Cindy
Lou, her favorite doll. Ira, Lester, and Meyer moved slowly from the
wings toward her, sometimes pointing to a moving star and sometimes
ahead to Cindy Lou.

It was a long story and it was a sad story. I carefully pronounced 62
all the words about my lonesome childhood, while little Eddie Braun-
stein wandered upstage and down with his shepherd's stick, looking
for sheep. I brought up lonesomeness again, and not being understood
at all except by some women everybody hated. Eddie was too small for
that and Marty Groff took his place, wearing his father's prayer shawl. I
announced twelve friends, and half the boys in the fourth grade gathered round Marty, who stood on an orange crate while my voice
harangued. Sorrowful and loud, I declaimed about love and God and
Man, but because of the terrible deceit of Abie Stock we came suddenly to a famous moment. Marty, whose remembering tongue I was,
waited at the foot of the cross. He stared desperately at the audience. I
groaned, "My God, my God, why hast thou forsaken me?" The soldiers
who were sheiks grabbed poor Marty to pin him up to die, but he
wrenched free, turned again to the audience, and spread his arms aloft
to show despair and the end. I murmured at the top of my voice, "The
rest is silence, but as everyone in this room, in this city—in this
world—now knows, I shall have life eternal."

That night Mrs. Kornbluh visited our kitchen for a glass of tea.   63

"How's the virgin?" asked my father with a look of concern.   64

"For a man with a daughter, you got a fresh mouth, 65
Abramovitch."

"Here," said my father kindly, "have some lemon, it'll sweeten 66
your disposition."

They debated a little in Yiddish, then fell in a puddle of Russian   67
and Polish. What I understood next was my father, who said, "Still and
all, it was certainly a beautiful affair, you have to admit, introducing us
to the beliefs of a different culture."

"Well, yes," said Mrs. Kornbluh. "The only thing . . . you   68
know Charlie Turner—that cute boy in Celia's class—a couple
others? They got very small parts or no part at all. In very bad taste, it
seemed to me. After all, it's their religion."

"Ach," explained my mother, "what could Mr. Hilton do? They   69
got very small voices; after all, why should they holler? The English
language they know from the beginning by heart. They're blond like
angels. You think it's so important they should get in the play?
Christmas . . . the whole piece of goods . . . they own it."

I listened and listened until I couldn't listen any more. Too   70
sleepy, I climbed out of bed and kneeled. I made a little church of my
hands and said, "Here, O Israel . . ." Then I called out in Yiddish,
"Please, good night, good night. Ssh." My father said, "Ssh yourself,"
and slammed the kitchen door.

I was happy. I fell asleep at once. I had prayed for everybody: my   71
talking family, cousins far away, passersby, and all the lonesome Chris-
tians. I expected to be heard. My voice was certainly the loudest.

EXERCISES

Words to Know

dumb-waiter (paragraph 1), Coney Island—amusement park in New
York City (4), a tittle or a jot (8), monitor (11), stamina (20), demerit
(24), Palestine (28), pogroms (28), iota (32), pagan (48), Chanukah
(48), tonsillitis (51), tolerance (52), resonant (54), pantomime
(57), hayloft (61), harangued (62), declaimed (62), disposition
(66), Yiddish (67).

Some of the Issues

1. In paragraphs 1 through 8 Paley tells about "a certain place."
   How does she describe it? Do we know what it looked like? What
   it sounded like? How do we know that it is a place in Shirley's
   memory?
2. In paragraph 9 we move to another place, just around the corner.
   How are we told about that place?
3. Shirley has the loudest voice in the school, but at some points she
   whispers or talks softly. When and why?

4. Mr. Hilton has a number of ways of getting Shirley and the other children to do what he wants them to do. What technique does he use? How sincere do you think he is? How much does he, and the other teachers, seem to understand or care about the children in the school?

5. Shirley's mother and father disagree with one another at several points in the story. Find the points where they disagree. What position does the father take consistently? The mother?

6. In paragraph 24 Miss Glacé, the student teacher, makes a comment. Does she believe it is a compliment? Is it really? Does her remark, and others made by teachers in the school, give any indication of their attitudes toward the children and their families?

7. Read the last sentences of paragraph 24; who is referred to as "we"? As "they"?

8. Paragraphs 34 through 38 tell how the neighbors react to the upcoming school play. What is their reaction? Why does no one pay attention to the rabbi's wife?

9. Read paragraph 52. Explain the people's reaction to "the tree." Why is it a stranger in Egypt?

10. Paragraphs 57 through 62 tell about the actual performance of the Christmas play. What is the story being told in the play? What parts are each of the children playing? How well do the children seem to understand the story and their parts?

11. Examine the last paragraph. Whom does Shirley pray for and why? In what way can Shirley be said to have triumphed?

The Way We Are Told

12. Grace Paley is known for her good ear for dialog. She is said to create dialog that sounds natural and conveys a sense of her characters' personalities. A large part of this story is told through dialog. Examine it, and show how it conveys the sense of each character who speaks and how it carries the story along.

13. Did you find the story funny? If so, why? Does the humorous tone help or hinder its serious purpose?

Some Subjects for Essays

14. We know Shirley, and indeed all of the characters in the story, through their voices. Unlike many authors, Paley gives few visual descriptions. We are not told the color of Shirley's hair, or how tall she is, or even exactly how old she is. We may, however, be able to form images in our minds about what she and others are

like, from our knowledge of what they say and how they say it. Imagine that "The Loudest Voice" is to be filmed. You are the casting director. Tell how you would visualize Paley's characters: Shirley, her parents, and the various teachers.

15. In this story Paley describes people and places by means of sound, not appearance. Write a paragraph giving a vivid description of a place you know well, using primarily sounds to describe it, and avoiding visual details as much as possible.

16. Have you ever, as a child or as an adult, participated in a cultural or religious ceremony that was unfamiliar to you, in which you perhaps felt out of place? Describe it in an essay.

*17. Many teachers have come to believe that schools should be responsive to the culture and history of their particular students, in addition to teaching about American culture in general. Using Paley's story as support, write an essay arguing for this proposition. (You may want to read James Fallows's "Bilingual Education" before you plan your essay.)

*18. Like Paley, Maya Angelou in "Graduation" describes a school ceremony in which officials are insensitive to the lives of the children and their parents. How do the two situations differ? In what way are they the same? Explain in an essay.

*19. In Paley's story and in Maxine Hong Kingston's "Girlhood Among Ghosts" the image of voice plays a major role. In an essay compare and contrast the two central characters' experience in losing and finding a voice.

WE REAL COOL

Gwendolyn Brooks

Gwendolyn Brooks was born in Kansas in 1917 and has spent most of her life in Chicago. Her first volume of poetry, *A Street in Bronzeville*, was published in 1945. Many of her poems concern conditions in the black community, its feelings and attitudes. In 1950 she won the Pulitzer Prize for poetry. The poem reprinted here is from *Selected Poems* (1963). In 1972 she published her autobiography *Report from Part One*. The latest volume of her poetry is *Blacks* (1987).

> *The Pool Players*
> *Seven at the Golden Shovel*
>
> We real cool. We
> Left School. We
>
> Lurk late. We
> Strike straight. We
>
> Sing sin. We
> Thin gin. We
>
> Jazz June. We
> Die soon.

PART FIVE

Encounters

The United States is often referred to as a "melting pot" without sufficient thought given to what is being said. What is implied by the term? What does it really mean? Basically it implies that America functions as one vast sort of container in which different ingredients — people, in this case — are amalgamated. The resulting amalgam is the American. In a country composed of as many different ethnicities as America, it is tempting to use the image of amalgamation to express the idea that all these many different people can take on one unified identity. The image of the melting pot, however, does not do justice to another American idea: that the different nationalities or races contribute important ingredients to the total, that Americans often retain some of their pre-melted characteristics, and that their total culture is enriched by such diversity. Something is therefore to be said for a different image that has found some echoes in more recent times: that America is really more like a mixed salad.

We all know by the time we reach our teens, and sometimes much sooner, that the melt does not always meld, and that the pot may sometimes get too hot and burn. Part Five of *Crossing Cultures* presents a variety of encounters that describe the resulting conflagrations. Some are simply personal; others occur as part of a historical event. Piri Thomas recalls his memory of being on "Alien Turf," the new kid, a Puerto Rican, in an Italian neighborhood. Brent Staples's nighttime walks involve him with passersby to whom he presents a danger simply by being black. Walter White's family was a target of a race riot in Atlanta early in this century. Jeanne Wakatsuki Houston also records her part in a historical event, the internment of Japanese-Americans on the West Coast at the beginning of World War II. With Jonathan Schell's account of a raid by American infantrymen on a Vietnamese village we turn to the global encounters Americans have increasingly had since the Second World War.

The last two essays are not accounts of encounters but reflections on them. Michael Dorris describes the first Thanksgiving to which according to story the Pilgrims invited the Indians. Dorris characterizes the account as an example of the conqueror's view of history, adding that the later contacts between the two groups gave the Indians no cause for any further giving of thanks. Robert Claiborne defends WASPs (White Anglo-Saxon Protestants) against being dumped on by all the other nationalities in the mixed salad that is America. Dwight Okita's poem returns us to the internment of Japanese-Americans.

ALIEN TURF

Piri Thomas

Piri Thomas was born in Spanish Harlem in 1928 and grew up in
its world of gangs, drugs, and petty crime. In his teens he became
an addict, was convicted of attempted armed robbery, and served
six years of a 15-year sentence. After his release, he began to work
for drug rehabilitation programs in New York and Puerto Rico and
developed a career as a writer. The autobiographical *Down These
Mean Streets* (1967), from which the following selection is
taken, was his first book. A sequel, *Savior, Savior, Hold My Hand*,
was published in 1972.

Thomas tells the reader about an event in his childhood, one
that many young people will have experienced: being the new kid
on the block. But when the block is in a poor neighborhood and
when, moreover, the new kid is from a background different from
the prevailing culture, then the mix can turn explosive.

For some information about Puerto Rico, read the headnote
for Jack Agueros's "A Puerto Rican Pilgrimage."

Sometimes you don't fit in. Like if you're a Puerto Rican on an Italian   1
block. After my new baby brother, Ricardo, died of some kind of
germs, Poppa moved us from 111th Street to Italian turf on 114th
Street between Second and Third Avenue. I guess Poppa wanted to get
Momma away from the hard memories of the old pad.

I sure missed 111th Street, where everybody acted, walked, and   2
talked like me. But on 114th Street everything went all right for a
while. There were a few dirty looks from the spaghetti-an'-sauce cats,
but no big sweat. Till that one day I was on my way home from school
and almost had reached my stoop when someone called: "Hey, you
dirty fuckin' spic."

The words hit my ears and almost made me curse Poppa at the   3
same time. I turned around real slow and found my face pushing in the
finger of an Italian kid about my age. He had five or six of his friends
with him.

"Hey, you," he said, "What nationality are ya?"   4

I looked at him and wondered which nationality to pick. And one   5
of his friends said, "Ah, Rocky, he's black enuff to be a nigger. Ain't
that what you is, kid?"

My voice was almost shy in its anger. "I'm Puerto Rican," I said.   6
"I was born here." I wanted to shout it, but it came out like a whisper.

159

"Right here inna street?" Rocky sneered. "Ya mean right here   7
inna middle of da street?"

They all laughed. I hated them. I shook my head slowly from side   8
to side.

"Uh-uh," I said softly. "I was born inna hospital — inna bed."   9

"Umm, *paisan* — born inna bed," Rocky said.   10

I didn't like Rocky Italiano's voice. "Inna hospital," I whispered,   11
and all the time my eyes were trying to cut down the long distance
from this trouble to my stoop. But it was no good; I was hemmed in by
Rocky's friends. I couldn't help thinking about kids getting wasted for
moving into a block belonging to other people.

"What hospital, *paisan?*" Bad Rocky pushed.   12

"Harlem Hospital," I answered, wishing like all hell that it was 5   13
o'clock instead of just 3 o'clock, 'cause Poppa came home at 5. I
looked around for some friendly faces belonging to grown-up people,
but the elders were all busy yakking away in Italian. I couldn't help
thinking how much like Spanish it sounded. Shit, that should make us
something like relatives.

"Harlem Hospital?" said a voice. "I knew he was a nigger."   14

"Yeah," said another voice from an expert on color. "That's the   15
hospital where all them black bastards get born at."

I dug three Italian elders looking at us from across the street and I   16
felt saved. But that went out the window when they just smiled and
went on talking. I couldn't decide whether they had smiled because
this new whatever-he-was was gonna get his ass kicked or because they
were pleased that their kids were welcoming a new kid to their country. An older man nodded his head at Rocky, who smiled back. I
wondered if that was a signal for my funeral to begin.

"Ain't that right, kid?" Rocky pressed. "Ain't that where all black   17
people get born?"

I dug some of Rocky's boys grinding and pushing and punching   18
closed fists against open hands. I figured they were looking to shake
me up, so I straightened up my humble voice and made like proud.
"There's all kinds of people born there. Colored people, Puerto Ricans
like me, an' — even spaghetti-benders like you."

"That's a dirty fuckin' lie" — *bash*, I felt Rocky's fist smack into   19
my mouth — "You dirty fuckin' spic."

I got dizzy and then more dizzy when fists started to fly from   20
everywhere and only toward me. I swung back, *splat, bish* — my fist
hit some face and I wished I hadn't, 'cause then I started getting
kicked.

I heard people yelling in Italian and English and I wondered if   21
maybe it was 'cause I hadn't fought fair in having hit that one guy. But
it wasn't. The voices were trying to help me.

"Whas'sa matta, you no-good kids, leeva da kid alone," a man 22
said. I looked through a swelling eye and dug some Italians pushing
their kids off me with slaps. One even kicked a kid in the ass. I could
have loved them if I didn't hate them so fuckin' much.

"You all right, kiddo?" asked the man. 23
"Where you live, boy?" said another one. 24
"Is the *bambino* hurt?" asked a woman. 25

I didn't look at any of them. I felt dizzy. I didn't want to open my 26
mouth to talk, 'cause I was fighting to keep from puking up. I just
hoped my face was cool-looking. I walked away from the group of
strangers. I reached my stoop and started to climb the steps.

"Hey, spic," came a shout from across the street. I started to turn 27
to the voice and changed my mind. "Spic" wasn't my name. I knew
that voice, though. It was Rocky's. "We'll see ya again, spic, " he
said.

I wanted to do something tough, like spitting in their direction. 28
But you gotta have spit in your mouth in order to spit, and my mouth
was hurt dry. I just stood there with my back to them.

"Hey, your old man just better be the janitor in that fuckin' 29
building."

Another voice added, "Hey, you got any pretty sisters? We might 30
let ya stay onna block."

Another voice mocked, "Aw, fer Chrissake, where ya ever hear of 31
one of them black broads being pretty?"

I heard the laughter. I turned around and looked at them. Rocky 32
made some kind of dirty sign by putting his left hand in the crook of
his right arm while twisting his closed fist in the air.

Another voice said, "Fuck it, we'll just cover the bitch's face with 33
the flag an' fuck'er for old glory."

All I could think of was how I'd like to kill each of them two or 34
three times. I found some spit in my mouth and splattered it in their
direction and went inside.

Momma was cooking, and the smell of rice and beans was beating 35
the smell of Parmesan cheese from the other apartments. I let myself
into our new pad. I tried to walk fast past Momma so I could wash up,
but she saw me.

"My God, Piri, what happened?" she cried. 36
"Just a little fight in school, Momma. You know how it is, 37
Momma, I'm new in school an' . . ." I made myself laugh. Then I
made myself say, "But Moms, I whipped the living———outta two
guys, an' one was bigger'n me."

"*Bendito*, Piri, I raise my family in Christian way. Not to fight. 38
Christ says to turn the other cheek."

"Sure, Momma." I smiled and went and showered, feeling sore at 39

Poppa for bringing us into spaghetti country. I felt my face with easy
fingers and thought about all the running back and forth from school
that was in store for me.

I sat down to dinner and listened to Momma talk about Christian   40
living without really hearing her. All I could think of was that I hadda
go out in that street again. I made up my mind to go out right after I
finished eating. I had to, shook up or not; cats like me had to show
heart.

"Be back, Moms," I said after dinner, "I'm going out on the   41
stoop." I got halfway to the stoop and turned and went back to our
apartment. I knocked.

"Who is it?" Momma asked.   42

"Me, Momma."   43

She opened the door. *"¿Qué pasa?"* she asked.   44

"Nothing, Momma, I just forgot something," I said. I went into   45
the bedroom and fiddled around and finally copped a funny book and
walked out the door again. But this time I made sure the switch on the
lock was open, just in case I had to get back real quick. I walked out on
that stoop as cool as could be, feeling braver with the lock open.

There was no sign of Rocky and his killers. After awhile I saw   46
Poppa coming down the street. He walked like beat tired. Poppa hated
his pick-and-shovel job with the WPA. He couldn't even hear the name
WPA without getting a fever. *Funny*, I thought, *Poppa's the same like
me, a stone Puerto Rican, and nobody in this block even pays him a
mind. Maybe older people get along better'n us kids.*

Poppa was climbing the stoop. "Hi, Poppa," I said.   47

"How's it going, son? Hey, you sure look a little lumped up.   48
What happened?"

I looked at Poppa and started to talk it outta me all at once and   49
stopped, 'cause I heard my voice start to sound scared, and that was no
good.

"Slow down, son," Poppa said. "Take it easy." He sat down on   50
the stoop and made a motion for me to do the same. He listened and I
talked, I gained confidence. I went from a tone of being shook up by
the Italians to a tone of being a better fighter than Joe Louis and Pedro
Montanez lumped together, with Kid Chocolate thrown in for extra.

"So that's what happened," I concluded. "And it looks like only   51
the beginning. Man, I ain't scared, Poppa, but like there's nothin' but
Italianos on this block and there's no me's like me except me an' our
family."

Poppa looked tight. He shook his head from side to side and   52
mumbled something about another Puerto Rican family that lived a
coupla doors down from us.

I thought, *What good would that do me, unless they prayed*   53 *over my dead body in Spanish?* But I said, "Man! That's great. Before ya know it, there'll be a whole bunch of us moving in, huh?"

Poppa grunted something and got up. "Staying out here, son?" 54

"Yeah, Poppa, for a little while longer." 55

From that day on I grew eyes all over my head. Anytime I hit that 56 street for anything, I looked straight ahead, behind me and from side to side all at the same time. Sometimes I ran into Rocky and his boys — the cat was never without his boys — but they never made a move to snag me. They just grinned at me like a bunch of hungry alley cats that could get to their mouse anytime they wanted. That's what they made me feel like — a mouse. Not like a smart house mouse but like a white house pet that ain't got no business in the middle of cat country but don't know better 'cause he grew thinking he was a cat — which wasn't far from wrong 'cause he'd end up as part of the inside of some cat.

Rocky and his fellas got to playing a way-out game with me called 57 "One-finger-across-the-neck-inna-slicing-motion," followed by such gentle words as "It won't be long, spico." I just looked at them blank and made it to wherever I was going.

I kept wishing those cats went to the same school I went to, a 58 school that was on the border between their country and mine, and I had *amigos* there — and there I could count on them. But I couldn't ask two or three *amigos* to break into Rocky's block and help me mess up his boys. I knew 'cause I had asked them already. They had turned me down fast, and I couldn't blame them. It would have been murder, and I guess they figured one murder would be better than four.

I got through the days trying to play it cool and walk on by Rocky 59 and his boys like they weren't there. One day I passed them and nothing was said. I started to let out my breath. I felt great; I hadn't been seen. Then someone yelled in a high, girlish voice, "Yoo-hoo . . . Hey, *paisan* . . . we see yoo . . ." And right behind that voice came a can of evaporated milk — whoosh, clatter. I walked cool for ten steps then started running like mad.

This crap kept up for a month. They tried to shake me up. Every 60 time they threw something at me, it was just to see me jump. I decided that the next fucking time they threw something at me I was gonna play bad-o and not run. That next time came about a week later. Momma sent me off the stoop to the Italian market on 115th Street and First Avenue, deep in Italian country. Man, that was stompin' territory. But I went, walking in the style which I had copped from the colored cats I had seen, a swinging and stepping down hard at every step. Those cats were so down and cool that just walking made a way-out sound.

Ten minutes later I was on my way back with Momma's stuff. I 61 got to the corner of First Avenue and 114th Street and crushed myself right into Rocky and his fellas.

"Well-l, fellas," Rocky said, "Lookee who's here."   62

I didn't like the sounds coming out of Rocky's fat mouth. And I   63
didn't like the sameness of the shitty grins spreading all over the boys' faces. But I thought, *No more! No more! I ain't gonna run no more.* Even so, I looked around, like for some kind of Jesus miracle to happen. I was always looking for miracles to happen.

"Say, *paisan*," one guy said, "you even buying from us *paisans*,   64
eh? Man, you must wantta be Italian."

Before I could bite that dopey tongue of mine, I said, "I wouldn't   65
be a guinea on a motherfucking bet."

"Wha-at?" said Rocky, really surprised. I didn't blame him; I was   66
surprised myself. His finger began digging a hole in his ear, like he hadn't heard me right. "Wha-at? Say that again?"

I could feel a thin hot wetness cutting itself down my leg. I had   67
been so ashamed of being so damned scared that I had peed on myself. And then I wasn't scared any more; I felt a fuck-it-all attitude. I looked real bad at Rocky and said, "Ya heard me. I wouldn't be a guinea on a bet."

"Ya little sonavabitch, we'll kick the shit outta ya," said one guy,   68
Tony, who had made a habit of asking me if I had any sen-your-ritas for sisters.

"Kick the shit outta me yourself if you got any heart, you mother   69
fuckin' fucker," I screamed at him. I felt kind of happy, the kind of feeling that you get only when you got heart.

Big-mouth Tony just swung out, and I swung back and heard all   70
of Momma's stuff plopping all over the street. My fist hit Tony smack dead in the mouth. He was so mad he threw a fist at me from about three feet away. I faked and jabbed and did fancy dance steps. Big-mouth put a stop to all that with a punch in my mouth. I heard the home cheers of "Yea, yea, bust that spic wide open!" Then I bloodied Tony's nose. He blinked and sniffed without putting his hands to his nose, and I remembered Poppa telling me, "Son, if you're ever fighting somebody an' you punch him in the nose, and he just blinks an' sniffs without holding his nose, you can do one of two things: fight like hell or run like hell — 'cause that cat's a fighter."

Big-mouth came at me and we grabbed each other and pushed   71
and pulled and shoved. *Poppa*, I thought, *I ain't gonna cop out. I'm a fighter, too.* I pulled away from Tony and blew my fist into his belly. He puffed and butted my nose with his head. I sniffed back. *Poppa, I didn't put my hands to my nose.* I hit Tony again in that same weak spot. He bent over in the middle and went down to his knees.

Big-mouth got up as fast as he could, and I was thinking how   72 much heart he had. But I ran toward him like my life depended on it; I wanted to cool him. Too late. I saw his hand grab a fistful of ground asphalt which had been piled nearby to fix a pothole in the street. I tried to duck; I should have closed my eyes instead. The shitty-gritty stuff hit my face, and I felt the scrappy pain make itself a part of my eyes. I screamed and grabbed for two eyes with one hand, while the other I beat some kind of helpless tune on air that just couldn't be hurt. I heard Rocky's voice shouting, "Ya scum bag, ya didn't have to fight the spic dirty; you could've fucked him up fair and square!" I couldn't see. I heard a fist hit a face, then Big-mouth's voice: "Whatta ya hittin' me for?" and then Rocky's voice: "*Putana!* I ought ta knock all your fuckin' teeth out."

I felt hands grabbing at me between my screams. I punched out.   73
I'm gonna get killed, I thought. Then I heard many voices: "Hold it, kid." "We ain't gonna hurt ya." "Je-*sus*, don't rub your eyes." "ooooohhhh, shit, his eyes is fulla that shit."

You're fuckin' right, I thought, *and it hurts like* coño.   74

I heard a woman's voice now: "Take him to a hospital." And an   75
old man asked: "How did it happen?"

"Momma, Momma," I cried.   76

"Comon, kid," Rocky said, taking my hand. "Lemme take ya   77
home." I fought for the right to rub my eyes. "Grab his other hand, Vincent," Rocky said. I tried to rub my eyes with my eyelids. I could feel hurt tears cutting down my cheeks. "Come on, kid, we ain't gonna hurt ya," Rocky tried to assure me. "Swear to our mudders. We just wanna take ya home."

I made myself believe him, and trying not to make pain noises, I   78
let myself be led home. I wondered if I was gonna be blind like Mr. Silva, who went around from door to door selling dish towels and brooms, his son leading him around.

"You okay, kid?" Rocky asked.   79

"Yeah," what was left of me said.   80

"A-huh," mumbled Big-mouth.   81

"He got much heart for a nigger," somebody else said.   82

A *spic*, I thought.   83

"For anybody," Rocky said. "Here we are, kid," he added.   84
"Watch your step."

I was like carried up the steps. "What's your apartment number?"   85
Rocky asked.

"One-B — inna back — ground floor," I said, and I was led there.   86
Somebody knocked on Momma's door. Then I heard running feet and Rocky's voice yelling back, "Don't rat, huh, kid?" And I was alone.

I heard the door open and Momma say, "*Bueno*, Piri, come in." I   87
didn't move. I couldn't. There was a long pause; I could hear Momma's

fright. "My God," she said finally. "What's happened?" Then she took a closer look. "Aieeee," she screamed. "*¡Dios mío!*"

"I was playing with some kids, Momma," I said, "an' I got some dirt in my eyes." I tried to make my voice come out without the pain, like a man.   88

"*Dios eterno*—your eyes!"   89

"What's the matter? What's the matter?" Poppa called from the bedroom.   90

"*¡Está ciego!*" Momma screamed. "He is blind!"   91

I heard Poppa knocking things over as he came running. Sis began to cry. Blind, hurting tears were jumping out of my eyes. "Whattya mean, he's blind?" Poppa said as he stormed into the kitchen. "What happened?" Poppa's voice was both scared and mad.   92

"Playing, Poppa."   93

"Whatta ya mean, 'playing'?" Poppa's English sounded different when he got warm.   94

"Just playing, Poppa."   95

"Playing? Playing got all that dirt in your eyes? I bet my ass. Them damn Ee-ta-liano kids ganged up on you again." Poppa squeezed my head between the fingers of one hand. "That settles it—we're moving outta this damn section, outta this damn block, outta this damn shit."   96

Shit, I thought, *Poppa's sure cursin' up a storm.* I could hear him slapping the side of his leg, like he always did when he got real mad.   97

"Son," he said, "you're gonna point them out to me."   98

"Point who out, Poppa? I was playin' an'—"   99

"Stop talkin' to him and take him to the hospital!" Momma screamed.   100

"*Pobrecito*, poor Piri," cooed my little sister.   101

"You sure, son?" Poppa asked. "You was only playing?"   102

"Shit, Poppa, I said I was."   103

Smack—Poppa was so scared and mad, he let it out in the slap to the side of my face.   104

"*¡Bestia!* ani-*mul!*" Momma cried. "He's blind, and you hit him!"   105

"I'm sorry, son, I'm sorry," Poppa said in a voice like almost crying. I heard him running back into the bedroom, yelling, "Where's my pants?"   106

Momma grabbed away fingers that were trying to wipe away the hurt in my eyes. "*Caramba*, no rub, no rub," she said, kissing me. She told Sis to get a rag and wet it with cold water.   107

Poppa came running back into the kitchen. "Let's go, son, let's go. Jesus! I didn't mean to smack ya, I really didn't," he said, his big hand rubbing and grabbing my hair gently.   108

"Here's the rag, Momma," said Sis.   109

"What's that for?" asked Poppa.   110

"To put on his eyes," Momma said.   111

I heard the smack of a wet rag, *blapt*, against the kitchen wall.   112
"We can't put nothing on his eyes. It might make them worse. Come
on, son," Poppa said nervously, lifting me up in his big arms. I felt like
a little baby, like I didn't hurt so bad. I wanted to stay there, but I said,
"Let me down, Poppa, I ain't no kid."

"Shut up," Poppa said softly. "I know you ain't but it's faster this   113
way."

"Which hospeetal are you taking him to?" Momma asked.   114

"Nearest one," Poppa answered as we went out the door. He   115
carried me through the hall and out into the street, where the bright
sunlight made a red hurting color through the crap in my eyes. I heard
voices on the stoop and on the sidewalk: "Is that the boy?"

"A-huh. He's probably blinded."   116

"We'll get a cab, son," Poppa said. His voice loved me. I heard   117
Rocky yelling from across the street, "We're pulling for ya, kid. Remember what we . . ." The rest was lost to Poppa's long legs running
down to the corner of Third Avenue. He hailed a taxi and we zoomed
off toward Harlem Hospital. I felt the cab make all kinds of sudden
stops and turns.

"How do you feel, *hijo?*" Poppa asked.   118

"It burns like hell."   119

"You'll be okay," he said, and as an afterthought added, "Don't   120
curse, son."

I heard cars honking and the Third Avenue el roaring above us. I   121
knew we were in Puerto Rican turf, 'cause I could hear our language.

"Son."   122

"Yeah, Poppa."   123

"Don't rub your eyes, fer Christ sake." He held my skinny wrists   124
in his one hand, and everything got quiet between us.

The cab got to Harlem Hospital. I heard change being handled   125
and the door opening and Poppa thanking the cabbie for getting here
fast. "Hope the kid'll be okay," the driver said.

I will be, I thought, *I ain't gonna be like Mr. Silva.*   126

Poppa took me in his arms again and started running. "Where's   127
emergency, mister?" he asked someone.

"To your left and straight away," said a voice.   128

"Thanks a lot," Poppa said, and we were running again.   129

"Emergency?" Poppa said when we stopped.   130

"Yes, sir," said a girl's voice. "What's the matter?"   131

"My boy's got his eyes full of ground-up tar an' — "   132

"What's the matter?" said a man's voice.   133

"Youngster with ground tar in his eyes, doctor."   134

"We'll take him, mister. You just put him down here and go with   135
the nurse. She'll take down the information. Uh, you the father?"

"That's right, doctor."   136

"Okay, just put him down here."   137

"Poppa, don't leave me," I cried.   138

"Sh, son, I ain't leaving you. I'm just going to fill out some   139
papers, an' I'll be right back."

I nodded my head up and down and was wheeled away. When the   140
rolling stretcher stopped, somebody stuck a needle in me and I got
sleepy and started thinking about Rocky and his boys, and Poppa's
slap, and how great Poppa was, and how my eyes didn't hurt no
more . . .

I woke up in a room blind with darkness. The only lights were   141
the ones inside my head. I put my fingers to my eyes and felt bandages.
"Let them be, sonny," said a woman's voice.

I wanted to ask the voice if they had taken my eyes out, but I   142
didn't. I was afraid the voice would say yes.

"Let them be, sonny," the nurse said, pulling my hand away from   143
the bandages. "You're all right. The doctor put the bandages on to
keep the light out. They'll be off real soon. Don't you worry none,
sonny."

I wished she would stop calling me sonny. "Where's Poppa?" I   144
asked cool like.

"He's outside, sonny. Would you like me to send him in?"   145

I nodded. "Yeah." I heard walking-away shoes, a door opening, a   146
whisper, and shoes walking back toward me. "How do you feel, *hijo?*"
Poppa asked.

"It hurts like shit, Poppa."   147

"It's just for awhile, son, and then off come the bandages. Every-   148
thing's gonna be all right."

I thought, *Poppa didn't tell me to stop cursing.*   149

"And son, I thought I told you to stop cursing," he added.   150

I smiled. Poppa hadn't forgotten. Suddenly I realized that all I   151
had on was a hospital gown. "Poppa, where's my clothes?" I asked.

I got them. I'm taking them home an'—"   152

"Whatta ya mean, Poppa?" I said, like scared. "You ain't leavin'   153
me here? I'll be damned if I stay." I was already sitting up and feeling
my way outta bed. Poppa grabbed me and pushed me back. His voice
wasn't mad or scared any more. It was happy and soft, like Momma's.

"Hey," he said, "get your ass back in bed or they'll have to put a   154
bandage there too."

"Poppa," I pleaded. "I don't care, wallop me as much as you   155
want, just take me home."

"Hey, I thought you said you wasn't no kid. Hell, you ain't scared   156
of being alone?"

Inside my head there was a running of *Yeah, yeah, yeah*, but I   157
answered, "Naw, Poppa, it's just that Momma's gonna worry and she'll
get sick an' everything, and—"

"Won't work, son," Poppa broke in with a laugh.   158

I kept quiet.   159

"It's only for a couple days. We'll come and see you an' every-   160
body'll bring you things."

I got interested but played it smooth. "What kinda things,   161
Poppa?"

Poppa shrugged his shoulders and spread his big arms apart and   162
answered me like he was surprised that I should ask. "Uh . . . fruits
and . . . candy and ice cream. And Momma will probably bring you
chicken soup."

I shook my head sadly. "Poppa, you know I don't like chicken   163
soup."

"So we won't bring chicken soup. We'll bring what you like.   164
Goddammit, whatta ya like?"

"I'd like the first things you talked about, Poppa," I said softly.   165
"But instead of soup I'd like"—I held my breath back, then shot it
out—"some roller skates!"

Poppa let out a whistle. Roller skates were about $1.50, and that   166
was rice and beans for more than a few days. Then he said, "All right,
son, soon as you get home, you got 'em."

But he had agreed too quickly. I shook my head from side to side.   167
Shit, I was gonna push all the way for the roller skates. It wasn't every
day you'd get hurt bad enough to ask for something so little like a pair
of roller skates. I wanted them right away.

"Fer Christ sakes," Poppa protested, "you can't use 'em in here.   168
Why, some kid will probably steal 'em on you." But Poppa's voice
died out slowly in a "you win" tone as I just kept shaking my head
from side to side. "Bring 'em tomorrow," he finally mumbled, "but
that's it."

"Thanks, Poppa."   169

"Don't ask for no more."   170

My eyes were starting to hurt like mad again. The fun was starting   171
to go outta the game between Poppa and me. I made a face.

"Does it hurt, son?"   172

"Naw, Poppa. I can take it." I thought how I was like a cat in a   173
movie about Indians, taking it like a champ, tied to a stake and getting
like burned toast.

Poppa sounded relieved. "Yeah, it's only at first it hurts." His   174
hand touched my foot. "Well, I'll be going now . . ." Poppa rubbed

my foot gently and then slapped me the same gentle way on the side of
my leg. "Be good, son," he said and walked away. I heard the door
open and the nurse telling him about how they were gonna move me
to the ward 'cause I was out of danger. "Son," Poppa called back,
"you're *un hombre.*"

I felt proud as hell.   175
"Poppa."   176
"Yeah, son?"   177
"You won't forget to bring the roller skates, huh?"   178
Poppa laughed. "Yeah, son."   179
I heard the door close.   180

EXERCISES

Words to Know

paisan—kid (paragraph 10), *bambino*—baby, child (25), *bendito*
—stupid (38), *¿qué pasa?*—What's going on? (44), *putana*—
whore (72), *¡Dios mío!*—my God! (87), *Dios eterno*—eternal God
(89), *está ciego*—he's blind (91), *pobrecito*—you poor boy (101),
hijo—son (118), *hombre*—man (174).

Some of the Issues

1. How do the first two sentences set the scene?
2. Piri wants to project a certain self-image in front of the gang.
   Characterize it.
3. Until the climactic fight, the cat-and-mouse game that Rocky's
   gang plays goes through several stages. Determine what these
   stages are and how Piri reacts to them.
4. How do the grown-ups (those in the street as well as Piri's parents) react to the situation at the various stages? How does Piri
   deal with his parents' reactions in particular?
5. How does Rocky's attitude toward Piri change after one of the
   gang members throws the asphalt? What causes the change?
6. Explain Piri's reaction to "spic" and "nigger." Is Piri's desire to
   be identified as a Puerto Rican a matter of pride or practicality?
7. What is the importance of being *"un hombre,"* of having
   "heart"? How does Piri prove himself a man? By whose standards?

The Way We Are Told

8. There is almost no description in this selection. It is all action and
   dialog. Thomas nevertheless manages to convey some strong im-

pressions of individuals and their attitudes How does he do it? Cite some examples.

* 9. Both Angelou ("Graduation") and Thomas tell their stories from an adolescent's point of view. Apart from the content, how do the two stories differ? What causes the differences?

Some Subjects for Essays

10. Write about a conflict that you have had. Set the scene and then use mostly dialog to tell your story. See if you can make the voices authentic.

* 11. *Rite de passage*, a French term, is usually used to indicate the ceremony marking the formal change of a young person from childhood to adulthood, such as a confirmation or *bar mitzvah*. Usually it is a religious ceremony. Write an essay arguing that Angelou's graduation and Thomas's big fight (or one or the other) were such rites of passage.

* 12. Both Jack Agueros ("Halfway to Dick and Jane") and Thomas describe growing up Puerto Rican in New York City. Write an essay comparing and contrasting the way they talk about their childhoods.

* 13. Use the photograph on page 156 as the basis for constructing a story about the situation and the attitudes of the characters in the picture, assuming that it represents some kind of conflict. What is the man with the headband reacting to? Relate his attitude to that of the narrator in "Alien Turf."

NIGHT WALKER

Brent Staples

Brent Staples was born in 1951 in Chester, Pennsylvania. He holds
a Ph.D. degree in psychology from the University of Chicago and is
a member of the editorial board of the *New York Times* and the
author of *Parallel Times: A Memoir* (1991). The selection reprinted here appeared originally in *Ms* magazine in September
1986. In it Staples describes repeated experiences he had when he
was taking walks at night. A tall black man, he aroused the fear of
other pedestrians as well as drivers who saw him as the stereotypical mugger.

    For Norman Podhoretz, whom Staples refers to in paragraph
11, reads Podhoretz's essay "The Brutal Bargain."

My first victim was a woman — white, well dressed, probably in her 1
early twenties. I came upon her late one evening on a deserted street in
Hyde Park, a relatively affluent neighborhood in an otherwise mean,
impoverished section of Chicago. As I swung onto the avenue behind
her, there seemed to be a discreet, uninflammatory distance between
us. Not so. She cast back a worried glance. To her, the youngish black
man — a broad six feet two inches with a beard and billowing hair,
both hands shoved into the pockets of a bulky military jacket —
seemed menacingly close. After a few more quick glimpses, she picked
up her pace and was soon running in earnest. Within seconds she
disappeared into a cross street.

    That was more than a decade ago. I was 22 years old, a graduate 2
student newly arrived at the University of Chicago. It was in the echo
of that terrified woman's footfalls that I first began to know the unwieldy inheritance I'd come into — the ability to alter public space in
ugly ways. It was clear that she thought herself the quarry of a mugger,
a rapist, or worse. Suffering a bout of insomnia, however, I was stalking
sleep, not defenseless wayfarers. As a softy who is scarcely able to take
a knife to a raw chicken — let alone hold it to a person's throat — I was
surprised, embarrassed, and dismayed all at once. Her flight made me
feel like an accomplice in tyranny. It also made it clear that I was
indistinguishable from the muggers who occasionally seeped into the
area from the surrounding ghetto. That first encounter, and those that
followed, signified that a vast, unnerving gulf lay between nighttime
pedestrians — particularly women — and me. And I soon gathered that
being perceived as dangerous is a hazard in itself. I only needed to turn

172

a corner into a dicey situation, or crowd some frightened, armed person in a foyer somewhere, or make an errant move after being pulled over by a policeman. Where fear and weapons meet — and they often do in urban America — there is always the possibility of death.

In that first year, my first away from my hometown, I was to become thoroughly familiar with the language of fear. At dark, shadowy intersections in Chicago, I could cross in front of a car stopped at a traffic light and elicit the *thunk, thunk, thunk, thunk* of the driver —black, white, male, or female — hammering down the door locks. On less traveled streets after dark, I grew accustomed to but never comfortable with people who crossed to the other side of the street rather than pass me. Then there were the standard unpleasantries with police, doormen, bouncers, cab drivers, and others whose business it is to screen out troublesome individuals *before* there is any nastiness.

I moved to New York nearly two years ago and I have remained an avid night walker. In central Manhattan, the near-constant crowd cover minimizes tense one-on-one street encounters. Elsewhere — visiting friends in SoHo, where sidewalks are narrow and tightly spaced buildings shut out the sky — things can get very taut indeed.

After dark on the warrenlike streets of Brooklyn where I live, women seem to set their faces on neutral and, with their purse straps strung across their chests bandolier style, they forge ahead as though bracing themselves against being tackled. I understand, of course, that the danger they perceive is not a hallucination. Women are particularly vulnerable to street violence, and young black males are drastically overrepresented among the perpetrators of that violence. Yet these truths are no solace against the kind of alienation that comes of being ever the suspect, against being set apart, a fearsome entity with whom pedestrians avoid making eye contact.

It is not altogether clear to me how I reached the ripe old age of 22 without being conscious of the lethality nighttime pedestrians attributed to me. Perhaps it was because in Chester, Pennsylvania, the small, angry industrial town where I came of age in the 1960s, I was scarcely noticeable against a backdrop of gang warfare, street knifings, and murders. I grew up one of the good boys, had perhaps a half-dozen fist fights. In retrospect, my shyness of combat has clear sources.

Many things go into the making of a young thug. One of those things is the consummation of the male romance with the power to intimidate. An infant discovers that random flailings send the baby bottle flying out of the crib and crashing to the floor. Delighted, the joyful babe repeats those motions again and again, seeking to duplicate the feat. Just so, I recall the points at which some of my boyhood friends were finally seduced by the perception of themselves as tough guys. When a mark cowered and surrendered his money without resistance, myth and reality merged—and paid off. It is, after all, only manly to embrace the power to frighten and intimidate. We, as men, are not supposed to give an inch of our lane on the highway; we are to seize the fighter's edge in work and in play and even in love; we are to be valiant in the face of hostile forces.

Unfortunately, poor and powerless young men seem to take all this nonsense literally. As a boy, I saw countless tough guys locked away; I have since buried several, too. They were babies, really—a teenage cousin, a brother of 22, a childhood friend in his mid-twenties—all gone down in episodes of bravado played out in the streets. I came to doubt the virtues of intimidation early on. I chose, perhaps even unconsciously, to remain a shadow—timid, but a survivor. 8

The fearsomeness mistakenly attributed to me in public places often has a perilous flavor. The most frightening of these confusions occurred in the late 1970s and early 1980s when I worked as a journalist in Chicago. One day, rushing into the office of a magazine I was writing for with a deadline story in hand, I was mistaken for a burglar. The office manager called security and, with an ad hoc posse, pursued me through the labyrinthine halls, nearly to my editor's door. I had no way of proving who I was. I could only move briskly toward the company of someone who knew me. 9

Another time I was on assignment for a local paper and killing time before an interview. I entered a jewelry store on the city's affluent Near North Side. The proprietor excused herself and returned with an enormous red Doberman pinscher straining at the end of a leash. She stood, the dog extended toward me, silent to my questions, her eyes bulging nearly out of her head. I took a cursory look around, nodded, and bade her good night. Relatively speaking, however, I never fared as badly as another black male journalist. He went to nearby Wauke-gan, Illinois, a couple of summers ago to work on a story about a murderer who was born there. Mistaking the reporter for the killer, police hauled him from his car at gunpoint and but for his press credentials would probably have tried to book him. Such episodes are not uncommon. Black men trade tales like this all the time. 10

In "My Negro Problem—And Ours" Podhoretz writes that the hatred he feels for blacks makes itself known to him through a variety of avenues—one being his discomfort with that "special brand of paranoid touchiness" to which he says blacks are prone. No doubt he is speaking here of black men. In time, I learned to smother the rage I felt at so often being taken for a criminal. Not to do so would surely have led to madness—via that special "paranoid touchiness" that so annoyed Podhoretz at the time he wrote the essay. 11

I began to take precautions to make myself less threatening. I 12 move about with care, particularly late in the evening. I give a wide berth to nervous people on subway platforms during the wee hours, particularly when I have exchanged business clothes for jeans. If I happen to be entering a building behind some people who appear skittish, I may walk by, letting them clear the lobby before I return, so as not to seem to be following them. I have been calm and extremely congenial on those rare occasions when I've been pulled over by the police

And on late-evening constitutionals along streets less traveled by,   13 I employ what has proved to be an excellent tension-reducing measure: I whistle melodies from Beethoven and Vivaldi and the more popular classical composers. Even steely New Yorkers hunching toward nighttime destinations seem to relax, and occasionally they even join in the tune. Virtually everybody seems to sense that a mugger wouldn't be warbling bright, sunny selections from Vivaldi's *Four Seasons*. It is my equivalent of the cowbell that hikers wear when they know they are in bear country.

EXERCISES

Words to Know

affluent (paragraph 1), impoverished (1), discreet (1), uninflammatory (1), billowing (1), pace (2), unwieldy (2), alter (2), quarry (2), stalking (2), insomnia (2), wayfarers (2), dismayed (2), accomplice (2), indistinguishable (2), elicit (3), avid (4), taut (4), warrenlike (5), bandolier style (5), hallucination (5), vulnerable (5), perpetrators (5), solace (5), alienation (5), lethality (6), flailing (6), cowered (6), bravado (8), fearsomeness (9), perilous (9), ad hoc (9), posse (9), labryinthine (9), cursory (10), paranoid (11), wide berth (12), skittish (12), congenial (12), constitutionals (13), warbling (13).

Some of the Issues

1. How does Staples first discover his "ability to alter public space" (paragraph 2)?
2. What is Staples's reaction to the way he is perceived by strangers on his nightly walks? Does he show that he understands the feelings of some of those who fear him? Does he also show anger? Where?
3. What does Staples tell us about himself? About his childhood? How does this knowledge emphasize the contrast between his real self and the way he is often perceived by strangers?

4. How does Staples respond to Norman Podhoretz's contention that black men have a "special brand of paranoid touchiness" (paragraph 11)?
5. What has Staples learned to do to reduce the tension of passersby? Why does he choose the music he does? Does it solve his problem?

The Way We Are Told

6. Staples starts with an anecdote. Why does he use the word "victim" in the first sentence? Is there really a "victim"?
7. Identify examples drawn from Staples's own experience. How are they used to support the generalizations he makes?

Some Subjects for Essays

8. Write telling about a time when someone misjudged you or something you did. What were the circumstances? How did you feel? What was the resolution? What did you learn from the experience?

I LEARN WHAT I AM

Walter White

Walter White was born in Atlanta, Georgia, in 1893. He joined the
NAACP early in its development and served as its head from 1931
until his death in 1955. The following excerpt is taken from his
autobiography, *A Man Called White* (1948).

  The events White describes took place in his childhood, at
the beginning of the twentieth century. The year was 1906 and he
was living in Atlanta with his large family, near the line that
separated the white community from his own. His father, an employee of the U.S. Postal Service, kept the house in immaculate
repair, its white picket fence symbolizing the American Dream.
When a race riot erupted in Atlanta, their house became a target of
the mob. White tells the dramatic story of those two days.

There were nine light-skinned Negroes in my family: mother, father, 1
five sisters, an older brother, George, and myself. The house in which I
discovered what it meant to be a Negro was located on Houston Street,
three blocks from the Candler Building, Atlanta's first skyscraper,
which bore the name of the ex-drug clerk who had become a million-
aire from the sale of Coca-Cola. Below us lived none but Negroes;
toward town all but a very few were white. Ours was an eight room,
two-story frame house which stood out in its surroundings not because
of its opulence but by contrast with the drabness and unpaintedness of
the other dwellings in a deteriorating neighborhood.

  Only Father kept his house painted, the picket fence repaired, 2
the board fence separating our place from those on either side whitewashed, the grass neatly trimmed, and flower beds abloom. Mother's
passion for neatness was even more pronounced and it seemed to me
that I was always the victim of her determination to see no single blade
of grass longer than the others or any one of the pickets in the front
fence less shiny with paint than its mates. This spic-and-spanness
became increasingly apparent as the rest of the neighborhood became
more down-at-heel, and resulted, as we were to learn, in sullen envy
among some of our white neighbors. It was the violent expression of
that resentment against a Negro family neater than themselves which
set the pattern of our lives.

  On a day in September 1906, when I was thirteen, we were 3
taught that there is no isolation from life. The unseasonably oppressive

heat of an Indian summer day hung like a steaming blanket over Atlanta. My sisters and I had casually commented upon the unusual quietness. It seemed to stay Mother's volubility and reduced Father, who was more taciturn, to monosyllables. But, as I remember it, no other sense of impending trouble impinged upon our consciousness.

I had read the inflammatory headlines in the *Atlanta News* and   4 the more restrained ones in the *Atlanta Constitution* which reported alleged rapes and other crimes committed by Negroes. But these were so standard and familiar that they made — as I look back on it now — little impression. The stories were more frequent, however, and consisted of eight-column streamers instead of the usual two- or four-column ones.

Father was a mail collector. His tour of duty was from three to   5 eleven P.M. He made his rounds in a little cart into which one climbed from a step in the rear. I used to drive the cart for him from two until seven, leaving him at the point nearest our home on Houston Street, to return home either for study or sleep. That day Father decided that I should not go with him. I appealed to Mother, who thought it might be all right, provided Father sent me home before dark because, she said, "I don't think they would dare start anything before nightfall." Father told me as we made the rounds that ominous rumors of a race riot that night were sweeping the town. But I was too young that morning to understand the background of the riot. I became much older during the next thirty-six hours, under circumstances which I now recognize as the inevitable outcome of what had preceded. . . .

During the afternoon preceding the riot little bands of sullen,   6 evil-looking men talked excitedly on street corners all over downtown Atlanta. Around seven o'clock my father and I were driving toward a mail box at the corner of Peachtree and Houston Streets when there came from near-by Pryor Street a roar the like of which I had never heard before, but which sent a sensation of mingled fear and excitement coursing through my body. I asked permission of Father to go and see what the trouble was. He bluntly ordered me to stay in the cart. A little later we drove down Atlanta's main business thoroughfare, Peachtree Street. Again we heard the terrifying cries, this time near at hand and coming toward us. We saw a lame Negro bootblack from Herndon's barber shop pathetically trying to outrun a mob of whites. Less than a hundred yards from us the chase ended. We saw clubs and fists descending to the accompaniment of savage shouting and cursing. Suddenly a voice cried, "There goes another nigger!" Its work done, the mob went after the new prey. The body with the withered foot lay dead in a pool of blood on the street.

Father's apprehension and mine steadily increased during the   7 evening, although the fact that our skins were white kept us from attack. Another circumstance favored us — the mob had not yet grown violent enough to attack United States government property. But I could see Father's relief when he punched the time clock at eleven P.M. and got into the cart to go home. He wanted to go the back way down Forsyth Street, but I begged him, in my childish excitement and ignorance, to drive down Marietta to Five Points, the heart of Atlanta's business district, where the crowds were densest and the yells loudest. No sooner had we turned into Marietta Street, however, than we saw careening toward us an undertaker's barouche. Crouched in the rear of the vehicle were three Negroes clinging to the sides of the carriage as it lunged and swerved. On the driver's seat crouched a white man, the reins held taut in his left hand. A huge whip was gripped in his right. Alternately he lashed the horses and, without looking backward, swung the whip in savage swoops in the faces of members of the mob as they lunged at the carriage determined to seize the three Negroes.

There was no time for us to get out of its path, so sudden and swift was the appearance of the vehicle. The hub cap of the right rear wheel of the barouche hit the right side of our much lighter wagon. Father and I instinctively threw our weight and kept the cart from turning completely over. Our mare was a Texas mustang which, frightened by the sudden blow, lunged in the air as Father clung to the reins. Good fortune was with us. The cart settled back on its four wheels as Father said in a voice which brooked no dissent, "We are going home the back way and not down Marietta." 8

But again on Pryor Street we heard the cry of the mob. Close to us and in our direction ran a stout and elderly woman who cooked at a downtown white hotel. Fifty yards behind, a mob which filled the street from curb to curb was closing in. Father handed the reins to me and, though he was of slight stature, reached down and lifted the woman into the cart. I did not need to be told to lash the mare to the fastest speed she could muster. 9

The church bells tolled the next morning for Sunday service. But no one in Atlanta believed for a moment that the hatred and lust for blood had been appeased. Like skulls on a cannibal's hut the hats and caps of victims of the mob of the night before had been hung on the iron hooks of telegraph poles. None could tell whether each hat represented a dead Negro. But we knew that some of those who had worn the hats would never again wear any. 10

Late in the afternoon friends of my father's came to warn of more trouble that night. They told us that plans had been perfected for a mob to form on Peachtree Street just after nightfall to march down Houston Street to what the white people called "Darktown," three blocks or so below our house, to "clean out the niggers." There had never been a firearm in our house before that day. Father was reluctant 11 even in those circumstances to violate the law, but he at last gave in at Mother's insistence.

We turned out the lights early, as did all our neighbors. No one   12
removed his clothes or thought of sleep. Apprehension was tangible. We could almost touch its cold and clammy surface. Toward midnight the unnatural quiet was broken by a roar that grew steadily in volume. Even today I grow tense in remembering it.

Father told Mother to take my sisters, the youngest of them only   13
six, to the rear of the house, which offered more protection from stones and bullets. My brother George was away, so Father and I, the only males in the house, took our places at the front windows of the parlor. The windows opened on a porch along the front side of the house, which in turn gave onto a narrow lawn that sloped down to the street and a picket fence. There was a crash as Negroes smashed the street lamp at the corner of Houston and Piedmont Avenue down the street. In a very few minutes the vanguard of the mob, some of them bearing torches, appeared. A voice which we recognized as that of the son of the grocer with whom we had traded for many years yelled, "That's where that nigger mail carrier lives! Let's burn it down! It's too nice for a nigger to live in!" In the eerie light Father turned his drawn face toward me. In a voice as quiet as though he were asking me to pass him the sugar at the breakfast table, he said, "Son, don't shoot until the first man puts his foot on the lawn and then—don't you miss!"

In the flickering light the mob swayed, paused, and began to flow   14
toward us. In that instant there opened up within me a great awareness; I knew then who I was. I was a Negro, a human being with an invisible pigmentation which marked me a person to be hunted, hanged, abused, discriminated against, kept in poverty and ignorance, in order that those whose skin was white would have readily at hand a proof of their superiority, a proof patent and inclusive, accessible to the moron and the idiot as well as to the wise man and the genius. No matter how low a white man fell, he could always hold fast to the smug conviction that he was superior to two-thirds of the world's population, for those two-thirds were not white.

It made no difference how intelligent or talented my millions of   15
brothers and I were, or how virtuously we lived. A curse like that of Judas was upon us, a mark of degradation fashioned with heavenly authority. There were white men who said Negroes had no souls, and who proved it by the Bible. Some of these now were approaching us, intent upon burning our house.

Theirs was a world of contrasts in values: superior and inferior,   16
profit and loss, cooperative and noncooperative, civilized and aboriginal, white and black. If you were on the wrong end of the compari-

son, if you were inferior, if you were noncooperative, if you were aboriginal, if you were black, then you were marked for excision, expulsion, or extinction. I was a Negro; I was therefore that part of history which opposed the good, the just, and the enlightened. I was a Persian, falling before the hordes of Alexander. I was a Carthaginian, extinguished by the Legions of Rome. I was a Frenchman at Waterloo, an Anglo-Saxon at Hastings, a Confederate at Vicksburg. I was the defeated, wherever and whenever there was a defeat.

Yet as a boy there in the darkness amid the tightening fright, I 17 knew the inexplicable thing — that my skin was as white as the skin of those who were coming at me.

The mob moved toward the lawn. I tried to aim my gun, wonder- 18 ing what it would feel like to kill a man. Suddenly there was a volley of shots. The mob hesitated, stopped. Some friends of my father's had barricaded themselves in a two-story brick building just below our house. It was they who had fired. Some of the mobsmen, still blood-thirsty, shouted, "Let's go get the nigger." Others, afraid now for their safety, held back. Our friends, noting the hesitation, fired another volley. The mob broke and retreated up Houston Street.

In the quiet that followed I put my gun aside and tried to relax. 19 But a tension different from anything I had ever known possessed me. I was gripped by the knowledge of my identity, and in the depths of my soul I was vaguely aware that I was glad of it. I was sick with loathing for the hatred which had flared before me that night and come so close to making me a killer; but I was glad I was not one of those who hated; I was glad I was not one of those made sick and murderous by pride. I was glad I was not one of those whose story is in the history of the world, a record of bloodshed, rapine, and pillage. I was glad my mind and spirit were part of the races that had not fully awakened, and who therefore had still before them the opportunity to write a record of virtue as a memorandum to Armageddon.

It was all just a feeling then, inarticulate and melancholy, yet 20 reassuring in the way that death and sleep are reassuring, and I have clung to it now for nearly half a century.

EXERCISES

Words to Know

opulence (paragraph 1), volubility (3), taciturn (3), impinged (3), apprehension (7), patent (14), degradation (15), enlightened (16), Carthaginian (16), Waterloo (16), Hastings (16), Armageddon (19).

Some of the Issues

1. In paragraph 1 White explains the location of his house in Atlanta. What is most important about the location?
2. In paragraph 2 White describes the appearance of the house and yard. Why is it important for him to stress the difference between it and its surroundings?
3. What does White mean when he says in paragraph 3, "we were taught that there is no isolation from life"?
4. In paragraph 4 White describes the headlines in the newspapers. How do they change in the days before the riot? Does he imply that his family believed what the papers said or not?
5. In paragraphs 5 through 13 there are indications that the riots are neither new nor isolated, unique occasions. Find these indicators.
6. In what ways do the actions of the mob differ between the first and second day of the rioting?
7. Where are the police?
8. In paragraphs 14 through 17 White interrupts his account of the mob's actions to describe his thoughts and his feelings of bitterness. Contrast them to his thoughts in paragraphs 19 and 20, after the mob had fled and the danger was — temporarily — past.

The Way We Are Told

9. Why does White give his description of home and neighborhood in two paragraphs (1 and 2)? How do the paragraphs differ?
10. How does White begin to build suspense in paragraph 3? How do paragraphs 4 and 5 also prepare the reader for what is to come?
11. Paragraph 6 gives the first description of a specific event, using several words and phrases that have emotional impact. Cite four or five of these.
12. In paragraph 9 White describes another episode of rescue. See if there are any words here, like those in paragraph 6, that have emotional connotations.
13. How does White heighten the suspense in the final paragraphs of the essay?

Some Subjects for Essays

14. Have you ever felt yourself in real danger? If so, try to describe the circumstances in two ways: give an objective description of the events and then rewrite your essay, trying to heighten the effect by the careful use of emotionally effective words and phrases. (You will find that the overuse of emotional words diminishes rather than enhances the effect.)

15. White describes his experience in the Atlanta riots as a turning point in his life. Describe an experience in your own life that profoundly changed your values.

* 16. Read Lillian Smith's "When I Was a Child." Then write a paragraph giving your view of what Smith's parents' attitude would likely have been toward the riots and the rioters. Explain what made you reach your conclusions.

* 17. Read Angelou's "Graduation." Both she and White record bad experiences that turned into a kind of victory in the end; both indicate that the victory is not final but needs to be fought for again and again. Write an essay in which you compare these experiences and their meaning to White and Angelou.

ARRIVAL AT MANZANAR

Jeanne Wakatsuki Houston and James D. Houston

Like Walter White in the preceding selection, Jeanne Wakatsuki was caught up in a historical event. The year was 1942, the place California. A few months before, the Japanese had attacked the United States, bombing Pearl Harbor and overrunning U.S. possessions in the Pacific. The war was going badly, the U.S. forces and those of her allies were in retreat all over the area. Popular anger and fear turned against the Japanese Americans living on the West Coast. President Franklin D. Roosevelt signed an executive order to intern those thousands of U.S. citizens — men, women, and children. They were rounded up at short notice, had to leave their homes and businesses, either selling them or abandoning them outright. They were shipped off to internment camps; Manzanar was one of them. They had to spend the war years there, all except those men who volunteered for the army. The battalion formed by these nisei, fighting in Italy, became the most decorated U.S. Army unit in the war.

The internment of Americans of Japanese descent increasingly became a subject of controversy and criticism in the decades following the war. In 1987 the U.S. Congress finally passed an act that made some restitution to the former internees; it acknowledged that what was done to them had been wrong and included a payment of $20,000 to each of the survivors of the camps, that is, to those who were still alive after more than forty years.

Jeanne Wakatsuki, born in California in 1935, was seven years old when she, together with her family, was sent to the internment camp at Manzanar. She remained there until age eleven. After high school she studied sociology and journalism at San Jose State College, where she met her husband, James D. Houston, a novelist. Together they wrote *Farewell to Manzanar*, published in 1973, as a record of life in the camp and of its impact on her and her family. The following is a selection from it.

In December of 1941 Papa's disappearance didn't bother me nearly so 1
much as the world I soon found myself in.

He had been a jack-of-all-trades. When I was born he was farming   2
near Inglewood. Later, when he started fishing, we moved to Ocean
Park, near Santa Monica, and until they picked him up, that's where we
lived, in a big frame house with a brick fireplace, a block back from
the beach. We were the only Japanese family in the neighborhood.
Papa liked it that way. He didn't want to be labeled or grouped by
anyone. But with him gone and no way of knowing what to expect, my
mother moved all of us down to Terminal Island. Woody already lived
there, and one of my older sisters had married a Terminal Island boy.
Mama's first concern now was to keep the family together; and once
the war began, she felt safer there than isolated racially in Ocean Park.
But for me, at age seven, the island was a country as foreign as India or
Arabia would have been. It was the first time I had lived among other
Japanese, or gone to school with them, and I was terrified all the time.

This was partly Papa's fault. One of his threats to keep us younger   3
kids in line was "I'm going to sell you to the Chinaman." When I had
entered kindergarten two years earlier, I was the only Oriental in the
class. They sat me next to a Caucasian girl who happened to have very
slanted eyes. I looked at her and began to scream, certain Papa had sold
me out at last. My fear of her ran so deep I could not speak of it, even to
Mama, couldn't explain why I was screaming. For two weeks I had
nightmares about this girl, until the teachers finally moved me to the
other side of the room. And it was still with me, this fear of Oriental
faces, when we moved to Terminal Island.

In those days it was a company town, a ghetto owned and con-   4
trolled by the canneries. The men went after fish, and whenever the
boats came back — day or night — the women would be called to
process the catch while it was fresh. One in the afternoon or four in
the morning, it made no difference. My mother had to go to work right
after we moved there. I can still hear the whistle — two toots for
French's, three for Van Camp's — and she and Chizu would be out of
bed in the middle of the night, heading for the cannery.

The house we lived in was nothing more than a shack, a barracks   5
with single plank walls and rough wooden floors, like the cheapest
kind of migrant workers' housing. The people around us were hard-
working, boisterous, a little proud of their nickname, *yo-go-re*, which
meant literally *uncouth one*, or roughneck, or dead-end kid. They not
only spoke Japanese exclusively, they spoke a dialect peculiar to
Kyushu, where their families had come from in Japan, a rough, fisher-
man's language, full of oaths and insults. Instead of saying *ba-ka-ta-re*,
a common insult meaning *stupid*, Terminal Islanders would say
ba-ka-ya-ro, a coarser and exclusively masculine use of the word,
which implies gross stupidity. They would swagger and pick on out-
siders and persecute anyone who didn't speak as they did. That was

what made my own time there so hateful. I had never spoken anything but English, and the other kids in the second grade despised me for it. They were tough and mean, like ghetto kids anywhere. Each day after school I dreaded their ambush. My brother Kiyo, three years older, would wait for me at the door, where we would decide whether to run straight home together, or split up, or try a new and unexpected route.

None of these kids every actually attacked. It was the threat that frightened us, their fearful looks, and the noises they would make, like miniature Samurai, in a language we couldn't understand.   6

At the time it seemed we had been living under this reign of fear for years. In fact, we lived there about two months. Late in February the navy decided to clear Terminal Island completely. Even though most of us were American-born, it was dangerous having that many Orientals so close to the Long Beach Naval Station, on the opposite end of the island. We had known something like this was coming. But, like Papa's arrest, not much could be done ahead of time. There were four of us kids still young enough to be living with Mama, plus Granny, her mother, sixty-five then, speaking no English, and nearly blind. Mama didn't know where else she could get work, and we had nowhere else to move *to*. On February 25 the choice was made for us. We were given forty-eight hours to clear out.   7

The secondhand dealers had been prowling around for weeks, like wolves, offering humiliating prices for goods and furniture they knew many of us would have to sell sooner or later. Mama had left all but her most valuable possessions in Ocean Park, simply because she had nowhere to put them. She had brought along her pottery, her silver, heirlooms like the kimonos Granny had brought from Japan, tea sets, lacquered tables, and one fine old set of china, blue and white porcelain, almost translucent. On the day we were leaving, Woody's car was so crammed with boxes and luggage and kids we had just run out of room. Mama had to sell this china.   8

One of the dealers offered her fifteen dollars for it. She said it was a full setting for twelve and worth at least two hundred. He said fifteen was his top price. Mama started to quiver. Her eyes blazed up at him. She had been packing all night and trying to calm down Granny, who didn't understand why we were moving again and what all the rush was about. Mama's nerves were shot, and now navy jeeps were patrolling the streets. She didn't say another word. She just glared at this man, all the rage and frustration channeled at him through her eyes.   9

He watched her for a moment and said he was sure he couldn't pay more than seventeen fifty for that china. She reached into the red velvet case, took out a dinner plate and hurled it at the floor right in front of his feet.   10

The man leaped back shouting, "Hey! Hey, don't do that! Those   11
are valuable dishes!"

Mama took out another dinner plate and hurled it at the floor,   12
then another and another, never moving, never opening her mouth,
just quivering and glaring at the retreating dealer, with tears streaming
down her cheeks. He finally turned and scuttled out the door, heading
for the next house. When he was gone she stood there smashing cups
and bowls and platters until the whole set lay in scattered blue and
white fragments across the wooden floor.

The name Manzanar meant nothing to us when we left Boyle   13
heights. We didn't know where it was or what it was. We went because
the government ordered us to. And, in the case of my older brothers
and sisters, we went with a certain amount of relief. They had all heard
stories of Japanese homes being attacked, of beatings in the streets of
California towns. They were as frightened of the Caucasians as Caucasians were of us. Moving, under what appeared to be government
protection, to an area less directly threatened by the war seemed not
such a bad idea at all. For some it actually sounded like a fine
adventure.

Our pickup point was a Buddhist church in Los Angeles. It was   14
very early, and misty, when we got there with our luggage. Mama had
bought heavy coats for all of us. She grew up in eastern Washington
and knew that anywhere inland in early April would be cold. I was
proud of my new coat, and I remember sitting on a duffel bag trying to
be friendly with the Greyhound driver. I smiled at him. He didn't
smile back. He was befriending no one. Someone tied a numbered tag
to my collar and to the duffel bag (each family was given a number,
and that became our official designation until the camps were closed),
someone else passed out box lunches for the trip, and we climbed
aboard.

I had never been outside Los Angeles County, never traveled   15
more than ten miles from the coast, had never even ridden on a bus. I
was full of excitement, the way any kid would be, and wanted to look
out the window. But for the first few hours the shades were drawn.
Around me other people played cards, read magazines, dozed, waiting.
I settled back, waiting too, and finally fell asleep. The bus felt very
secure to me. Almost half its passengers were immediate relatives.
Mama and my older brothers had succeeded in keeping most of us
together, on the same bus, headed for the same camp. I didn't realize
until much later what a job that was. The strategy had been, first, to
have everyone living in the same district when the evacuation began,
and then to get all of us included under the same family number, even
though names had been changed by marriage. Many families weren't as

lucky as ours and suffered months of anguish while trying to arrange transfers from one camp to another.

We rode all day. By the time we reached our destination, the shades were up. It was late afternoon. The first thing I saw was a yellow swirl across a blurred, reddish setting sun. The bus was being pelted by what sounded like splattering rain. It wasn't rain. This was my first look at something I would soon know very well, a billowing flurry of dust and sand churned up by the wind through Owens Valley.

We drove past a barbed-wire fence, through a gate, and into an   17
open space where trunks and sacks and packages had been dumped from the baggage trucks that drove out ahead of us. I could see a few tents set up, the first rows of black barracks, and beyond them, blurred by sand, rows of barracks that seemed to spread for miles across this plain. People were sitting on cartons or milling around, with their backs to the wind, waiting to see which friends or relatives might be on this bus. As we approached, they turned or stood up, and some moved toward us expectantly. But inside the bus no one stirred. No one waved or spoke. They just stared out the windows, ominously silent. I didn't understand this. Hadn't we finally arrived, our whole family intact? I opened a window, leaned out, and yelled happily "Hey! This whole bus is full of Wakatsukis!"

Outside, the greeters smiled. Inside there was an explosion of   18
laughter, hysterical, tension-breaking laughter that left my brothers choking and whacking each other across the shoulders.

We had pulled up just in time for dinner. The mess halls weren't   19
completed yet. An outdoor chow line snaked around a half-finished building that broke a good part of the wind. They issued us army mess kits, the round metal kind that fold over, and plopped in scoops of canned Vienna sausage, canned string beans, steamed rice that had been cooked too long, and on top of the rice a serving of canned apricots. The Caucasian servers were thinking the fruit poured over rice would make a good dessert. Among the Japanese, of course, rice is never eaten with sweet foods, only with salty or savory foods. Few of us could eat such a mixture. But at this point no one dared protest. It would have been impolite. I was horrified when I saw the apricot syrup seeping through my little mound of rice. I opened my mouth to complain. My mother jabbed me in the back to keep quiet. We moved on through the line and joined the others squatting in the lee of half-raised walls, dabbing courteously at what was, for almost everyone there, an inedible concoction.

After dinner we were taken to Block 16, a cluster of fifteen   20
barracks that had just been finished a day or so earlier—although finished was hardly the word for it. The shacks were built of one

thickness of pine planking covered with tarpaper. They sat on concrete footings, with about two feet of open space between the floorboards and the ground. Gaps showed between the planks, and as the weeks passed and the green wood dried out, the gaps widened. Knotholes gaped in the uncovered floor.

Each barracks was divided into six units, sixteen by twenty feet, 21 about the size of a living room, with one bare bulb hanging from the ceiling and an oil stove for heat. We were assigned two of these for the twelve people in our family group; and our official family "number" was enlarged by three digits — 16 plus the number of this barracks. We were issued steel army cots, two brown army blankets each, and some mattress covers, which my brothers stuffed with straw.

The first task was to divide up what space we had for sleeping. 22 Bill and Woody contributed a blanket each and partitioned off the first room: one side for Bill and Tomi, one side for Woody and Chizu and their baby girl. Woody also got the stove, for heating formulas.

The people who had it hardest during the first few months were 23 young couples like these, many of whom had married just before the evacuation began, in order not to be separated and sent to different camps. Our two rooms were crowded, but at least it was all in the family. My oldest sister and her husband were shoved into one of those sixteen-by-twenty-foot compartments with six people they had never seen before — two other couples, one recently married like themselves, the other with two teenage boys. Partitioning off a room like that wasn't easy. It was bitter cold when we arrived, and the wind did not abate. All they had to use for room dividers were those army blankets, two of which were barely enough to keep one person warm. They argued over whose blanket should be sacrificed and later argued about noise at night — the parents wanted their boys asleep by 9:00 P.M. — and they continued arguing over matters like that for six months, until my sister and her husband left to harvest sugar beets in Idaho. It was grueling work up there, and wages were pitiful, but when the call came through camp for workers to alleviate the wartime labor shortage, it sounded better than their life at Manzanar. They knew they'd have, if nothing else, a room, perhaps a cabin of their own.

That first night in Block 16, the rest of us squeezed into the 24 second room — Granny, Lillian, age fourteen, Ray, thirteen, May, eleven, Kiyo, ten, Mama, and me. I didn't mind this at all at the time. Being youngest meant I got to sleep with Mama. And before we went to bed I had a great time jumping up and down on the mattress. The boys had stuffed so much straw into hers, we had to flatten it some so we wouldn't slide off. I slept with her every night after that until Papa came back.

EXERCISES

Words to Know

Caucasian (paragraph 3), Samurai (6), ominously (17), abate (23).

Some of the Issues

1. What do the first three paragraphs tell us about Houston's family?
2. Paragraphs 3 through 7 explain her fears. What are they? What would you imagine would be the mother's fears in this period?
3. What does the story about the secondhand dealer (paragraphs 8 through 12) tell us about the situation of Japanese-Americans at that time? What does it tell us about Houston's mother?
4. Examine the actions of the camp officials. To what extent can the authorities be said to be deliberately cruel? unthoughtful? or uninformed about cultural differences? Cite specific details to support your view.
* 5. Read Maxine Hong Kingston's "Girlhood Among Ghosts." Both Kingston and Houston grew up in California at about the same time. In what way are the two experiences similar? How do they differ?

The Way We Are Told

6. In paragraphs 20 through 24 Houston gives a detailed description of the barracks. Does her description contain any words or phrases that express emotions? Justify their presence or absence.

Some Subjects for Essays

7. Jeanne Houston describes the bus ride to Manzanar from a child's point of view, as an adventure, almost fun, and not as a tragedy. Recall an incident of your childhood that would look different to you now (a fire, getting lost in a strange neighborhood). Describe it from a child's point of view and end with a paragraph explaining how you view the same incident as an adult.
8. Jeanne Wakatsuki Houston recalls her childhood just before internment and during its initial phase. Examine her attitude toward her experiences; how does it reflect her bicultural background?

THE VILLAGE OF
BEN SUC

Jonathan Schell

Jonathan Schell, a journalist and frequent contributor to *The New Yorker*, is the author of *The Time of Illusion* (1976), *The Fate of the Earth* (1982), an analysis of the possible effects of atomic warfare, *The Abolition* (1984), and *The Village of Ben Suc* (1967), from which the following selection is taken.

Schell here records one of his experiences as a journalist during the Vietnam War. He went along with a squadron of helicopters ferrying some platoons of American infantry on a raid on the village of Ben Suc. He gives the reader a carefully detailed description of the raid; it seems to be a routine operation, one of many like it, but Schell's account of it raises some fundamental questions about the war, and even about war in general.

Indochina, consisting of Vietnam, Cambodia, and Laos, was part of the French colonial empire until World War II. After the defeat of France by Germany in 1940, the Japanese occupied the colony until their own defeat and surrender in 1945. At that time France tried to re-establish its colonial authority, but met with stiff Vietnamese resistance by communist forces under the leadership of Ho Chi Minh. In 1954 the French finally gave up their attempt and Vietnam was partitioned. The northern half went to Ho Chi Minh's forces. The United States, which had supported the French with arms and supplies, now became increasingly involved in trying to sustain the southern, noncommunist half, until, by the late 1960s, about half a million U.S. military personnel were involved in that effort. In the 1970s the United States gradually withdrew its armed forces, having concluded an agreement with the northern government. In 1972 the southern government collapsed and the country was reunited under communist rule.

The men got up at five-thirty in the morning and were guided in the 1 dark to a mess tent in a different part of the rubber grove, where they had a breakfast of grapefruit juice, hot cereal, scrambled eggs, bacon, toast, and coffee. At about six-thirty, the sky began to grow light, and they were led back to the airstrip. Strings of nine and ten helicopters with tapered bodies could be seen through the treetops, filing across the gray early-morning sky like little schools of minnows. In the distance, the slow beat of their engines sounded soft and almost peaceful, but when they rushed past overhead the noise was fearful and deafening. By seven o'clock, sixty helicopters were perched in formation on the airstrip, with seven men assembled in a silent group beside each one. When I arrived at the helicopter assigned to me — No. 47 — three engineers and three infantrymen were already there, five of them standing or kneeling in the dust checking their weapons. One of them, a sergeant, was a small, wiry American Indian, who spoke in short, clipped syllables. The sixth man, a stocky infantryman with blond hair and a red face, who looked to be about twenty and was going into action for the first time, lay back against an earth embankment with his eyes closed, wearing an expression of boredom, as though he wanted to put these wasted minutes of waiting to some good use by catching up on his sleep. Two of the other six men in the team were also going into combat for the first time. The men did not speak to each other.

At seven-fifteen, our group of seven climbed up into its helicopter, a UH-1 (called Huey), and the pilot, a man with a German accent, told us that four of us should sit on the seat and three on the floor in front, to balance the craft. He also warned us that the flight might be rough, since we would be flying in the turbulent wake of the helicopter in front of us. At seven-twenty, the engines of the sixty helicopters started simultaneously, with a thunderous roar and a storm of dust. After idling his engine for three minutes on the airstrip, our pilot raised his right hand in the air, forming a circle with the forefinger and thumb, to show that he hoped everything would proceed perfectly from then on. The helicopter rose slowly from the airstrip right after the helicopter in front of it had risen. The pilot's gesture was the only indication that the seven men were on their way to something more than a nine-o'clock job. Rising, one after another, in two parallel lines of thirty, the fleet of sixty helicopters circled the base twice, gaining altitude and tightening their formation as they did so, until each machine was not more than twenty yards from the one immediately in front of it. Then the fleet, straightening out the two lines, headed south, toward Ben Suc.

In Helicopter No. 47, one of the men shouted a joke, which only one other man could hear, and they both laughed. The soldier who had earlier been trying to catch a nap on the runway wanted to get a picture of the sixty helicopters with a Minolta camera he had hanging from a strap around his neck. He was sitting on the floor, facing backward, so he asked one of the men on the seat to try to get a couple of shots. "There are sixty choppers here," he shouted, "and every one of them costs a quarter of a million bucks!" The Huey flies with its doors open, so the men who sat on the outside seats were perched right next to the drop. They held tightly to ceiling straps as the helicopter rolled and pitched through the sky like a ship plunging through a heavy sea. Wind from the rotors and from the forward motion blasted into the men's faces, making them squint. At five minutes to eight, the two lines of the fleet suddenly dived, bobbing and swaying from the cruising altitude of twenty-five hundred feet down to treetop level, at a point about seven miles from Ben Suc but heading away from it, to confuse enemy observers on the ground. Once at an altitude of fifty or sixty feet, the fleet made a wide U turn and headed directly for Ben Suc at a hundred miles an hour, the helicopters' rails raised slightly in forward flight. Below, the faces of scattered peasants were clearly visible as they looked up from their water buffalo at the sudden, earsplitting incursion of sixty helicopters charging low over their fields.

All at once, helicopter No. 47 landed, and from both sides of it   4
the men jumped out on the run into a freshly turned vegetable plot in the village of Ben Suc — the first Vietnamese village that several of them had ever set foot in. The helicopter took off immediately, and another settled in its place. Keeping low, the men I was with ran single file out into the center of the little plot, and then, spotting a low wall of bushes on the side of the plot they had just left, ran back there for cover and filed along the edges of the bushes toward several soldiers who had landed a little while before them. For a minute, there was silence. Suddenly a single helicopter came clattering overhead at about a hundred and fifty feet, squawking Vietnamese from two stubby speakers that stuck out, winglike, from the thinnest part of the fuse-lage, near the tail. The message, which the American soldiers could not understand, went, "Attention, people of Ben Suc! You are surrounded by Republic of South Vietnam and Allied Forces. Do not run away or you will be shot as V.C. Stay in your homes and wait for further instructions." The metallic voice, floating down over the fields, huts, and trees, was as calm as if it were announcing a flight departure at an air terminal. It was gone in ten seconds, and the soldiers again moved on in silence. Within two minutes, the young men from No. 47 reached a little dirt road marking the village perimeter, which they were to hold, but there were no people in sight except American soldiers. The young men lay down on the sides of embankments and in little hollows in the small area it had fallen to them to control. There was no sign of an enemy.

For the next hour and a half, the six men from No. 47 were to be   5
the masters of a small stretch of vegetable fields which was divided down the center by about fifty yards of narrow dirt road — almost a path — and bounded on the front and two sides (as they faced the road and, beyond it, the center of the village) by several small houses behind copses of low palm trees and hedges and in back by a small graveyard giving onto a larger cultivated field. The vegetable fields,

most of them not more than fifty feet square and of irregular shape, were separated by neatly constructed grass covered ridges, each with a path running along its top. The houses were small and trim, most of them with one side open to the weather but protected from the rain by the deep eaves of a thatch-grass roof. The houses were usually set apart by hedges and low trees, so that one house was only half visible from another and difficult to see from the road; they were not unlike a wealthy American suburb in the logic of their layout. An orderly small yard, containing low-walled coops for chickens and a shed with stalls for cows, adjoined to each house. Here and there, between the fields and in the copses, stood the whitewashed waist-high columns and brick walls of Vietnamese tombs, which look like small models of the ruins of once-splendid palaces. It was a tidy, delicately wrought small-scale landscape with short views — not overcrowded but with every square foot of land carefully attended to.

Four minutes after the landing, the heavy crackle of several auto- 6
matic weapons firing issued from a point out of sight, perhaps five hundred yards away. The men, who had been sitting or kneeling, went down on their bellies, their eyes trained on the confusion of hedges, trees, and houses ahead. A report that Mike Company had made light contact came over their field radio. At about eight-ten, the shock of tremendous explosions shattered the air and rocked the ground. The men hit the dirt again. Artillery shells crashed somewhere in the woods, and rockets from helicopters thumped into the ground. When a jet came screaming low overhead, one of the men shouted, ''They're bringing in air strikes!'' Heavy percussions shook the ground under the men, who were now lying flat, and shock waves beat against their faces. Helicopter patrols began to wheel low over the treetops outside the perimeter defended by the infantry, spraying the landscape with long bursts of machine-gun fire. After about five minutes, the explosions became less frequent, and the men from the helicopters, realizing that this was the planned bombing and shelling of the northern woods, picked themselves up, and two of them, joined by three soldiers from another helicopter, set about exploring their area.

Three or four soldiers began to search the houses behind a nearby 7
copse. Stepping through the doorway of one house with his rifle in firing position at his hip, a solidly built six-foot-two Negro private came upon a young woman standing with a baby in one arm and a little girl of three or four holding her other hand. The woman was barefoot and was dressed in a white shirt and rolled-up black trousers; a bandana held her long hair in a coil at the back of her head. She and her children intently watched each of the soldier's movements. In English, he asked, ''Where's your husband?'' Without taking her eyes off the

soldier, the woman said something in Vietnamese, in an explanatory tone. The soldier looked around the inside of the one-room house and, pointing to his rifle, asked, "You have same-same?" The woman shrugged and said something else in Vietnamese. The soldier shook his head and poked his hand into a basket of laundry on the table between him and the woman. She immediately took all the laundry out of the basket and shrugged again, with a hint of impatience, as though to say, "It's just laundry!" The soldier nodded and looked around, appearing unsure of what to do next in this situation. Then, on a peg on one wall, he spotted a pair of men's pants and a shirt hanging up to dry. "Where's *he?*" he asked, pointing to the clothes. The woman spoke in Vietnamese. The soldier took the damp clothing down and, for some reason, carried it outside, where he laid it on the ground.

The house was clean, light, and airy, with doors on two sides and   8
the top half of one whole side opening out onto a grassy yard. On the table, a half-eaten bowl of rice stood next to the laundry basket. A tiny hammock, not more than three feet long, hung in one corner. At one side of the house, a small, separate wooden roof stood over a fireplace with cooking utensils hanging around it. On the window ledge was a row of barley sprouting plants, in little clods of earth wrapped in palm leaves. Inside the room, a kilnlike structure, its walls and top made of mud, logs, and large stones, stood over the family's bedding. At the rear of the house, a square opening in the ground led to an underground bomb shelter large enough for several people to stand in. In the yard, a cow stood inside a third bomb shelter, made of tile walls about a foot thick.

After a minute, the private came back in with a bared machete at   9
his side and a field radio on his back. "Where's your husband, huh?" he asked again. This time, the woman gave a long answer in a complaining tone, in which she pointed several times at the sky and several times at her children. The soldier looked at her blankly. "What do I do with her?" he called to some fellow-soldiers outside. There was no answer. Turning back to the young woman, who had not moved since his first entrance, he said, "O.K., lady, you stay here," and left the house.

Several other houses were searched, but no other Vietnamese   10
were found, and for twenty minutes the men on that particular stretch of road encountered no one else, although they heard sporadic machine-gun fire down the road. The sky, which had been overcast, began to show streaks of blue, and a light wind stirred the trees. The bombing, the machine-gunning from helicopters, the shelling, and the rocket firing continued steadily. Suddenly a Vietnamese man on a bicycle appeared, pedalling rapidly along the road from the direction

of the village. He was wearing the collarless, pajamalike black garment that is both the customary dress of the Vietnamese peasant and the uniform of the National Liberation Front, and although he was riding away from the center of the village — a move forbidden by the voices from the helicopters — he had, it appeared, already run a long gantlet of American soldiers without being stopped. But when he had ridden about twenty yards past the point where he first came in sight, there was a burst of machine-gun fire from a copse thirty yards in front of him, joined immediately by a burst from a vegetable field to one side, and he was hurled off his bicycle into a ditch a yard from the road. The bicycle crashed into a side embankment. The man with the Minolta camera, who had done the firing from the vegetable patch, stood up after about a minute and walked over to the ditch, followed by one of the engineers. The Vietnamese in the ditch appeared to be about twenty, and he lay on his side without moving, blood flowing from his face, which, with the eyes open, was half buried in the dirt at the bottom of the ditch. The engineer leaned down, felt the man's wrist, and said, "He's dead." The two men — both companions of mine on No. 47 — stood still for a while, with folded arms, and stared down at the dead man's face, as though they were giving him a chance to say something. Then the engineer said, with a tone of finality, "That's a V.C. for you. He's a V.C., all right. That's what they wear. He was leaving town. He had to have some reason."

The two men walked back to a ridge in the vegetable field and sat   11
down on it, looking off into the distance in a puzzled way and no longer bothering to keep low. The man who had fired spoke suddenly, as though coming out of deep thought. "I saw this guy coming down the road on a bicycle," he said. "And I thought, you know, Is this it? Do I shoot? Then some guy over there in the bushes opened up, so I cut loose."

The engineer raised his eyes in the manner of someone who has   12
made a strange discovery and said, "I'm not worried. You know, that's the first time I've ever seen a dead guy, and I don't feel bad. I just don't, that's all." Then, with a hard edge of defiance in his voice, he added, "Actually, I'm glad. I'm glad we killed the little V.C."

Over near the copse, the man who had fired first, also a young   13
soldier, had turned his back to the road. Clenching a cigar in his teeth, he stared with determination over his gun barrel across the wide field, where several water buffaloes were grazing but no human beings had yet been seen. Upon being asked what had happened, he said, "Yeah, he's dead. Ah shot him. He was a fuckin' V.C."

EXERCISES

Words to Know

tapered (paragraph 1), turbulent (2), wake (2), choppers (3), perched (3), pitched (3), incursion (3), V.C. — Vietcong, communist guerrilla soldier (4), copses (5), perimeter (6), explanatory tone (7), machete (9), sporadic (10), National Liberation Front (10), gantlet (10).

Some of the Issues

1. We learn very little about the soldiers who fly Huey No. 47. How would the story change if we knew more about them as individuals?
2. Numbers play a considerable role in the first two paragraphs. Why?
3. Paragraph 8 seems to interrupt the episode that is taking place in 7 and 9. What is its contribution to that episode?
4. What is the evidence that leads the soldiers to decide that the bicyclist was a V.C.?
· * 5. Read George Orwell's "Shooting an Elephant." In it the narrator is under the same kind of pressure to take action as the soldier with the Minolta. Do you see any differences in their situations?

The Way We Are Told

6. Consider the details Schell singles out in the first three paragraphs: the anonymity of the soldiers as contrasted to the references to specific numbers, times, or to the Minolta camera. Why does Schell not record the names of any of the soldiers?
7. Why does Schell single out the fact that No. 47 lands in "a freshly turned vegetable plot" (paragraph 4) and describe the six men as "masters of a small stretch of vegetable fields" (paragraph 5)?
8. In paragraph 5 Schell describes the village. How does he place his emphasis through his selection of details, and what effect does the description achieve? Contrast it particularly with what we are told in paragraph 6.
9. In paragraphs 7 through 9 (the encounter between the soldiers and the woman), what would you say are the dangers in the kind of communication that is taking place? How does this episode prepare for the events in paragraphs 10 through 12?
10. Does the way in which Schell describes the whole raid change in paragraphs 10 through 12? If so, in what way?

11. Is Schell giving an objective, factual rendering of the events he witnessed, or not? Support your conclusion.

Some Subjects for Essays

12. Write an essay in which you examine in detail Schell's view of what war is like. Use the details of the selection as evidence.
13. Write an account of a specific event, using sensory detail of different kinds to make the reader "feel" the event as much as possible. Like Schell in this selection, avoid direct judgment and do not include yourself in the story.

FOR THE INDIANS, NO THANKSGIVING

Michael Dorris

Michael Dorris, born in 1945, is a professor of anthropology at Dartmouth College. He is the author of several books, including *Native Americans 500 Years After* (1975) and the novel *A Yellow Raft in Blue Water* (1987). In 1989 Dorris published *The Broken Cord*, the story of Adam, a Sioux Indian boy born of an alcoholic mother whom Dorris and his wife, the novelist Louise Erdrich, adopted and tried to cure of secondary alcoholic syndrome.

The selection included here appeared in the *Chicago Tribune* at Thanksgiving, 1988. With bitter humor Dorris, a member of the Modoc tribe, explains why Indians have no reason to give thanks on that Thursday in November. He describes how mainstream Americans have shaped the image of the Native American to suit their purpose. You may want to read Vine Deloria's "Custer Died for Your Sins," which discusses a related topic.

King Philip's War, referred to in paragraph 2, was fought between the settlers in Massachusetts and the Wampanoags led by their chief Metacomet, who had taken the name Philip at a time when he befriended the colonists, and before he came to see them as enemies who would destroy his people. The Indians were defeated by the New England Confederation and Philip was killed.

Maybe those Pilgrims and Wampanoags actually got together for a November picnic, maybe not. It matters only as a facile, ironical footnote. 1

For the former group, it would have been a celebration of a precarious hurdle successfully crossed on the path to the political domination first of a continent and eventually of a planet. For the latter, it would have been, at best, a naïve extravaganza — the last meeting as equals with invaders who, within a few years, would win King Philip's War and decorate the city limits of their towns with rows of stakes, each topped with an Indian head. 2

The few aboriginal survivors of the ensuing violence were either sold into Caribbean slavery by their better armed, erstwhile hosts, or were ruthlessly driven from their Cape Cod homes. Despite the symbolic idealism of the first potluck, New England — from the emerging 3

199

European point of view — simply wasn't big enough for two sets of societies.

An enduring benefit of success, when one culture clashes with 4 another, is that the victorious group controls the record. It owns not only the immediate spoils but also the power to edit, embellish and concoct the facts of the original encounter for the generations to come. Events, once past, reside at the small end of the telescope, the vague and hazy antecedents to accepted reality.

Our collective modern fantasy of Thanksgiving is a case in point. 5 It has evolved into a ritual pageant in which almost everyone of us, as children, either acted or were forced to watch a 17th century vision that we can conjure whole in the blink of an eye.

The cast of stock characters is as recognizable as those in any 6 Macy's parade: long-faced Pilgrim men, pre-N.R.A. muskets at their sides, sitting around a rude outdoor table while their wives, dressed in long dresses, aprons and linen caps, bustle about lifting the lids off steaming kettles — pater and materfamilias of New World hospitality.

They dish out the turkey to a scattering of shirtless Indian invi- 7 tees. But there is no ambiguity as to who is in charge of the occasion, who could be asked to leave, whose protocol prevails.

Only good Indians are admitted into this tableau, of course: those 8 who accept the manifest destiny of a European presence and are prepared to adopt English dining customs and, by inference, English everything else.

These compliant Hollywood extras are, naturally enough, among 9 the blessings the Pilgrims are thankful for — and why not? They're colorful, bring the food and vanish after dessert. They are something exotic to write home about, like a visit to Frontierland. In the sound bite of national folklore, they have metamorphosed into icons, totems of America as evocative, and ultimately as vapid, as a flag factory.

And these particular Indians did not all repair to the happy 10 hunting grounds during the first Christmas rush. They lived on, smoking peace pipes and popping up at appropriate crowd-pleasing moments.

They lost mock battles from coast to coast in Wild West shows. In 11 19th century art, they sat bareback on their horses and watched a lot of sunsets. Whole professional teams of them take the home field every Sunday afternoon in Cleveland or Washington.

They are the sources of merit badges for Boy Scouts and the 12 emblem of purity for imitation butter. They are, and have been from the beginning, predictable, manageable, domesticated cartoons, inventions without depth or reality apart from that bestowed by their creators.

These appreciative Indians, as opposed to the pesky flesh and 13 blood native peoples on whom they are loosely modeled, did not question the enforced exchange of their territories for a piece of pie. They did not protest when they died by the millions of European diseases.

They did not resist — except for the "bad" ones, the renegades 14 —when solemn pacts made with them were broken or when their religions and customs were declared illegal. They did not make a fuss in courts in defense of their sovereignty. They never expected all the fixings anyway.

As for Thanksgiving 1988, the descendants of those first party- 15 goers sit at increasingly distant tables, the pretense of equity all but abandoned. Against great odds, native Americans have maintained political identity — hundreds of tribes have Federal recognition as "domestic, dependent nations."

But, in a country so insecure about heterogeneity that it votes its 16 dominant language as "official," this refusal to melt into the pot has been an expensive choice.

A majority of reservation Indians reside in among the most impov- 17 erished counties in the nation. They constitute the ethnic group at the wrong peak of every scale: most undernourished, most short-lived, least educated, least healthy.

For them, that long ago Thanksgiving was not a milestone, not a 18 promise. It was the last full meal.

EXERCISES

Words to Know

Pilgrims (paragraph 1), Wampanoags (1), facile (1), ironical (1), precarious (2), naïve (2), extravaganza (2), aboriginal (3), ensuing (3), erstwhile (3), symbolic (3), idealism (3), potluck (3), emerging (3), enduring (4), spoils (4), edit (4), embellish (4), concoct (4), vague (4), antecedents (4), fantasy (5), ritual pageant (5), vision (5), conjure (5), stock characters (6), pre-N.R.A. muskets (6), rude (6), pater and materfamilias (6), scattering (7), ambiguity (7), protocol (7), prevails (7), tableau (8), manifest destiny (8), inference (8), compliant (9), Hollywood extras (9), exotic (9), sound bite (9), metamorphosed (9), icons (9), totems (9), evocative (9), vapid (9), happy hunting grounds (10), mock (11), emblem of purity (12), domesticated (12), bestowed (12), appreciative (13), pesky (13), loosely modeled (13), renegade (14), solemn pacts (14), sovereignty (14), equity (15), heterogeneity (16), undernourished (17), milestone (18).

Some of the Issues

1. What is the "November picnic"? If it did indeed take place, what does it signify for each group of participants?
2. What does Dorris mean by saying that the victor controls the record (paragraph 4)? How do the following paragraphs expand on that statement?
3. What, according to Dorris, is the definition of "good" Indians (paragraph 8)? What roles do they play? Who assigns them those roles?
4. In paragraphs 11–13 Dorris refers to various ways that the Indians' image has been used. What is his purpose?
5. What does Dorris mean in paragraph 15 when he says that the descendants of those first party-goers sit at increasingly distant tables?
* 6. Both Dorris and Vine Deloria, Jr. in "Custer Died for Your Sins" compare the myth and the reality of the Indian. Do they differ in any significant ways? How?

The Way We Are Told

7. What kind of tone does the first paragraph set for the essay?
8. Dorris calls Thanksgiving "our collective modern fantasy" (paragraph 5). What terms does he use in the following paragraphs that amplify that idea of fantasy?
9. Consider the tone of the essay. Would you call it funny? Bitter? Angry? How does Dorris's language create that tone? Cite examples.

Some Subjects for Essays

10. In recent years Native American groups have raised objections to the use of Indian names for sports teams (Cleveland Indians, Milwaukee Braves) and the use of Indian symbols such as the tomahawk in advertising. Find examples and discuss whether the objections are justified.

A WASP STINGS BACK

Robert Claiborne

Born in England, Robert Claiborne has spent much of his adult life in the United States. His professional activities have largely been concerned with making science understandable to general audiences, as associate editor of the *Scientific American*, editor of the Life Science Library, and the author of a number of books, including *Climate, Man and History* (1970), *The First Americans* (1973), *God or Beast: Evolution and Human Nature* (1974), and *Astronomy for Absolute Beginners* (1975). He has also written many articles for *Harper's*, the *Nation*, the *New York Times*, and other publications.

The selection which follows was published in the "My Turn" section of *Newsweek* in 1974. It is a spirited defense of WASPs, White Anglo-Saxon Protestants, who, Claiborne asserts, are every other American ethnic group's favorite whipping boy. He makes his case by means of a counterattack based on historical evidence. WASPs, he says, are responsible for developing the civil protections of representative democracy which give those critics the chance to launch their attacks with impunity.

Over the past few years, American pop culture has acquired a new folk antihero: the Wasp. One slick magazine tells us that the White Anglo-Saxon Protestants rule New York City, while other media gurus credit (or discredit) them with ruling the country—and, by inference, ruining it. A Polish-American declares in a leading newspaper that Wasps have "no sense of honor." *Newsweek* patronizingly describes Chautauqua as a cital of "Wasp values," while other folklorists characterize these values more explicitly as a compulsive commitment to the work ethic, emotional uptightness and sexual inhibition. The Wasps, in fact, are rapidly becoming the one minority that every other ethnic group —blacks, Italians, chicanos, Jews, Poles and all the rest—feels absolutely free to dump on. I have not yet had a friend greet me with "Did you hear the one about the two Wasps who . . . ?"—but any day now!

I come of a long line of Wasps; if you disregard my French great-great-grandmother and a couple of putatively Irish ancestors of the same vintage, a rather pure line. My mother has long been one of

203

the Colonial Dames, an organization some of whose members consider the Daughters of the American Revolution rather parvenu. My
umpty-umpth Wasp great-grandfather, William Claiborne, founded the
first European settlement in what is now Maryland (his farm and
trading post were later ripped off by the Catholic Lord Baltimore,
Maryland politics being much the same then as now).

As a Wasp, the mildest thing I can say about the stereotype   3
emerging from the current wave of anti-Wasp chic is that I don't
recognize myself. As regards emotional uptightness and sexual inhibition, modesty forbids comment — though I dare say various friends
and lovers of mine could testify on these points if they cared to. I will
admit to enjoying work — because I am lucky enough to be able to
work at what I enjoy — but not, I think, to the point of compulsive-
ness. And so far as ruling America, or even New York, is concerned, I
can say flatly that (a) it's a damn lie because (b) if I *did* rule them,
both would be in better shape than they are. Indeed I and all my Wasp
relatives, taken in a lump, have far less clout with the powers that run
this country than any one of the Buckleys or Kennedys (Irish Catholic),
the Sulzbergers or Guggenheims (Jewish), or the late A. P. Giannini
(Italian) of the Bank of America.

Admittedly, both corporate and (to a lesser extent) political   4
America are dominated by Wasps — just as (let us say) the garment
industry is dominated by Jews, and organized crime by Italians. But to
conclude from this that The Wasps are the American elite is as silly as
to say that The Jews are cloak-and-suiters or The Italians are gangsters.
Wasps, like other ethnics, come in all varieties, including criminals —
political, corporate and otherwise.

More seriously, I would like to say a word for the maligned   5
"Wasp values," one of them in particular. As a matter of historical fact,
it was we Wasps — by which I mean here the English-speaking
peoples — who invented the idea of *limited governments*: that there
are some things that no king, President or other official is allowed to
do. It began more than seven centuries ago, with Magna Carta, and
continued (to cite only the high spots) through the wrangles between
Parliament and the Stuart kings, the Puritan Revolution of 1640, the
English Bill of Rights of 1688, the American Revolution and our own
Bill of Rights and Constitution.

The Wasp principle of limited government emerged through   6
protracted struggle with the much older principle of unlimited government. This latter was never more cogently expressed than at the
trial of Charles I, when the hapless monarch informed his judges that,
as an anointed king, he was not accountable to any court in the land. A
not dissimilar position was taken more recently by another Wasp head

of state — and with no more success; Executive privilege went over no better in 1974 than divine right did in 1649. The notion that a king, a President or any other official can do as he damn well pleases has never played in Peoria — or Liverpool or Glasgow, Melbourne or Toronto. For more than 300 years, no Wasp nation has endured an absolute monarchy, dictatorship or any other form of unlimited government — which is something no Frenchman, Italian, German, Pole, Russian or Hispanic can say.

It is perfectly true, of course, that we Wasps have on occasion   7 imposed unlimited governments on other (usually darker) peoples. We have, that is, acted in much the same way as have most other nations that possessed the requisite power and opportunity — including many Third World nations whose leaders delight in lecturing us on political morality (for recent information on this point, consult the files on Biafra, Bangladesh and Brazil, Indian tribes of). Yet even here, Wasp values have played an honorable part. When you start with the idea that Englishmen are entitled to self-government, you end by conceding the same right to Africans and Indians. If you begin by declaring that all (white) men are created equal, you must sooner or later face up to the fact that blacks are also men — and conform your conduct, however reluctantly, to your values.

Keeping the Wasp faith hasn't always been easy. We Wasps, like   8 other people, don't always live up to our own principles, and those of us who don't, if occupying positions of power, can pose formidable problems to the rest of us. Time after time, in the name of anti-Communism, peace with honor or some other slippery shibboleth, we have been conned or bullied into tolerating government interference with our liberties and privacy in all sorts of covert — and sometimes overt —ways; time after time we have had to relearn the lesson that eternal vigilance is the price of liberty.

It was a Wasp who uttered that last thought And it was a congress   9 of Wasps who, about the same time, denounced the executive privileges of George III and committed to the cause of liberty their lives, their fortunes and — *pace* my Polish-American compatriot — their sacred honor.

EXERCISES

Words to Know

Wasp (title), Chautauqua (paragraph 1), parvenu (2), stereotype (3), chic (3), maligned (5), Magna Carta (5), Stuart kings (5), protracted

(6), cogently (6), Charles I (6), hapless (6), anointed (6), Biafra (7), shibboleth (8), *pace* (9).

Some of the Issues

1. Find the topic sentence of paragraph 1.
2. What is the point Claiborne makes about ethnic jokes (paragraph 1)?
3. In what way does Claiborne establish his credentials?
4. In paragraph 3 Claiborne says that "it's a damn lie" that he rules New York, let alone America. In paragraph 4, however, he says "Admittedly, both corporate and (to a lesser extent) political America are dominated by Wasps." Is he contradicting himself in these two paragraphs?
5. Paragraph 5 changes the tone. How does Claiborne move from defense of Wasps (paragraphs 1 through 4) to a counterattack? What is the main point of that counterattack?
6. After discussing King Charles I (who was executed for treason), Claiborne refers to president Richard Nixon, who tried in vain to use claims of "executive privilege" and "national security" in his defense when he was accused of complicity in the Watergate break-in. Explain how Claiborne uses these two cases as part of his argument that Wasps are responsible for the development of limited government.
7. Consider the last sentence of paragraph 6 and the first of paragraph 7. Does Claiborne feel he has to defend the Wasp role further?
8. What is the topic of the last sentence of paragraph 7? Is it true historically as well as logically?
9. What does Claiborne mean by "slippery shibboleth" (paragraph 8)?

The Way We Are Told

10. Find words and phrases in paragraph 1 that Claiborne uses to lay the groundwork for his defense of Wasps, or for his counterattack.
11. Find the main thesis that Claiborne advances and show how he supports and defends it. Make an outline of his essay for this purpose.
12. Show how, in paragraph 5, Claiborne builds to his major point.

Some Subjects for Essays

13. If you feel that your nationality (ethnicity, race, religion) has been, as Claiborne puts it, "dumped on," explain the dumping and write a defense.
14. In an essay advance the thesis that the knowledge of history is important in developing national, ethnic, racial, or religious pride and coherence. Develop your thesis through the use of logical argument and examples.

IN RESPONSE TO EXECUTIVE ORDER 9066: ALL AMERICANS OF JAPANESE DESCENT MUST REPORT TO RELOCATION CENTERS

Dwight Okita

Dwight Okita was born in Chicago in 1958. He has written poetry and plays, created poetry videos, and currently writes a weekly column on Chicago's bustling theater scene. His mother was among the thousands of Japanese Americans who were interned shortly after the United States entered the Second World War. This poem is written in his mother's voice. His new play, "The Rainy Season," also touches on the Japanese relocation experience. To learn more about that internment, read Jeanne Wakatsuki Houston's "Arrival at Manzanar."

Dear Sirs:
Of course I'll come. I've packed my galoshes
and three packets of tomato seeds. Janet calls them
"love apples." My father says where we're going
they won't grow.

I am a fourteen-year-old girl with bad spelling
and a messy room. If it helps any, I will tell you
I have always felt funny using chopsticks
and my favorite food is hot dogs.
My best friend is a white girl named Denise—
we look at boys together. She sat in front of me
all through grade school because of our names:
O'Connor, Ozawa. I know the back of Denise's head very well.

I tell her she's going bald. She tells me I copy on tests.
We are best friends.

I saw Denise today in Geography class.
She was sitting on the other side of the room.
"You're trying to start a war," she said, "giving secrets away
to the Enemy, Why can't you keep your big mouth shut?"
I didn't know what to say.
I gave her a packet of tomato seeds
and asked her to plant them for me, told her
when the first tomato ripened
she'd miss me.

PART SIX

New Worlds

The New World—that designation for America has had a wider meaning than simply the name of the continent that Columbus ran into on his way to find the western passage to Asia. America has been an idea, or rather different ideas at different times. To the Spaniards who were the first arrivals nearly five hundred years ago, it was a source of unimagined wealth. Large-scale Spanish expeditions searched prairies and deserts for El Dorado and the Fountain of Youth. In some of the early English descriptions, often by writers who had never laid eyes on the New World, it resembled the Lost World—the Garden of Eden, Paradise, or the closest approach to it. Some of that impression survives in the description of America by Michel Guillaume St. Jean de Crèvecoeur: a New World America, prosperous, rational, a land in which every person can reach whatever position in life his abilities and his industry will allow. He contrasts that happy state to the Old World, the Europe he knew, with its ingrained social order in which men or women were born to high status or poverty, with few possibilities to change their fate.

The idea of America in the late nineteenth century was that of a beacon of liberty and refuge for the poor. It was the destination of "the huddled masses yearning to breathe free," in the words of Emma Lazarus's poem inscribed at the foot of the newly installed Statue of Liberty. Alistair Cooke's description

211

which follows Crèvecoeur represents that picture of America, of the downtrodden poor leaving the bad old world for a better life in the new one.

The four selections which follow approach the meaning of new worlds from an entirely different perspective. Here are worlds — civilizations — that are by no means new, but that present eye-opening new perspectives to the observer. The selections differ widely from each other, but they have a common idea: We need to understand that different cultures may have different answers to the same questions and that these answers may be as logical as the ones we are used to hearing.

The first two of these selections are observations made by Americans. For Mark Salzman, China is a new world full of surprises. The Tiv in Africa show Laura Bohannan that a story she considers universal can also be seen from a very different angle. George Orwell, as a British colonial officer in Burma, discovers, as he says, "the real motive for which despotic governments act." Boon, the central character in John David Morley's "Living in a Japanese Home," discovers how Japanese culture is mirrored in the design of the Japanese home. All four selections discuss discoveries that show the increasing need to understand cultural differences in our shrinking world.

Joseph Bruhac's poem "Ellis Island" tells about the huddled masses that Alistair Cooke describes. It reminds us that the masses who came seeking freedom and prosperity in America also eliminated the freedom of others.

WHAT IS AN AMERICAN?

Michel Guillaume St. Jean de Crèvecoeur

Michel Guillaume St. Jean de Crèvecoeur (1735–1813) came as a young man to the New World, settling at first in the French colony of *Louisiane*, which at that time stretched in a huge arc from the mouth of the St. Lawrence River in the north to the mouth of the Mississippi in the south. In the Seven Years War (1756–1763), called the French and Indian Wars in America, he fought under Montcalm against the British. When the colonies passed into British hands, he remained and settled as a farmer in Vermont. The Revolutionary War found him on the side of the loyalists. Crèvecoeur returned to France permanently in 1790. His *Letters from an American Farmer*, written in French, was published in 1782 and is among the earliest descriptions of life in American.

Crèvecoeur defines and describes what he sees as the virtues and advantages America possesses as compared to the Europe of his day. He sees a prosperous agricultural society, virtually classless, in which persons can reach whatever position in life their abilities allow. He contrasts this to the Old World with its ingrained class structure, where a man (or woman) is born to wealth and high status or to poverty and lifelong drudgery, with no way to escape. He sees America as a young, mobile society in contrast to the static world from which the new man, the American, has made his escape.

I wish I could be acquainted with the feelings and thoughts which 1 must agitate the heart and present themselves to the mind of an enlightened Englishman, when he first lands on this continent. He must greatly rejoice, that he lived at a time to see this fair country discovered and settled; he must necessarily feel a share of national pride, when he views the chain of settlements which embellishes these extended shores. When he says to himself, this is the work of my countrymen, who, when convulsed by factions, afflicted by a variety of miseries and wants, restless and impatient, took refuge here. They brought along with them their national genius, to which they principally owe what liberty they enjoy, and what substance they possess. Here he sees

213

the industry of his native country, displayed in a new manner, and traces in their works the embryos of all the arts, sciences, and ingenuity which flourish in Europe. Here he beholds fair cities, substantial villages, extensive fields, an immense country filled with decent houses, good roads, orchards, meadows, and bridges, where an hundred years ago all was wild, woody, and uncultivated!

What a train of pleasing ideas this fair spectacle must suggest! It is 2 a prospect which must inspire a good citizen with the most heartfelt pleasure. The difficulty consists in the manner of viewing so extensive a scene. He is arrived on a new continent; a modern society offers itself to his contemplation, different from what he had hitherto seen. It is not composed, as in Europe, of great lords who possess every thing, and of a herd of people who have nothing. Here are no aristocratical families, no courts, no kings, no bishops, no ecclesiastical dominion, no invisible power giving to a few a very visible one; no great manufacturers employing thousands, no great refinements of luxury. The rich and the poor are not so far removed from each other as they are in Europe.

Some few towns excepted, we are all tillers of the earth, from 3 Nova Scotia to West Florida. We are a people of cultivators, scattered over an immense territory, communicating with each other by means of good roads and navigable rivers, united by the silken bands of mild government, all respecting the laws without dreading their power, because they are equitable. We are all animated with the spirit of industry, which is unfettered, and unrestrained, because each person works for himself. If he travels through our rural districts, he views not the hostile castle, and the haughty mansion, contrasted with the clay-built hut and miserable cabin, where cattle and men help to keep each other warm, and dwell in meanness, smoke, and indigence. A pleasing uniformity of decent competence appears throughout our habitations. The meanest of our log-houses is a dry and comfortable habitation. Lawyer or merchant are the fairest titles our towns afford; that of a farmer is the only appellation of the rural inhabitants of our country. It must take some time ere he can reconcile himself to our dictionary, which is but short in words of dignity, and names of honour. There, on a Sunday, he sees a congregation of respectable farmers and their wives, all clad in neat homespun, well mounted, or riding in their own humble waggons. There is not among them an esquire, saving the unlettered magistrate. There he sees a parson as simple as his flock, a farmer who does not riot on the labour of others. We have no princes, for whom we toil, starve, and bleed: we are the most perfect society now existing in the world. Here man is free as he ought to be; nor is this pleasing equality so transitory as many others are. Many ages will not see the shores of our great lakes replenished with inland nations, nor the unknown bounds of North America entirely peopled. Who can tell how far it extends? Who can tell the millions of men whom it will feed and contain? for no European foot has as yet travelled half the extent of this mighty continent?

The next wish of this traveller will be to know whence came all these people? They are a mixture of English, Scotch, Irish, Dutch, Germans, and Swedes. From this promiscuous breed, the race now called Americans have arisen. The eastern provinces must indeed be excepted, as being the unmixed descendants of Englishmen. I have heard many wish they had been more intermixed also: for my part, I am no wisher; and think it much better as it has happened. They exhibit a most conspicuous figure in this great and variegated picture; they too enter for a great share in the pleasing perspective displayed in these thirteen provinces. I know it is fashionable to reflect on them; but I respect them for what they have done; for the accuracy and wisdom with which they have settled their territory; for the decency of their manners; for their early love of letters; their ancient college, the first in this hemisphere; for their industry, which to me, who am but a farmer, is the criterion of every thing. There never was a people, situated as they are, who, with so ungrateful a soil, have done more in so short a time. Do you think that the monarchical ingredients which are more prevalent in other governments, have purged them from all foul stains? Their histories assert the contrary.

In this great American asylum, the poor of Europe have by some means met together, and in consequence of various causes; to what purpose should they ask one another, what countrymen they are? Alas, two thirds of them had no country. Can a wretch who wanders about, who works and starves, whose life is a continual scene of sore afflic- tion of pinching penury; can that man call England or any other kingdom his country? A country that had no bread for him, whose fields procured him no harvest, who met with nothing but the frowns of the rich, the severity of the laws, with jails and punishments; who owned not a single foot of the extensive surface of this planet? No! Urged by a variety of motives, here they came. Everything has tended to regenerate them; new laws, a new mode of living, a new social system; here they are become men: in Europe they were as so many useless plants, wanting vegetative mould, and refreshing showers; they withered, and were mowed down by want, hunger, and war: but now, by the power of transplantation, like all other plants, they have taken root and flourished! Formerly they were not numbered in any civil list of their country, except in those of the poor; here they rank as citizens. By what invisible power has this surprizing metamorphosis been per- formed? By that of the laws and that of their industry. The laws, the indulgent laws, protect them as they arrive, stamping on them the symbol of adoption; they receive ample rewards for their labours; these accumulated rewards procure them lands; those lands confer on them the title of freemen; and to that title every benefit is affixed which men can possibly require. This is the great operation daily performed by our laws. From whence proceed these laws? From our government. Whence that government? It is derived from the original genius and strong desire of the people, ratified and confirmed by government. This is the great chain which links us all, this is the picture which every province exhibits.

What attachment can a poor European emigrant have for a coun-   6
try where he had nothing? The knowledge of the language, the love of a few kindred as poor as himself, were the only cords that tied him: his country is now that which gives him land, bread, protection, and consequence: *Ubi panis ibi patria*, is the motto of all emigrants. What then is the American, this new man? He is either an European, or the descendant of an European; hence that strange mixture of blood, which you will find in no other country. I could point out to you a man, whose grandfather was an Englishman, whose wife was Dutch, whose son married a French woman, and whose present four sons have now four wives of different nations. *He* is an American, who, leaving behind him all his ancient prejudices and manners, receives new ones from the new mode of life he has embraced, the new government he obeys, and the new rank he holds. He becomes an American by being received in the broad lap of our great *Alma Mater*.

Here individuals of all nations are melted into a new race of men,   7
whose labours and posterity will one day cause great change in the world. Americans are the western pilgrims, who are carrying along with them that great mass of arts, sciences, vigour, and industry, which began long since in the east; they will finish the great circle. The Americans were once scattered all over Europe; here they are incorporated into one of the finest systems of population which has ever appeared, and which will hereafter become distinct by the power of the different climates they inhabit. The American ought, therefore, to love this country much better than that wherein either he or his forefathers were born. Here the rewards of his industry follow with equal steps the progress of his labour; his labour is founded on the basis of nature, *self-interest*; can it want a stronger allurement? Wives and children, who before in vain demanded of him a morsel of bread, now, fat and frolicsome, gladly help their father to clear those fields whence exuberant crops are to arise to feed and to clothe them all; without any part being claimed, either by a despotic prince, a rich abbot, or a mighty lord. Here religion demands but little of him; a small voluntary salary to the minister, and gratitude to God; can he refuse these? The American is a new man, who acts upon new princi-

ples; he must therefore entertain new ideas, and form new opinions. From involuntary idleness, servile dependence, penury, and useless labour, he has passed to toils of a very different nature, rewarded by ample subsistence. — This is an American.

EXERCISES

Words to Know

enlightened (paragraph 1), factions (1), ecclesiastical (2), dominion (2), unfettered (3), indigence (3), habitation (3), homespun (3), replenished (3), variegated (4), monarchical (4), metamorphosis (5), *ubi panis ibi patria* — where bread is, there is my country (6), frolicsome (7), exuberant (7), penury (7).

Some of the Issues

1. Why should the "enlightened Englishman" rejoice at landing in America?
2. What is the central idea of the second paragraph? How does it relate to the first? How does it carry Crèvecoeur's ideas beyond the first paragraph?
3. Consider the last sentence in paragraph 2 and explain how it is expanded upon in paragraph 3.
4. Paragraph 3 makes its point by means of contrasts. What are they?
5. Paragraphs 4 and 5 classify the people who came to America, but in two different ways. Paragraph 4 discusses national origins. How are Americans described in paragraph 5?
6. In paragraphs 6 and 7 Crèvecoeur asserts that these diverse Europeans are "melted into a new race of men" — Americans. How does that process take place? (Note the word "melted.")
7. Make a list of the contrasts Crèvecoeur makes or clearly implies between Europe and America. Then attempt to organize and classify them into major groupings.
8. Crèvecoeur omits two groups of inhabitants of America. Who are they? Why do you think he omits them when he is clearly concerned about the well-being of ordinary people?

The Way We Are Told

9. Why does Crèvecoeur create the character of the "enlightened Englishman" to report on America in paragraph 1, instead of

continuing to use the first person singular, as he does in the opening sentence?

10. Crèvecoeur tries to convince the reader of the superiority of Americans and their institutions. Who, would you say, are his readers? What are their likely beliefs? How does Crèvecoeur respond to these beliefs?

11. Crèvecoeur uses rhetorical questions, exclamations, and repetition of words and phrases to strengthen his case. Find examples of each.

Some Subjects for Essays

12. Write an essay in praise of some institution that you admire. Select those aspects that seem important to you, organize them in some logical order, and write your description, stressing the favorable facts rather than giving your opinions.

13. Crèvecoeur presents the American as an ideal "new man," free of the shackles of history imposed on him in Europe. In an essay examine the extent to which the American can still be described in Crèvecoeur's terms today.

14. Crèvecoeur may have been the first to use the word *melt* to describe the fusion of people of different nationalities into a new "race of men" — Americans. The term *melting pot* has become a cliché representing that process. More recently some observers have cast doubts on the extent of that process and preferred the analogy of the salad bowl to the melting pot. Write an essay "American Society — Melting Pot or Salad Bowl?"

THE HUDDLED MASSES

Alistair Cooke

Alistair Cooke is probably best known as the host of the PBS
television series "Masterpiece Theater," a function he has fulfilled
since 1971. In the 1970s he also hosted "Alistair Cooke's America" on PBS, a narrative history of the growth of the United States.
The following selection is taken from the book based on that
series, and describes immigration to the United States at the height
of the influx of Europeans in the late nineteenth and early twentieth centuries.

Cooke, born in Manchester, England, in 1908, is himself an
immigrant, having left his native England for America in 1937. As
a broadcaster, journalist, and commentator he has concentrated
his attention on interpreting America, its culture and institutions,
to the world. He has written a number of books in that field and
holds honorary degrees from several universities, including Edin-
burgh, Manchester, and St. Andrews.

For another view of immigration, see Joseph Bruchac's poem
"Ellis Island."

"We call England the Mother country," Robert Benchley once re-   1
marked, "because most of us come from Poland or Italy." It's not quite
as drastic as that, but today the chances of an American being of wholly
English stock are, outside the South, no more than one in four. Only
the English visitor is still surprised by this palpable fact. When a
German makes his first trip across the Atlantic, he can go into almost
any large city between southern Pennsylvania and the Great Lakes, and
on across the prairie into the small towns of Kansas, and he will find
himself among people whose physique is familiar, who share many of
his values and his tastes in food and drink. The Scandinavian will be
very much at home with the landscape and the farming of Minnesota,
and he will not be surprised to hear that the state is represented in
Congress by men named Langen and Olson and Nelsen. A Polish Catholic would easily pass as a native among the sandy potato fields, the
lumbering wooden churches, and the Doroskis and Stepnoskis of eastern Long Island.

For three quarters of the population that hears itself so often   2
hailed as "the American people" are the descendants of immigrants
from Asia and Africa and, most of all, from the continent of Europe.
They brought over with them their religions and folkways and their

national foods, not least their national prejudices, which for a long time in the new country turned the cities of the Northeast and the Midwest into adjoining compounds of chauvinists, distrustful not only of immigrants from other nations everywhere but too often of their neighbors three or four blocks away.

But even the most clannish of them sooner or later had to mix   3
with the peoples already there and learn among other things a new kind of politics, in which the dominant power went to men who knew how to balance the needs of one national group against another. The American delicatessen became an international store for the staples that the old immigrant could not do without. Few American children, certainly in the cities, need to be told that goulash comes from Hungary, liverwurst from Germany, borscht from Russia, and lasagne from Italy. And even Gentiles who never tasted the combination probably know that lox — smoked salmon — and the doughnut-shaped rolls called bagels are as inseparable, in Jewish households of any nationality, as an Englishman's — and an Anglo-Saxon American's — bacon and eggs.

Why did they come? Why do they still come? For a mesh of   4
reasons and impulses that condition any crucial decision in life. But the most powerful was one common to most of the immigrants from the 1840s on — hard times in the homeland. They chose America because, by the early nineteenth century, Europeans, especially if they were poor, had heard that the Americans had had a revolution that successfully overthrew the old orders of society. Madame de Staël could tell a Boston scholar, in 1817, "You are the advance guard of the human race." And Goethe, ten years later, wrote for anybody to read: "Amerika, du hast es besser als unser Kontinent" (which may be loosely translated as: "America, you have things better over there.") He was thinking of the freedom from the binding force of "useless traditions." But people who had never heard of Madame de Staël and Goethe picked up the new belief that there was a green land far away preserved "from robbers, knights and ghosts affrighting." Whenever life could hardly be worse at home, they came to believe that life was better in America.

In Ireland in the middle 1840s human life had touched bottom.   5
Ironically, two causes of the Irish plight came *from* America. The rising competition of American agriculture made thousands of very small farmers (300,000 of Ireland's 685,000 farms had less than three acres) shift from tillage to grazing, on barren ground. And the potato blight, which was to putrefy vast harvest in a few weeks, had crossed the Atlantic from America in 1845. Within five years the potato famine had claimed almost a million Irish lives, over twenty thousand of them dropping in the fields from starvation.

The young Queen Victoria was informed that the state of Ireland   6
was "alarming" and that the country was so full of "inflammable
matter" that it could explode in rebellion. So she paid a royal visit,
serenely admired the beauty of the scenery, and was relieved that the
people "received us with the greatest enthusiasm." Nevertheless, at
Kingston and at Cork she noted: "You see more ragged and wretched
people here than I ever saw anywhere else." One of those ragged
people could well have been a bankrupt farmer from Wexford County
who had gone to Cork. Most such, with any energy left over after the
famine, retreated to the towns and either joined sedition societies or
headed for America. This one chose America, and, like very many of
the Irish who came after, his destination was chosen for him by the
simple fact that Boston was the end of the Cunard line. His name was
Patrick Kennedy, great-grandfather of the thirty-fifth President of the
United States. He was one of the 1,700,000 Irish — a little less than
one quarter of the whole population when the famine began — who
left for America in the 1840s and 1850s.

Hunger, then, was the spur in Ireland. There were other, equally   7
fearful incentives. In the single year of 1848 political storms swept
across Europe — in Austria, an abdication, arrests, and executions; in
Italy, a revolution and a declaration of war by the Pope against Austria;
in Sicily, an uprising against the King of Naples; in Germany, a liberal
revolution that failed. Both then and throughout the rest of the century
and on into our own, in any troubled country, whether or not its
mischief could be laid to known culprits, there was always the ancient
scapegoat of the Jew. In eastern and central Europe the ghettos had
long been routine targets for the recruiting sergeant and the secret
police, and their inhabitants were acquainted from childhood with
what one of them called "the stoniest sound in the world: the midnight knock on the door." It would be hard to calculate but easy to
guess at the millions of American Jews whose forefathers were harried
and haunted by these persecutors. It is something hardly thought of by
most of us who came here by free choice, or were born here without
ever having to make a choice.

In some cities of Europe, Jews were permitted to practice their   8
religion in compounds. But in many more places, where the Jews had
been systematically vilified for fifteen hundred years, authorities considered their rituals to be a sinister as black magic, and the more daring
or devout worshiped in stealth. In America, they had heard, they could
worship openly in their own fashion, Orthodox, Reform, Conservative
—or, as radical Reconstructionists, they could look to the United
States as a permitted rallying ground on which to muster the faithful
for the return to Palestine. I dwell on the Jews because, in the great
tidal wave of the late nineteenth- and early twentieth-century immi-

gration, they were the most numerous of those who saw America as the Land of Canaan; because their story offers the most dramatic and arduous exercise in the struggle to assimilate; and because, as much or more than other peoples, they created the American polyglot metropolis against which, in 1924, the Congress protested with restrictive legislation that tried, too late, to restore the United States to its northern European origins.

So late as 1880, there were only a quarter of a million Jews in the United States. By 1924 there were four and a half million, the product of a westward movement that started in the early nineteenth century with their exodus from the ghettos of eastern Europe into the new factories of western Europe. They had moved in that direction earlier throughout the Thirty Years War and then after the later Cossack massacres and peasant revolts. But the factory system provided them with a legal right to flee from their inferior citizenship in Germany and from pogroms in Russia, Poland, and Romania. In the last quarter of the nineteenth century, both city and rural Jews were the willing quarry of emigration agents from America carrying glowing broadsides from house to house about the high wages, good clothes, abundant food, and civil liberties available in the New World. The sweet talk of these promoters might be sensibly discounted, but not the bags of mail containing "America letters" from relatives who had made the voyage and whose more practical accounts of an attainable decent life were read aloud in cottages, markets, and factories.

The word spread beyond the factories and the ghettos to the farmers of southern and central Europe. And whereas before 1890 the immigrant stream had flowed out of Scandinavia, Germany, Ireland, England, and Canada, in the next thirty years the mass of immigrants came from Italy, Austria-Hungary, Russia, and again and always Ireland.

The Germans formed a strong and special current in the mainstream of immigration. There were already a quarter of a million of them in the United States at the time of the Declaration of Independence, and in the thirty years between 1860 and 1890 they contributed more refugees than any other nation, among them more varied social types, more professionals, and more scholars than the others. They also settled far and wide. The German Jews, beginning as small merchants, prospered more conspicuously and founded many of the great banking families of New York. Wherever the Germans went, they tended to establish themselves, both by superiority of talent and a marked gift of clannishness, at the head of the social hierarchy of Jewry. The Sephardic Jews and the German Jews were at the top, and at the bottom were the Lithuanians and the Hungarians, elements in a social system that discouraged intermarriage between its upper and lower strata the defiance of which has probably caused as much snobbish anguish as the love matches of Jews and Gentiles in other immigrant families.

All told, in the first two decades of this century, an unbelievable fourteen and a half million immigrants arrived. They were mostly the persecuted and the poor, "the wretched refuse of your teeming shore" apostrophized by Emma Lazarus, a wealthy and scholarly young lady whose poetic dramas and translations of Heine are forgotten in the thunder of five lines inscribed on the Statue of Liberty. These unlettered millions were, for the most part, to become the "huddled masses" who, in the tenements of the American cities, would have quite a time of it "yearning to breathe free." They had never heard of Thomas Jefferson or George Washington. But they were the easy victims of the absurd myth that the streets of America were paved with gold — not much, perhaps, but enough to offer striking proof, in sepia photographs sent back to Poland or Hungary, of well-fed families who looked you in the eye, of a father or a cousin wearing a suit and shiny shoes, just like a doctor or a merchant in the old country. 12

Long before they arrived at the ports of embarkation — Constantinople, Piraeus, Antwerp, Bremen — emigrant trains had started deep inside Russia. Most of them were linked box cars, sometimes with benches, the men in one car, the women and children in another. Every few hundred miles the train would be shunted on to a siding in order to pick up other new armies, of Austrians, Hungarians, Lithuanians, and finally a troop of Germans, before they came to, say, Hamburg. There they were corralled and checked to see if they had the three essential passports to America: an exit paper, twenty-five spare dollars to prevent their becoming a public charge, and the price of the passage. By the 1890s lively rate wars between steamship lines had halved the steerage fare from about twenty dollars to ten. In an enclosure outside Hamburg they would be bathed, de-loused, and fed, and their baggage and clothes fumigated. Then they were ferried out to the big ship and stowed aboard, as many as nine hundred in steerage. 13

In the floating commune of the emigrant ship, the status symbols were few but well defined. A suitcase, however battered, was most likely the mark of a city man. To a poor peasant, a wicker basket was elegance enough. Most people tied everything up in a blanket or a sheet. They had brought with them what they thought to be indispensable to a decent life afloat. First, the necessity of a pillow, goosefeather, if they were lucky — a point of pride, a relic, and a symbol that some families kept throughout their lives. Village girls took along their only certain dowry, a special extra petticoat and, for formal occasions, a corset. Many of the young women were engaged to men from the home town on the other side of the Atlantic. It was well understood 14 that the ambitious male, engaged or already married, went on ahead to stake out the fortune, which was more often the bare living that could sustain a family. Many of these engagements were broken once for all on the way over by the rude proximity of the males in steerage.

Like all travelers, both simple and sophisticated, they were 15 deeply suspicious of the other nation's food. It was a common thing to take along a cooking pot, a few raw vegetables, and a hunk of sausage or some other final reminder of the favorite snack. The religious invariably took with them the tokens of their faith, a cross or a prayer book or phylacteries; and a member of a closely-knit family would cherish an heirloom yielded up in the moment of parting. It could be nothing more pretentious than a brass candlestick or a lock of hair.

For two weeks or eight days, depending on the size of the ship, 16 they sewed, played cards, sang to harmonicas or tin whistles, counted their savings, continually checked their exit papers, complained about the atrocious food and the ubiquity of the rats. The ones who could read, probably less than half the flock, recited the cheering promise of the emigrant agents' broadsides and pamphlets. The young women nursed the elders and the chronically seasick and resisted, or succumbed to, the advances of spry bachelors. There was no possibility of privacy in the swarm of steerage.

But as America came nearer, some of them suffered from nervous 17 recall of the stratagems that had got them this far. Bright youngsters who had carefully failed their high school examinations in order to prove their unfitness for military service. Oldsters who began to mask a fever with massive doses of medicine. Embezzlers, petty criminals, and betrothed men skipping breach-of-promise suits who had obviously had the wit to fake an exit pass or steal the passage money. A lot of people had a lot to hide.

Far down in the lower bay of New York City, they crowded to the 18 rail to eye their first Americans in the persons of the immigration inspectors, two men and a woman in uniform clambering up a ladder from a cutter that had nosed alongside. The captain was required to note on the ship's manifest the more flagrant cases of contagious disease, for only seventy years ago they were still on the lookout for yellow fever and leprosy. The unlucky victims of such ailments were taken off in a quarantine boat to a special island to be deported as soon as possible.

The harbor was sometimes choked with ships at anchor. In the 19 early 1900s there could be as many as fifteen thousand immigrants arriving in one day, and the ships had to drop anchor and wait. But eventually the engines would rumble again, and there, like a battleship on the horizon, stood what the song calls "Manhattan, an isle of joy." Closer, it grew into a cluster of pinnacles known as skyscrapers.

And then the midtown skyscrapers topped the ones first seen. It was unlike any other city, and to the European it was always audacious and magical, and threatening.

Soon the newcomers would be on the docks sorting their bundles and baggage in a babble of languages, and when that was done they were tagged with numbers. Until 1892 they were cleared for entry at Castle Garden, once a fort, then a theater and a public amusement place down at the Battery. However, the volume of immigrants grew so great, and so many of them managed to disappear into Manhattan before being "processed," that a larger and more isolated sorting point had to be found. So, from 1892 on, once the immigrants had been tagged with numbers they were shipped aboard a ferry or a barge to what was to be known in several languages as "the isle of tears," the clearing station, Ellis Island. [20]

It had been used by the early Dutch as a picnic ground. Much later its three acres were increased by landfill into twenty-seven, and it became a government arsenal. Today, it looks like a rather imposing college recently gutted by fire. It is totally derelict, a frowzy monument to the American habit of junking and forgetting whatever wears out. But wandering through its great central hall and tattered corridors, seeing the offices with their rusting files, the broken lavatories, and upturned dining tables, one can imagine the bedlam of its heyday, when the milling swarm of strangers was served and interrogated by hundreds of inspectors, wardens, interpreters, doctors, nurses, waiters, cooks, and agents of immigrant aid societies; and all the while a guerrilla army of con men, land swindlers, and hackmen passed out fresh broadsides boosting the heavenly prospects of the inland towns and unheard-of settlements on the prairie. [21]

The newcomers crowded into the main building and the first thing they heard over the general bedlam were the clarion voices of inspectors bellowing out numbers in Italian, German, Polish, Hungarian, Russian, and Yiddish. According to assigned numbers they were herded into groups of thirty and led through long tiled corridors up a wide staircase into the biggest hall most of them had ever seen. Its dimensions, its pillars, its great soaring windows still suggest the grand ballroom of some abdicated monarch. Once they were assembled there in their thousands, the clearance procedure began. I recently pressed an aged immigrant to describe it. "Procedure?" he squealed incredulously. "Din, confusion, bewilderment, madness!" [22]

They moved in single file through a stockyard maze of passageways and under the eye of a doctor in a blue uniform who had in his hand a piece of chalk. He was a tough instant diagnostician. He would look at the hands, the hair, the faces and rap out a few questions. He might spot a panting old man with purple lips, and he would chalk on [23] his back a capital "H" for suspected heart disease. Any facial blotches, a hint of gross eczema brought forth a chalked "F," for facial rash. Children in arms were made to stand down to see if they rated an "L" for the limp of rickets or some other deficiency disease. There was one chalk mark that every family dreaded, for it guaranteed certain deportation. It was a circle with a cross in the middle, and it indicated "feeble-minded."

Next they moved on to two doctors dipping into bowls of disin- 24 fectant and snapping back the eyelids of suspects, usually with a buttonhook. They were looking for a disease very common then in southern and eastern Europe, trachoma. If you had it, an "E" was chalked on your back, and your first days in the New World were surely your last.

About eight in ten survived this scrutiny and passed to the final 25 ordeal, the examination before an immigration inspector standing with an interpreter. Not noticeably gracious types, for they worked ten hours a day, seven days a week, they droned out an unchanging catechism: Who paid your passage? How many dependents? Ever been in prison? Can you read and write? (There was for a long time no legal obligation to be able to do either.) Is there a job waiting for you? (This was a famous catch, since a law called the Contract Labor Law forbade immigrants from signing up abroad for any work at all.) Finally, your name was checked against the ship's manifest. Many people were lucky to emerge into the new life with their old name. An Irish inspector glancing down at what to him was the gobbledygook of "Ouspenska" wrote on the landing card "Spensky." A Norwegian with an unpronounceable name was asked for the name of the town he had left. It was Dröbak. The inspector promptly wrote down what he thought he'd heard. Another Norwegian standing nearby philosophically realized that his own name was just as unmanageable and decided that what was good enough for his friend was good enough for him. To this day the progeny of both families rejoice in the name of Robeck.

But a new identity was better than none, and it gave you a landing 26 card. With it you were now ready to pay a visit to a currency booth to change your lire or drachmas, or whatever, into dollars. This exchange could entail prolonged haggling and not a few fist fights with the cashiers, who for many years were short-change artists. But at last you were handed over to the travel agent or the railroad men, if you were going far afield, or you sought the help of an aid society or a beckoning politician, if New York was to be the end of the line. Most immigrants could speak hardly a word of English except the one they had memorized as the town of their destination. A man would unfold a scrap of paper and point to a block-printed word: "Pringvilliamas." Maybe he eventually arrived in Springfield, Massachusetts, and maybe he didn't. But at this point the immigrants' only concern was to get off Ellis Island. All of them looked in relief for the door that was marked "Push to New York." And they pushed.

EXERCISES

Words to Know

palpable (paragraph 1), chauvinists (2), Gentiles (3), Anglo-Saxon (3), Madame de Staël (4), Goethe (4), tillage (5), putrefy (5), Queen Victoria (6), sedition (6), abdication (7), ghettos (7), vilified (8), Land of Canaan (8), polyglot (8), metropolis (8), exodus (9), Thirty Years War (9), Cossack (9), pogroms (9), quarry (9), broadsides (9), clannishness (11), social hierarchy (11), Sephardic Jews (11), strata (11), apostrophized (12), Emma Lazarus (12), Heinrich Heine (12), tenements (12), sepia (12), steerage (13), fumigated (13), relic (14), dowry (14), phylacteries (15), ubiquity (16), swarm (16), stratagem (17), embezzlers (17), betrothed (17), breech-of-promise (17), clambering (18), ship's manifest (18), flagrant (18), quarantine (18), pinnacles (19), babble (20), Ellis Island (20), derelict (21), bedlam (21), guerrilla army (21), clarion (22), trachoma (24), catechism (25), gobbledygook (25), progeny (25).

Some of the Issues

1. In paragraphs 2 and 3 Cooke singles out several consequences of Americans' diverse origins. What are the most significant ones?
2. What according to Cooke was the most powerful reason for immigrants to come to the United States in the nineteenth and early twentieth centuries?
3. The author singles out two groups in particular, the Irish and the Jews. What reasons for coming did they have? In what ways did their reasons differ?
4. In the first twelve paragraphs the topic is: who came from Europe and why? What is the major topic in the second part of the essay (paragraphs 13 – 26)?
5. What obstacles did prospective immigrants have to cope with in order to be admitted to the United States?

The Way We Are Told

6. The first three paragraphs are all concerned with the diversity of the origins of Americans. Each paragraph has a specific subtopic, however. What is the logic of their sequence?
7. Examine paragraph 6. What do you think was the author's purpose in telling the reader about Queen Victoria and Patrick Kennedy? What contrasts does he try to evoke by pairing them in the same paragraph?
8. In paragraphs 3 and 15, the author refers to food. How would you say he uses those references to demonstrate the effects of diversity?

Some Subjects for Essays

9. In the last twenty to thirty years the pattern of immigration has increasingly deviated from the one Cooke describes. A majority of immigrants now come from Asia and Latin America. Using newspapers and magazines as resources, discuss the countries of origin of these more recent immigrants and examine what causes them to come. Do you see any similarities to the earlier waves of immigrants whom Cooke discusses?
* 10. Analyze the photograph on page 210 of immigrants arriving in America in the early years of the twentieth century. How does Alistair Cooke's essay contribute to your understanding of the picture? How does the picture contribute to your understanding of the essay?

TEACHER MARK

Mark Salzman

As Mark Salzman tells you in the following selection from his autobiographical memoir *Iron and Silk*, he was graduated from Yale in 1982. He studied Chinese language and literature and is "fluent in Mandarin and nearly so in Cantonese," the two most widely spoken Chinese dialects. Not long after his graduation he took a job teaching English in Changsha, an industrial city of a million, the capital of Hunan province in China.

The early and mid-1980s were marked by rapid changes in the People's Republic of China. The country, with more than one billion people — by far the most populous on earth — was rapidly opening up to the outside world, particularly the industrialized West. Tens of thousands of Chinese university students were coming to study in Western countries, including the United States. Western corporations were encouraged to develop commerce and industry with, and in, China. The communist government that ruled the country since the revolution in 1949 was experimenting with capitalist incentives for economic development. The country seemed to be moving from a rigidly socialist system under a dictatorial regime to an intellectual opening up that promised changes in a democratic direction. In 1989 the impatience with the slow pace of that opening-up process, as well as anger about corruption and favoritism in the government, led to huge protest demonstrations led by hundreds of thousands of students. In the late spring of 1989 these movements were harshly suppressed.

Mark Salzman describes a time when the opening-up seemed in full flower and likely to continue. The teachers he talks about may be less willing to talk freely in the 1990s than they were in the mid-1980s, but they may also be less willing to trust their own news media as they did then. But that, it must be understood, is merely a conjecture.

The Cultural Revolution referred to in paragraph 41 was a time of great upheaval and destruction in the 1960s. Bands of young women and men, called the Red Guards, roamed the country out of control, dispensing what they considered justice. Education came to a standstill as millions of teachers, students, and professionals were sent to work as peasants in the countryside under the harshest conditions.

The Gulag Archipelago (paragraph 50) by the Russian novelist Aleksandr Solzhenitsyn is a description — and severe indictment — of the concentration camps in the Soviet Union under

229

Josef Stalin, in which millions of people lived and died. Its author lives in exile in the United States. The camps themselves, however, have essentially disappeared.

In 1982, I graduated from Yale University as a Chinese literature 1 major. I was fluent in Mandarin and nearly so in Cantonese, had struggled through a fair amount of classical Chinese and had translated the works of Huang Po-Fei, a modern poet. Oddly, though, I had no real desire to go to China; it sounded like a giant penal colony to me, and besides, I have never liked traveling much. I applied to the Yale-China Association because I needed a job, and was assigned to teach English at Hunan Medical College in Changsha, a sooty, industrial city of more than a million people and the capital of the southern province of Hunan.

When I arrived in Changsha, the temperature was above 100 2 degrees. I was 22 years old and homesick. The college assigned three classes to me: 26 doctors and teachers of medicine; four men and one woman identified as "the Middle-Aged English Teachers," and 25 medical students, ages 22 to 28. I was entirely unsure what to expect from them; the reverse, I would learn, was also true.

Their English ability ranged from nearly fluent to practically 3 hopeless. At the end of the first week the Class Monitor for the class of doctors read aloud the results of their "Suggestions for Better Study" meeting: "Dear Teacher Mark. You are an active boy! Your lessons are very humorous and very wonderful. To improve our class, may we suggest that in the future, we (1) spend more time reading (2) spend more time listening (3) spend more time writing, and (4) spend more time speaking. Also, some students feel you are moving too quickly through the book. However, some students request that you speed up a little, because the material is too elementary. We hope we can struggle together to overcome these contradictions! Thank you, our dear teacher."

On the first day of class, when I asked the Middle-Aged English 4 Teachers to introduce themselves to me, each chose instead to introduce the person sitting next to him. Teacher Xu began: "Teacher Cai was a wonderful dancer when he was a young man. He is famous in our college because he has a beautiful wife." Teacher Cai hit Teacher Xu and said, "Teacher Xu is always late to class, and he is afraid of his wife!"

"I am not!" 5

"Oh, but you are!" 6

Teacher Zhang pointed to Teacher Zhu. "Teacher Zhu was a navy 7 man," he said. "But he can't swim! And Teacher Du is very fat. So we

call her Fatty Du — she has the most powerful voice in our college!"
Fatty Du beamed with pride and said, "And Teacher Zhang's special
characteristic is that he is afraid of me!"

"I am not!"   8

"Oh, but you are!"   9

On an afternoon some week later, I asked them to open their   10
textbooks to a chapter entitled "War," which contained photographs
of World War II, including one of the atomic bomb explosion over
Hiroshima.

"Teacher Zhu," I said, "Can you tell us something about your   11
experiences during the war?"

Teacher Zhu, an aspiring Communist Party member, stood up   12
and smiled.

"Yes," he said. Then he hesitated. "This is a picture of the atom 13
bomb, isn't it?"

"Yes."   14

He smiled stiffly. "Teacher Mark — how do you feel, knowing   15
your country dropped an atom bomb on innocent people?"

My face turned red with embarrassment at having the question   16
put so personally, but I tried to remain detached.

"This is a good question, Teacher Zhu. I can tell you that in   17
America, many people disagree about this. Not everyone thinks it was
the right thing to do, although most people think that it saved lives."

"How did it save lives?"   18

"Well, by ending the war quickly."   19

Here, Teacher Zhu looked around the room at his classmates.   20

"But Teacher Mark. It is a fact that the Japanese had already   21
surrendered to the Communist Eighth Route Army of China. America
put the bomb on Japan to make the world think America was the . . ."

"The victor!" shouted Fatty Du.   22

"Yes, the victor," said Teacher Zhu.   23

I must have stood gaping for a long time, for the other students 24
began to laugh.

"Teacher Zhu," I asked, "how do you know this is a fact?"   25

"Because that is what our newspapers say!"   26

"I see. But our newspapers tell a different story. How can we   27
know which newspaper has told the truth?"

Here he seemed relieved.   28

"That is easy! Our newspapers are controlled by the people, but   29
your newspapers are owned by capitalist organizations, so of course
they make things up to support themselves."

My mouth opened and closed a few times. Fatty Du, appar-   30
ently believing that the truth had been too much for me, came to my
aid.

"It doesn't matter! Any capitalist country would do that. It is not just your country!"   31

My head swimming, I asked her if she thought only capitalist countries lied in the papers.   32

"Oh, of course not! The Russians do it, too. But here in China, we have no reason to lie in the papers. When we make a mistake, we admit it! As for war, there is nothing to lie about. China has never attacked a nation. It has only defended its borders. We love peace. If we were the most powerful country in the world, think how peaceful the world would be!"   33

I agreed that war was a terrible thing and said I was glad that China and the United States had become friendly. The class applauded my speech.   34

"Teacher Mark — can I trouble you? I have a relative. She is my wife's cousin. She is a doctor visiting from Harbin. She speaks very good English and is very interested in learning more. Could I take her here to practice with you? It would only be once or twice."   35

Because of the overwhelming number of relatives and friends of students, not to mention perfect strangers, who wanted to learn English, I had to be protective of my time. I explained this to my student and apologized for not being able to help him.   36

"This is terrible," he said, smiling sheepishly.   37

"Why?" I asked.   38

"Because . . . I already told her you would."   39

I tried to let my annoyance show, but the harder I frowned, the more broadly he smiled, so at last I agreed to meet with her once.   40

"Her name is Little Mi," he said, much relieved. "She is very smart and strong-willed. She was always the leader of her class and was even the head of the Communist Youth League in her school. During the Cultural Revolution, she volunteered to go to the countryside. There she almost starved to death. At last she had a chance to go to medical school. She was the smartest in her class."   41

Little Mi sounded like a terrific bore; I cleared my throat, hoping that my student would simply arrange a time and let me be, but he continued. "Her specialty was pediatrics. She wanted to work with children. When the time came for job assignments after graduation, though, some people started a rumor that she and some of the other English students read Western literature in their spare time instead of studying medicine. They were accused of *fang yang pi*!" — imitating Westerners.   42

"So instead of being sent to a good hospital, she was sent to a small family planning clinic outside of the city. There she mostly   43 assists doctors with abortions. That is how she works with children. But saddest of all, she has leukemia. Truly, she has eaten bitter all her life. When can I bring her?''

I told him they could come to my office in the Foreign Languages Building that evening. He thanked me extravagantly and withdrew. 44

At the appointed time someone knocked. I braced myself for an hour of grammar questions and opened the door. There stood Little Mi, who could not have been much older than I, with a purple scarf wrapped around her head like a Russian peasant woman. She was petite, unsmiling and beautiful. She looked at me without blinking. 45

"Are you Teacher Mark?" she asked in an even, low voice. 46

"Yes — please come in." She walked in, sat down and said in fluent English, "My cousin's husband apologizes for not being able to come. His adviser called him in for a meeting. Do you mind that I came alone?'' 47

"Not at all. What can I do for you?'' 48

"Well," she said, looking at the bookshelf next to her, "I love to read, but it is difficult to find good books in English. I wonder if you would be so kind as to lend me a book or two, which I can send back to you from Harbin as soon as I finish them." I told her to pick whatever she liked from my shelf. As she went through the books she talked about the foreign novels she had enjoyed; "Of Mice and Men,'' "From Here To Eternity" and "The Gulag Archipelago.'' 49

"How did you get 'The Gulag Archipelago'?" I asked her. 50

"It wasn't easy," she answered. "I hear that Americans are shocked by what they read in it. Is that true?'' 51

"Yes, weren't you?'' 52

"Not really," she answered quietly. 53

I remembered the story of her life my student had told. "You are a pretty tough girl, aren't you? I said. 54

She looked up from the magazine she had been leafing through with a surprised expression, then covered her mouth with her hand and giggled nervously. "How terrible! I'm not like that at all!'' 55

We talked for over an hour, and she picked a few books to take with her. When she got up to leave, I asked her when she would return to Harbin. 56

"The day after tomorrow.'' 57

Against all better judgment I asked her to come visit me again the next evening. She eyed me closely, said "Thank you — I will," then disappeared into the unlit hallway. I listened to her footsteps as she made her way down the stairs and out of the deserted building. Then from the window I watched her shadowy figure cross the athletic field. 58

She came the next night at exactly the same time. I had brought 59 for her a few books of photographs of the United States, and she marveled at the color pictures taken in New England during the fall. "How beautiful," she said. "Just like a dream."

I could not openly stare at her, so I gazed at her hand as she   60 turned the pages of the book, listened to her voice, and occasionally glanced at her face when she asked me something.

We talked and talked, then she seemed to remember something   61 and looked at her watch. It was after 10 o'clock—nearly two hours had passed. She gasped, suddenly worried. "I've missed the last bus!"

She was staying in a hospital on the other side of the river, at least   62 a two-hour walk. It was a bitter cold night. On foot, she would get back after midnight and arouse considerable suspicion. The only thing to do was put her on the back of a bicycle and ride her. That in itself would not attract attention, since that is how most Chinese families travel around town. I had seen families of five on one bicycle many times, and young couples ride this way for want of anything else to do at night. The woman usually rides sidesaddle on the rack over the rear wheel with her arms around the man's waist, leaning her shoulder and face against his back.

A Chinese woman riding that way on a bicycle powered by a   63 Caucasian male would attract attention, however. I put on my thick padded Red Army coat, tucked my hair under a Mao hat, wore a surgical mask (as many Chinese do, to keep dust out of their lungs), and put on a pair of Chinese sunglasses, the kind that *liumang*— young punks—wear. Little Mi wrapped her scarf around her head and left the building first.

Five minutes later, I went out, rode fast through the gate of our   64 college, and saw her down the street, shrouded in the haze of dust kicked up by a coal truck. I pulled alongside her and she jumped on before I stopped.

The street was crowded. Neither of us said a word. Trucks, buses   65 and jeeps flung themselves madly through the streets, bicycles wove around us, and pedestrians darted in front of us, cursing the *liumang*. Finally I turned onto the road that ran along the river, and the crowd thinned out. It was a horrible road, with potholes everywhere that I could not see in time to avoid. She, too shy to put her arms around my waist, had been balancing herself across the rack, but when we hit an especially deep rut I heard her yelp and felt her grab on to me. Regaining her balance, she began to loosen her grip, but I quickly steered into another pothole and told her to hold on. Very slowly, I felt her leaning her shoulder against my back. When at last her face touched my coat, I could feel her cheek through it.

We reached the steep bridge and I started the climb. About   66 halfway up she told me to stop riding, that we could walk up the bridge to give me a rest. At the top, we stopped to lean against the rail and look at the lights of the city. Trucks and jeeps were our only company.

"Does this remind you of America?" she asked, gesturing toward the city lights with her chin.   67

"Yes, a little."   68

"Do you miss home?"   69

"Very much. But I'll be home very soon. And when I get home, I will miss Changsha."   70

"Really? But China is so . . . no you tell me—what is China like?"   71

"The lights are dimmer here."   72

"Yes," she said quietly, "and we are boring people, aren't we?" Only her eyes showed above the scarf wrapped around her face. I asked her if she thought she was boring, and her eyes wrinkled with laughter.   73

"I am not boring. I believe I am a very interesting girl. Do you think so?"   74

"Yes, I think so." She had pale skin, and I could see her eyelids blush.   75

"When you go back to America, will you live with your parents?"   76

"No."   77

"Why not?"   78

"I'm too old! They would think it was strange if I didn't live on my own."   79

"How wonderful! I wish my parents felt that way. I will have to live with them forever."   80

"Forever?"   81

"Of course! Chinese parents love their children, but they also think that children are like furniture. They own you, and you must make them comfortable until they decide to let you go. I cannot marry, so I will have to take care of them forever. I am almost 30 years old, and I must do whatever they say. So I sit in my room and dream. In my imagination I am free, and I can do wonder things!"   82

"Like what?"   83

She cocked her head to one side and raised one eyebrow.   84

"Do you tell people your dreams?"   85

"Yes, sometimes."   86

She laughed and said, "I'm not going to tell you my dreams."   87

We were silent awhile, then she suddenly asked me if I was a sad man or a happy man.   88

"That's hard to say—sometimes I'm happy, sometimes I'm sad. Mostly, I just worry."   89

"Worry? What do you worry about?"   90

"I don't know—everything, I guess. Mostly about wasting   91
time."

"How strange! My cousin's husband says that you work very   92
hard."

"I like to keep busy. That way I don't have time to worry."   93

"I can't understand that. You are such a free man—you can   94
travel all over the world as you like, make friends everywhere. You are
a fool not to be happy, especially when so many people depend on it."

"What do you mean?"   95

"My relative says that your nickname in the college is *huo-*   96
shenxian—an immortal in human form—because you are
so . . . different. Your lectures make everyone laugh, and you make
people feel happy all the time. This is very unusual."

I asked her if she was happy or sad. She raised one eyebrow again,   97
looking not quite at me.

"I don't have as many reasons to be happy as you." She looked at   98
her watch and shook her head. "I must get back—we have to hurry."
As I turned toward the bicycle she leaned very close to me, almost
touching her face against mine, looking straight into my eyes, and said,
"I have an idea."

I could feel her breath against my throat.   99

"Let's coast down the bridge," she said. "Fast! No brakes!"   100

I got on the bicycle.   101

"Are you getting on?" I asked her.   102

"Just a minute. At the bottom I'll get off, so I'll say goodbye   103
now."

"I should at least take you to the gate of the hospital."   104

"No, that wouldn't be a good idea. Someone might see me and   105
ask who you were. At the bottom of the bridge I'll hop off, and you
turn around. I won't see you again, so thank you. I was fun meeting
you. You should stop worrying." She jumped on, pressed her face
against my back, held me like a vice, and said, "Now—go! As fast as
you can!"

EXERCISES

Words to Know

Mandarin (paragraph 1), Cantonese (1), penal colony (1), detached
(16), gaping (24), capitalist (29), sheepishly (37), Cultural Revolution (41), pediatrics (42), leukemia (43), extravagantly (44), petite
(45), The Gulag Archipelago (49), sidesaddle (62), Caucasian (63),
shrouded (64), immortal (96).

Some of the Issues

1. How did Salzman feel about going to China before traveling there? What was his preparation for the job of teaching English?
2. Describe Salzman's English classes. How appropriate are the doctors' suggestions? How did the middle-aged English teachers introduce each other?
3. What differing views of history are revealed in paragraphs 13 to 34?
4. What impression did Salzman have of Little Mi before meeting her? What do you learn about her past? About the effects of the Cultural Revolution?
5. What is Salzman's reaction when he finds out that Little Mi has read *The Gulag Archipelago*?
6. How is Little Mi's personality revealed to us? What indications are there of a change in Salzman's feelings?
7. The final conversation between Salzman and Little Mi reveals many differences in their lives and attitudes toward living. What are they? Do you think Salzman and Little Mi understand each other in spite of their differences?

The Way We Are Told

8. At first sight Salzman seems simply to be recording his conversations and impressions. Yet, in doing so, he lets the reader know quite clearly what he feels. How does Salzman express his point of view? Try to find some examples.
9. In paragraph 15 Teacher Zhu confronts Salzman with a question about dropping the atom bomb on Hiroshima. Examine the rest of the discussion between Salzman and the teachers. How does Salzman show that they, far from wanting a confrontation on that topic, go out of their way to "help" him understand?

Some Subjects for Essays

10. Salzman and Little Mi lead lives that are very far apart. Before their meeting Salzman expects her to be a bore. Yet, in the few hours they spend together, they bridge the wide gap between them. Describe a situation in which your own anticipation or first impression of someone turned out to be wrong.

SHAKESPEARE IN
THE BUSH

Laura Bohannan

Laura Bohannan, born in New York City in 1922, is a professor of anthropology at the University of Illinois in Chicago. She received her doctorate from Oxford University and later did field work with various peoples in Africa, including the Tiv, a tribe in central Nigeria, with whom this story is concerned. Under the pseudonym Elenore Smith Bowen, she has published a novel about anthropological field work, *Return to Laughter*.

   The Tiv, who have a tradition of story telling (accompanied by beer drinking) during the rainy season, asked their visitor to tell a story. She chose Shakespeare's *Hamlet*, believing that its universality would make it comprehensible, even in a culture very different from the one in which it was originally conceived. This assumption turned out to be quite wrong.

Just before I left Oxford for the Tiv in West Africa, conversation turned to the season at Stratford, "You Americans," said a friend, "often have difficulty with Shakespeare. He was, after all, a very English poet, and one can easily misinterpret the universal by misunderstanding the particular." 1

   I protested that human nature is pretty much the same the whole world over; at least the general plot and motivation of the greater tragedies would always be clear — everywhere — although some details of custom might have to be explained and difficulties of translation might produce other slight changes. To end an argument we could not conclude, my friend gave me a copy of *Hamlet* to study in the African bush: it would, he hoped, lift my mind above its primitive surroundings, and possibly I might, by prolonged meditation, achieve the grace of correct interpretation. 2

   It was my second field trip to that African tribe, and I thought myself ready to live in one of its remote sections — an area difficult to cross even on foot. I eventually settled on the hillock of a very knowledgeable old man, the head of a homestead of some hundred and forty people, all of whom were either his close relatives or their wives and children. Like the other elders of the vicinity, the old man spent most of his time performing ceremonies seldom seen these days in the more 3 accessible parts of the tribe. I was delighted. Soon there would be three months of enforced isolation and leisure, between the harvest that takes place just before the rising of the swamps and the clearing of new farms when the water goes down. Then, I thought, they would have even more time to perform ceremonies and explain them to me.

I was quite mistaken. Most of the ceremonies demanded the presence of elders from several homesteads. As the swamps rose, the old men found it too difficult to walk from one homestead to the next, and the ceremonies gradually ceased. As the swamps rose even higher, all activities but one came to an end. The women brewed beer from maize and millet. Men, women, and children sat on their hillocks and drank it. 4

People began to drink at dawn. By midmorning the whole homestead was singing, dancing, and drumming. When it rained, people had to sit inside their huts: there they drank and sang or they drank and told stories. In any case, by noon or before, I either had to join the party or retire to my own hut and my books. "One does not discuss serious matters when there is beer. Come, drink with us." Since I lacked their capacity for the thick native beer, I spent more and more time with *Hamlet*. Before the end of the second month, grace descended on me. I was quite sure that *Hamlet* had only one possible interpretation, and that one universally obvious. 5

Early every morning, in the hope of having some serious talk before the beer party, I used to call on the old man at his reception hut—a circle of posts supporting a thatched roof above a low mud wall to keep out wind and rain. One day I crawled through the low doorway and found most of the men of the homestead sitting huddled in their ragged cloths on stools, low plank beds, and reclining chairs, warming themselves against the chill of the rain around a smoky fire. In the center were three pots of beer. The party had started. 6

The old man greeted me cordially. "Sit down and drink." I accepted a large calabash full of beer, poured some into a small drinking gourd, and tossed it down. Then I poured some more into the same gourd for the man second in seniority to my host before I handed my calabash over to a young man for further distribution. Important people shouldn't ladle beer themselves. 7

"It is better like this," the old man said, looking at me approvingly and plucking at the thatch that had caught in my hair. "You should sit and drink with us more often. Your servants tell me that when you are not with us, you sit inside your hut looking at a paper." 8

The old man was acquainted with four kinds of "papers": tax receipts, bride price receipts, court fee receipts, and letters. The messenger who brought him letters from the chief used them mainly as 9 a badge of office, for he always knew what was in them and told the old man. Personal letters for the few who had relatives in the government or mission stations were kept until someone went to a large market where there was a letter writer and reader. Since my arrival, letters were brought to me to be read. A few men also brought me bride price receipts, privately, with requests to change the figures to a higher sum. I found moral arguments were of no avail, since in-laws are fair game, and the technical hazards of forgery difficult to explain to an illiterate people. I did not wish them to think me silly enough to look at any such paper for days on end, and I hastily explained that my "paper" was one of the "things of long ago" of my country.

"Ah," said the old man. "Tell us."   10

I protested that I was not a storyteller. Storytelling is a skilled art   11
among them; their standards are high, and the audiences critical — and vocal in their criticism. I protested in vain. This morning they wanted to hear a story while they drank. They threatened to tell me no more stories until I told them one of mine. Finally, the old man promised that no one would criticize my style "for we know you are struggling with our language." "But," put in one of the elders, "you must explain what we do not understand, as we do when we tell you our stories." Realizing that here was my chance to prove *Hamlet* universally intelligible, I agreed.

The old man handed me some more beer to help me on with my   12
storytelling. Men filled their long wooden pipes and knocked coals from the fire to place in the pipe bowls; then, puffing contentedly, they sat back to listen. I began in the proper style.

"Not yesterday, not yesterday, but long ago, a thing occurred.   13
One night three men were keeping watch outside the homestead of the great chief, when suddenly they saw the former chief approach them."

"Why was he no longer their chief?"   14

"He was dead," I explained. "That is why they were troubled   15
and afraid when they saw him."

"Impossible," began one of the elders, handing his pipe on to his   16
neighbor, who interrupted, "Of course it wasn't the dead chief. It was an omen sent by a witch. Go on."

Slightly shaken, I continued. "One of these three was a man who   17
knew things" — the closest translation for scholar, but unfortunately it also meant witch. The second elder looked triumphantly at the first. "So he spoke to the dead chief saying, 'Tell us what we must do so you may rest in your grave,' but the dead chief did not answer. He vanished, and they could see him no more. Then the man who knew things — his name was Horatio — said this event was the affair of the dead chief's son, Hamlet."

*   *   *

There was a general shaking of heads round the circle. "Had the 18
dead chief no living brothers? Or was this son the chief?"

"No," I replied. "That is, he had one living brother who became 19
the chief when the elder brother died."

The old men muttered: such omens were matters for chiefs and 20
elders, not for youngsters; no good could come of going behind a
chief's back; clearly Horatio was not a man who knew things.

"Yes, he was," I insisted, shooing a chicken away from my beer. 21
"In our country the son is next to the father. The dead chief's younger
brother had become the great chief. He had also married his elder
brother's widow only about a month after the funeral."

"He did well," the old man beamed and announced to the others, 22
"I told you that if we knew more about Europeans, we would find
they really were very like us. In our country also," he added to me,
"the younger brother marries the elder brother's widow and becomes the father of his children. Now, if your uncle, who married
your widowed mother, is your father's full brother, then he will
be a real father to you. Did Hamlet's father and uncle have one
mother?"

His question barely penetrated my mind; I was too upset and 23
thrown too far off balance by having one of the most important elements of *Hamlet* knocked straight out of the picture. Rather uncer-
tainly I said that I thought they had the same mother, but I wasn't
sure — the story didn't say. The old man told me severely that these
genealogical details made all the difference and that when I got home I
must ask the elders about it. He shouted out the door to one of his
younger wives to bring his goatskin bag.

Determined to save what I could of the mother motif, I took a 24
deep breath and began again. "The son Hamlet was very sad because
his mother had married again so quickly. There was no need for her to
do so, and it is our custom for a widow not to go to her next husband
until she has mourned for two years."

"Two years is too long," objected the wife, who had appeared 25
with the old man's battered goatskin bag. "Who will hoe your farms for
you while you have no husband?"

"Hamlet," I retorted without thinking, "was old enough to hoe 26
his mother's farms himself. There was no need for her to remarry." No
one looked convinced. I gave up. "His mother and the great chief told
Hamlet not to be sad, for the great chief himself would be a father to
Hamlet. Furthermore, Hamlet would be the next chief: therefore he
must stay to learn the things of a chief. Hamlet agreed to remain, and
all the rest went off to drink beer."

While I paused, perplexed at how to render Hamlet's disgusted 27
soliloquy to an audience convinced that Claudius and Gertrude had

behaved in the best possible manner, one of the younger men asked me who had married the other wives of the dead chief.

"He had no other wives," I told him.   28

"But a chief must have many wives! How else can be brew beer   29
and prepare food for all his guests?"

I said firmly that in our country even chiefs had only one wife,   30
that they had servants to do their work, and that they paid them from
tax money.

It was better, they returned, for a chief to have many wives and   31
sons who would help him hoe his farms and feed his people; then
everyone loved the chief who gave much and took nothing — taxes
were a bad thing.

I agreed with the last comment, but for the rest fell back on their   32
favorite way of fobbing off my questions: "That is the way it is done, so
that is how we do it."

I decided to skip the soliloquy. Even if Claudius was here   33
thought quite right to marry his brother's widow, there remained the
poison motif, and I knew they would disapprove of fratricide. More
hopefully I resumed, "That night Hamlet kept watch with the three
who had seen his dead father. The dead chief again appeared, and
although the others were afraid, Hamlet followed his dead father off to
one side. When they were alone, Hamlet's dead father spoke."

"Omens can't talk!" The old man was emphatic.   34

"Hamlet's dead father wasn't an omen. Seeing him might have   35
been an omen, but he was not." My audience looked as confused as I
sounded. "It *was* Hamlet's dead father. It was a thing we call a
'ghost.'" I had to use the English word, for unlike many of the neigh-
boring tribes, these people didn't believe in the survival after death of
any individuating part of the personality.

"What is a 'ghost'? An omen?"   36

"No, a 'ghost' is someone who is dead but who walks around and   37
can talk, and people can hear him and see him but not touch him."

They objected. "One can touch zombis."   38

"No, no! It was not a dead body the witches had animated to   39
sacrifice and eat. No one else made Hamlet's dead father walk. He did
it himself."

"Dead men can't walk," protested my audience as one man.   40

I was quite willing to compromise. "A 'ghost' is the dead man's   41
shadow."

But again they objected. "Dead men cast no shadows."   42

"They do in my country," I snapped.   43

The old man quelled the babble of disbelief that arose immedi-   44
ately and told me with that insincere, but courteous, agreement one
extends to the fancies of the young, ignorant, and superstitious, "No

doubt in your country the dead can also walk without being zombis."
From the depths of his bag he produced a withered fragment of kola
nut, bit off one end to show it wasn't poisoned, and handed me the rest
as a peace offering.

"Anyhow," I resumed, "Hamlet's dead father said that his own   45
brother, the one who became chief, had poisoned him. He wanted
Hamlet to avenge him. Hamlet believed this in his heart, for he did not
like his father's brother." I took another swallow of beer. "In the
country of the great chief, living in the same homestead, for it was a
very large one, was an important elder who was often with the chief to
advise and help him. His name was Polonius. Hamlet was courting his
daughter, but her father and her brother . . . [I cast hastily about for
some tribal analogy] warned her not to let Hamlet visit her when she
was alone on her farm, for he would be a great chief and so could not
marry her."

"Why not?" asked the wife, who had settled down on the edge of   46
the old man's chair. He frowned at her for asking stupid questions and
growled, "They live in the same homestead."

"That was not the reason," I informed them. "Polonius was a   47
stranger who lived in the homestead because he helped the chief, not
because he was a relative."

"Then why couldn't Hamlet marry her?"   48

"He could have," I explained, "But Polonius didn't think he   49
would. After all, Hamlet was a man of great importance who ought to
marry a chief's daughter, for in his country a man could have only one
wife. Polonius was afraid that if Hamlet made love to his daughter,
then no one else would give a high price for her."

"That might be true," remarked one of the shrewder elders, "but   50
a chief's son would give his mistress's father enough presents and
patronage to more than make up the difference. Polonius sounds like a
fool to me."

"Many people think he was," I agreed. "Meanwhile Polonius   51
sent his son Laertes off to Paris to learn the things of that country, for it
was the homestead of a very great chief indeed. Because he was afraid
that Laertes might waste a lot of money on beer and women and
gambling, or get into trouble by fighting, he sent one of his servants to
Paris secretly, to spy out what Laertes was doing. One day Hamlet came
upon Polonius's daughter Ophelia. He behaved so oddly he frightened
her. Indeed" — I was fumbling for words to express the dubious quality of Hamlet's madness — "the chief and many others had also noticed
that when Hamlet talked one could understand the words but not what
they meant. Many people thought that he had become mad." My
audience suddenly became much more attentive. "The great chief
wanted to know what was wrong with Hamlet, so he sent for two of

Hamlet's age mates [school friends would have taken long explanation] to talk to Hamlet and find out what troubled his heart. Hamlet, seeing that they had been bribed by the chief to betray him, told them nothing. Polonius, however, insisted that Hamlet was mad because he had been forbidden to see Ophelia, whom he loved."

"Why," inquired a bewildered voice, "should anyone bewitch Hamlet on that account?" 52

"Bewitch him?" 53

"Yes, only witchcraft can make anyone mad, unless, of course, one sees the beings that lurk in the forest." 54

I stopped being a storyteller, took out my notebook and demanded to be told more about these two causes of madness. Even while they spoke and I jotted notes, I tried to calculate the effect of this new factor on the plot. Hamlet had not been exposed to the beings that lurk in the forests. Only his relatives in the male line could bewitch him. Barring relatives not mentioned by Shakespeare, it had to be Claudius who was attempting to harm him. And, of course, it was. 55

For the moment I staved off questions by saying that the great chief also refused to believe that Hamlet was mad for the love of Ophelia and nothing else. "He was sure that something much more important was troubling Hamlet's heart." 56

"Now Hamlet's age mates," I continued, "had brought with them a famous storyteller. Hamlet decided to have this man tell the chief and all his homestead a story about a man who had poisoned his brother because he desired his brother's wife and wished to be chief himself. Hamlet was sure the great chief could not hear the story without making a sign if he was indeed guilty, and then he would discover whether his dead father had told him the truth." 57

The old man interrupted, with deep cunning, "Why should a father lie to his son?" he asked. 58

I hedged: "Hamlet wasn't sure that it really was his dead father." It was impossible to say anything, in that language, about devil-inspired visions. 59

"You mean," he said, "it actually was an omen, and he knew witches sometimes send false ones. Hamlet was a fool not to go to one skilled in reading omens and divining the truth in the first place. A man-who-sees-the-truth could have told him how his father died, if he really had been poisoned, and if there was witchcraft in it; then Hamlet could have called the elders to settle the matter." 60

The shrewd elder ventured to disagree. "Because his father's brother was a great chief, one-who-sees-the-truth might therefore have been afraid to tell it. I think it was for that reason that a friend of Hamlet's father—a witch and an elder—sent an omen so his friend's son would know. Was the omen true?" 61

"Yes," I said, abandoning ghosts and the devil; a witch-sent omen   62
it would have to be. "It was true, for when the storyteller was telling
his tale before all the homestead, the great chief rose in fear. Afraid
that Hamlet knew his secret he planned to have him killed."

The stage set of the next bit presented some difficulties of trans-   63
lation. I began cautiously. "The great chief told Hamlet's mother to
find out from her son what he knew. But because a woman's children
are always first in her heart, he had the important elder Polonius hide
behind a cloth that hung against the wall of Hamlet's mother's
sleeping hut. Hamlet started to scold his mother for what she had
done."

There was a shocked murmur from everyone. A man should never   64
scold his mother.

"She called out in fear, and Polonius moved behind the cloth.   65
Shouting, 'A rat!' Hamlet took his machete and slashed through the
cloth." I paused for dramatic effect. "He had killed Polonius!"

The old men looked at each other in supreme disgust. "That   66
Polonius truly was a fool and a man who knew nothing! What child
would not know enough to shout, 'It's me!'" With a pang, I remembered that these people are ardent hunters, always armed with bow,
arrow, and machete; at the first rustle in the grass an arrow is aimed
and ready, and the hunter shouts "Game!" If no human voice answers
immediately, the arrow speeds on its way. Like a good hunter Hamlet
had shouted, "A rat!"

I rushed in to save Polonius's reputation. "Polonius did speak.   67
Hamlet heard him. But he thought it was the chief and wished to kill
him to avenge his father. He had meant to kill him earlier that
evening. . . ." I broke down, unable to describe to these pagans,
who had no belief in individual afterlife, the difference between
dying at one's prayers and dying "unhousell'd, disappointed,
unaneled."

This time I had shocked my audience seriously. "For a man to   68
raise his hand against his father's brother and the one who had become
his father — that is a terrible thing. The elders ought to let such a man
be bewitched."

I nibbled at my kola nut in some perplexity, then pointed out   69
that after all the man had killed Hamlet's father.

"No," pronounced the old man, speaking less to me than to the   70
young men sitting behind the elders. "If your father's brother has
killed your father, you must appeal to your father's age mates; *they*
may avenge him. No man may use violence against his senior relatives." Another thought struck him. "But if his father's brother had
indeed been wicked enough to bewitch Hamlet and make him mad
that would be a good story indeed, for it would be his fault that

Hamlet, being mad, no longer had any sense and thus was ready to kill his father's brother.''

There was a murmur of applause. *Hamlet* was again a good story   71
to them, but it no longer seemed quite the same story to me. As I thought over the coming complications of plot and motive, I lost courage and decided to skim over dangerous ground quickly.

"The great chief," I went on, "was not sorry that Hamlet had   72
killed Polonius. It gave him a reason to send Hamlet away, with his two treacherous age mates, with letters to a chief of a far country, saying that Hamlet should be killed. But Hamlet changed the writing on their papers, so that the chief killed his age mates instead." I encountered a reproachful glare from one of the men whom I had told undetectable forgery was not merely immoral but beyond human skill. I looked the other way.

"Before Hamlet could return, Laertes came back for his father's   73
funeral. The great chief told him Hamlet had killed Polonius. Laertes swore to kill Hamlet because of this, and because his sister Ophelia, hearing her father had been killed by the man she loved, went mad and drowned in the river."

"Have you already forgotten what we told you?" The old man was   74
reproachful. "One cannot take vengeance on a madman; Hamlet killed Polonius in his madness. As for the girl, she not only went mad, she was drowned. Only witches can make people drown. Water itself can't hurt anything. It is merely something one drinks and bathes in."

I began to get cross. "If you don't like the story, I'll stop."   75

The old man made soothing noises and himself poured me some   76
more beer. "You tell the story well, and we are listening. But it is clear that the elders of your country have never told you what the story really means. No, don't interrupt! We believe you when you say your marriage customs are different, or your clothes and weapons. But people are the same everywhere; therefore, there are always witches and it is we, the elders, who know how witches work. We told you it was the great chief who wished to kill Hamlet, and now your own words have proved us right. Who were Ophelia's male relatives?"

"There were only her father and her brother." Hamlet was   77
clearly out of my hands.

"There must have been many more; this also you must ask of your   78
elders when you get back to your country. From what you tell us, since Polonius was dead, it must have been Laertes who killed Ophelia, although I do not see the reason for it."

We had emptied one pot of beer, and the old men argued the   79 point with slightly tipsy interest. Finally one of them demanded of me, "What did the servant of Polonius say on his return?"

With difficulty I recollected Reynaldo and his mission. "I don't   80 think he did return before Polonius was killed."

"Listen," said the elder, "and I will tell you how it was and how   81 your story will go, then you may tell me if I am right. Polonius knew his son would get into trouble, and so he did. He had many fines to pay for fighting, and debts from gambling. But he had only two ways of getting money quickly. One was to marry off his sister at once, but it is difficult to find a man who will marry a woman desired by the son of a chief. For if the chief's heir commits adultery with your wife, what can you do? Only a fool calls a case against a man who will someday be his judge. Therefore Laertes had to take the second way: he killed his sister by witchcraft, drowning her so he could secretly sell her body to the witches."

I raised an objection. "They found her body and buried it. Indeed   82 Laertes jumped into the grave to see his sister once more — so, you see, the body was truly there. Hamlet, who had just come back, jumped in after him."

"What did I tell you?" The elder appealed to the others. "Laertes   83 was up to no good with his sister's body. Hamlet prevented him, because the chief's heir, like a chief, does not wish any other man to grow rich and powerful. Laertes would be angry, because he would have killed his sister without benefit to himself. In our country he would try to kill Hamlet for that reason. Is this not what happened?"

"More or less," I admitted. "When the great chief found Hamlet   84 was still alive, he encouraged Laertes to try to kill Hamlet and arranged a fight with machetes between them. In the fight both the young men were wounded to death. Hamlet's mother drank the poisoned beer that the chief meant for Hamlet in case he won the fight. When he saw his mother die of poison, Hamlet, dying, managed to kill his father's brother with his machete."

"You see, I was right!" exclaimed the elder.   85

"That was a very good story," added the old man, "and you told   86 it with very few mistakes. There was just one more error, at the very end. The poison Hamlet's mother drank was obviously meant for the survivor of the fight, whichever it was. If Laertes had won, the great chief would have poisoned him, for no one would know that he arranged Hamlet's death. Then, too, he need not fear Laertes' witchcraft; it takes a strong heart to kill one's only sister by witchcraft.

"Sometime," concluded the old man, gathering his ragged toga   87 about him, "you must tell us some more stories of your country. We, who are elders, will instruct you in their true meaning, so that when you return to your own land your elders will see that you have not been sitting in the bush, but among those who know things and who have taught you wisdom."

EXERCISES

Words to Know

meditation (paragraph 2), homesteads (4), calabash (7), gourd (7), bride price (9), no avail (9), intelligible (11), omen (16), genealogical (23), motif (24), retorted (26), soliloquy (27), fobbing off (32), fratricide (33), quelled (44), babble (44), dubious (51), cunning (58), hedged (59), unhousell'd (67), unaneled (67), toga (87).

Some of the Issues

1. In paragraphs 1 and 2 Bohannan and a friend discuss human nature in relation to Shakespeare's *Hamlet*. What are their opinions?
2. Read paragraphs 3 through 6. What were Bohannan's expectations for her second field trip to the Tiv, and why were they mistaken? How do her plans change?
3. What is the significance of the discussion about "papers" in paragraphs 8 and 9? How does it foretell that the Tivs' interpretation of *Hamlet* may differ from Bohannan's (and ours)?
4. In a number of instances, Bohannan shows that she is knowledgeable about the social customs of the Tiv and is trying to conform to them. Give some specific instances.
5. In paragraphs 24 through 32 two differences between the Tiv and the West are made clear: they relate to the period of mourning for the dead and to the number of wives a chief may have. In what way does the Tivs' view on these matters differ from Western views? Does their view have any advantages for their culture?
6. The Tiv elders are shocked — morally upset — at several parts of the story of *Hamlet*. What specific instances can you cite? Do their moral perceptions differ from ours in those instances?
7. Bohannan makes several efforts to make *Hamlet* more intelligible or acceptable to the Tiv. What are some of these? Does she succeed?
8. Both Bohannan (paragraph 2) and the chief (paragraph 76) say that human nature is much the same everywhere. What evidence do you find in the essay to support or contradict these assertions?

The Way We Are Told

9. Why does Bohannan begin her essay with the conversation with a friend at Oxford?

10. Several times in her essay Bohannan expresses surprise at the Tivs' reaction to her story. Is it possible that she was in reality not as surprised as she indicates?

Some Subjects for Essays

11. Bohannan does her best to adapt the story of Hamlet to the experiences, customs, and feelings of the Tiv. Have you ever had the experience of having to adapt yourself in some way to a situation in which the rules and assumptions differed greatly from your own? Tell the story.

12. Practice writing short, accurate summaries of stories, plays, movies, or television shows you know.

13. Describe a particular American event or activity to someone who has never experienced it. Topics might be Thanksgiving, a rock concert, a commencement exercise.

* 14. Read Clyde Kluckhohn's "Customs." He, like Bohannan, discusses the question of the universality of human nature. Write an essay in which you describe the view of each writer and compare their arguments.

* 15. Read "A Modest Proposal" by Jonathan Swift. In an essay demonstrate that both Bohannan and Swift adopt poses in order to make their arguments effectively.

SHOOTING AN ELEPHANT

George Orwell

George Orwell was born Eric Arthur Blair in India in 1903, of English parents. He was sent to England to attend one of its most famous public (that is, private) schools, Eton, on a scholarship, and hated it. Afterwards he returned to India and joined the Imperial Police, quitting it after five years. "Shooting an Elephant" recounts one experience he had in that service. In itself a minor event, it leads him to consider the role of colonial rule and rulers, and the steps they believe they must take to uphold their rule.

In Orwell's time Burma, where he was stationed, was a part of the Indian Empire under British rule. It was occupied by Japan during the Second World War. When India gained her independence, Burma became a separate, sovereign state in early 1948. A country about the size of Texas with a population of forty million, Burma, ruled by a heavy-handed military dictatorship, is largely closed off from the rest of the world.

After leaving India, Orwell turned to writing but with little success. He lived in great poverty for some time, as described in his first published book, *Down and Out in Paris and London* (1933). In the mid-1930s he fought on the side of the Republic in the Spanish Civil War, was wounded, and wrote of his experience in *Homage to Catalonia* (1938). Success finally came late in his life with *Animal Farm* (1945) and *1984*, both of which expressed his disillusionment with communism. *1984* was published in 1949, the year before his death from tuberculosis.

In Moulmein, in lower Burma, I was hated by large numbers of people 1
—the only time in my life that I have been important enough for this
to happen to me. I was sub-divisional police officer of the town, and in
an aimless, petty kind of way anti-European feeling was very bitter. No
one had the guts to raise a riot, but if a European woman went through
the bazaars alone somebody would probably spit betel juice over her
dress. As a police officer I was an obvious target and was baited
whenever it seemed safe to do so. When a nimble Burman tripped me
up on the football field and the referee (another Burman) looked the
other way, the crowd yelled with hideous laughter. This happened
more than once. In the end the sneering yellow faces of young men

that met me everywhere, the insults hooted after me when I was at a safe distance, got badly on my nerves. The young Buddhist priests were the worst of all. There were several thousands of them in the town and none of them seemed to have anything to do except stand on street corners and jeer at Europeans.

All this was perplexing and upsetting. For at that time I had already made up my mind that imperialism was an evil thing and the sooner I chucked up my job and got out of it the better. Theoretically — and secretly, of course — I was all for the Burmese and all against their oppressors, the British. As for the job I was doing, I hated it more bitterly than I can perhaps make clear. In a job like that you see the dirty work of Empire at close quarters. The wretched prisoners huddling in the stinking cages of the lockups, the grey, cowed faces of the long-term convicts, the scarred buttocks of the men who had been flogged with bamboos — all these oppressed me with an intolerable sense of guilt. But I could get nothing into perspective. I was young and ill-educated and I had had to think out my problems in the utter silence that is imposed on every Englishman in the East. I did not even know that the British Empire is dying, still less did I know that it is a great deal better than the younger empires that are going to supplant it. All I knew was that I was stuck between my hatred of the empire I served and my rage against the evil-spirited little beasts who tried to make my job impossible. With one part of my mind I thought of the British Raj as an unbreakable tyranny, as something clamped down, in *saecula saeculorum*, upon the will of prostrate peoples; with another part I thought that the greatest joy in the world would be to drive a bayonet into a Buddhist priest's guts. Feelings like these are the normal by-products of imperialism; ask any Anglo-Indian official, if you can catch him off duty.

One day something happened which in a roundabout way was enlightening. It was a tiny incident in itself, but it gave me a better glimpse than I had had before of the real nature of imperialism — the real motives for which despotic governments act. Early one morning the sub-inspector at a police station the other end of the town rang me up on the 'phone and said that an elephant was ravaging the bazaar. Would I please come and do something about it? I did not know what I could do, but I wanted to see what was happening and I got on to a pony and started out. I took my rifle, an old .44 Winchester and much too small to kill an elephant, but I thought the noise might be useful *in terrorem*. Various Burmans stopped me on the way and told me about the elephant's doings. It was not, of course, a wild elephant, but a tame one which had gone "must." It had been chained up, as tame elephants always are when their attack of "must" is due, but on the previous night it had broken its chain and escaped. Its mahout, the only person who could manage it when it was in that state, had set out in pursuit, but had taken the wrong direction and was now twelve hours' journey away, and in the morning the elephant had suddenly reappeared in the town. The Burmese population had no weapons and were quite helpless against it. It had already destroyed somebody's bamboo hut, killed a cow and raided some fruit-stalls and devoured the stock; also it had met the municipal rubbish van and, when the driver jumped out and took to his heels, had turned the van over and inflicted violences upon it.

The Burmese sub-inspector and some Indian constables were 4 waiting for me in the quarter where the elephant had been seen. It was a very poor quarter, a labyrinth of squalid bamboo huts, thatched with palm-leaf, winding all over a steep hillside. I remember that it was a cloudy, stuffy morning at the beginning of the rains. We began questioning the people as to where the elephant had gone and, as usual, failed to get any definite information. That is invariably the case in the East; a story always sounds clear enough at a distance, but the nearer you get to the scene of events the vaguer it becomes. Some of the people said that the elephant had gone in one direction, some said that he had gone in another, some professed not even to have heard of any elephant. I had almost made up my mind that the whole story was a pack of lies, when we heard yells a little distance away. There was a loud, scandalized cry of "Go away, child! Go away this instant!" and an old woman with a switch in her hand came round the corner of a hut, violently shooing away a crowd of naked children. Some more women followed, clicking their tongues and exclaiming; evidently there was something that the children ought not to have seen. I rounded the hut and saw a man's dead body sprawling in the mud. He was an Indian, a black Dravidian coolie, almost naked, and he could not have been dead many minutes. The people said that the elephant had come suddenly upon him round the corner of the hut, caught him with its trunk, put its foot on his back and ground him into the earth. This was the rainy season and the ground was soft; and his face had scored a trench a foot deep and a couple of yards long. He was lying on his belly with arms crucified and head sharply twisted to one side. His face was coated with mud, the eyes wide open, the teeth bared and grinning with an expression of unendurable agony. (Never tell me, by the way, that the dead look peaceful. Most of the corpses I have seen looked devilish.) The friction of the great beast's foot had stripped the skin from his back as neatly as one skins a rabbit. As soon as I saw the dead man I sent an orderly to a friend's house nearby to borrow an elephant rifle. I had already sent back the pony, not wanting it to go mad with fright and throw me if it smelt the elephant.

The orderly came back in a few minutes with a rifle and five 5 cartridges, and meanwhile some Burmans had arrived and told us that the elephant was in the paddy fields below, only a few hundred yards away. As I started forward practically the whole population of the quarter flocked out of the houses and followed me. They had seen the rifle and were all shouting excitedly that I was going to shoot the elephant. They had not shown much interest in the elephant when he was merely ravaging their homes, but it was different now that he was going to be shot. It was a bit of fun to them, as it would be to an English crowd; besides they wanted the meat. It made me vaguely uneasy. I had no intention of shooting the elephant — I had merely sent for the rifle to defend myself if necessary — and it is always unnerving to have a crowd following you. I marched down the hill, looking and feeling a fool, with the rifle over my shoulder and an ever-growing army of people jostling at my heels. At the bottom, when you got away from the huts, there was a metalled road and beyond that a miry waste of paddy fields a thousand yards across, not yet ploughed but soggy from the first rains and dotted with coarse grass. The elephant was standing eight yards from the road, his left side towards us. He took not the slightest notice of the crowd's approach. He was tearing up bunches of grass, beating them against his knees to clean them and stuffing them into his mouth.

I had halted on the road. As soon as I saw the elephant I knew   6 with perfect certainty that I ought not to shoot him. It is a serious matter to shoot a working elephant — it is comparable to destroying a huge and costly piece of machinery — and obviously one ought not to do it if it can possibly be avoided. And at that distance, peacefully eating, the elephant looked no more dangerous than a cow. I thought then and I think now that his attack of "must" was already passing off; in which case he would merely wander harmlessly about until the mahout came back and caught him. Moreover, I did not in the least want to shoot him. I decided that I would watch him for a little while to make sure that he did not turn savage again, and then go home.

But at that moment I glanced round at the crowd that had fol-   7 lowed me. It was an immense crowd, two thousand at the least and growing every minute. It blocked the road for a long distance on either side. I looked at the sea of yellow faces above the garish clothes — faces all happy and excited over this bit of fun, all certain that the elephant was going to be shot. They were watching me as they would watch a conjurer about to perform a trick. They did not like me, but with the magical rifle in my hands I was momentarily worth watching. And suddenly I realized that I should have to shoot the elephant after all. The people expected it of me and I had got to do it; I could feel their two thousand wills pressing me forward, irresistibly. And it was at this moment, as I stood there with the rifle in my hands, that I first grasped the hollowness, the futility of the white man's dominion in the East. Here was I, the white man with his gun, standing in front of the unarmed native crowd — seemingly the leading actor of the piece; but in reality I was only an absurd puppet pushed to and fro by the will of those yellow faces behind. I perceived in this moment that when the white man turns tyrant it is his own freedom that he destroys. He becomes a sort of hollow, posing dummy, the conventionalized figure of a sahib. For it is the condition of his rule that he shall spend his life in trying to impress the "natives," and so in every crisis he has got to do what the "natives" expect of him. He wears a mask, and his face grows to fit it. I had got to shoot the elephant. I had committed myself to doing it when I sent for the rifle. A sahib has got to act like a sahib; he has got to appear resolute, to know his own mind and do definite things. To come all that way, rifle in hand, with two thousand people marching at my heels, and then to trail feebly away, having done nothing — no, that was impossible. The crowd would laugh at me. And my whole life, every white man's life in the East, was one long struggle not to be laughed at.

But I did not want to shoot the elephant. I watched him beating   8
his bunch of grass against his knees, with that preoccupied grand-motherly air that elephants have. It seemed to me that it would be murder to shoot him. At that age I was not squeamish about killing animals, but I had never shot an elephant and never wanted to. (Some-how it always seems worse to kill a *large* animal.) Besides, there was the beast's owner to be considered. Alive, the elephant was worth at least a hundred pounds; dead, he would only be worth the value of his tusks, five pounds, possibly. But I had got to act quickly. I turned to some experienced-looking Burmans who had been there when we arrived, and asked them how the elephant had been behaving. They all said the same thing: he took no notice of you if you left him alone, but he might charge if you went too close to him.

It was perfectly clear to me what I ought to do. I ought to walk up   9
to within, say, twenty-five yards of the elephant and test his behavior. If he charged, I could shoot; if he took no notice of me, it would be safe to leave him until the mahout came back. But also I knew that I was going to do no such thing. I was a poor shot with a rifle and the ground was soft mud into which one would sink at every step. If the elephant charged and I missed him, I should have about as much chance as a toad under a steam-roller. But even then I was not thinking particularly of my own skin, only of the watchful yellow faces behind. For at that moment, with the crowd watching me, I was not afraid in the ordinary sense, as I would have been if I had been alone. A white man mustn't be frightened in front of "natives"; and so, in general, he isn't frightened. The sole thought in my mind was that if anything went

wrong those two thousand Burmans would see me pursued, caught, trampled on and reduced to a grinning corpse like that Indian up the hill. And if that happened it was quite probable that some of them would laugh. That would never do. There was only one alternative. I shoved the cartridges into the magazine and lay down on the road to get a better aim.

The crowd grew very still, and a deep, low, happy sigh, as of   10
people who see the theatre curtain go up at last, breathed from innumerable throats. They were going to have their bit of fun after all. The rifle was a beautiful German thing with cross-hair sights. I did not then know that in shooting an elephant one would shoot to cut an imaginary bar running from ear-hole to ear-hole. I ought, therefore, as the elephant was sideways on, to have aimed straight at his ear-hole; actually I aimed several inches in front of this, thinking the brain would be further forward.

When I pulled the trigger I did not hear the bang or feel the   11
kick — one never does when a shot goes home — but I heard the devilish roar of glee that went up from the crowd. In that instant, in too short a time, one would have thought, even for the bullet to get there, a mysterious, terrible change had come over the elephant. He neither stirred nor fell, but every line of his body had altered. He looked suddenly stricken, shrunken, immensely old, as though the frightful impact of the bullet had paralysed him without knocking him down. At last, after what seemed a long time — it might have been five seconds, I dare say — he sagged flabbily to his knees. His mouth slobbered. An enormous senility seemed to have settled upon him. One could have imagined him thousands of years old. I fired again into the same spot. At the second shot he did not collapse but climbed with desperate slowness to his feet and stood weakly upright, with legs sagging and head drooping. I fired a third time. That was the shot that did for him. You could see the agony of it jolt his whole body and knock the last remnant of strength from his legs. But in falling he seemed for a moment to rise, for as his hind legs collapsed beneath him he seemed to tower upward like a huge rock toppling, his trunk reaching skywards like a tree. He trumpeted, for the first and only time. And then down he came, his belly towards me, with a crash that seemed to shake the ground even where I lay.

I got up. The Burmans were already racing past me across the   12
mud. It was obvious that the elephant would never rise again, but he was not dead. He was breathing very rhythmically with long rattling gasps, his great mound of a side painfully rising and falling. His mouth was wide open — I could see far down into caverns of pale pink throat. I waited a long time for him to die, but his breathing did not weaken. Finally I fired my two remaining shots into the spot where I thought

his heart must be. The thick blood welled out of him like red velvet, but still he did not die. His body did not even jerk when the shots hit him, the tortured breathing continued without a pause. He was dying, very slowly and in great agony, but in some world remote from me where not even a bullet could damage him further. I felt that I had got to put an end to that dreadful noise. It seemed dreadful to see the great beast lying there, powerless to move and yet powerless to die, and not even to be able to finish him. I sent back for my small rifle and poured shot after shot into his heart and down his throat. They seemed to make no impression. The tortured gasps continued as steadily as the ticking of a clock.

In the end I could not stand it any longer and went away. I heard   13
later that it took him half an hour to die. Burmans were bringing dahs and baskets even before I left, and I was told they had stripped his body almost to the bones by the afternoon.

Afterwards, of course, there were endless discussions about the   14
shooting of the elephant. The owner was furious, but he was only an Indian and could do nothing. Besides, legally I had done the right thing, for a mad elephant has to be killed, like a mad dog, if its owner fails to control it. Among the Europeans opinion was divided. The older men said I was right, the younger men said it was a damn shame to shoot an elephant for killing a coolie, because an elephant was worth more than any damn Coringhee coolie. And afterwards I was very glad that the coolie had been killed; it put me legally in the right and it gave me a sufficient pretext for shooting the elephant. I often wondered whether any of the others grasped that I had done it solely to avoid looking a fool.

EXERCISES

Words to Know

perplexing (paragraph 2), imperialism (2), supplant (2), British Raj (2), *saecula saeculorum*—for all time (2), prostrate (2), ravaging (3), bazaar (3), *in terrorem*—to spread terror (3), mahout (3), rubbish (3), Dravidian (4), jostling (5), conjurer (7), conventionalized (7), sahib (7), flabbily (11), senility (11), dahs (13).

Some of the Issues

1. Before Orwell begins to tell the story of the shooting of the elephant, he uses two paragraphs to talk about feelings: the feelings of

the Burmese toward him as a colonial officer, and his own "perplexing and unsettling" feelings toward the Burmese. Why are Orwell's feelings complex and contradictory? How does this discussion of attitudes set the scene for the narrative that follows?

2. The main topic or theme of the essay is stated in the first few sentences of paragraph 3. After reading the whole essay, explain why the incident Orwell describes gave him "a better glimpse of the real nature of imperialism." What, according to Orwell, are "the real motives for which despotic governments act"?

3. In paragraph 7 Orwell says, "I perceived in this moment that when the white man turns tyrant it is his own freedom he destroys." Explain the meaning of this sentence; how does it apply to the story Orwell tells?

The Way We Are Told

4. When Orwell begins to tell the story of the elephant, in paragraph 3, he continues to reveal his attitude toward the Burmese in various indirect ways. Try to show how he does this.

5. In paragraph 4 Orwell describes the dead coolie in considerable detail. Compare that description to the one of the elephant's death. How do the descriptions differ? What are some of the words and phrases that show the difference?

6. In paragraphs 5 through 9 Orwell discusses his plans and options regarding the elephant. Paragraphs 5 and 6, however, differ greatly from 7, 8, and 9, both in content and treatment. Characterize the difference.

Some Subjects for Essays

7. Have you ever been placed in a situation in which you were forced to do something that you did not entirely agree with? For example, an employee must often carry out the policies of his or her employer even while disagreeing with them. Write an essay describing such an incident and detail your feelings before, during, and after.

8. Orwell is placed in a position of authority but finds that it restricts his scope of action rather than expands it. Write an essay that asserts the truth of this apparent contradiction. Try to find examples of other situations in which the possession of power limits the possessor.

LIVING IN A
JAPANESE HOME

John David Morley

John David Morley was born in Singapore in 1948, of British parents, and educated at Oxford University. His earliest job was as tutor to the children of Elizabeth Taylor and Richard Burton when they were filming in Mexico. His interest in the theater led him to Japanese theater and eventually to Japanese culture in general. He taught himself Japanese, studied at the Language Research Institute at Waseda University in Tokyo, and then went to work for Japanese Television as liaison officer, interpreter, and researcher, stationed in Munich, Germany. In 1985 he published a novel, *Pictures from the Water Trade: Adventures of a Westerner in Japan*, from which the present selection is taken. The novel is based on some of his own experiences.

The Japanese island empire successfully managed to isolate itself from foreign influences until the middle of the nineteenth century. Once that isolation had been breached, however, Japan moved rapidly to catch up with the Western world, not only by industrializing but also by following the major powers' expansionist policies. Japan fought a successful war with Russia (1905), occupied and eventually annexed Korea (1910), and in the 1930s, occupied Manchuria and large parts of China. After her surprise attack on Pearl Harbor (December 7, 1941), Japan had spectacular initial successes in World War II, occupying the Philippines, Indochina, Indonesia, Burma, and Singapore. Defeated and virtually destroyed in the later phases of the war, Japan was occupied by the U.S. Army under General Douglas MacArthur, whose administration of the islands is primarily responsible for converting Japan into a constitutional monarchy with a parliamentary government. Japan's economic recovery has been spectacular —today the country is the second most powerful industrial nation in the world. Japan's success is all the more remarkable when one considers that the country has almost no natural resources of its own on its crowded islands. With its size smaller than California, it has 122 million inhabitants, half as many as the United States.

Japanese society is highly homogeneous, has a very low crime rate, a very high level of literacy, and is considered very hard-working. To learn more about the causes of Japan's industrial prowess, read Adam Smith's "The Japanese Model"; to learn more about Japanese life, read Ian Buruma's "Public Life in Japan."

The introduction was arranged through a mutual acquaintance, Yo-   1
shida, at the private university where Boon was taking language
courses and where Sugama was employed on the administrative staff.
They met one afternoon in the office of their acquaintance and in-
spected each other warily for ten minutes.

"Nice weather," said Boon facetiously as he shook hands with   2
Sugama. Outside it was pouring with rain.

"Nice weather?" repeated Sugama doubtfully, glancing out of the   3
window. "But it's raining."

It was not a good start.   4

Sugama had just moved into a new apartment. It was large   5
enough for two, he said, but he was looking for someone to share the
expenses. This straightforward information arrived laboriously, in bits
and pieces, sandwiched between snippets of Sugama's personal history
and vague professions of friendship, irritating to Boon, because at the
time he felt they sounded merely sententious. All this passed back and
forth between Sugama and Boon through the mouth of their mutual
friend, as Boon understood almost no Japanese and Sugama's English,
though well-intentioned, was for the most part impenetrable.

It made no odds to Boon where he lived or with whom. All he   6
wanted was a Japanese-speaking environment in order to absorb the
language as quickly as possible. He had asked for a family, but none
was available.

One windy afternoon in mid-October the three of them met   7
outside the gates of the university and set off to have a look at Sugama's
new apartment. It was explained to Boon that cheap apartments in
Tokyo were very hard to come by, the only reasonable accommodation
available being confined to housing estates subsidised by the government. Boon wondered how a relatively prosperous bachelor like Sugama managed to qualify for government-subsidised housing. Sugama
admitted that this was in fact only possible because his grandfather
would also be living there. It was the first Boon had heard of the matter
and he was rather taken aback.

It turned out, however, that the grandfather would "very sel-   8
dom" be there — in fact, that he wouldn't live there at all. He would
only be there on paper, he and his grandson constituting a "family."
That was the point. "You must *say* he is there," said Sugama
emphatically.

The grandfather lived a couple of hundred miles away, and al-   9
though he never once during the next two years set foot in the apartment he still managed to be the bane of Boon's life. A constant stream
of representatives from charities, government agencies and old people's clubs, on average one or two a month, came knocking on the
door, asking to speak to grandfather. At first grandfather was simply

"not in" or had "gone for a walk," but as time passed and the flow of visitors never faltered, Boon found himself having to resort to more drastic measures. Grandfather began to make long visits to his home in the country; he had not yet returned because he didn't feel up to making the journey; his health gradually deteriorated. Finally Boon decided to have him invalided, and for a long time his condition remained "grave". On grandfather's behalf Boon received the condolences of all these visitors, and occasionally even presents.

Two years later grandfather did in fact die. Boon was thus exonerated, but in the meantime he had got to know grandfather well and had become rather fond of him. He attended his funeral with mixed feelings. 10

Sugama had acquired tenure of his government-subsidised apartment by a stroke of luck. He had won a ticket in a lottery. These apartments were much sought after, and in true Japanese style their distribution among hundreds of thousands of applicants was discreetly left to fate. The typical tenant was a young couple with one or two children, who would occupy the apartment for ten or fifteen years, often under conditions of bleak frugality, in order to save money to buy a house. Although the rent was not immoderate, prices generally in Tokyo were high, and it was a mystery to Boon how such people managed to live at all. Among the lottery winners there were inevitably also those people for whom the acquisition of an apartment was just a prize, an unexpected bonus, to be exploited as a financial investment. It was no problem for these nominal tenants to sub-let their apartments at prices well above the going rate. 11

Boon had never lived on a housing estate and his first view of the tall concrete compound where over fifty thousand people lived did little to reassure him. Thousands of winner families were accommodated in about a dozen rectangular blocks, each between ten and fifteen stories high, apparently in no way different (which disappointed Boon most of all) from similar housing compounds in Birmingham or Berlin. He had naively expected Japanese concrete to be different, to have a different colour, perhaps, or a more exotic shape. 12

But when Sugama let them into the apartment and Boon saw the interior he immediately took heart: this was unmistakably Japanese. Taking off their shoes in the tiny box-like hall, the three of them padded reverently through the kitchen into the *tatami* rooms. 13

"Smell of fresh *tatami*," pronounced Sugama, wrinkling his nose. 14

Boon was ecstatic. Over the close-woven pale gold straw matting lay a very faint greenish shimmer, sometimes perceptible and sometimes not, apparently in response to infinitesimal shifts in the texture of the falling light. The *tatami* was quite unlike a carpet or any other 15 form of floor-covering he had ever seen. It seemed to be alive, humming with colours he could sense rather than see, like a greening tree in the brief interval between winter and spring. He stepped on to it and felt the fibres recoil, sinking under the weight of his feet, slowly and softly.

"You can see green?" asked Sugama, squatting down.   16

"Yes indeed."   17

"Fresh *tatami*. Smell of grass, green colour. But not for long, few weeks only."   18

"What exactly is it?"   19

"Yes."   20

Boon turned to Yoshida and repeated the question, who in turn asked Sugama and conferred with him at length.   21

"*Tatami* comes from *oritatamu*, which means to fold up. So it's a kind of matting you can fold up."   22

"Made of straw."   23

"Yes."   24

"How long does it last?"   25

Long consultation.   26

"He says this is not so good quality. Last maybe four, five years."   27

"And then what?"   28

"New *tatami*. Quite expensive, you see. But very practical."   29

The three *tatami* rooms were divided by a series of *fusuma*, sliding screens made of paper and light wood. These screens were decorated at the base with simple grass and flower motifs; a natural extension, it occurred to Boon, of the grass-like *tatami* laid out inbetween. Sugama explained that the *fusuma* were usually kept closed in winter, and in summer, in order to have "nice breeze", they could be removed altogether. He also showed Boon the *shoji*, a type of sliding screen similar to the *fusuma* but more simple: an open wooden grid covered on one side with semi-transparent paper, primitive but rather beautiful. There was only one small section of *shoji* in the whole apartment; almost as a token, thought Boon, and he wondered why.   30

With the exception of a few one- and two-room apartments every house that Boon ever visited in Japan was designed to incorporate these three common elements: *tatami, fusuma* and *shoji*. In the houses of rich people the *tatami* might last longer, the *fusuma* decorations might be more costly, but the basic concept was the same. The interior design of all houses being much the same, it was not surprising to find certain similarities in the behaviour and attitudes of the people who lived in them.   31

The most striking feature of the Japanese house was lack of privacy; the lack of individual, inviolable space. In winter, when the   32 *fusuma* were kept closed, any sound above a whisper was clearly audible on the other side, and of course in summer they were usually removed altogether. It is impossible to live under such conditions for very long without a common household identity emerging which naturally takes precedence over individual wishes. This enforced family unity was still held up to Boon as an ideal, but in practice it was ambivalent, as much a yoke as a bond.

There was no such thing as the individual's private room, no 33 bedroom, dining- or sitting-room as such, since in the traditional Japanese house there was no furniture determining that a room should be reserved for any particular function. A person slept in a room, for example, without thinking of it as a bedroom or as his room. In the morning his bedding would be rolled up and stored away in a cupboard; a small table known as the *kotatsu*, which could also be plugged into the mains to provide heating, was moved back into the centre of the room and here the family ate, drank, worked and relaxed for the rest of the day. Although it was becoming standard practice in modern Japan for children to have their own rooms, many middle-aged and nearly all older Japanese still lived in this way. They regarded themselves as "one flesh", their property as common to all; the *uchi* (household, home) was constituted according to a principle of indivisibility. The system of moveable screens meant that the rooms could be used by all the family and for all purposes: walls were built round the *uchi*, not inside it.

Boon later discovered analogies between this concept of house 34 and the Japanese concept of self. The Japanese carried his house around in his mouth and produced it in everyday conversation, using the word *uchi* to mean "I", the representative of my house in the world outside. His self-awareness was naturally expressed as corporate individuality, hazy about quite what that included, very clear about what it did not.

Ittaikan, the traditional view of the corporate *uchi* as one flesh, 35 had unmistakably passed into decline in modern Japan. A watery sentiment remained, lacking the conviction that had once made the communal *uchi* as self-evident in practice as it was in principle. This was probably why people had become acutely aware of the problem of space, although they did not necessarily have less space now than they had had before. A tendency to restrict the spatial requirements of daily life quite voluntarily had been evident in Japan long before land became scarce. When the tea-room was first introduced during the Muromachi period (early fourteenth to late sixteenth century) the specification of its size was four and a half mats, but in the course of time this was reduced to one mat (two square metres). The reasons for this kind of scaling down were purely aesthetic. It was believed that only within a space as modest as this could the spirit of *wabi*, a taste for the simple and quiet, be truly cultivated.

The almost wearying sameness about all the homes which Boon   36
visited, despite differences in the wealth and status of their owners, prompted a rather unexpected conclusion: the classlessness of the Japanese house. The widespread use of traditional materials, the preservation of traditional structures, even if in such contracted forms as to have become merely symbolic, suggested a consensus about the basic requirements of daily life which was very remarkable, and which presumably held implications for Japanese society as a whole. Boon's insight into that society was acquired very slowly, after he had spent a great deal of time sitting on the *tatami* mats and looking through the sliding *fusuma* doors which had struck him as no more than pleasing curiosities on his first visit to a Japanese-style home.

EXERCISES

Words to Know

warily (paragraph 1), facetiously (2), laboriously (5), snippets (5), professions of friendship (5), sententious (5), impenetrable (5), prosperous (7), bane (9), faltered (9), deteriorated (9), invalided (9), condolences (9), exonerated (10), tenure (11), bleak frugality (11), exploited (11), nominal (12), naively (12), exotic (12), *tatami*— woven straw matting used as floor covering in Japanese homes (13), ecstatic (15), perceptible (15), infinitesimal (15), recoil (15), token (30), inviolable (32), audible (32), precedence (32), ambivalent (32), yoke (32), analogies (34), corporate individuality (34), consensus (36).

Some of the Issues

1. Describe the first meeting of Boon and Sugama. Why did Boon consider it "not a good start"?
2. Describe the selection process for government-subsidized housing in Japan — very different from Western practices. Can you find a rationale for the Japanese system?
3. On entering the new apartment Sugama wrinkles his nose while Boon is ecstatic. What accounts for their difference in attitude?
4. What are the key elements of the Japanese home? What are the advantages of this mode of living? What disadvantages does it have?

5. How does the arrangement condition the lives of the people who live in it? How does it reflect Japanese values?
6. Morley says that the most striking feature of the Japanese house is lack of privacy. Later he speaks of the classlessness of the Japanese home. How does he illustrate his two points?
* 7. Read Marcus Mabry's "Living in Two Worlds." Both Morley (through Boon) and Mabry are concerned with privacy, Morley when he joins Sugama and Mabry when he goes home to New Jersey. How and why are their attitudes different?

The Way We are Told

8. The author does not at any time refer to Western conditions and attitudes; yet they are constantly implied in his discussion of events, contacts with people, and descriptions of living conditions. Give some examples.
9. What does the author achieve by his gradual revelation of the truth about Sugama's grandfather?
10. The story is told by Boon, a fictional British visitor, but the experiences presumably reflect Morley's own. What does the author gain by creating Boon to tell his story?

Some Subjects for Essays

11. Compare and contrast the Western or American concept of privacy to the Japanese view as described by Morley. How does the physical environment of the Japanese home support Japanese notions of privacy? In describing the American living space, you might think of the "ideal" American family home, a bedroom for each child, preferably with a private bath, and a kitchen and family room as places for the family to gather.
12. How important is privacy to you? How did the physical environment in which you grew up shape your attitudes?

ELLIS ISLAND

Joseph Bruchac

Joseph Bruchac, born in 1942, is of mixed immigrant and native American ancestry. He teaches English at Hamilton College in Clinton, New York. He has written poetry and fiction and translated West African and Iroquois literature. He is the editor of *Breaking Silence*, a collection of Asian-American poetry.

Ellis Island in New York harbor became the main point of entry for immgrants to the United States in 1892. As many as a million people a year pased through its vast sheds in the early twentieth century, up to fifteen thousand being herded through in one day. (For more on the immigrants and the immigration procedures at Ellis Island, read Alistair Cooke's "The Huddled Masses.") Finally closed in 1954, it was abandoned and allowed to decay. In 1965 Ellis Island was declared a national landmark, but it was not until the 1980s that interest in its place in history became sufficiently strong to encourage moves toward its restoration. Work on it was begun in earnest at the time the Statue of Liberty, its neighbor, was being restored. In 1990 Ellis Island, partially restored as a museum of immigration and a national monument, was reopened to the public.

In his poem Joseph Bruchac concerns himself not only with the waves of immigration but with one of its results: the displacement of Native Americans from their ancestral lands.

Beyond the red brick of Ellis Island
where the two Slovak children
who became my grandparents
waited the long days of quarantine,
after leaving the sickness,
the old Empires of Europe,
a Circle Line ship slips easily
on its way to the island
of the tall woman, green
as dreams of forests and meadows
waiting for those who'd worked
a thousand years
yet never owned their own.

Like millions of others,
I too come to this island,

nine decades the answerer
of dreams.

Yet only one part of my blood loves that memory.
Another voice speaks
of native lands
within this nation.
Lands invaded
when the earth became owned.
Lands of those who followed
the changing Moon,
knowledge of the season
in their veins.

PART SEVEN

Customs

Mention the word *culture*, and the first thing that is likely to come to many people's minds will be museums, classical music, Shakespeare, or climbing about ancient ruins. Some may feel inspired by these thoughts while others may find them boring. However, culture has another basic definition, the one Clyde Kluckhohn uses in the first essay: culture is, quite simply, "the total life way of a people." In other words, in all that we say or do, believe or disbelieve, love or hate, find natural or unnatural, we are largely conditioned by our particular society—that is to say, by our culture.

Most people accept that increasing our knowledge of widely differing cultures sharpens our sense of the consequences of cultural differences. We find that most people will tolerate the idea of cultural differences at least as long as it remains an idea. Americans may not mind, for example, the fact that some people in Asia consider dogs desirable to eat. Eating dogs, defined as a custom, may seem strange, even offensive, but not of central concern as long as one is not obliged to participate. However, when cultural differences touch upon values we consider central, we may find them harder to accept.

Part Seven contains examples of cultural differences and their consequences. Clyde Kluckhohn, already mentioned, cites examples, both of the kind that create no particular problems of acceptance and those that do. Next, Leonore Tiefer develops a specific case. Americans and Europeans, who find kissing a natural expression of affection or even simply of greeting, may be surprised that in some other cultures kissing is merely considered an unsanitary habit. Ashley Montagu asserts that shedding tears, which many Americans think is "unmanly," that is, unnatural for a man, can on the other hand be seen as a healthy expression of feeling that should not be suppressed. Customs, or cultural attitudes, may have unexpected consequences: Conrad Phillip Kottak asserts that Brazil's relatively poor showing in the Olympics as compared to the United States is largely due to cultural differences. Ian Buruma cites two detailed examples taken from work situations in Japan which demonstrate some basic differences in attitude between that culture and accepted notions of behavior in the West.

The final selections in Part Seven are examples taken from an area of American life that has become more and more significant worldwide: television. The soap opera and the commercial are two cultural phenomena of American origin. How do they reflect the culture from which they come?

CUSTOMS

Clyde Kluckhohn

Clyde Kluckhohn (1905–1960) was at the time of his death a professor of anthropology at Harvard. As an undergraduate at Princeton, he became ill and was sent to New Mexico to recover. There he spent a great deal of time in Navaho country, learned the Navaho language, and developed a lifelong interest in Indian peoples. As a Rhodes scholar he studied at Oxford and received an M.A. from that university. At Harvard he played a major role in establishing its Russian Research Center. Among Kluckhohn's books are *To the Foot of the Rainbow* (1972), and several studies of the Navaho.

The selection included here is an excerpt from *Mirror for Man* (1949). In it Kluckhohn first defines the meaning of culture as "that part of the environment that is the creation of man." We may think of our way of doing things, our customs, as "natural" (and those of others that deviate from ours as "unnatural"). Kluckhohn, however, gives several examples to show that our reactions to people and events are culturally conditioned.

Why do the Chinese dislike milk and milk products? Why would the 1 Japanese die willingly in a Banzai charge that seemed senseless to Americans? Why do some nations trace descent through the father, others through the mother, still others through both parents? Not because different peoples have different instincts, not because they were destined by God or Fate to different habits, not because the weather is different in China and Japan and the United States. Sometimes shrewd common sense has an answer that is close to that of the anthropologist: "because they were brought up that way." By "culture" anthropology means the total life way of a people, the social legacy the individual acquires from his group. Or culture can be regarded as that part of the environment that is the creation of man.

This technical term has a wider meaning than the "culture" of 2 history and literature. A humble cooking pot is as much a cultural product as is a Beethoven sonata. In ordinary speech a man of culture is a man who can speak languages other than his own, who is familiar with history, literature, philosophy, or the fine arts. In some cliques that definition is still narrower. The cultured person is one who can talk about James Joyce, Scarlatti, and Picasso. To the anthropologist, however, to be human is to be cultured. There is culture in general,

271

and then there are the specific cultures such as Russian, American, British, Hottentot, Inca. The general abstract notion serves to remind us that we cannot explain acts solely in terms of the biological properties of the people concerned, their individual past experience, and the immediate situation. The past experience of other men in the form of culture enters into almost every event. Each specific culture constitutes a kind of blueprint for all of life's activities.

One of the interesting things about human beings is that they try   3
to understand themselves and their own behavior. While this has been particularly true of Europeans in recent times, there is no group which has not developed a scheme or schemes to explain man's actions. To the insistent human query "why?" the most exciting illumination anthropology has to offer is that of the concept of culture. Its explanatory importance is comparable to categories such as evolution in biology, gravity in physics, disease in medicine. A good deal of human behavior can be understood, and indeed predicted, if we know a people's design for living. Many acts are neither accidental nor due to personal peculiarities nor caused by supernatural forces nor simply mysterious. Even those of us who pride ourselves on our individualism follow most of the time a pattern not of our own making. We brush our teeth on arising. We put on pants — not a loincloth or a grass skirt. We eat three meals a day — not four or five or two. We sleep in a bed — not in a hammock or on a sheep pelt. I do not have to know the individual and his life history to be able to predict these and countless other regularities, including many in the thinking process of all Americans who are not incarcerated in jails or hospitals for the insane.

To the American woman a system of plural wives seems "instinc-   4
tively" abhorrent. She cannot understand how any woman can fail to be jealous and uncomfortable if she must share her husband with other women. She feels it "unnatural" to accept such a situation. On the other hand, a Koryak woman of Siberia, for example, would find it hard to understand how a woman could be so selfish and so undesirous of feminine companionship in the home as to wish to restrict her husband to one mate.

Some years ago I met in New York City a young man who did not   5
speak a word of English and was obviously bewildered by American ways. By "blood" he was as American as you or I, for his parents had gone from Indiana to China as missionaries. Orphaned in infancy, he was reared by a Chinese family in a remote village. All who met him found him more Chinese than American. The facts of his blue eyes and light hair were less impressive than a Chinese style of gait, Chinese arm and hand movements, Chinese facial expression, and Chinese modes of thought. The biological heritage was American, but the cultural training had been Chinese. He returned to China.

Another example of another kind: I once knew a trader's wife in   6
Arizona who took a somewhat devilish interest in producing a cultural
reaction. Guests who came her way were often served delicious sand-
wiches filled with a meat that seemed to be neither chicken nor tuna
fish yet was reminiscent of both. To queries she gave no reply until
each had eaten his fill. She then explained that what they had eaten
was not chicken, not tuna fish, but the rich, white flesh of freshly
killed rattlesnakes. The response was instantaneous — vomiting, often
violent vomiting. A biological process is caught in a cultural web.

A highly intelligent teacher with long and successful experience   7
in the public schools of Chicago was finishing her first year in an
Indian school. When asked how her Navaho pupils compared in intelligence with Chicago youngsters, she replied, "Well, I just don't
know. Sometimes the Indians seem just as bright. At other times they
just act like dumb animals. The other night we had a dance in the high
school. I saw a boy who is one of the best students in my English class
standing off by himself. So I took him over to a pretty girl and told
them to dance. But they just stood there with their heads down. They
wouldn't even say anything." I inquired if she knew whether or not
they were members of the same clan. "What difference would that
make?"

"How would you feel about getting into bed with your brother?"   8
The teacher walked off in a huff, but, actually, the two cases were
quite comparable in principle. To the Indian the type of bodily contact involved in our social dancing has a directly sexual connotation.
The incest taboos between members of the same clan are as severe as
between true brothers and sisters. The shame of the Indians at the
suggestion that a clan brother and sister should dance and the indigna-
tion of the white teacher at the idea that she should share a bed with an
adult brother represent equally nonrational responses, culturally standardized unreason.

All this does not mean that there is no such thing as raw human   9
nature. The very fact that certain of the same institutions are found in
all known societies indicates that at bottom all human beings are very
much alike. The files of the Cross-Cultural Survey at Yale University
are organized according to categories such as "marriage ceremonies,"
"life crisis rites," "incest taboos." At least seventy-five of these categories are represented in every single one of the hundreds of cultures
analyzed. This is hardly surprising. The members of all human groups
have about the same biological equipment. All men undergo the same
poignant life experiences such as birth, helplessness, illness, old age,
and death. The biological potentialities of the species are the blocks
with which cultures are built. Some patterns of every culture crystallize around focuses provided by the inevitables of biology: the differ-

ence between the sexes, the presence of persons of different ages, the varying physical strength and skill of individuals. The facts of nature also limit culture forms. No culture provides patterns for jumping over trees or for eating iron ore.

EXERCISES

Words to Know

Banzai charge (paragraph 1), shrewd (1), cliques (2), James Joyce (2), Scarlatti (2), Picasso (2), Hottentot (2), Inca (2), insistent (3), query (3), illumination (3), incarcerated (3), instinctively (4), abhorrent (4), gait (5), reminiscent (6), connotation (8), incest taboos (8), clan (8), life crisis rites (9), poignant (9), potentialities (9), species (9), crystallize (9), inevitable (9).

Some of the Issues

1. In the opening paragraphs Kluckhohn gives us two different definitions of the word "culture." Explain the difference between them.
2. Read the opening sentences of paragraph 3. What "illumination," according to Kluckhohn, does anthropology offer to "the insistent human query 'Why?'"
3. In the same paragraph Kluckhohn asserts that the "concept of culture" is comparable to concepts such as evolution or gravity. Do you think he is right to give it such importance?
4. Explain the meaning of the two anecdotes in paragraphs 5 and 6. Are they simply to present examples of cultural differences? Do they indicate more than that?
5. In what way does the anecdote in paragraphs 7 and 8 differ from the preceding two?
6. What is the point Kluckhohn tries to make when, at the end of paragraph 8, he sums up with the term "culturally standardized unreason"? Can you cite additional examples?
7. In paragraph 9, after citing several examples of cultural differences, Kluckhohn asserts that "at bottom all human beings are very much alike." Is he contradicting himself? Sum up Kluckhohn's arguments for both diversity and similarity.
8. Kluckhohn starts his essay with several questions. Does he answer them? What do you think is his purpose in beginning in this way?

The Way We Are Told

9. Read once more the three anecdotes told in paragraphs 5 through 8 and consider the order in which they are told. Is there a purpose in this order?

Some Subjects for Essays

10. Cultural differences can occur in many ways, often near to home. Describe a time when you encountered cultural differences — in a friend's house, with a fellow student, in some unfamiliar setting — and examine the effect on you as well as, perhaps, yours on the others involved.

11. The last twenty years have brought several major changes in customs in America; some of these reflect changes in attitude toward sex, women's roles, or religion. Select one major change; describe and analyze it.

* 12. Read John David Morley's "The Japanese Home" and Ian Buruma's "Public Life in Japan." Select two or three specific customs that differ from those usual in your culture. Examples may be Morley's description of the way recipients of public housing are selected or Buruma's account of business contacts. Compare and contrast these with related customs in your culture. How do the differences in custom reflect differences in values?

* 13. The photograph on page 268 shows a Japanese-American mother and son in California at a traditional festival, Obon. The boy is dressed to participate in the event. Cite, if you can, similar examples of the continuation of a traditional culture by people who have otherwise moved away from it. How important do you think is the continuation of such customs to the maintenance of a culture?

THE KISS

Leonore Tiefer

Leonore Tiefer is a professor of psychiatry at the Downstate Medical Center in Brooklyn, New York, where she also directs the Center for Human Sexuality. Her research is concerned with the complex psychological, social, and political causes of human behavior. She is the author of *Human Sexuality: Feelings and Functions*. "The Kiss" appeared in *Human Nature* magazine in July 1978. Here Tiefer asserts that, like all human customs, a kiss is not "natural" but learned behavior. She demonstrates this by describing cultures in which kissing is considered a strange, unnatural act.

Nothing seems more natural than a kiss. Consider the French kiss, also known as the soul kiss, deep kiss, or tongue kiss (to the French, it was the Italian kiss, but only during the Renaissance). Western societies regard this passionate exploration of mouths and tongues as an instinctive way to express love and to arouse desire. To a European who associates deep kisses with erotic response, the idea of one without the other feels like summer without sun. 1

Yet soul kissing is completely absent in many cultures of the world, where sexual arousal may be evoked by affectionate bites or stinging slaps. Anthropology and history amply demonstrate that, depending on time and place, the kiss may or may not be regarded as a sexual act, a sign of friendship, a gesture of respect, a health threat, a ceremonial celebration, or a disgusting behavior that deserves condemnation. 2

In my pursuit of the story of the kiss, two themes most appealed to me: the remarkable cultural and historical variation in styles and purposes of kissing; and the anatomical, evolutionary underpinning that has made the kiss such a successful signal. In spite of its cultural variants, the kiss is not an accident of civilization, an arbitrary gesture. There are reasons we kiss instead of bumping shoulders or tugging each other's ear lobes. 3

One of the first modern studies to dispel the belief that sexual behavior is universally the same (and therefore instinctive) was *Patterns of Sexual Behavior*, written in 1951 by Clellan Ford and Frank Beach. Ford and Beach compared many of the sexual customs of 190 4 tribal societies that were recorded in the Human Relations Area Files at Yale University.

Unfortunately, few of the field studies mentioned kissing customs at all. Of the 21 that did, some sort of kissing accompanied intercourse in 13 tribes — the Chiricahua, Cree, Crow, Gros Ventre, Hopi, Huichol, Kwakiutl, and Tarahumara of North America; the Alorese, Keraki, Trobrianders, and Trukese of Oceania; and in Eurasia, among the Lapps. Ford and Beach noted some variations: The Kwakiutl, Trobrianders, Alorese, and Trukese kiss by sucking the lips and tongue of their partners; the Lapps like to kiss the mouth and nose at the same time. (I would add Margaret Mead's observation of the Arapesh. They "possess the true kiss," she wrote: they touch lips, but instead of pressing, they mutually draw the breath in.)

But sexual kissing is unknown in many societies, including the Balinese, Chamorro, Manus, and Tinguian of Oceania; the Chewa and Thonga of Africa; the Siriono of South America; and the Lepcha of Eurasia. In such cultures the mouth-to-mouth kiss is considered dangerous, unhealthy, or disgusting, the way most Westerners would regard a custom of sticking one's tongue into a lover's nose. Ford and Beach report that when the Thonga first saw Europeans kissing they laughed, remarking, "Look at them — they eat each other's saliva and dirt."

Deep kissing apparently has nothing to do with the degree of sexual inhibition or repression in a culture. Donald S. Marshall, an anthropologist who studied a small Polynesian island he called Mangaia, found that all Mangaian woman are taught to be orgasmic and sexually active; yet kissing, sexual and otherwise, was unknown until Westerners (and their popular films) arrived on the island. In contrast, John C. Messenger found that on a sexually repressed Irish island where sex is considered dirty, sinful, and, for women, a duty to be endured, tongue kissing was unknown as late as 1966.

Many tribes across the African continent and elsewhere believe that the soul enters and leaves through the mouth and that a person's bodily products can be collected and saved by an enemy for harmful purposes. In these societies, Sir James Frazer wrote in *The Golden Bough*, the possible loss of saliva would cause a kiss to be regarded as a dangerous gesture. The "soul kiss" is taken literally. (It was taken figuratively in Western societies; recall Marlowe's "Sweet Helen, make me immortal with a kiss! Her lips suck forth my soul. . . .")

Although the deep kiss is relatively rare around the world as a part of sexual intimacy, other forms of mouth or nose contact are common — particularly the "oceanic kiss," named for its prevalence among cultures in Oceania, but not limited to them. The Tinguians place their lips near the partner's face and suddenly inhale. Balinese lovers bring their faces close enough to catch each other's perfume and to feel the warmth of the skin, making contact as they move their heads slightly. Paul d'Enjoy, a French anthropologist writing in 1897, described a kiss practiced by the Chinese, Yakuts, and Mongolians: The nose is pressed to the cheek, followed by a nasal inhalation and finally a smacking of lips.

The oceanic kiss may be varied by the placement of nose and cheek, vigor of the inhalation, the nature of accompanying sounds, action of the arms, and so on; and it is used for affectionate greeting as well as for sexual play. Some observers think that the so-called Eskimo or Malay kiss of rubbing noses is actually a mislabeled oceanic kiss: The kisser is simply moving his or her nose rapidly from one cheek to the other of the partner, bumping noses en route.   10

Small tribes and obscure Irish islanders are not the only groups to echew tongue kissing. The advanced civilizations of China and Japan, which regarded sexual proficiency as high art, apparently cared little about it. In their voluminous production of erotica — graphic displays of every possible sexual position, angle of intercourse, variation of partner and setting — mouth-to-mouth kissing is conspicuous by its absence. Japanese poets have rhapsodized for centuries about the allure of the nape of the neck, but they have been silent on the mouth; indeed, kissing is acceptable only between mother and child. (The Japanese have no word for kissing — though they recently borrowed from English to create "kissu.") Intercourse is "natural"; a kiss, pornographic. When Rodin's famous sculpture, *The Kiss*, came to Tokyo in the 1920s as part of a show of European art, it was concealed from public view behind a bamboo curtain.   11

Among cultures of the West, the number of nonsexual uses of the kiss is staggering. The simple kiss has served any or all of several purposes: greeting and farewell, affection, religious or ceremonial symbolism, deference to a person of higher status. (People also kiss icons, dice, and other objects, of course, in prayer, for luck, or as part of a ritual.) Kisses make the hurt go away, bless sacred vestments, seal a bargain. In story and legend a kiss has started wars and ended them, and awakened Sleeping Beauty and put Brunnhilde to sleep.   12

EXERCISES

Words to Know

dispel (paragraph 4), repression (7), Marlowe (8), prevalence (9), eschew (11), nape (11), Rodin (11), icon (12), Brunnhilde (12).

Some of the Issues

1. What is Tiefer's basic assertion about kissing? What evidence does she present?
2. Tiefer lists several different kinds of kisses "natural" to different societies. What are they?
3. A number of cultures consciously avoid or oppose kissing. What reasons do they have?

The Way We Are Told

4. Consider the opening sentence of paragraph 1. Why does Tiefer use "seems" rather than "is"?

Some Subjects for Essays

5. Tiefer uses a common device in presenting information: she begins by describing a commonly held assumption; in this case, that kissing is "natural," universal. Then she goes on to disprove this assumption by citing contrary evidence. Write an essay in which you try to disprove a commonly held assumption.
6. Select a group of products, activities, or type of persons of which you have some knowledge: bicycles, sports, teachers, and so on. Establish the main sets and subsets, and write an essay using your classification as an organizing principle.

AMERICAN SPACE, CHINESE PLACE

Yi-Fu Tuan

Yi-Fu Tuan was born in Tientsin (Tianjin), China, in 1930, the son of a diplomat. He received an M.A. from Oxford University and continued his education in the United States, earning a Ph.D. in geography from the University of California at Berkeley. He is Kirkland Wright Professor of Geography at the University of Wisconsin, having previously taught at several universities in the United States and Canada. Among his books are *Space and Place: The Perspective of Experience* (1977) and *Dominance and Affection: The Making of Pets* (1984).

The selection reprinted here appeared in *Harper's Magazine* in July 1974. In it Tuan explains the differences between a Chinese and an American house and shows that these differences reflect basic contrasts in the outlook of members of the two cultures.

For information about China, read Mark Salzman's "Teacher Mark." You may also want to read John David Morley's "Living in a Japanese Home" for yet another perspective on living space.

Americans have a sense of space, not of place. Go to an American home in exurbia, and almost the first thing you do is drift toward the picture window. How curious that the first compliment you pay your host inside his house is to say how lovely it is outside his house! He is pleased that you should admire his vistas. The distant horizon is not merely a line separating earth from sky, it is a symbol of the future. The American is not rooted in his place, however lovely: his eyes are drawn by the expanding space to a point on the horizon, which is his future.

By contrast, consider the traditional Chinese home. Blank walls enclose it. Step behind the spirit wall and you are in a courtyard with perhaps a miniature garden around the corner. Once inside the private compound you are wrapped in an ambiance of calm beauty, an ordered world of buildings, pavement, rock, and decorative vegetation. But you have no distant view: nowhere does space open out before you. Raw nature in such a home is experienced only as weather, and the only open space is the sky above. The Chinese is rooted in his place. When he has to leave, it is not for the promised land on the

280

terrestrial horizon, but for another world altogether along the vertical, religious axis of his imagination.

The Chinese tie to place is deeply felt. Wanderlust is an alien   3
sentiment. The Taoist classic *Tao Te Ching* captures the ideal of rootedness in place with these words: "Though there may be another country in the neighborhood so close that they are within sight of each other and the crowing of cocks and barking of dogs in one place can be heard in the other, yet there is no traffic between them; and through-out their lives the two peoples have nothing to do with each other." In theory if not in practice, farmers have ranked high in Chinese society. The reason is not only that they are engaged in the "root" industry of producing food but that, unlike pecuniary merchants, they are tied to the land and do not abandon their country when it is in danger.

Nostalgia is a recurrent theme in Chinese poetry. An American   4
reader of translated Chinese poems may well be taken aback — even put off — by the frequency, as well as the sentimentality of the lament for home. To understand the strength of this sentiment, we need to know that the Chinese desire for stability and rootedness in place is prompted by the constant threat of war, exile, and the natural disasters of flood and drought. Forcible removal makes the Chinese keenly aware of their loss. By contrast, Americans move, for the most part, voluntarily. Their nostalgia for home town is really longing for child-hood to which they cannot return: in the meantime the future beckons and the future is "out there," in open space. When we criticize American rootlessness we tend to forget that it is a result of ideals we admire, namely, social mobility and optimism about the future. When we admire Chinese rootedness, we forget that the word "place" means both location in space and position in society: to be tied to place is also to be bound to one's station in life, with little hope of betterment. Space symbolizes hope; place, achievement and stability.

EXERCISES

Words to Know

exurbia (paragraph 1), vistas (1), ambiance (2), terrestrial (2), axis (2), Taoist (3), Wanderlust (3), rootedness (3), pecuniary (3), nos-talgia (4), lament (4), stability (4), forcible (4), rootlessness (4), social mobility (4), symbolizes (4).

Some of the Issues

1. What does the author mean when he says that Americans have "a sense of space"? How does he support that statement?
2. Why does he call that sense of space "a symbol of the future"? How is the American attitude toward the future linked to a sense of space?
3. What are the physical differences between the American and the Chinese home?
4. What according to Tuan do these physical contrasts signify with respect to attitudes? How does he support the assertion that the Chinese are rooted in one place?
5. In paragraph 4 Tuan differentiates between Chinese and American nostalgia for home. What does he indicate are the differences?
6. In the end Tuan defends, in a way, the American attitude toward roots by asserting that it is the result of "ideals we admire." What are these ideals?

The Way We Are Told

7. Americans do not find it "curious" to admire the view through the picture window. Why does Tuan use that word?
8. How does Tuan convey the feeling of the Chinese home to a visitor? What visitor does he have in mind? In other words, who is addressed in this essay?
9. Tuan links the attitude toward the home in America to a sense of mobility, of optimism. Does he give the reader any grounds for the assumption that the Chinese home, by contrast, is linked to an attitude of pessimism?

Some Subjects for Essays

10. Describe the design and location of your ideal home, focusing not on comforts and conveniences but on the kind of space that fits your personality and the life you want to lead.
11. Tuan contrasts the Chinese idea of rootedness and stability as expressed in the design of the Chinese home with the American desire to travel light and look to the future. Compare and contrast these two lifestyles, indicating your personal choice and your reasons for it.

SWIMMING IN CROSS-CULTURAL CURRENTS

Conrad Phillip Kottak

Conrad Phillip Kottak is a professor of anthropology at the University of Michigan in Ann Arbor. He has done field work in Brazil and Madagascar and has investigated life in contemporary America from an anthropological perspective. He is editor of *Research in American Culture* and the author of several textbooks in anthropology. The article reprinted here first appeared in *Natural History* magazine in May 1985.

Here Kottak writes both as an anthropologist and as the father of a competitive swimmer. He starts out by asking why Brazil managed to garner only six Olympic medals in 1984 while the United States won 174, in spite of the many similarities between the two countries: their size, their population, and their ethnic diversity. Kottak finds the answer in differences in culture.

With 3.5 million square miles, Brazil is only slightly smaller than the United States. Its population is currently estimated at 145 million (as compared with 240 million in the United States). In contrast to the rest of Latin America, its dominant language is Portuguese.

After World War II, Brazil began to develop into an industrial power. However, along with this development has come widespread ecological damage and disruption and death for many indigenous peoples in the vast rain forests away from the developed coastal areas. Industrialization also has done little to better the lives of many poor Brazilians in urban centers. For a description of life in the "favelas" surrounding Rio de Janeiro see the diary of Carolina Maria de Jesus.

In the 1980s, after years of military rule, Brazil began to move toward a democratic government with an elected president.

Why do athletes from some countries excel at particular sports? Why do certain nations pile up dozens of Olympic medals while others win only a handful or none at all? It isn't simply a matter of being rich or poor, developed or underdeveloped. Cultural values and social conditions also play a role in international sports success. The United States and Brazil, giants of the Western Hemisphere, with populations of about 235 million and 135 million, respectively, offer a good contrast

283

in Olympic success. Both are countries of almost continental proportions; both have people of ethnically diverse backgrounds, with roots
in Europe, Africa, Asia, and Native America. Each is the major economic power of its continent. However, in the 1984 Summer Olympics, the United States won 174 medals, while Brazil managed only 8.
The contrast was particularly noticeable in swimming, where the
United States won 34 medals and Brazil one.

From early August 1983 to late August 1984, I was in Rio de   2
Janeiro to set up a research project on the impact of nationwide
commercial television on traditional Brazilian culture. Among other
aspects of the project, I was interested in television sports coverage,
but I also had a personal connection with swimming because my son is
a competitive swimmer. During those thirteen months, I noticed many
striking contrasts between Brazilian and American swimming. Since
most successful international swimmers begin their training in childhood, a closer look at the cultural values affecting children's swimming may help us understand some of the reasons that the United
States excels at that sport and Brazil doesn't.

The most obvious contrasts between competitive swimming in   3
the United States and Brazil have to do with different cultural attitudes
toward time, which is valued more highly and calculated more carefully in the United States. Many Brazilians find the American obsession
with time to be the outstanding contrast between the two cultures.
Brazilians don't make appointments for such punctual times as 1:45 or
2:15, and they react suspiciously to the precision offered by digital
watches. As they point out, delays are common in traffic-jammed cities
such as Rio de Janeiro; no one arrives, or is expected to arrive, on time.

I have been following children's competitive swimming since my   4
son, an age-group swimmer in the USS (United States Swimming, formerly AAU) program, was 7. (Age-group refers to the organization of
most events by age-based categories: 8 and under, 9–10, 11–12,
13–14, and 15–16. Age groups in the United States don't have ages
similar to those of everyone else. In the tribal vocabulary, instead of
being 6 or 7, one is "8 and under"; my son just turned "13–14.")
During a period of six years, I have attended dozens of swimming
practices and meets. I have discussed swimming with other parents
and coaches, have chaired the swim committee of a local club, and
have helped out at swimming meets. USS swim meets, which take
place throughout the winter and summer, lead to state and national
championships.

A swimmer's objective in a given meet is not just to win but to   5
better his or her time. One's time for any event is always the fastest
time yet achieved in that event. At a given meet, swimmers may
participate in all events in which they have made certain cutoff times

announced at the beginning of the season. There are A meets for swimmers who have achieved A cutoff times, B meets for those whose times are slower, and C events for the slowest. One's time for any event can only get better, never worse.

Within the swimmer's world, time is paramount. Even winners are disappointed if they don't better their times, since a new time means progress compared with other swimmers and a step toward state and national championships—and toward that final goal, Olympic gold and a new world record. I have watched small children sob on discovering that a win did not better their time. On the adult level, a gold-medal-winning American backstroker in the 1984 Summer Olympics reacted similarly when he won the finals without beating his own previously set world record. 6

Conversation among swimmers could be mistaken for chitchat at a convention of time and motion study experts, so frequent are the references to hundredths of a second. Kids who haven't yet studied long division routinely reel off "19.16s" (nineteen and sixteen-hundredths seconds) and "35.97s." The most common question among American swimmers is probably, "What's your time for the 50 free?" Swimmers not only know their own times but also those of their teammates and their fiercest rivals. 7

It's easy to find out swimmers' times. Just buy a mimeographed program at a meet. This program lists, by numbered event, the name of each swimmer and his or her time for each event. In this way, an American swimmer's times become public knowledge. Parents consult the program as they watch each event, comparing previous best times with those achieved that day. As they monitor their own child's performance, parents also comment favorably to other moms and dads whose children have done well. Parents sit in silent embarrassment or make audible excuses when their children don't match or better their former best times. 8

American children are motivated to keep on swimming because they know that even if they don't achieve a new time in one event that day, they might better their time in another. Because they are allowed to swim in as many events as they have A times (for an A meet) or B times (for a B meet), most swimmers usually have something to be happy about when they get home. 9

An American swimming meet closely mirrors the larger society in that most people have good and bad moments, strong and weak performances, and despite disappointments, generally find rewards. Swimming is a particularly appropriate sport for a competitive, achievement-oriented society in which lines of social class are not clearly and rigidly drawn. Status within the American swimmer's world is like the form of social organization that anthropologists call the 10 chiefdom, common a century ago in the Polynesian islands. In the chiefdom, slight gradations in prestige and power, rather than demarcated social classes, meant that everyone had a distinctive social status, just a bit higher or lower than anyone else's. A swimmer's unique status is the end result of a complex scoring process that takes into account a series of constantly changing times in different events. Like a Polynesian, every swimmer has a social status slightly different from everyone else's.

Time, then, is the basis of social status in American swimming.   11
Public recognition of excellent times is, in itself, a potent reward. The more tangible prizes — medals and ribbons — got to only a small number of finalists (normally six, eight, or twelve), but everyone has a best time.

Since precious commodities usually have guardians, the swim-   12
mer's world has guardians of time (for example, parents armed with the most modern stopwatches). Even when electronic timing pads are used, each lane always has two human timers. There are also finish judges to determine finish order in close races and, for important meets, winning-lane timers. At the end of each heat, times are written on cards, which are used to determine and list finish order, official times, and winners. The results of each race are posted one by one in the halls of the building (usually a high school) where the meet takes place. By consulting these sheets, parents can compare their children's times with previous bests and with those of other swimmers. In this way the adult members of the society monitor whether their young are keeping up with their peers and whether they are bettering themselves in terms of the values emphasized in American culture, including individual achievement and hard work.

Swimmers' times — these public, precious symbols of   13
achievement — are tended, guarded, enshrined in print, and transmitted from local to state to national levels, where they are used to establish rankings. The most important source of information about times and national rankings is the monthly magazine *Swimming World*. *Swimming World* also publishes results of meets held throughout the country, and sells a popular T-shirt, proclaiming "I made it in *Swimming World*," an achievement that confers considerable prestige among fellow swimmers. The particularly American character of the swimmer's world just described emerges crystal clear when we consider the same sport in Brazil.

Before enrolling my son in a competitive swim program in Rio de   14
Janeiro in 1983, I accepted the above procedure as part of swimming per se — not as an illustration of distinctive American cultural values. Even though I am accustomed to comparing American institutions and behavior with those of other cultures, I had not thought much about

how swim programs might be run differently elsewhere or what the meets might tell me about different values and traditions. But striking differences between Brazilian and American swimming were soon apparent. First, Brazilian swim teams are associated with private, money-making professional clubs, such as the Fluminense Football (soccer) Club, for which my son swam. Most of the soccer clubs that battle for city, state, and national championships have divisions of amateur sports, which manage swimming, gymnastics, and other competitive programs for children.

The clubs are commercial organizations, rather than the high school, college, age-group, and sports-club teams that dominate competitive swimming in the United States. It was as though my son were swimming for the Detroit Tigers. One of the tasks of the vice-president for amateur sports of a Brazilian club is to find rich sponsors, businesses or individuals, national or foreign, for the swim team. The soccer rivalry between such teams as Fluminense, Flamengo, and Vasco spills over into amateur sports. In Rio de Janeiro, swimmers and gymnasts play their own small parts in an ongoing battle for sports supremacy, and the system is similar in other Brazilian cities. 15

Daily practices are held in the Olympic-sized pools of different clubs, and the competition is stiffer in a city of eight million than in the Detroit metropolitan area. Many Brazilian national champion age-group swimmers live in Rio, and their times (at least through the early teens) are comparable to those of top American swimmers. Cutoffs are much more stringent, however, and there are fewer meets — which means that swimmers lack opportunities to better their times and to gain experience. 16

Compared with the United States, Brazilian meets are badly organized. In the United States, meets are planned a year in advance; in Brazil, coaches often don't know until a day or two before the meet where it will be held, and sites are frequently changed at the last minute — for example, from a convenient pool a few blocks away to a suburb requiring an hour's drive. Cariocas (residents of Rio de Janeiro) are accustomed to associating with family and friends, but not with such strangers as the parents of their children's colleagues. There is no tradition of car pooling, and swimmers frequently miss meets because of last-minute changes. For American swimmers, to miss a meet is practically unheard of; mild illnesses or relatives' birthday parties are not acceptable excuses for letting down one's teammates. If one is scheduled to swim a relay, to miss a meet is considered especially unfair to other team members. 17

American swim meets almost always have relays — freestyle and medley (backstroke, breast stroke, butterfly, and freestyle, or crawl). Brazilian meets, however, rarely include relays; only one of the half 18 dozen meets I attended in Rio had them. Perhaps relays are almost always a part of American meets because they embody key American values so well. The free relay is based on pure speed; it is the fastest of the races because everyone swims the fastest stroke, the crawl, normally called "the free."

The medley relay tests speed through specialization; each of four   19 specialized swimmers tries for a best time to bring his or her team in first. It shows specialized individuals working rapidly together, like an efficient industrial or managerial team. Making the relay through a best time is a valued achievement. In relays, the win is more important than in individual events. Since relay members can change from week to week, swimmers have a less accurate recollection of relay times than personal ones. In these events, swimming celebrates certain American values: winning organization, competition through speed, efficiency, and specialization with other, similar groups. These values have spread out from the American economy to the larger society and are well represented in competitive swimming. In Brazil, the absence of relays helps focus attention on the individual win.

Even more noteworthy, however, than capricious meet planning   20 and the absence of relays is the treatment of time in Brazilian swimming. In the United States, times are recorded electronically, as well as by people with stopwatches, and are publicly posted. In Brazil, however, times are not published in the mimeographed meet program. The swimmers' names and club affiliations are listed for each event, but their times are not. At first I supposed that, as in the United States, names were listed in an order established by prior best times and that the fastest swimmers swam in the last heat. After observing the results of several races in different meets, I learned this was not the case. Swimmers in the first or second heat were as likely to win as those in the last one.

Since times are not listed, parents and swimmers can concentrate   21 only on who wins, not on who betters former times, which means that, rather than several possible winners, each event has only one. Public recognition of improvement — a key reward and powerful reason to keep on swimming — is missing. Nor are times publicly posted after each race. They are announced by loudspeaker after finish order is determined, beginning with the slowest swimmer and laboriously moving up to the winner — sometimes through twenty or thirty names. In this way parents and swimmers are reminded, not that many swimmers have improved, but that there are twenty times as many losers as winners.

Another feature of the Brazilian meet illustrates different cultural   22 values about time. Where were the many guardians of time? I saw no attentive parents with stopwatches; there were no frantic winning-lane timers. Each lane had a single timer—even when the electronic pads weren't working. And, since timers often chatted as swimmers raced home, times were occasionally lost, an unheard-of-occurrence in USS swimming. Times are not gathered, tended, and cherished as in the United States. This is one of many symbolic statements in the swimmer's world of the different values attached to time in the cultures of the two Western giants.

Brazilian coaches do keep track of their swimmers' times, which   23
they use to determine who will swim what events in the next meet. But in contrast to USS swimming, in which kids are normally entered in all races for which they have made cutoff times, in Brazil they are limited to three or four races. This further reduces their opportunities for meet experience.

Why are there so few opportunities to swim competitively in   24
Brazil? One reason is the absence of public school, particularly high school, athletic programs. Another is the reduced level of parental involvement in organizing and running meets, compared with that in the United States. There are simply too few volunteers to provide the needed chances to compete, particularly in a city of eight million where thousands of young people train as swimmers.

The pattern of stiff cutoffs and restricted competition is persist-   25
ent and has unfortunate consequences for Brazil in international competition. For example, the Brazilian Olympic Committee did not send female swimmers to Los Angeles in 1984 because none had made arbitrarily established cutoffs. This excluded a South American record holder, while swimmers with no better times were attending the Olympics as representatives of other South American countries. The attitude was that only swimmers who had made the cutoffs had any chance to place in Los Angeles. No one imagined that the power of Olympic excitement might spur swimmers to extraordinary efforts. During television coverage of the 1984 South American Championships, held in Rio, I was aghast to hear commentators downgrade chances that any Brazilian other than Ricardo Prado might win a medal. More than once I heard this comment about a new champion: "He doesn't have a chance to win at Los Angeles because his time isn't good enough"—as though it could never get better.

American coverage, in contrast, dotes on unexpected results,   26
showing adherence to an American sports credo: "It's not over till it's over." In Brazil, the credo seems to be "It's over before it's begun."

Winning, of course, is an important American cultural value, and   27
this is particularly true for college and professional team sports like football, basketball, and baseball. Football coaches are fond of making such comments as "Winning isn't a good thing; it's the only thing" and "Show me a good loser and I'll show you a loser." For sports such as

running and swimming, however, in which the focus is on the individual, American culture also recognizes and admires moral victories, personal bests, comeback athletes, and special Olympics, and commends those who run good races without finishing first. In amateur sports, personal improvement can be as important as winning.

Americans have been told so many times that their culture over-   28
emphasizes winning that they may find it hard to believe that Brazilians seem to value winning even more. Prior to the 1984 Summer Olympics, swimmer Ricardo Prado (instead of the eventual Brazilian gold medalist, Joaquim Cruz) was touted by the media as Brazil's most likely gold medal winner (he was a silver medalist). Prado had won 200- and 400-meter individual medley (IM) events in the 1983 Pan American Games and, until 1984, held the world record for the 400 IM. Commenting on his massive press coverage, Prado observed that only winning athletes were noticed in Brazil — only number ones, never number twos. He blasted the press for formerly neglecting his achievements and those of other Brazilian swimmers who were not, or not yet, world record holders.

Perhaps Brazilians value winning so much because it is so rare. In   29
USS swimming, the focus on times means there are always multiple winners. This may be the key to the relationship of swimming to cultural values. In American society, where poverty is less pervasive, resources more abundant, social classes less marked, opportunities for achievement more numerous, and individual social mobility easier than in Brazil, there can be multiple winners. Brazilian society is more stratified; a much smaller middle class and elite group makes up at most 30 percent of the population. Brazilian swimming echoes lessons from the larger society: victories are scarce and reserved for the few.

But there is another dimension to the relationship between com-   30
petitive swimming and society. Even in the United States the opportunity to swim competitively is limited, generally to people of the middle class and above. To swim seriously in America requires money, time, and parental involvement. American children begin swimming competitively for sports clubs or country clubs, which have membership fees. Success in summer swimming may then lead them to join Y or USS programs, for winter competition. The United States is an automobile-oriented culture. Cars and parents' time are necessary to drive to practices and meets. During Michigan winters, in order to arrive at distant meets for 8:00 A.M. warmups, my son and I have sometimes spent the night in a motel. Swimmers' parents have money to spend on gas, food, lodging, and club memberships. Children whose parents can afford to belong to clubs are more likely to get interested in swimming in the first place.

In Brazil the situation is somewhat different. Public transporta-   31 tion is better in Brazilian cities than in most parts of the United States. There is less residential segregation of rich and poor, black and white. Given the dense urban populations and that the major soccer clubs — and therefore their swimming pools — are located right in the city, poor kids, including black children, can work out as swim-team members almost as easily as children from middle-class families. As a result, in contrast to the United States, where it is rare to see a black swimmer at a USS meet or in a state championship, swimmers with dark skins and fast times are present at virtually any carioca swimming meet.

Some Americans think that blacks and whites excel in particular 32 sports because of biological and physiological differences, but Brazil, which has proportionately as many blacks as the United States, demonstrates that sports abilities reflect culture rather than biology. When blacks have opportunities to do well in swimming, soccer, or tennis, they are physically capable of doing as well as whites. In schools, parks, and city playgrounds in the United States, blacks have access to baseball diamonds, basketball courts, football fields, and tracks. However, because of restricted economic opportunities, black families have traditionally lacked the resources to invest in hockey or ski equipment or join clubs with tennis courts and swimming pools. But as Brazilian swimming demonstrates, when these opportunities are available, blacks do well.

Here then is a different way in which the swimmer's world 33 provides a microcosm of the surrounding culture. Despite the emphasis in the United States on the possibility of rising through hard work and individual achievement, in swimming, as in society, success is easiest for those who are better off to begin with.

What can we conclude about the different cultural models for 34 competitive swimming? Perhaps the more relaxed approach to swimming encountered in Brazil reflects a culture in which there is less emphasis on time, measurement, comparison, and achievement. Brazilians may even experience fewer stresses and be happier because they live in a less competitive, less achievement-oriented society. Whatever the case, one thing is eminently clear: the United States is a better training ground than Brazil for international competitive swimming. As we know from years of Olympic games and a glance at today's world records, the countries that do best at swimming are the United States, East Germany, and the Soviet Union. State support of Soviet and East German swimmers is a powerful incentive for talented young people in those countries. Other nations that do well in international competition — Australia, Canada, Great Britain, the Netherlands — are more like the United States than Brazil in their cultural backgrounds and current socioeconomic conditions.

Despite pride in country, Brazilian swimmers know that it wasn't 35 accidental that the South American giant could manage only one medal while its North American counterpart was winning thirty-four. Recognizing this, most of the Brazilian men who swam in the 1984 Olympics, including silver-medalist Ricardo Prado, are now training in the United States.

EXERCISES

Words to Know

excel (paragraph 1), developed (1), underdeveloped (1), ethnically diverse (1), obsession (3), punctual (3), paramount (6), chitchat (7), monitor (8), audible (8), achievement-oriented (10), demarcated (10), status (10), anthropologists (10), Polynesian (10), gradations (10), tangible (11), commodities (12), enshrined (13), supremacy (15), sites (17), relay (17), embody (18), capricious (20), prior (20), laboriously (21), tended (22), cherished (22), symbolic (22), arbitrarily (25), aghast (25), dotes (26), adherence (26), stratified (29), elite (29), virtually (31), microcosm (33), incentive (34), socioeconomic (34).

Some of the Issues

1. In paragraph 1 Kottak attempts to establish that there are many important similarities between the United States and Brazil. Cite several of them and consider why it is important for the writer to stress such similarities from the start of the essay.
2. Attitudes toward time often differ from culture to culture; Brazilians and (North) Americans have different attitudes. What are they? How are they reflected in competitive swimming? What, according to Kottak, are some of the advantages of United States attitudes toward time over the Brazilian? Are there any disadvantages?
3. In paragraph 10 Kottak makes a comparison between the American swimmer's world and the social organization in the Polynesian islands a hundred years ago. At first sight it would seem that those two groups have little in common. What resemblance does Kottak find?
4. In paragraph 10 Kottak also describes why, in his view, an American swimming meet "closely mirrors the larger society." What does he mean by that statement?
5. Read paragraph 29, which describes Brazilian society, and try to spell out the ways in which its attitudes toward competitive swimming mirror it.

6. What is the importance of the relay (paragraphs 18 and 19)? Why is it significant that Brazilian meets have few relays?
7. What aspects of Brazilian culture are mirrored in the "stiff cut-offs" (paragraph 24) and the expressed belief that a swimmer "doesn't have a chance . . . because his time isn't good enough"?
8. In which of the two countries is swimming training more "demo-cratically" available — that is, in which is swimming training more easily accessible to young people irrespective of parental income? Why?

The Way We Are Told

9. What is the effect of the two questions with which Kottak starts his essay? Are they answered?
10. In paragraph 4 Kottak refers to the phrase "age-group" as part of the "tribal vocabulary." What impression does the word "tribal" convey?
11. What effect does Kottak achieve in paragraph 12 by using the somewhat strange expression "guardians of time" to describe American parents at swim meets?
12. In the essay Kottak establishes his authority to discuss his subject on two grounds: as an anthropologist and as the parent of a swim-mer. How does he do each?
13. There are two basic patterns of organizing a comparison-and-con-trast essay such as this. One pattern is to make an item-by-item comparison, as Kottak does in paragraph 1. The second, used by the author in the rest of the essay, is to develop the first example completely, and then add the second comparatively. Make an outline of the essay that shows its development of comparisons and contrasts. Indicate what paragraphs are devoted to each sub-topic and when transitions occur.

Some Subjects for Essay

14. Select a sport or leisure-time activity you participate in or know well. In an essay examine how it reflects cultural values like the ones Kottak discusses: attention to time, competitiveness, team organization, individual or group achievement.
15. Select a sport — it may be the same as in the previous topic. Examine to what extent it is available to everybody: consider what is needed in terms of free time, money, facilities, equipment, or other resources to succeed in it. Try to determine what the effect of such various constraints seems to be.

BODY RITUAL AMONG THE NACIREMA

Horace Miner

Horace Miner, born in 1912 in St. Paul, Minnesota, served as
professor of sociology and anthropology at the University of Michigan until his retirement. He received his Ph.D. from the University
of Chicago. He has researched and written extensively about a
number of West and Central African cultures. The selection reprinted here was first published in the *American Anthropologist*
in 1956. It describes a North American tribe whose customs will
seem strange to the reader—or will they?

The anthropologist has become so familiar with the diversity of ways   1
in which different peoples behave in similar situations that he is not
apt to be surprised by even the most exotic customs. In fact, if all of
the logically possible combinations of behavior have not been found
somewhere in the world, he is apt to suspect that they must be present
in some yet undescribed tribe. This point has, in fact, been expressed
with respect to clan organization by Murdock (1949:71). In this light,
the magical beliefs and practices of the Nacirema present such unusual
aspects that it seems desirable to describe them as an example of the
extremes to which human behavior can go.

Professor Linton first brought the ritual of the Nacirema to the   2
attention of anthropologists twenty years ago (1936:326), but the
culture of this people is still very poorly understood. They are a North
American group living in the territory between the Canadian Cree, the
Yaqui and Tarahumare of Mexico, and the Carib and Arawak of the
Antilles. Little is known of their origin, although tradition states that
they came from the east. According to Nacirema mythology, their
nation was originated by a culture hero, Notgnihsaw, who is otherwise
known for two great feats of strength—the throwing of a piece of
wampum across the river Pa-To-Mac and the chopping down of a
cherry tree in which the Spirit of Truth resided.

Nacirema culture is characterized by a highly developed market   3
economy which has evolved in a rich natural habitat. While much of
the people's time is devoted to economic pursuits, a large part of the
fruits of these labors and a considerable portion of the day are spent in

ritual activity. The focus of this activity is the human body, the appearance and health of which loom as a dominant concern in the ethos of the people. While such a concern is certainly not unusual, its ceremonial aspects and associated philosophy are unique.

The fundamental belief underlying the whole system appears 4
to be that the human body is ugly and that its natural tendency is to debility and disease. Incarcerated in such a body, man's only hope is to avert these characteristics through the use of the powerful influences of ritual and ceremony. Every household has one or more shrines devoted to this purpose. The more powerful individuals in the society have several shrines in their houses and, in fact, the opulence of a house is often referred to in terms of the number of such ritual centers it possesses. Most houses are of wattle and daub construction, but the shrine rooms of the more wealthy are walled with stone. Poorer families imitate the rich by applying pottery plaques to their shrine walls.

While each family has at least one such shrine, the rituals asso- 5
ciated with it are not family ceremonies but are private and secret. The rites are normally only discussed with children, and then only during the period when they are being initiated into these mysteries. I was able, however, to establish sufficient rapport with the natives to examine these shrines and to have the rituals described to me.

The focal point of the shrine is a box or chest which is built into 6
the wall. In this chest are kept the many charms and magical potions without which no native believes he could live. These preparations are secured from a variety of specialized practitioners. The most powerful of these are the medicine men, whose assistance must be rewarded with substantial gifts. However, the medicine men do not provide the curative potions for their clients, but decide what the ingredients should be and then write them down in an ancient and secret language. This writing is understood only by the medicine men and by the herbalists who, for another gift, provide the required charm.

The charm is not disposed of after it has served its purpose, but is 7
placed in the charm-box of the household shrine. As these magical materials are specific for certain ills, and the real or imagined maladies of the people are many, the charm-box is usually full to overflowing. The magical packets are so numerous that people forget what their purposes were and fear to use them again. While the natives are very vague on this point, we can only assume that the idea in retaining all the old magical materials is that their presence in the charm-box, before which the body rituals are conducted, will in some way protect the worshipper.

Beneath the charm-box is a small font. Each day every member of 8
the family, in succession, enters the shrine room, bows his head before the charm-box, mingles different sorts of holy water in the font, and

proceeds with a brief rite of ablution. The holy waters are secured from the Water Temple of the community, where the priests conduct elaborate ceremonies to make the liquid ritually pure.

In the hierarchy of magical practitioners, and below the medi-   9
cine men in prestige, are specialists whose designation is best trans-lated "holy-mouth-men." The Nacirema have an almost pathological horror of and fascination with the mouth, the condition of which is believed to have a supernatural influence on all social relationships. Were it not for the rituals of the mouth, they believe that their teeth would fall out, their gums bleed, their jaws shrink, their friends desert them, and their lovers reject them. They also believe that a strong relationship exists between oral and moral characteristics. For exam-ple, there is a ritual ablution of the mouth for children which is supposed to improve their moral fiber.

The daily body ritual performed by everyone includes a mouth-   10
rite. Despite the fact that these people are so punctilious about care of the mouth, this rite involves a practice which strikes the uninitiated stranger as revolting. It was reported to me that the ritual consists of inserting a small bundle of hog hairs into the mouth, along with certain magical powders, and then moving the bundle in a highly formalized series of gestures.

In addition to the private mouth-rite, the people seek out a   11
holy-mouth-man once or twice a year. These practitioners have an impressive set of paraphernalia, consisting of a variety of augers, awls, probes, and prods. The use of these objects in the exorcism of the evils of the mouth involves almost unbelievable ritual torture of the client. The holy-mouth-man opens the client's mouth and, using the above mentioned tools, enlarges any holes which decay may have created in the teeth. Magical materials are put into these holes. If there are no naturally occurring holes in the teeth, large sections of one or more teeth are gouged out so that the supernatural substance can be applied. In the client's view, the purpose of these ministrations is to arrest decay and to draw friends. The extremely sacred and traditional char-acter of the rite is evident in the fact that the natives return to the holy-mouth-men year after year, despite the fact that their teeth con-tinue to decay.

It is to be hoped that, when a thorough study of the Nacirema is   12
made, there will be careful inquiry into the personality structure of these people. One has but to watch the gleam in the eye of a holy-mouth-man, as he jabs an awl into an exposed nerve, to suspect that a certain amount of sadism is involved. If this can be established, a very interesting pattern emerges, for most of the population shows definite masochistic tendencies. It was to these that Professor Linton referred in discussing a distinctive part of the daily body ritual which is per-

formed only by men. This part of the rite involves scraping and lacerating the surface of the face with a sharp instrument. Special women's rites are performed only four times during each lunar month, but what they lack in frequency is made up in barbarity. As part of this ceremony, women bake their heads in small ovens for about an hour. The theoretically interesting point is that what seems to be a preponderantly masochistic people have developed sadistic specialists.

The medicine men have an imposing temple, or *latipso*, in every community of any size. The more elaborate ceremonies required to treat very sick patients can only be performed at this temple. These ceremonies involve not only the *thaumaturge* but a permanent group of vestal maidens who move sedately about the temple chambers in distinctive costume and headdress.   13

The *latipso* ceremonies are so harsh that it is phenomenal that a fair proportion of the really sick natives who enter the temple ever recover. Small children whose indoctrination is still incomplete have been known to resist attempts to take them to the temple because "that is where you go to die." Despite this fact, sick adults are not only willing but eager to undergo the protracted ritual purification if they can afford to do so. No matter how ill the supplicant or how grave the emergency, the guardians of many temples will not admit a client if he cannot give a rich gift to the custodian. Even after one has gained admission and survived the ceremonies, the guardians will not permit the neophyte to leave until he makes still another gift.   14

The supplicant entering the temple is first stripped of all his or her clothes. In every-day life the Nacirema avoids exposure of his body and its natural functions. Bathing and excretory acts are performed only in the secrecy of the household shrine, where they are ritualized as part of the body-rites. Psychological shock results from the fact that body secrecy is suddenly lost upon entry into the *latipso*. A man, whose own wife has never seen him in an excretory act, suddenly finds himself naked and assisted by a vestal maiden while he performs his natural functions into a sacred vessel. This sort of ceremonial treatment is necessitated by the fact that the excreta are used by a diviner to ascertain the course and nature of the client's sickness. Female clients, on the other hand, find their naked bodies are subjected to the scrutiny, manipulation and prodding of the medicine men.   15

Few supplicants in the temple are well enough to do anything but lie on their hard beds. The daily ceremonies, like the rites of the holy-mouth-men, involve discomfort and torture. With ritual precision, the vestals awaken their miserable charges each dawn and roll them about on their beds of pain while performing ablutions, in the formal movements of which the maidens are highly trained. At other times they insert magic wands in the supplicant's mouth or force him   16 to eat substances which are supposed to be healing. From time to time the medicine men come to their clients and jab magically treated needles into their flesh. The fact that these temple ceremonies may not cure, and may even kill the neophyte, in no way decreases the people's faith in the medicine men.

There remains one other kind of practitioner, known as a "lis-   17
tener." This witchdoctor has the power to exorcise the devils that lodge in the heads of people who have been bewitched. The Nacirema believe that parents bewitch their own children. Mothers are particularly suspected of putting a curse on children while teaching them the secret body rituals. The counter-magic of the witch doctor is unusual in its lack of ritual. The patient simply tells the "listener" all his troubles and fears, beginning with the earliest difficulties he can remember. The memory displayed by the Nacirema in these exorcism sessions is truly remarkable. It is not uncommon for the patient to bemoan the rejection he felt upon being weaned as a babe, and a few individuals even see their troubles going back to the traumatic effects of their own birth.

In conclusion, mention must be made of certain practices which   18
have their base in native esthetics but which depend upon the pervasive aversion to the natural body and its functions. There are ritual fasts to make fat people thin and ceremonial feasts to make thin people fat. Still other rites are used to make women's breasts larger if they are small, and smaller if they are large. General dissatisfaction with breast shape is symbolized in the fact that the ideal form is virtually outside the range of human variation. A few women afflicted with almost inhuman hyper-mammary development are so idolized that they make a handsome living by simply going from village to village and permitting the natives to stare at them for a fee.

Reference has already been made to the fact that excretory func-   19
tions are ritualized, routinized, and relegated to secrecy. Natural reproductive functions are similarly distorted. Intercourse is taboo as a topic and scheduled as an act. Efforts are made to avoid pregnancy by the use of magical materials or by limiting intercourse to certain phases of the moon. Conception is actually very infrequent. When pregnant, women dress so as to hide their condition. Parturition takes place in secret, without friends or relatives to assist, and the majority of women do not nurse their infants.

Our review of the ritual life of the Nacirema has certainly shown   20
them to be a magic-ridden people. It is hard to understand how they have managed to exist so long under the burdens which they have imposed upon themselves. But even such exotic customs as these take on real meaning when they are viewed with the insight provided by Malinowski when he wrote:

"Looking from far and above, from our high places of safety in   21
the developed civilization, it is easy to see all the crudity and irrele-
vance of magic. But without its power and guidance early man could
not have mastered his practical difficulties as he has done, nor could
man have advanced to the higher stages of civilization."

EXERCISES

Words to Know

anthropologist (paragraph 1), diversity (1), exotic (1), clan (1), culture (2), mythology (2), wampum (2), market economy (3), evolved
(3), focus (3), loom (3), ethos (3), ceremonial (3), debility (4),
incarcerated (4), avert (4), shrines (4), opulence (4), wattle and
daub (4), initiated (5), rapport (5), focal point (6), practitioners (6),
herbalists (6), maladies (7), font (8), ablution (8), designation (9),
pathological (9), oral (9), moral fiber (9), punctilious (10) uninitiated (10), paraphernalia (11), exorcism (11), gouged (11), ministrations (11), sadism (12), masochistic (12), lacerating (12), lunar
(12), barbarity (12), thaumaturge (13), vestal maidens (13), sedately
(13), phenomenal (14), indoctrination (14), protracted (14), supplicant (14), custodian (14), neophyte (14), excretory (15), diviner
(15), ascertain (15), scrutiny (15), manipulation (15), prodding
(15), bemoan (17), traumatic (17), esthetics (18), pervasive (18),
aversion (18), hyper-mammary (18), routinized (19), relegated (19),
conception (19), parturition (19).

Some of the Issues

1. At what point did you realize that Miner was putting you on? What
   specifically tipped you off?
2. Where do the Nacirema live? How is their geographic location
   described?
3. Describe the "culture hero" Notgnihsaw in the way you usually
   read or hear about him, especially with respect to the "two great
   feats of strength." Account for the differences in description.
4. What are the activities described as "ceremonies" and "rituals" in
   paragraphs 3 through 8?
5. Describe the contents and uses of the "charm-box" (paragraphs 6
   and 7), the focal point of the Naciremas' shrine.
6. Establish the "hierarchy of magical practitioners" and translate it.
7. Describe the routines of the "latipso," stressing in particular the

activities outlined in paragraph 15, and the sudden change in attitude toward body rituals that takes place.

8. Sadistic and masochistic tendencies are observed among the Nacirema. Do you agree that the rituals Miner describes should be characterized in that way?

The Way We Are Told

9. Miner uses two basic devices for disguising words and ideas. One is spelling words backwards or distorting them as in Pa-To-Mac. The other device is renaming: dentists, for example, become holy-mouth-men. Give several examples of each of these disguises or renamings and provide a translation for each.

10. Miner uses the devices of a scholarly paper or research report, including references and bibliography. The writers and works he cites are in fact real. What advantages does he gain by including the real with the fake?

11. Assuming that you find the essay funny—what makes it so?

* 12. Read Jonathan Swift's "Modest Proposal." Both Miner and Swift, as narrators, assume poses. Compare and contrast these poses.

Some Subjects for Essays

13. In describing American behavior in "Nacirema" terms, Miner has a purpose beyond amusing us: he wants us to question what we assume to be the logic of our customs and behavior. Your essay should explain, with examples, how he goes about that, and evaluate the truth of his assertions.

14. The proverbial man from outer space has just landed, left his spaceship, and now observes a very strange, possibly magical, ritual: the natives call it "football." You, in the role of the person from outer space, describe what you witness, leaving nothing out. You may, if you prefer, witness other rituals: "Rock Concert," for example, or "Game Show."

AMERICAN MEN DON'T CRY

Ashley Montagu

Ashley Montagu was born in London in 1905 and came to the
United States in 1917. He has served as a professor of anthropology at several universities, including Rutgers, Harvard, and Princeton. His many books include *On Being Human* (1950), *The Natural Superiority of Women* (1953), *Culture and the Evolution of
Man* (1962), *The Nature of Human Aggression* (1962), *Man
and the Computer* (1972), and *The American Way of Life*
(1952), from which the following selection is an excerpt.

American men don't cry because it is considered unmasculine to do so.   1
Only sissies cry. Crying is a "weakness" characteristic of the female,
and no American male wants to be identified with anything in the least
weak or feminine. Crying, in our culture, is identified with childish-
ness, with weakness and dependence. No one likes a crybaby, and we
disapprove of crying even in children, discouraging it in them as early
as possible. In a land so devoted to the pursuit of happiness as ours,
crying really is rather un-American. Adults must learn not to cry in
situations in which it is permissible for a child to cry. Women being
the "weaker" and "dependent" sex, it is only natural that they should
cry in certain emotional situations. In women, crying is excusable. But
in men, crying is a mark of weakness. So goes the American credo with
regard to crying.

"A little man," we impress on our male children, "never cries.   2
Only sissies and crybabies do." And so we condition males in America
not to cry whenever they feel like doing so. It is not that American
males are unable to cry because of some biological time clock within
them which causes them to run down in that capacity as they grow
older, but that they are trained not to cry. No "little man" wants to be
like that "inferior creature," the female. And the worst thing you can
call him is a sissy or a crybaby. And so the "little man" represses his
desire to cry and goes on doing so until he is unable to cry even when
he wants to. Thus do we produce a trained incapacity in the American
male to cry. And this is bad. Why is it bad? Because crying is a natural
function of the human organism which is designed to restore the
emotionally disequilibrated person to a state of equilibrium. The re-

turn of the disequilibrated organ systems of the body to steady states or dynamic stability is known as homeostasis. Crying serves a homeostatic function for the organism as a whole. Any interference with homeostatic mechanisms is likely to be damaging to the organism. And there is good reason to believe that the American male's trained incapacity to cry is seriously damaging to him.

It is unnecessary to cry whenever one wants to cry, but one should be able to cry when one ought to cry—when one needs to cry. For to cry under certain emotionally disequilibrating conditions is necessary for the maintenance of health. 3

To be human is to weep. The human species is the only one in the whole of animated nature that sheds tears. The trained inability of any human being to weep is a lessening of his capacity to be human—a defect which usually goes deeper than the mere inability to cry. And this, among other things, is what American parents—with the best intentions in the world—have achieved for the American male. It is very sad. If we feel like it, let us all have a good cry—and clear our minds of those cobwebs of confusion which have for so long prevented us from understanding the ineluctable necessity of crying. 4

EXERCISES

Words to Know

represses (paragraph 2), disequilibrated (2), equilibrium (2), dynamic (2), homeostasis (2), ineluctable (4).

Some of the Issues

1. Montagu makes an assertion in the first line of the essay. How does he support it?
2. Define the difference between the topics of paragraph 1 and paragraph 2. How do they relate to one another?
3. Montagu attributes American men's reluctance to cry not to nature but to environment and training. Does he give evidence to support his view or does he present it as a given?

The Way We Are Told

4. Montagu uses repetition extensively, usually with some variations. Find examples. (Look, for instance, at the second sentences of both paragraphs 1 and 2.)

5. Montagu uses quotation marks extensively. Define the effect they have.

Some Subjects for Essays

6. In American culture certain assumptions are often made about men's or women's fitness to assume certain roles: A woman's place is in the home. Girls aren't good in math. Men aren't the caring, loving creatures that women are. Only mothers know how to mother, not fathers. Agree or disagree with any one such assumption. Do not be neutral. Come down on one side or the other and provide as much evidence for your opinion as you can.

7. Montagu explains how young boys in America are trained not to cry. Consider how children are raised in America or in another country you know well. How does the typical upbringing of boys and girls differ? Consider such factors as the selection of toys, attention given to appearance and keeping clean, restrictions or encouragement of physical activity, acceptance of anger or fighting. Write an essay commenting on the similarities and differences you find in the raising of boys and girls, and evaluate the results of different kinds of upbringing.

8. Recent years have seen an increase in the number of women in traditionally "male" professions such as engineering and a somewhat lesser growth in the number of men in traditionally "female" jobs such as nursing and elementary school teaching. Write an essay giving your opinion of these trends.

CONFORMITY AND INDIVIDUALITY IN JAPAN

Ian Buruma

Ian Buruma is the author of *Behind the Mask*, a study of contemporary Japanese culture, and of *God's Dust: A Modern Asian Journey* (1989). He is the cultural editor of the *Far Eastern Review* in Hong Kong, and a frequent contributor to American magazines.

The selection below was first published in *Tokyo: Form and Spirit* (1986), edited by Mildred Friedman. Buruma uses two examples, an elevator operator and a "salaryman" (middle rank businessman), to demonstrate the impact of conformity and "human relations based on hierarchy" in the Japanese workplace. Buruma goes on to discuss the role of talent, the obstacles to its rise, and the loneliness that the talented are likely to face. Nevertheless, "originality and creativity do exist in Japan." However, as Buruma points out, the Japanese preference for skill over originality results in pride being taken in routine work.

To learn more about Japan, read John David Morley's "The Japanese Home" and Adam Smith's "The Japanese Model."

The repetitive zeal with which Japanese go about honing their skills 1
makes them seen obsessed with form, with mechanics rather than content. A rather touching example of this is the first reaction of Japanese audiences to moving pictures: they turned round their chairs to watch the projector, a source of much more fascination than the images flickering on the screen. Added to their reputation as copycats is their image as robots. This, too, is missing the point. The preoccupation with style does not necessarily mean the lack of a soul; just as Japanese do not feel that good manners make a human being less "real," "himself," "natural" or whatever term one wishes to use for that elusive inner core of man. Style, in the post-romantic West, is largely an extension of man's ego; traditional style in Japan — and China, for that matter — is more a transformation of the ego: to acquire a perfect technique, one eliminates, as it were, one's individuality, only to regain it by transcending the skill. This new individuality is not

the expression of one's real private life, but an individual interpretation of something already there and thus in the public domain.

Private life in Japan is just that: private. An artist or, for that matter, a waitress, is not expected to reveal his — or her — private "self," but his public one. The borderline between public and private worlds is much clearer in Japan than it is in the West (as in China, many Japanese houses have walls around them). Thus, the public self is not seen as a humiliating infringement on the "real" self. Of course, in certain periods, Japanese artists have rebelled against this division and the rigidity of style by going to the opposite extreme: writers of the "natural" school saw it as their vocation to burden the reader with the minutest details of their private lives. One key, I think, to the public aesthetic is the skill of an elevator girl.

Yoko Sato is nineteen and she is being trained to be an elevator girl in a department store. She lives at home with her parents but needs the extra money she earns to buy clothes and go to discos on Saturday nights. It's hard being an elevator girl for, as Yoko is ceaselessly told, she is the face of the store. If she does something wrong or displeases a customer, the company loses face.

Yoko does not much enjoy the lectures on company loyalty or philosophy written in fussy Chinese characters by the owner of the store, who likes to expound at length on the uniqueness of his firm. Still, Yoko learned all the lines by heart and recites them every morning with her colleagues. It may be a lot of boring nonsense, but this is the way things are done, and Yoko wants to do a good job.

The voice and bowing lessons are a little more interesting. Yoko always prides herself on being a good mimic — her imitations of the pompous section chief make her friends laugh. The perfect elevator girl's voice is high-pitched, on the verge of falsetto, and seeming to bubble over into merry laughter, without actually doing so. This is not an easy effect to achieve and it takes hours of drilling. Yoko's name was called out by the teacher, asking her to come forward. She was told to speak the following lines: this lift is going up, this lift is going down; and again: this lift is going up . . . and again. Her pitch was too low and her delivery not quite sprightly enough. The teacher told her to practice at home.

Bowing lessons are a more mechanical exercise. An inventive young engineer in the design department devised a bowing machine. It is a steel contraption a bit like those metal detectors through which one must pass at international airports. An electronic eye, built into the machine, registers exactly the angle of the bow and lights flicker on at fifteen degrees, thirty degrees and forty-five degrees. The teacher of the bowing class explained that the "fifteen bow" was for an informal greeting to colleagues. The "thirty bow" was appropriate for meeting senior members of the store, and the deepest bow essential when welcoming clients, shoppers and other visitors. Much of the average day of an elevator girl is spent at a perfect forty-five degree angle.

Yoko does not find this in the least humiliating, or even dull.   7
Learning a skill like this is a challenge, and she is eager to get it just right. The girls were lined up in front of the machine and one by one, like pupils at a gymnastics class, they walked up to make three bows. Yoko missed the first one by several degrees; the disapproving noise of an electronic buzzer told her so. She blushed. The second, thirty degrees, she got wrong again, by inches. Determined to get it right the next time, she bent down, back straight, fingers together and eyes trained to the floor about three feet from her toes — the light flashed, she did it, a smile of contentment spread across her face.

This is an extreme — though in Japan by no means despised —   8
example of the insistence on form and of the way it is taught. The training of elevator girls also points to another constant factor in Japanese attitudes to work: form in human relations. The importance of etiquette and ritual in Japanese work is vital. When male bosses tell their female staff that serving tea, bowing to clients and other such ceremonial functions are as necessary as the jobs usually reserved for men, they are only being partly hypocritical. To be sure, many men would feel threatened if too many women encroached on their traditional domains. It is much safer to insist that women should stick to the home after marriage or, in the case of unmarried "office ladies" (OLs), stick to making tea or other ceremonies. But, at the same time, Japanese do attach far more importance to such decorative functions than Westerners tend to do; and they genuinely feel that women do them best. Although some Western tourists might find the artificial ways of elevator girls grating, humiliating or, at best, quaint, Japanese feel comfortable with them and indeed miss such service when it is not provided.

Men, too, spend much of their time on the rites of human rela-   9
tions. Although Japanese have a strong sense of hierarchy, decisions are based upon at least a show of consensus. This makes it difficult to take individual initiatives, and passing the buck is therefore a national sport. Consensus, as indeed all forms of Japanese business, is built on personal relations. These relations are based on mutual obligations: if I do this for you, you do that for me. Such favors are rarely expressed directly and relations take much time and effort to cement. This is where most salarymen — the middle-ranking samurai of today — come in. Because there are so many salarymen and so many relations to cement, many hours are spent in coffee shops during the day and bars

and restaurants at night. This may seem inconsequential or even parasitic to the Western mind. It certainly does not make for efficiency. But just as the trade of rugs in the Middle East cannot proceed without endless cups of tea, the coffee shop workers are the backbone of the Japanese miracle. Let us turn again to an example.

Every table at the Café L'Etoile, a coffee shop in the Ginza, was   10 occupied. Through the thick screen of cigarette smoke one could just discern Kazuo Sasaki, a young employee of one of the largest advertising companies. He was exchanging *meishi* (name cards) with three men from a small public relations firm. All four of them studied the cards carefully, made polite hissing noises and sat down. Sasaki ordered his tenth cup of coffee and lit his thirteenth filter-tipped cigarette.

His order was taken by a uniformed young waiter who yelled out   11 the command to another waiter, who shouted it to another link in the chain. The effect was highly theatrical — a spectacle of work, as it were. This particular gimmick was unique to L'Etoile and new waiters were drilled endlessly until they got it just right.

So much of Sasaki's day was spent meeting people in coffee shops   12 that it was easier to reach him at Café L'Etoile than at his office. He has been working for his company for four years. His main job is to delegate commissions taken by his company to smaller companies, who then often delegate them to even smaller firms.

Business was not much discussed at Café L'Etoile. It would be   13 indelicate to come directly to the point. Instead, Sasaki had become expert at discussing golf handicaps — the nearest he got to a golf course himself was one of those practicing ranges where one spent hours hitting balls into a giant net. He also had an endless supply of jokes about last night's hangover, or jocular comments on his client's sexual prowess. He always knew the latest baseball results and could talk for hours about television programs. On those rare occasions when an eccentric client insisted on talking about politics or books, Sasaki was at least a good listener. He has, in short, the social graces of a very superior barber.

In a country where so much depends on social graces, this is not   14 to be despised. It is, I think rightly, argued that human relationships in Japan transcend abstract ideals of right and wrong. This is not true, for instance, in the Judeo-Christian tradition, where God is the final arbiter, in whose eyes we shall be judged. To commit perjury in a Japanese court, to protect one's boss, is the moral thing to do. Loyalty transcends a mere law.

Human relations based on hierarchy are a comfort to many, espe-   15 cially in a highly competitive world. In most Japanese companies seniority counts for more than competence and, ideally, one's job is forever assured. This works best for mediocrity — which, for face-saving reasons, is rarely exposed — and worst for talented mavericks.

Talent, being highly individualistic and thus socially troublesome, is not always highly regarded in Japan. Hard work and skill, especially in the sense of dexterity (*kiyō*), are the two qualities Japanese pride themselves on as a people. The traditional Japanese stress on refining and miniaturizing everything — the Korean critic Yi O Ryong argues that this is the key to Japanese culture — may explain the modern success in transistor, microchip or camera making. But although manual dexterity, the appearance of consensus and the discipline — not to say docility — of the Japanese rank and file account for some of Japan's success story, no country can succeed without talented mavericks. Despite the Japanese saying that nails that stick out must be hammered in, there are those odd, talented exceptions, even in Japan, who refuse to be hammered in. Though sometimes respected, such people are rarely liked. The great Japanese filmmaker Akira Kurosawa, known in Japan as The Emperor, is a case in point. He is undoubtedly one of the greatest artists of the century, but Japanese critics have consistently tried to pull him off his pedestal, often in snide personal attacks. He has consistently refused to toe the social line; he has neither masters nor pupils; the ritual of human relations is less important to him than his talent. He is, in short, a loner, as is almost every truly gifted man or woman in this collectivist society.

But the creative force in Japan comes from these loners. They tend to come to the fore mostly in periods of social instability. The immediate aftermath of World War II seems to have been especially congenial to nonconformist entrepreneurs. Akio Morita, founder of Sony, Konosuke Matsushita of Matsushita and Soichirō Honda, the grand old man behind the motor cars, immediately come to mind. The interesting thing about such creative oddballs is that once they make it to the top, they almost invariably become traditional masters, laying down the rules for the young to follow. They are more than teachers of technical skills or business methods, in the manner of such figures as Lee Iacocca. In fact, they conform more closely to the image of the classical Confucian sage, concerned with ethics and moral philosophy rather than technique. Matsushita wrote a kind of bible, expounding his philosophy; and Honda's autobiography has an equally lofty tone.

Recently the enormous success of high technology industries has spurred a new generation of mavericks — whiz kids, laying the paths to Japanese versions of Silicon Valley. Such people are especially interesting as they combine the old Japanese penchant for miniature refinement and uncommon individualism. They often get their start in research and development departments of large companies, but proceed to break with the time-honored tradition of company loyalty to start their own firms. According to an official at the Ministry of International Trade and Industry there are now about five thousand "highly innovative" small companies with the potential to emerge as future Sonys or Hondas. No doubt their leaders, too, will one day write their books and become masters.

Although the difference between artist and craftsmen has never   19 been as clear in Japan as in the post-romantic West, there have always been mavericks in the arts as well. But those who do not follow masters often pay a heavy price. The number of suicides among Japanese writers in this century cannot be a mere romantic aberration. Such artists, like the gung-ho entrepreneurs, also thrive in times of unrest. The turbulent early nineteenth century produced such highly eccentric playwrights as Tsuruya Namboku and artists such as Ekin, who rejected every traditional school and persisted in a highly individualistic style. Two famous eccentric geniuses of our own time are Kurosawa and the author Yukio Mishima (1925–1970), Japan's most celebrated twentieth-century novelist, who ended his life at forty-five in a dramatic suicide.

Creative loners are by no means limited to men. In some periods   20 of Japanese history women had more freedom to express themselves than men, paradoxically because they had less freedom to engage in other public pursuits. Perhaps the greatest period for Japanese literature was the Heian (794–1185), particularly the tenth century, when the *kana* syllabary, a truly indigenous script, was developed. While educated men—virtually restricted to the aristocracy—still wrote in literary Chinese, talented women expressed themselves in the vernacular; the obvious example being Murasaki Shikibu (978–1015/31?), the author of *Genji monogatari (The Tale of Genji)*. One of the greatest writers of modern Japan was also a woman: Higuchi Ichiyō (1872–1896), who lived and died—very young—at the end of the nineteenth century. Both women wrote mostly about loneliness—a common theme in literature and a usual fate of writers anywhere, to be sure, but especially in Japan, where isolation from the common herd is particularly keenly felt.

So originality and creativity do exist in Japan. But they are all too   21 often stifled by the pressure to conform. It takes tremendous courage to continue on in one's individual course. Let us be thankful for those few who do. But while such gifted eccentrics are rarer than in countries where individualism is fostered, there is an advantage to the Japanese preference for skill over originality. In places where everyone wants to be a star, but mediocrity necessarily prevails, there is a disturbing lack of pride in an ordinary job well done. In Western Europe there is even a perverse tendency to be proud of sloppiness.

Japan may have fewer Nobel Prize winners than, say, Britain, but to see a shop girl wrap a package or a factoryworker assemble a bike is to see routine work developed to a fine art. This, the lack of Nobel Prizes not withstanding, may be Japan's grandest tradition.

EXERCISES

Words to Know

repetitive (paragraph 1), zeal (1), honing (1), preoccupation (1), elusive (1), ego (1), transcending (1), public domain (1), infringement (2), minutest (2), aesthetic (2), pompous (5), falsetto (5), sprightly (5), hypocritical (8), encroached (8), domains (8), quaint (8), hierarchy (9), consensus (9), initiatives (9), passing the buck (9), samurai (9), parasitic (9), indelicate (13), jocular (13), eccentric (13), Judeo-Christian tradition (14), arbiter (14), perjury (14), transcends (14), seniority (15), mediocrity (15), mavericks (15), dexterity (16), miniaturizing (16), docility (16), pedestal (16), collectivist society (16), social instability (17), entrepreneurs (17), Confucian sage (17), expounding (17), spawned (18), Silicon Valley (18), penchant (18), post-romantic West (19), aberration (19), gung-ho entrepreneurs (19), eccentric (19), paradoxically (20), syllabary (20), indigenous (20), fostered (21), perverse (21).

Some of the Issues

1. In paragraph 1 Buruma cites two character traits commonly attributed to the Japanese. What are they?
2. In what way does the traditional Japanese notion of a personal style differ from that in the West?
3. How do private and public selves differ from each other in Japan, according to the author?
4. What, according to Buruma, is the particular importance of being an elevator girl?
5. Describe the process of training an elevator girl. Why would Yoko find it challenging? How does the author relate the challenge to the importance of style in human relations in Japan?
6. The story about the salaryman Kazuo Sasaki also concerns personal style. What leads Buruma so say that Sasaki has "the social graces of a very superior barber"? Why are such social graces valuable in Japanese culture?
7. How does Buruma account for the rise of the great entrepreneurs? What is the general attitude toward them?

8. What according to Buruma are the results of the Japanese preference for skill over originality?
9. Why would loneliness be a persistent theme in Japanese literature?
10. In paragraph 21 Buruma cites the advantages of the Japanese
    outlook on work. What are they?
* 11. Read Robert N. Bellah's "American Individualism." Compare his
    concept of the loner in American culture to Buruma's analysis of
    the position of the loner in Japan.
* 12. Read John David Morley's "The Japanese Home." What do you
    learn about Japanese style there that relates to Buruma's views?

The Way We Are Told

13. How does the author try to show that Yoko's training is not viewed
    as humiliating or at least boring, but as challenging?
14. In the description of Kazuo Sasaki at the Café L'Etoile, how does
    Buruma demonstrate the importance of style over substance?
15. How does Buruma show the ambivalent attitude toward the per-
    son of talent, the loner? How does he distinguish him or her from
    the American type?

Some Subjects for Essays

16. If you have ever been trained for a job, describe the training. What
    would you say was its aim? How did it differ in its purpose from
    the training given to Yoko?
17. Read John David Morley's "The Japanese Home." In what re-
    spects, would you say, does the Japanese home reflect, as well as
    contribute, to the ambivalent attitude toward the person who
    stands out from the crowd?

SIN, SUFFER
AND REPENT

Donna Woolfolk Cross

Donna Woolfolk Cross was born in New York City in 1947 and
teaches English at Onondaga Community College. Her books are
concerned with the uses and abuses of language, especially in
advertising and the media: *Speaking of Words* (1977, with James
MacKillup), *Word Abuse: How the Words We Use Abuse Us*
(1979), and *Mediaspeak* (1981), from which the following selection is taken. It describes and analyzes an American cultural
phenomenon that has spread across the globe: the soap opera.

Soap operas reverse Tolstoy's famous assertion in Anna Karenina *that
"Happy families are all alike; every unhappy family is unhappy in its
own way." On soaps, every family is unhappy, and each is unhappy
in more or less the same way.*

— Marjory Perloff

*It is the hope of every advertiser to habituate the housewife to an
engrossing narrative whose optimum length is forever and at the
same time to saturate all levels of her consciousness with the miracle
of a given product, so she will be aware of it all the days of her life
and mutter its name in her sleep.*

— James Thurber

In July 1969, when the entire nation was glued to television sets 1
watching the first man walk on the moon, an irate woman called a
Wausau, Wisconsin, TV station to complain that her favorite soap
opera was not being shown that day and why was that. The station
manager replied, "This is probably the most important news story of
the century, something you may never again see the equal of." Unim-
pressed, the lady replied, "Well, I hope they crash."

One can hardly blame her. For weeks, she had been worrying that 2
Audrey might be going blind, that Alice would marry that scoundrel
Michael, and that Dr. Hardy might not discover his patient Peter to be
his long-lost natural son before the boy died of a brain tumor. Suddenly, in the heat of all these crises, she was cut off from all informa-

312

tion about these people and forced to watch the comings and goings of men in rubber suits whom she had never met. It was enough to unhinge anybody.

Dedicated watchers of soap operas often confuse fact with fic-   3
tion.* Sometimes this can be endearing, sometimes ludicrous. During the Senate Watergate hearings (which were broadcast on daytime television), viewers whose favorite soap operas were preempted simply adopted the hearings as substitute soaps. Daniel Shorr reports that the listeners began "telephoning the networks to criticize slow-moving sequences, suggesting script changes and asking for the return of favorite witnesses, like 'that nice John Dean.'"

Stars of soap operas tell hair-raising stories of their encounters   4
with fans suffering from this affliction. Susan Lucci, who plays the promiscuous Erica Kane on "All My Children," tells of a time she was riding in a parade: "We were in a crowd of about 250,000, traveling in an antique open car moving ver-r-ry slowly. At that time in the series I was involved with a character named Nick. Some man broke through, came right up to the car and said to me, 'Why don't you give *me* a little bit of what you've been giving Nick?'" The man hung onto the car, menacingly, until she was rescued by the police. Another time, when she was in church, the reverent silence was broken by a woman's astonished remark, "Oh, my god, Erica prays!" Margaret Mason, who plays the villainous Lisa Anderson in "Days of Our Lives," was accosted by a woman who poured a carton of milk all over her in the supermarket. And once a woman actually tried to force her car off the Ventura Freeway.

Just as viewers come to confuse the actors with their roles, so too   5
they see the soap opera image of life in America as real. The National Institutes of Mental Health reported that a majority of Americans actually adopt what they see in soap operas to handle their own life problems. The images are not only "true to life"; they are a guide for living.

What, then, is the image of life on soap operas? For one thing,   6
marriage is touted as the *ne plus ultra* of a woman's existence. Living together is not a respectable condition and is tolerated only as long as one of the partners (usually the woman) is bucking for eventual marriage. Casual sex is out; only the most despicable villains engage in

---

*Contrary to popular belief, soap operas are not the harmless pastime of lonely housewives only. Recent surveys show that many high school and college students, as well as many working and professional people, are addicted to soaps. A sizable chunk of the audience is men. Such well-known people as Sammy Davis, Jr., Van Cliburn, John Connally, and Supreme Court Justice Thurgood Marshall admit to being fans of one or more soap operas.

it: "Diane has no respect for marriage or any of the values we were
brought up with. She's a vicious, immoral woman." Occasionally, a
woman will speak out against marriage, but it's clear that in her heart
of hearts she really wants it. Women who are genuinely not interested
in marriage do not appear on soap operas except as occasional caricatures, misguided and immature in their thinking. Reporter Martha
McGee appeared on "Ryan's Hope" just long enough to titillate the
leading man with remarks like, "I don't know if you're my heart's
desire, but you're sexy as hell." Punished for this kind of heretical
remark, she was last seen sobbing brokenly in a telephone booth.

No, love and marriage still go together like a horse and carriage   7
in soap operas, though many marriages don't last long enough for the
couple to put away all the wedding gifts. As Cornell professor Rose
Goldsen says, this is a world of "fly-apart marriages, throwaway husbands, throwaway wives." There is rarely any clear logic behind the
dissolution of these relationships; indeed, the TV formula seems to be:
the happier the marriage, the more perilous the couple's future. A
blissful marriage is the kiss of death: "I just can't believe it about Alice
and Steve. I mean, they were the *perfect* couple, the absolute *perfect*
couple!"

Most marriages are not pulled apart by internal flaws but by   8
external tampering — often by a jealous rival: "C'mon, Peter. Stay for
just one more drink. Jan won't mind. And anyway, the night's still
young. Isn't it nice to be together all nice and cozy like this?"

Often the wife has willfully brought this state of affairs on herself   9
by committing that most heinous of all offenses: neglecting her man.
"NHM" almost always occurs when the woman becomes too wrapped
up in her career. Every time Rachel Corey went to New York City for a
weekend to further her career as a sculptress, her marriage tottered. At
this writing, Ellen Dalton's marriage to Mark appears to be headed for
big trouble as a result of her business trip to Chicago:

> ERICA: I warned you, Ellen, not to let your job interfere with
> your marriage.
> ELLEN: I have tried to do my best for my marriage *and* my
> job . . . Mark had no right to stomp out of here just now.
> ERICA: Don't you understand? He just couldn't take anymore.
> ELLEN: What do you mean?
> ERICA: It's not just the trip to Chicago that Mark resents. It's
> your putting your job before having a family.
> ELLEN: I demand the right to be treated as an equal. I don't have
> to apologize because I don't agree to have a child the minute
> my husband snaps his fingers. I'm going to Chicago like a big
> girl and I'm going to do the job I was hired to do. (stalks out
> the door)

ERICA: (musing, to herself) Well, I may be old-fashioned, but
that's no way to hold onto your man.

Career women do appear frequently on soap operas, but the ones   10
who are romantically successful treat their careers as a kind of side-
line. Female cardiologists devote fifteen years of their lives to advanced medical training, then spend most of their time in the hospital
coffee shop. One man remarked to a career woman who was about to
leave her job, "Oh, Kate, you'll miss working. Those long lunches,
those intimate cocktail hours!" Women residents apparently schedule
all their medical emergencies before dinnertime, because if they
should have to stay late at the hospital, it's the beginning of the end for
their marriages. It's interesting to speculate how they might work this
out:

NURSE: Oh my God, Dr. Peterson, the patient's hemorrhaging!
DR. PETERSON: Sorry, nurse, it'll just have to wait. If I don't get
my meat loaf in by a quarter to six, it'll never be ready before
my husband gets home.

Husbands, weak-minded souls, cannot be expected to hold out   11
against the advances of any attractive woman, even one for whom they
have contempt, if their wives aren't around. Meatloafless, they are very
easily seduced. The clear suggestion is that they could hardly have
been expected to do otherwise:

"Well, after all, Karen, you weren't around very much during
that time. It's not surprising that Michael turned to Pat for a
little comfort and understanding."

If, in the brief span of time allotted to them, a couple manage to   12
have intercourse, the woman is certain to become pregnant. Contraception on soap operas is such a sometime thing that even the Pope
could scarcely object to it. The birthrate on soaps is eight times as high
as the United States birthrate; indeed it's higher than the birthrate of
any underdeveloped nation in the world. This rabbitlike reproduction
is fraught with peril. One recent study revealed that out of nineteen
soap opera pregnancies, eight resulted in miscarriages and three in
death for the mother. Rose Goldsen has estimated that the odds are 7 to
10 against any fetus making it to full term, worse if you include getting
through the birth canal. Women on soap operas miscarry at the drop of
a pin. And, of course, miscarriages are rarely caused by any defect with
mother or baby: again, external forces are to blame. Often, miscarriage
is brought on by an unappreciative or unfaithful mate. For example, on
"Another World," Alice the heroine, suffered a miscarriage when her
husband visited his ex-wife Rachel. One woman lost her baby because
her husband came home drunk. This plot twist is no doubt particularly

appealing to women viewers because of the instant revenge visited upon the transgressing mate. They can fantasize about similar punishment for husbandly malfeasance in their own lives — and about his inevitable guilt and repentance:

> HUSBAND: (stonily) Jennifer, these potatoes are too gluey. I can't eat this!
> WIFE: (clutches her belly) Oh, no!
> HUSBAND: What? What is it?
> WIFE: It's the baby! Something's wrong — call the doctor!
> HUSBAND: Oh my god, what have I done?
> *Later, at the hospital*:
> DOCTOR: I'm sorry, Mr. Henson, but your wife has lost the baby.
> HUSBAND: (brokenly)I didn't know, I didn't know. How could I have attacked her potatoes so viciously with her in such a delicate condition!
> DOCTOR: Now, now. You musn't blame yourself. We still don't know exactly what causes miscarriages except that they happen for a complicated set of physical and emotional reasons.
> HUSBAND: Oh, thank you, Doctor.
> DOCTOR: Of course, carping about the potatoes couldn't have *helped*.

Miscarriage is effective as a punishment because it is one of the very worst things that can happen to a woman on a soap opera. In the world of soaps, the one thing every good and worthwhile woman wants is a baby. Soap operas never depict childless women as admirable. These "real people" do not include women like Katharine Hepburn, who once announced that she never wanted to have children because "the first time the kid said no to me, I'd kill it!" Childless women are either to be pitied, if there are physical reasons that prevent them from getting pregnant, or condemned, if they are childless by choice. [13]

Second only to neglecting her man in her hierarchy of female crime is having an abortion. No admirable character *ever* gets an abortion on a soap opera. Occasionally, however, a virtuous woman will consider it, usually for one of two reasons: she doesn't want the man she loves to feel "trapped" into marrying her; or she has been "violated" by her husband's best friend, a member of the underworld, or her delivery boy, who may also be her long-lost half brother. But she always "comes around" in the end, her love for "the new life growing inside me" conquering her misgivings. If the baby should happen to survive the perilous journey through the birth canal (illegitimate babies get miscarried at a far higher rate than legitimate ones), she [14] never has any regrets. Why should she? Babies on soap operas never drool, spit up, or throw scrambled eggs in their mothers' faces. Babyhood (and its inevitable counterpart, motherhood) is "sold" to American women as slickly as soap. Kimberly, of "Ryan's Hope," is so distressed when she finds out she is pregnant that she runs away from home. She has the baby, prematurely, while alone and unattended on a deserted houseboat. It is a difficult and dangerous birth. But once the baby is born, Kimberly is all maternal affection. "Where is she?" she shouts. "Why won't they let me see my little girl?" By the end of the day, she announces, "If anything happens to this baby, I don't know what I'll do!"

Under the surface of romantic complications, soap operas sell a   15
vision of morality and American family life, of a society where marriage is the highest good, sex the greatest evil, where babies are worshiped and abortion condemned, where motherhood is exalted and children ignored. It is a vision of a world devoid of social conflict. There are hardly any short-order cooks, bus drivers, mechanics, construction workers, or farmers on soap operas. Blue-collar problems do not enter these immaculate homes. No one suffers from flat feet or derrière spread from long hours spent at an unrewarding or frustrating job. The upwardly mobile professionals who populate soap operas love their work, probably because they are hardly ever at it—one lawyer clocked in at his office exactly once in three months. Their problems are those of people with time on their hands to covet the neighbor's wife, track down villains, betray friends, and enjoy what one observer has called "the perils of Country Club Place."

It is a world largely devoid of black people and black viewpoints.   16
When black characters do appear, they are doctors or lawyers whose problems, ambitions, and anxieties are identical to those of their white colleagues.* Racial discrimination and inequality do not exist, and the black romantic plotlines are indistinguishable from white—though, of course, the two *never* mix. Once, it is true, in a daring departure from the straight and narrow, "All My Children" showed a black-white romance which shocked a lot of viewers. But it wasn't really a romance in the usual sense. At least, it was perfectly clear that black Dr. Nancy Grant had turned to her white boyfriend Owen solely for comfort after the breakup of her marriage to black Dr. Frank Grant. They were not—gasp!—sleeping together. Anyway, the whole mess was re-

---

*"All My Children" has recently introduced a "lower-class" black character—a streetwise teenager named Jesse, who is the despair of his black aunt and uncle, both doctors. It is clear, however, that Jesse's scorn for Establishment values is merely a defense against rejection, and his eventual conversion and admittance to Pine Valley society seems inevitable.

solved when Owen considerately died just minutes after marrying
Nancy to save her from disgrace because she was pregnant with black
Dr. Frank Grant's baby. Another experiment with a black-white flirta-
tion was abruptly ended when the black family moved to another
town. Still another such plotline was resolved when it turned out that
the white woman in an interracial relationship was actually a light-
skinned black woman who had been "ashamed" of her heritage.

The world of soap operas is without doubt white, upper middle-   17
class—and decidedly small-town. Emerging out of the mists of the
American heartland as mysteriously as Brigadoon are towns like Oak-
dale, Pine Valley, Rosehill. On soap operas, towns never have real-life
names like Secaucus or Weedsport. The great American myth of the
Good, Clean, Safe Small Town, which some thought had been laid to
rest by the likes of Sinclair Lewis and Sherwood Anderson, has been
resurrected on the soaps. Only in small towns, the daily message is,
can one find true happiness and fulfillment:

> CAROL: I've wondered sometimes if you don't get bored living
>   in Oakdale? Living in New York or on the Coast can be so
>   much more exciting.
> SANDY: Excitement is one thing. Real feelings are another.

One half expects her to add, "Oh, Auntie Em, there's no place like
home!"

EXERCISES

Words to Know

Quotations: assertion, habituate, engrossing, optimum, saturate, mutter. irate (paragraph 1), scoundrel (2), natural son (2), unhinge (2),
endearing (3) ludicrous (3), Watergate (3), preempted (3), affliction
(4), promiscuous (4), villainous (4), accosted (4), touted (6), *ne
plus ultra*—highest point (6), bucking (6), despicable (6), caricatures (6), titillate (6), heretical (6), dissolution (7), perilous (7),
tampering (8), heinous (9), sculptress (9), tottered (9), cardiologists
(10), hemorrhaging (10), allotted (12), contraception (12), underdeveloped (12), fraught (12), fetus (12), transgressing (12), fantasize
(12), malfeasance (12), inevitable (12), repentance (12), carping
(12), hierarchy (14), misgiving (14), perilous (14), exalted (15),
devoid (15), blue-collar (15), immaculate (15), derrière (15), upwardly mobile (15), covet (15), colleagues (16), Establishment (16,

footnote), inevitable (16, footnote), Brigadoon (17), Sinclair Lewis (17), Sherwood Anderson (17).

Some of the Issues

1. After you have read the essay examine its title: "Sin, Suffer and Repent." Who is it that sins, suffers, and repents?
2. Cross gives several instances of soap viewers confusing soap-opera life with real life. Cite them. What does the confusion consist of? Why is it important for her to convince us that there is confusion?
3. Cross cites several examples of characters who break the moral code of the soaps. What happens to them? Are the consequences different for male characters and female characters?
4. Summarize what the soaps say about working women. What kind of restrictions are they placed under? Are men's jobs portrayed in the same way?
5. What is the attitude toward motherhood expressed in soaps? Toward children? Why do you think there are so many miscarriages?
6. Why are husbands portrayed as "weak-minded souls"? Are men in soaps given more, or less, dignity than women?
7. Why do women in soap operas who carry illegitimate babies miscarry more often?
8. How, according to Cross, do the soaps treat abortion? Is it the worst crime?
9. How are members of minorities treated on soaps according to Cross?

The Way We Are Told

10. In several instances, Cross supports her arguments with citations from authorities. Find the ones in which a specific source is cited, and others which are more vague. How convincing is Cross's use of authorities?
11. Cross uses what are apparently actual excerpts from the soaps, but also makes up her own parodies of soap-opera dialog to convince us. Does she make the difference clear? Is what she does fair?
12. What is the effect of the abbreviation NHM (paragraph 9)?
13. In paragraph 14 several single words are emphasized by putting them in quotation marks. What is the effect of doing so?
14. Cross has a serious purpose in writing this essay. Are her uses of humor, irony, and exaggeration appropriate? Examine some specific examples.

Some Subjects for Essays

15. Write an essay justifying *one* of the following propositions:
    a. Soap operas are a harmless entertainment, and nobody is likely to confuse soap-opera life with real life.
    b. While soap operas may occasionally distort reality, on the whole they do provide an accurate picture of American life.
    c. Soaps have a detrimental effect on their audiences, and steps should be taken to discourage their production.
16. Soap operas are interspersed with commercials. Examine a daytime soap, looking at the picture of life in both the commercial messages and the drama. Can you see ways in which they reinforce each other?
17. Design a questionnaire about the soap-opera viewing habits of your classmates, and summarize and explain your findings in an essay. Include questions that can help you determine whether soap operas have changed in any of their basic values since the time of Cross's essay.
* 18. Read Michael Arlen's "Ring Around the Collar!" He talks about the portrayal of women in TV commercials. Compare and contrast his description with those of women's roles in soaps as defined by Cross.

RING AROUND
THE COLLAR!

Michael J. Arlen

Michael J. Arlen was born in London in 1930. He attended Harvard
University and became a reporter for *Life* magazine upon graduation in 1952. Since 1957 he has been television critic for the *New
Yorker*. Arlen's books include *The Living Room War* (1969),
Exiles (1970), *Passage to Ararat* (1975), *Thirty Seconds*
(1980), and *The Camera Age* (1980). He won a National Book
Award in 1976. The following selection comes from *The View
from Highway 1* (1976). Arlen's brief essay is an analysis of a
popular TV commercial; he describes the commercial and examines its impact and cultural context.

This half-minute commercial for a laundry detergent called Wisk ap-   1
pears fairly frequently on daytime and evening television. In a recent
version, a young woman and a young man are shown being led down
the corridor of a hotel by a bellman who is carrying suitcases. The
hotel seems to be an attractive one — not very elegant but definitely
not an ordinary motel. Similarly, the young man and woman are attractive, but with nothing either glamorous or working-class about their
appearance. Perhaps he is a junior executive. And she is probably his
wife, though there is nothing so far that says that the two people are
married. Since the framework of the drama is a commercial, the assumption is that they *are* married. On the other hand, against the
familiar framework of similar modern movie scenes, there is no such
assumption; possibly it is the beginning of an adventure. Then, suddenly, the bellman drops one of the suitcases in the corridor; some of
the contents of the suitcase spill out; the bellman crouches down on
the corridor carpet to put the items back in. He notices one of the
man's shirts and holds it up. "Ring around the collar!" he says accus-
ingly; these words are then taken up in the kind of singsong chant that
has become a feature of these ads. The man looks puzzled and let
down. The woman examines the offending shirt and looks mortified

and aghast. By now, whatever slight elegance or intimations of adventure may have existed at the beginning of the scene have totally disintegrated, and, indeed, have quickly re-formed themselves into the classic hubby-and-housewife focus of most television commercials. The wife admits her mistake — to the bellman and her husband — of having used an inadequate detergent, and the scene changes to what is apparently the laundry area of her house, where the wife (now back in her regular "wifely" clothes) discusses the merits of using Wisk when doing the family wash.

    In a number of ways, this is the most noticeably irritating of the 2 housewife commercials. There is a nagging, whiny quality to the "Ring around the collar!" chant which is almost a caricature of the nagging, whiny voices of earlier Hollywood and TV-commercial housewives but which deliberately stops before the point of caricature is reached. In the manner of certain other ads — especially those for aspirin and "cold remedies" — it is a commercial that expressly announces its own irritatingness. We are going to repeat and repeat and repeat, these commercials say, and we are going to grate on your nerves — and you are going to remember us. At times, this sales approach has been given various fine-sounding methodological names by advertisers, but essentially it is the voice of the small boy who wants something: I want, I want, I want, I want — and finally you give it to him. In this case, the small boy wants you to buy his detergent, and who is to tell him no?

    On the level of anti-female condescension, the "Ring around the 3 collar!" ad seems to go even beyond irritation. In most housewife commercials, the housewife is portrayed as little more than a simpering, brainless jelly, almost pathologically obsessed with the world of kitchen floors or laundry, or of the celebrated "bathroom bowl." But in the Wisk commercials the standard trivializing portrait is accompanied by quite unusual brutality. As if in a reverse Cinderella process, the young prince and his companion not only are stopped in their tracks by the hazard of the Dirty Shirt (and the curse cry of "Ring around the collar!") but, instantly, as if under a magic spell, are snatched from the hotel-palace and returned to their previous existence — she to profess folk-happiness among the laundry tubs, and he, presumably, to his northern New England sales route. Sex is back to what it used to be: the identityless woman in the traveling suit is replaced by the beaming housewife in housewifely attire. And it is all the result of *her* failure in not having properly attended to her husband's needs — in having exposed him to the scorn of the bellman who guarded the erotic corridor. The fable does not end in tragedy — for though Cinderella is back among the laundry tubs, she now has good magic on her side. But it has been a sobering experience.

EXERCISES

Words to Know

bellman (paragraph 1), mortified (1), aghast (1), intimations (1), disintegrated (1), caricature (2), grate (2), methodological (2), condescension (3), simpering (3), pathologically obsessed (3), trivializing (3), identityless (3), erotic (3), sobering (3).

Some of the Issues

1. Why must the couple in the commercial be neither glamorous nor working-class?
2. What do we assume about the relationship of the man and the woman when we first see them in the hotel corridor?
3. Explain the man's and the woman's differing reactions to the offending shirt.
4. When the locale changes at the end of the commercial, what do we then know about the couple?
5. Why is it important that the "Ring around the collar!" jingle is *almost* a caricature?
6. Explain why the level of "anti-female condescension" in this commercial is higher than in other, similar ones, according to Arlen?
7. Account for the reasons for Arlen's assertion that the Wisk commercial is "a reverse Cinderella process."

The Way We Are Told

8. This selection consists of three fairly long paragraphs, each with a specific function. Describe the function of each. How does Arlen make the transition from paragraph to paragraph?
9. Arlen is careful in paragraph 1 not to go beyond what the TV screen and sound track tell the viewer. Show what words and phrases he uses in order not to exceed the limits of the "story" told in the commercial.
10. Like the commercial itself, Arlen uses the device of repetition to make an impact on the reader. Find some examples where he either repeats outright or does so using slightly different phrasing.
11. Though it would probably be easy to caricature the Wisk commercial by humorously exaggerating some of its effects, Arlen tries to avoid that approach. There are, however, a few places where he uses a satirical tone. Find some of them.

Some Subjects for Essays

12. If you have seen a different version of the commercial, describe it in a manner similar to Arlen's. Is the same attitude toward women reflected in the version you have chosen? Or if "Ring around the collar!" is no longer being chanted in your area, analyze another commercial whose content and view of society are irritating to you.

13. Is the simpering housewife the only view of women we see in television commercials, or are there others? Select one, or a set, of commercials that give a different stereotypical view of women, and describe and analyze them.

* 14. Read Donna Woolfolk Cross's "Sin, Suffer and Repent." Then watch an installment or two of a soap opera, paying particular attention to the commercials that appear with it. In an essay try to analyze the relationship between soap and ad: Why, do you think, would a particular sponsor want to associate his product or service with the soap opera? Are there any links, in content or treatment, between soap and ad?

PART EIGHT

Reflections

The word *reflection* has a precise meaning in science: the moon reflects the light of the sun to the earth. A mirror reflects — gives back — an image placed in front of it. To reflect on something means to give it more careful, thoughtful consideration. The selections grouped in Part Eight of *Crossing Cultures* relate to each other not because they have a common theme like "Growing Up" or "Families" but because they are considerations or reconsiderations of basic cross-cultural issues. Each author looks at a topic from an angle that may seem unusual or surprising, and therefore thought-provoking.

Most Americans, if they have thought about Canada at all, are unlikely to have gone beyond considering that country a friendly neighbor, a country very much like ours in most ways, only colder in the winter. That, as the distinguished writer Margaret Atwood makes clear in the first selection, is not at all what Canadians think of themselves. Similarly, Vine Deloria confronts the reader with ideas about Indians and their relationship to other Americans that urge reconsideration. Adam Smith describes and analyzes the stunning development of Japan to become an industrial superpower and questions whether the United States could, or even would want to, follow Japan's example. Next, Michael Harrington examines the extent and persistence of poverty in America from a point of view that differs from the usual discussions of the subject. He argues that the poor are simply invisible to other, more affluent Americans.

The three selections which follow take the reader to other parts of the globe. Americans generally believe that our assistance to the less-developed countries of the Third World is designed to help them develop, that is, to become more like ourselves. Ivan Illich, in his essay "Effects of Development," argues that our help, far from being beneficial, may actually retard development. The next essay questions another belief widely held in industrialized countries. Most people assume that the steadily increasing industrialization of Third World countries is beneficial for their inhabitants because it frees them from the backbreaking labor in the fields and provides an abundance of new, better jobs in factories and workshops. Barbara Ehrenreich and Annette Fuentes, in their essay "Life on the Global Assembly Line," cast doubt on that assumption by discussing both the working conditions and the social and cultural problems created by that development.

The final selection in Part Eight reaches back two hundred and fifty years: Jonathan Swift, clergyman, suggests rather brutally to his fellow Englishmen of the mid-eighteenth century that they need to reflect on the consequences of the way they treat the people of Ireland.

CANADIANS:
WHAT DO THEY WANT?

Margaret Atwood

Margaret Atwood is one of Canada's foremost contemporary writers. She was born in Ottawa in 1939 and holds a B.A. degree from the University of Toronto and an M.A. from Radcliffe (Harvard). She has served as writer in residence at several universities and has received a number of honorary degrees and prizes for her writing. Poet, novelist, and essayist, she is best known for her novels, among them *The Edible Woman* (1970), *Lady Oracle* (1976), *Life Before Man* (1980), *The Handmaid's Tale* (1985), and *Cat's Eye* (1988).

With its ten provinces and vast Northern and Yukon Territories stretching toward the North Pole, Canada is larger than the United States. But with some twenty-four million inhabitants, the size of its population is just 10 percent of that of its southern (and only) neighbor. Canadians often complain that Americans know far too little about Canada, taking it for granted as an ally, a trading partner, and a fellow democracy. Canadians are concerned about dominance by its much more powerful neighbor, and not only economic but cultural dominance as well.

About one in four Canadians is French-speaking, most of them living in the province of Quebec, north of New York State and New England. Just as Canadians in general are concerned about being dominated by the United States, so French Canadians are concerned about being deprived of their culture by the English-speaking majority, which has led to a separatist movement and some legislation restricting the use of English in Quebec. (For more information on restrictions against English in Quebec read Robert McCrum, William Cran, and Robert MacNeil's "World Language: English.")

Last month, during a poetry reading, I tried out a short prose poem called "How to Like Men." It began by suggesting that one start with the feet. Unfortunately, the question of jackboots soon arose, and things went on from there. After the reading I had a conversation with a young man who thought I had been unfair to men. He wanted men to be liked totally, not just from the heels to the knees, and not just as individuals but as a group; and he thought it negative and inegalitarian of me to have alluded to war and rape. I pointed out that as far as any of us knew these were two activities not widely engaged in by women, but he was still upset. "We're both in this together," he protested. I admitted that this was so; but could he, maybe, see that our relative positions might be a little different.

This is the conversation one has with Americans, even, uh, *good* Americans, when the dinner-table conversation veers round to Canadian-American relations. "We're in this together," they like to say, especially when it comes to continental energy reserves. How do you *explain* to them, as delicately as possible, why they are not categorically beloved? It gets like the old Lifebuoy ads: even their best friends won't tell them. And Canadians are supposed to be their best friends, right? Members of the family?

Well, sort of. Across the river from Michigan, so near and yet so far, there I was at the age of eight, reading *their* Donald Duck comic books (originated however by one of *ours*; yes, Walt Disney's parents were Canadian) and coming at the end to Popsicle Pete, who promised me the earth if only I would save wrappers, but took it all away from me again with a single asterisk: Offer Good Only in the United States. Some cynical members of the world community may be forgiven for thinking that the same asterisk is there, in invisible ink, on the Constitution and the Bill of Rights.

But quibbles like that aside, and good will assumed, how does one go about liking Americans? Where does one begin? Or, to put it another way, why did the Canadian women lock themselves in the john during a '70s "international" feminist conference being held in Toronto? Because the American sisters were being "imperialist," that's why.

But then, it's always a little naive of Canadians to expect that Americans, of whatever political stamp, should stop being imperious. How can they? The fact is that the United States is an empire and Canada is to it as Gaul was to Rome.

It's hard to explain to Americans what it feels like to be a Canadian. Pessimists among us would say that one has to translate the experience into their own terms and that this is necessary because Americans are incapable of thinking in any other terms — and this in itself is part of the problem. (Witness all those draft dodgers who went into culture chock when they discovered to their horror that Toronto was not Syracuse.)

Here is a translation: Picture a Mexico with a population ten times larger than that of the United States. That would put it at about two billion. Now suppose that the official American language is Spanish, that 75 percent of the books Americans buy and 90 percent of the movies they see are Mexican, and that the profits flow across the border to Mexico. If an American does scrape it together to make a movie, the Mexicans won't let him show it in the States, because they own the distribution outlets. If anyone tries to change this ratio, not only the Mexicans but many fellow Americans cry "National chauvinism," or, even more effectively, "National socialism." After all, the American public prefers the Mexican product. It's what they're used to.

Retranslate and you have the current American-Canadian picture.   8
It's changed a little recently, not only on the cultural front. For instance, Canada, some think a trifle late, is attempting to regain control of its own petroleum industry. Americans are predictably angry. They think of Canadian oil as *theirs*.

"What's mine is yours," they have said for years, meaning exports: "What's yours is mine" means ownership and profits. Canadians   9
are supposed to do retail buying, not controlling, or what's an empire for? One could always refer Americans to history, particularly that of their own revolution. They objected to the colonial situation when they themselves were a colony; but then, revolution is considered one of a very few homegrown American products that definitely are not for export.

Objectively, one cannot become too self-righteous about this state of affairs. Canadians owned lots of things, including their souls,   10
before World War II. After that they sold, some say because they had put too much into financing the war, which created a capital vacuum (a position they would not have been forced into if the Americans hadn't kept out of the fighting for so long, say the sore losers). But for whatever reason, capital flowed across the border in the '50s, and Canadians, traditionally sock-under-the-mattress hoarders, were reluctant to invest in their own country. Americans did it for them and ended up with a large part of it, which they retain to this day. In every sellout there's a seller as well as a buyer, and the Canadians did a thorough job of trading their birthright for a mess.

That's on the capitalist end, but when you turn to the trade union   11
side of things you find much the same story, except that the sellout happened in the '30s under the banner of the United Front. Now Canadian workers are finding that in any empire the colonial branch plants are the first to close, and what could be a truly progressive labor movement has been weakened by compromised bargains made in international union headquarters south of the border.

Canadians are sometimes snippy to Americans at cocktail parties.   12
They don't like to feel owned and they don't like having been sold. But what really bothers them — and it's at this point that the United States

and Rome part company — is the wide-eyed innocence with which their snippiness is greeted.

Innocence becomes ignorance when seen in the light of interna-   13
tional affairs, and though ignorance is one of the spoils of conquest —
the Gauls always knew more about the Romans than the Romans knew
about them — the world can no longer afford America's ignorance. Its
ignorance of Canada, though it makes Canadians bristle, is a minor and
relatively harmless example. More dangerous is the fact that individual
Americans seem not to know that the United States is an imperial
power and is behaving like one. They don't want to admit that empires
dominate, invade and subjugate — and live on the proceeds — or,
if they do admit it, they believe in their divine right to do so. The export of divine right is much more harmful than the export of Coca-
Cola, though they may turn out to be much the same thing in the
end.

Other empires have behaved similarly (the British somewhat   14
better, Genghis Khan decidedly worse); but they have not expected to
be *liked* for it. It's the final Americanism, this passion for being liked.
Alas, many Americans are indeed likable; they are often more generous, more welcoming, more enthusiastic, less picky and sardonic than
Canadians, and it's not enough to say it's only because they can afford
it. Some of that revolutionary spirit still remains: the optimism, the
18th-century belief in the fixability of almost anything, the conviction
of the possibility of change. However, at cocktail parties and elsewhere one must be able to tell the difference between an individual
and a foreign policy. Canadians can no longer afford to think of Americans as only a spectator sport. If Reagan blows up the world, we will
unfortunately be doing more than watching it on television. "No
annihilation without representation" sounds good as a slogan, but if
we run it up the flagpole, who's going to salute?

We *are* all in this together. For Canadians, the question is how to   15
survive it. For Americans there is no question, because there does not
have to be. Canada is just that vague, cold place where their uncle
used to go fishing, before the lakes went dead from acid rain.

How do you like Americans? Individually, it's easier. Your aver-   16
age American is no more responsible for the state of affairs than your
average man is for war and rape. Any Canadian who is so narrow-
minded as to dislike Americans merely on principle is missing out on
one of the good things in life. The same might be said, to women, of
men. As a group, as a foreign policy, it's harder. But if you like men,
you can like Americans. Cautiously. Selectively. Beginning with the
feet. One at a time.

EXERCISES

Words to Know

jackboots (paragraph 1), inegalitarian (1), alluded (1), veers (2), categorically (2), asterisk (3), cynical (3), quibbles (4), imperious (5), Gaul (5), pessimists (6), draft dodgers (6), culture shock (6), chauvinism (7), self-righteous (10), progressive (11), compromised (11), snippy (12), spoils (13), subjugate (13), divine right (13), Genghis Khan (14), sardonic (14), annihilation (14), acid rain (15).

Some of the Issues

1. How does Atwood answer the young man who asserts that men and women "are in this together"? How does she respond as a Canadian when Americans tell her the same thing?
2. Why is it hard to explain to Americans what it feels like to be Canadian?
3. Atwood accuses Americans of being imperialists. Does she support that claim? How? Do you think most Americans would be surprised by her accusation? Do you agree with it? Why or why not?
4. Explain the analogy Atwood makes (paragraphs 7 and 8) to help Americans understand Canada's attitudes toward American dominance.
5. What according to Atwood is "one of the few homegrown American products . . . definitely not for export"?
6. In paragraphs 10 and 11 Atwood concedes that Canadians must share some blame for American domination. What specific examples does she give?
7. Atwood accuses Americans of ignorance. Of what in particular? What, according to Atwood, accounts for this ignorance?
8. Atwood admits that many Americans are likeable as individuals. Why is this not enough for her?

The Way We Are Told

9. Who is Atwood's audience? Can she afford to be critical of it? Does she make any concessions to her audience's sense of patriotism?
10. Consider Atwood's style. Does it often resemble speech? Make note of the use of italics, the phrase "even, uh, *good* Americans" and the choice of vocabulary.
11. How would you characterize the tone of Atwood's article? How does she use humor? Does humor help her to disarm the reader?

12. Atwood makes several references to slogans; for example, "even their best friends won't tell them" (paragraph 2). What is the effect? What is she referring to when she says "No annihilation without representation"?

13. In the last paragraph Atwood returns to a comment she made at the very beginning of the essay. What is the advantage of beginning and ending in this way?

Some Subjects for Essays

14. Atwood accused the United States of being an imperialist power in certain ways. Examine her claim. Do you agree or disagree?

* 15. Read Ngugi wa Thiong'o's "The Politics of Language." Both Ngugi and Atwood are concerned with imperialist pressures on their respective cultures exerted by much more formidable powers in each case. Examine what these pressures consist of in each case, and compare their impact.

CUSTER DIED FOR YOUR SINS

Vine Deloria, Jr.

Vine Deloria, Jr. is a Sioux Indian, born on the Pine Ridge Reservation in South Dakota in 1933. A graduate of the University of Iowa, he also has a law degree from the University of Colorado. Since 1978 he has been a professor of political science at the University of Arizona. He is active in the struggle for Indian rights and has served as executive director of the National Congress of American Indians. His books include *We Talk You Listen* (1970), *God Is Red* (1973), *American Indians: American Justice* (1983), *American Indian Policy in the Twentieth Century* (1985), and *Custer Died for Your Sins* (1969), from which this selection is taken. It is a bitter and often sarcastic attack on the stereotype other Americans have developed about Indians. For another view of Indian and white relations read Michael Dorris's "For the Indians, No Thanksgiving."

One of the finest things about being an Indian is that people are always interested in you and your "plight." Other groups have difficulties, predicaments, quandaries, problems, or troubles. Traditionally we Indians have had a "plight." 1

Our foremost plight is our transparency. People can tell just by looking at us what we want, what should be done to help us, how we feel, and what a "real" Indian is really like. Indian life, as it relates to the real world, is a continuous attempt not to disappoint people who know us. Unfulfilled expectations cause grief and we have already had our share. 2

Because people can see right through us, it becomes impossible to tell truth from fiction or fact from mythology. Experts paint us as they would like us to be. Often we paint ourselves as we wish we were or as we might have been. 3

The more we try to be ourselves the more we are forced to defend what we have never been. The American public feels most comfortable with the mythical Indians of stereotype-land who were always THERE. These Indians are fierce, they wear feathers and grunt. Most of us don't fit this idealized figure since we grunt only when overeating, which is seldom. 4

335

Indian reactions are sudden and surprising. One day at a confer-   5
ence we were singing "My Country 'Tis of Thee" and we came across
the part that goes:

> *Land where our fathers died*
> *Land of the Pilgrims' pride . . .*

Some of us broke out laughing when we realized that our fathers
undoubtedly died trying to keep those Pilgrims from stealing our land.
In fact, many of our fathers died because the Pilgrims killed them as
witches. We didn't feel much kinship with those Pilgrims, regardless
of who they did in.

We often hear "give it back to the Indians" when a gadget fails to   6
work. It's a terrible thing for a people to realize that society has set
aside all nonworking gadgets for their exclusive use.

American blacks had become recognized as a species of human   7
being by amendments to the Constitution shortly after the Civil War.
Prior to emancipation they had been counted as three-fifths of a person
in determining population for representation in the House of Representatives. Early Civil Rights bills nebulously state that other people
shall have the same rights as "white people," indicating there *were*
"other people." But Civil Rights bills passed during and after the Civil
War systematically excluded Indian people. For a long time an Indian
was not presumed capable of initiating an action in a court of law, of
owning property, or of giving testimony against whites in court. Nor
could an Indian vote or leave his reservation. Indians were America's
captive people without any defined rights whatsoever.

Then one day the white man discovered that the Indian tribes still   8
owned some 135 million acres of land. To his horror he learned that
much of it was very valuable. Some was good grazing land, some was
farm land, some mining land, and some covered with timber.

Animals could be herded together on a piece of land, but they   9
could not sell it. Therefore it took no time at all to discover that
Indians were really people and should have the right to sell their
lands. Land was the means of recognizing the Indian as a human being.
It was the method whereby land could be stolen legally and not
blatantly.

Once the Indian was thus acknowledged, it was fairly simple to   10
determine what his goals were. If, thinking went, the Indian was just
like the white, he must have the same outlook as the white. So the
future was planned for the Indian people in public and private life.
First in order was allotting them reservations so that they could sell
their lands. God's foreordained plan to repopulate the continent fit
exactly with the goals of the tribes as they were defined by their white
friends.

It is fortunate that we were never slaves. We gave up land instead   11
of life and labor. Because the Negro labored, he was considered a draft
animal. Because the Indian occupied large areas of land, he was considered a wild animal. Had we given up anything else, or had anything
else to give up, it is certain that we would have been considered some
other thing.

Whites have had different attitudes toward the Indians and the   12
blacks since the Republic was founded. Whites have always refused to
give nonwhites the respect which they have been found to legally
possess. Instead there has always been a contemptuous attitude that
although the law says one thing, "we all know better."

Thus whites steadfastly refused to allow blacks to enjoy the fruits   13
of full citizenship. They systematically closed schools, churches,
stores, restaurants, and public places to blacks or made insulting pro-
visions for them. For one hundred years every program of public and
private white America was devoted to the exclusion of the black. It
was, perhaps, embarrassing to be rubbing shoulders with one who had
not so long before been defined as a field animal.

The Indian suffered the reverse treatment. Law after law was   14
passed requiring him to conform to white institutions. Indian children
were kidnapped and forced into boarding schools thousands of miles
from their homes to learn the white man's ways. Reservations were
turned over to different Christian denominations for governing. Reservations were for a long time church operated. Everything possible was
done to ensure that Indians were forced into American life. The wild
animal was made into a household pet whether or not he wanted to be
one.

EXERCISES

Words to Know

plight (paragraph 1), quandary (1), allotting (10), foreordained (10),
draft animal (11).

Some of the Issues

1. What is the point Deloria makes about Indians' "transparency"?
2. Characterize the "mythical Indian" by adding details to what Deloria says. Where do these details come from?
3. What are according to Deloria the differences in the way that whites
   have looked at the blacks and the Indians? What are the causes of
   these differences?

The Way We Are Told

4. How does Deloria support his assertions?
5. Who would you say is Deloria's audience?
6. Find examples of irony in the article.

Some Subjects for Essays

* 7. Find one common stereotype in the media that bothers you, for example: the dumb secretary, the housewife worried about waxy buildup on the kitchen floor or about the whiteness of her neighbor's laundry. Describe the stereotyped role, trying to use a satirical tone. You may want to read Michael J. Arlen's "Ring Around the Collar!" as an example.
* 8. Examine advertisements in several magazines. Find one that makes use of a stereotype. Describe the advertisement and its effect. Read Myrna Knepler's "Sold at Fine Stores Everywhere, Naturellement."
* 9. Read Michael Dorris's "For the Indians, No Thanksgiving." Both Dorris and Deloria discuss the white man's view of Indians. Compare their respective attitudes as well as the way they state their views.

THE JAPANESE MODEL

Adam Smith

Adam Smith is the pseudonym of George J. W. Goodman (1930–),
who turned from fiction to writing about economics and finance,
particularly the impact of economic change on society. After getting a B.A. from Harvard, Goodman was awarded a Rhodes Scholarship and spent the years 1952–4 in England at Oxford University.
His books include *The Money Game* (1968), *Supermoney*
(1972), *Powers of Mind* (1975), and *Paper Money* (1981). He
appears frequently on Public Television and writes a regular feature for *Esquire*, in which the following selection appeared in
October 1980. It is a brief analysis of some of the causes for the
spectacular rise of Japan from maker of cheap merchandise in the
years immediately after World War II to its present eminence as
one of the major economic world powers.

 For some additional information about Japan see the headnote to John David Morley's "Living in a Japanese Home."

"Do you remember," said my visitor, "the stories about Usa?"   1

 My visitor was an old friend, an American who lives in the Far   2
East, where he drums up business for his American firm. As for Usa, it is
a town on the main southernmost Japanese island, Kyushu.

 "The story used to be," said my visitor, "that because Japanese   3
goods were so cheap and shoddy, they were all sent to Usa before they
were exported to be stamped MADE IN USA, so that people would
think they had been made in the United States."

 "I remember," I said. "That's like the story about how the Japa-   4
nese filched the plans for a battleship but got them just wrong enough
so that when the ship was launched it turned upside down."

 "Well," said the Far East hand, "you haven't heard stories like   5
that for twenty-five years. Detroit is reeling from Japanese imports, and
you see joggers wearing earphones and carrying little Japanese tape
decks not much larger than cigarette packs. I have to go meet some of
my Japanese associates in New York now. They think New York is
charming—and so *cheap*, they keep saying. Such *bargains*."

 The Far East hand left with me a book that is a huge best seller in   6
Japan. It was written by a Harvard professor, Ezra Vogel, and its English-language edition has sold a respectable twenty-five thousand
copies. But in Japan it is a runaway success: four hundred fifty-five

thousand copies sold. The title is *Japan as No. 1: Lessons for America*. "The very title," said Edwin Reischauer, a former ambassador to Japan, "will blow the minds of many Americans. Japan today has a more smoothly functioning society [than ours] and an economy that is running rings around ours." One Japanese official has said that the United States has now taken the place of Japan's prewar colonies. The United States supplies the raw materials — the coal, the grain and soybeans, the timber — to this superior modern industrial machine, and it gets back the machine's superior industrial products.

Japan's economic performance has been well documented in   7
Vogel's book. In 1952, Japan's gross national product was one third that of France. By the late 1970s, it was larger than those of France and Britain combined, and half as large as that of the United States. Japan is the leading automobile manufacturer. Of the world's twenty-two largest and most modern steel plants, fourteen are in Japan and none are in the United States.

Health? Japan has the world's lowest infant mortality rate. In   8
1967 the life expectancy of the average Japanese passed that of the average American, and in 1977 Japan's life expectancy rate passed Sweden's to become the highest in the world.

Education? About 90 percent of all Japanese graduate from high   9
school, and they generally spend sixty more days a year in high school than do their American counterparts.

Crime? In Japan the cities are safe, and the Japanese carry large   10
amounts of cash and don't even worry about it. Americans are accustomed to annual increases in the crime rate; in Japan, the crime rate is going *down*.

Labor? The Japanese visitors are shocked again. Professor Vogel   11
says that the American factory seems almost like an armed camp to them: "Foremen stand guard to make sure workers do not slack off. Workers grumble at foremen, and foremen are cross with workers. In the Japanese factory, employees seem to work even without the foreman watching."

What are the Japanese doing right? And how have they done it on   12
a crowded group of islands, without enough coal and oil, without significant natural resources, without adequate farmland?

The rather chilling answer is that they have done it by a social   13
process — by a kind of group behavior modification. An average Japanese who goes to work for a company is there for life. He works throughout the day in an atmosphere in which consensus is always the goal. If, as his career progresses, he needs retraining, the company will retrain him, so he need not get involved in the protection of rights that

American unions strive for. The company's goals are his. The people he sees socially are from the company.

The government works the same way, striving for consensus within itself and for consensus with business. Elite bureaucrats, their ties reinforced by social contacts in the geisha houses and on the golf course, form an elaborate old-boy network and move in lockstep through the age ranks.   14

And all this starts very early. Children are taught the value of cooperation, says Vogel, "however annoying they may find group pressures." The group pressure helps to explain the low crime rate. The policeman is part of the group: his little kiosk also contains the neighborhood bulletin board. The criminal, in fact, is encouraged to turn himself in. Even Japanese gangs exist in a consensus with the police.   15

The whole design of group activity is a conscious one. After World War II, the Japanese decided what they needed to survive, and they followed their decision. They even learned golf and baseball with the same sense of purpose that they applied to business and government. Americans win arguments; the Japanese win agreements. Americans try for victory; the Japanese try for consensus.   16

Nobody can deny Japan its success. What is so chilling is the implication of that success: Japan works and America doesn't. The Japanese leaped from feudalism to a modern corporate society without the intervening four hundred years of individualism that have characterized Western Europe and the United States. Our individualism was all very well in its time, but that was when energy was plentiful and the world was agricultural. But now we live in a postagrarian world, and individualism doesn't work anymore: "Our institutional practices promote adversary relations and litigation, divisiveness threatens our society," warns Vogel.   17

What we ought to do, he argues, is to borrow some of the models that have worked for the Japanese: more group direction, more "central leadership oriented to a modern economic order," more cooperation between business and government.   18

You can see why this is at once so provocative and so chilling. Should we all gather behind the banners of IBM and General Motors? When William H. Whyte Jr. wrote *The Organization Man*, the phenomenon he documented was considered alarming. Do we really want five hundred highly trained bureaucrats, a close-knit group from elite universities, to establish our goals and run our government? Our experience with the best and the brightest was not totally happy. Should we teach youngsters not to win, just to tie?   19

Japanophiles point out that America, too, had groups: New   20
England town meetings, farmers' granges, professional guilds. But in
our mobile society, solidarity has become attenuated. We have lost a
sense of community.

This is not the direction we are going in. Americans complain   21
that their government is too big and directs them too much. They are
more and more suspicious of big business. They distrust, the polls
show, all of their institutions.

There isn't any doubt that we are losing ground in the world, and   22
that we have forgotten what safe cities and a sense of community feel
like. Is the group model what it takes to survive? Could we adopt it?
More to the point, is it the way we want to live?

EXERCISES

Words to Know

shoddy (paragraph 3), filched (4), Far East hand (5), consensus (13),
kiosk (15), postagrarian (17), litigation (17), "the best and the
brightest" (19), Japanophiles (20), granges (20), guilds (20) attenuated (20).

Some of the Issues

1. In paragraphs 1 through 5 Smith cites a conversation with a "Far
   East hand." What specifics does it contribute to the essay? How
   does it set up the comparison between the United States and
   Japan?
2. What do the remarks of the former United States Ambassador and
   the unnamed Japanese official in paragraph 6 contribute to
   Smith's argument?
3. What, according to Smith, are the underlying causes of Japanese
   industrial superiority?
4. Explain the meaning of the sentence in paragraph 19: "Our experience with the best and the brightest was not totally happy.
   Should we teach our youngsters not to win, just to tie?"
5. What is Smith's main argument? That we should imitate the Japanese? That we cannot expect to follow their example? Try to
   determine Smith's direction, giving evidence from the essay.

The Way We Are Told

6. Smith's essay can be divided into four parts linked by transitional

paragraphs 6, 12, and 18. Write an outline of the essay using this
division.

7. Notice the presence of many sentences (and fragments) phrased as
questions. Why does Smith use this form? Consider the last paragraph in particular.

Some Subjects for Essays

8. Reread paragraph 19 and try to answer any one of the questions
asked in it. In your response, consider carefully the Japanese
examples Smith has cited and argue your answer from them as
well as from your own experience.
9. Write an essay about one or two products you have recently used.
Argue that they are either improvements on previous products or
they are not. Try to account for the change in various ways.
* 10. Read Ian Buruma's "Public Life in Japan." Then consider in particular two sections of Smith's essay: his remarks on labor (paragraph
11) and his conclusion (paragraph 22). Examine Buruma's descriptions of Yoko the elevator girl and Sasaki the "salaryman";
how do they confirm or contradict what Smith says?

THE INVISIBLE POOR

Michael Harrington

Michael Harrington (1928–89) was a professor of political science at Queens College, New York. He served as associate editor of *The Catholic Worker* in the early 1950s and was co-chair of the Democratic Socialists of America. His books of social criticism include *The Accidental Century* (1965), *Toward a Democratic Left* (1968), *The Vast Majority: A Journey to the World's Poor* (1977), *The Next America: The Decline and Rise of the United States* (1981), *The Politics at God's Funeral* (1983), *The New American Poverty* (1984), and *The New Left* (1987). *The Other America*, from which the following selection was taken, was first published in 1963. Harrington here discusses the separation of the poor from the rest of American society. His concept of their invisibility, of a segregated culture of poverty, was influential in drawing attention to the poor, leading not only to major social reforms in the 1960s but continuing its impact through the 1970s and 1980s.

The millions who are poor in the United States tend to become increasingly invisible. Here is a great mass of people, yet it takes an effort of the intellect and will even to see them. 1

I discovered this personally in a curious way. After I wrote my first article on poverty in America, I had all the statistics down on paper. I had proved to my satisfaction that there were around 50,000,000 poor in this country, Yet, I realized I did not believe my own figures. The poor existed in the Government reports; they were percentages and numbers in long, close columns, but they were not part of my experience. I could prove that the other America existed, but I had never been there. 2

There are perennial reasons that make the other America an invisible land. 3

Poverty is often off the beaten track. It always has been. The ordinary tourist never left the main highway, and today he rides interstate turnpikes. He does not go into the valleys of Pennsylvania where the towns look like movie sets of Wales in the thirties. He does not see the company houses in rows, the rutted roads (the poor always have bad roads whether they live in the city, in towns, or on farms), and everything is black and dirty. And even if he were to pass through such 4

344

a place by accident, the tourist would not meet the unemployed men in the bar or the women coming home from a runaway sweatshop.

Then, too, beauty and myths are perennial masks of poverty. The traveler comes to the Appalachians in the lovely season. He sees the hills, the streams, the foliage — but not the poor. Or perhaps he looks at a run-down mountain house and, remembering Rousseau rather than seeing with his eyes, decides that 'those people' are truly fortunate to be living the way they are and that they are lucky to be exempt from the strains and tensions of the middle class. The only problem is that 'those people,' the quaint inhabitants of those hills, are undereducated, underprivileged, lack medical care, and are in the process of being forced from the land into a life in the cities, where they are misfits. 5

These are normal and obvious causes of the invisibility of the poor. They operated a generation ago; they will be functioning a generation hence. It is more important to understand that the very development of American society is creating a new kind of blindness about poverty. The poor are increasingly slipping out of the very experience and consciousness of the nation. 6

If the middle class never did like ugliness and poverty, it was at least aware of them. 'Across the tracks' was not a very long way to go. There were forays into the slums at Christmas time; there were charitable organizations that brought contact with the poor. Occasionally, almost everyone passed through the Negro ghetto or the blocks of tenements, if only to get downtown to work or to entertainment. 7

Now the American city has been transformed. The poor still inhabit the miserable housing in the central area, but they are increasingly isolated from contact with, or sight of, anybody else. Middle-class women coming in from Suburbia on a rare trip may catch the merest glimpse of the other America on the way to an evening at the theater, but their children are segregated in suburban schools. The business or professional man may drive along the fringes of slums in a car or bus, but it is not an important experience to him. The failures, the unskilled, the disabled, the aged, and the minorities are right there, across the tracks, where they have always been. But hardly anyone else is. 8

In short, the very development of the American city has removed poverty from the living, emotional experience of millions upon millions of middle-class Americans. Living out in the suburbs, it is easy to assume that ours is, indeed, an affluent society. 9

This new segregation of poverty is compounded by a well-meaning ignorance. A good many concerned and sympathetic Americans are aware that there is much discussion of urban renewal. Suddenly, driving through the city, they notice that a familiar slum has been torn 10 down and that there are towering, modern buildings where once there had been tenements or hovels. There is a warm feeling of satisfaction, of pride in the way things are working out: the poor, it is obvious, are being taken care of.

The irony of this . . . is that the truth is nearly the exact oppo-   11
site to the impression. The total impact of the various housing pro-grams in postwar America has been to squeeze more and more people into existing slums. . . . Clothes make the poor invisible too: Amer-ica has the best-dressed poverty the world has ever known. For a variety of reasons, the benefits of mass production have been spread much more evenly in this area than in many others. It is much easier in the United States to be decently dressed than it is to be decently housed, fed, or doctored. Even people with terribly depressed in-comes can look prosperous.

This is an extremely important factor in defining our emotional   12
and existential ignorance of poverty. In Detroit the existence of social classes became much more difficult to discern the day the companies put lockers in the plants. From that moment on, one did not see men in work clothes on the way to the factory, but citizens in slacks and white shirts. This process has been magnified with the poor throughout the country. There are tens of thousands of Americans in the big cities who are wearing shoes, perhaps even a stylishly cut suit or dress, and yet are hungry. It is not a matter of planning, though it almost seems as if the affluent society had given out costumes to the poor so that they would not offend the rest of society with the sight of rags.

Then, many of the poor are the wrong age to be seen. A good   13
number of them (over 8,000,000) are sixty-five years of age or better; an even larger number are under eighteen. The aged members of the other America are often sick, and they cannot move. Another group of them live out their lives in loneliness and frustration: they sit in rented rooms, or else they stay close to a house in a neighborhood that has completely changed from the old days. Indeed, one of the worst aspects of poverty among the aged is that these people are out of sight and out of mind, and alone.

The young are somewhat more visible, yet they too stay close to   14
their neighborhoods. Sometimes they advertise their poverty through a lurid tabloid story about a gang killing. But generally they do not disturb the quiet streets of the middle class.

And finally, the poor are politically invisible. It is one of the   15
cruelest ironies of social life in advanced countries that the dispos-sessed at the bottom of society are unable to speak for themselves. The people of the other America do not, by far and large, belong to unions, to fraternal organizations, or to political parties. They are without

lobbies of their own; they put forward no legislative program. As a group, they are atomized. They have no face; they have no voice.

Thus, there is not even a cynical political motive for caring about the poor, as in the old days. Because the slums are no longer centers of powerful political organizations, the politicians need not really care about their inhabitants. The slums are no longer visible to the middle class, so much of the idealistic urge to fight for those who need help is gone. Only the social agencies have a really direct involvement with the other America, and they are without any great political power.   16

To the extent that the poor have a spokesman in American life, that role is played by the labor movement. The unions have their own particular idealism, an ideology of concern. More than that, they realize that the existence of a reservoir of cheap, unorganized labor is a menace to wages and working conditions throughout the entire economy. Thus, many union legislative proposals — to extend the coverage of minimum wage and social security, to organize migrant farm laborers — articulate the needs of the poor.   17

That the poor are invisible is one of the most important things about them. They are not simply neglected and forgotten as in the old rhetoric of reform; what is much worse, they are not seen.   18

EXERCISES

Words to Know

rutted (paragraph 4), sweatshop (4), myth (5), perennial (5), Rousseau (5), quaint (5), forays (7), affluent (9), compounded (10), existential (12), cynical (16), reservoir (17), articulate (17), rhetoric (18).

Some of the Issues

1. In order to establish that the poor are invisible, Harrington needs to establish first that poverty continues to exist in America. How does he do that?
2. In what way is rural poverty invisible?
3. What reasons does Harrington give for the invisibility of the urban poor?
4. How has the development of the American city increased the invisibility of the poor?
5. How has mass production affected that invisibility?

The Way We Are Told

6. In paragraph 2 Harrington uses the first person singular. Why does he refer to himself here but not elsewhere?
7. Paragraph 3 consists of one sentence. What is its function with respect to the organization of the selection? What is its effect?
8. Discuss the structure of paragraphs 4 and 5. How is their content developed? Find additional paragraphs that show the same structure.
9. Harrington discusses rural poverty before turning to its urban counterpart. What may be his reasons for that order?
10. What audience does Harrington address? (Consider, for example, his expression of surprise in paragraph 2 at his own findings about the extent of poverty.)

Some Subjects for Essays

11. Select a topic you feel competent to argue for, such as American (foreign) cars are a better buy than foreign (American) ones; private (public) colleges are preferable to public (private) ones; or city (suburban) living is preferable to suburban (city) living. Then make a list of all the arguments for your case you can think of. Next, sort your arguments into logical groups, subordinating items as needed. Arrange your groups in logical order. Finally, write your essay.
12. In paragraph 6 Harrington says that the causes of the invisibility of the poor "operated a generation ago: they will be functioning a generation hence." Harrington's book was published in the early 1960s, in other words, a generation ago. Do the poor continue to be invisible?

EFFECTS OF DEVELOPMENT

Ivan Illich

Ivan Illich was born in Vienna, Austria in 1926 and studied theology in Rome. He received a doctorate from the University of Salzburg in 1951 and was ordained a priest in the Catholic Church in the same year. From 1951 to 1956 he served as a parish priest in a Puerto-Rican neighborhood in New York City. He has served as visiting professor at Berkeley and other universities. He has written a number of books noted for their questioning of accepted values and ideas. Among them are *Deschooling Society* (1971), *Energy and Equity* (1974), *Medical Nemesis* (1976), *Disabling Professions* (1977), and *Toward a History of Needs* (1978). In the 1980s he published four books: *The Right to Useful Unemployment, Shadow Work, Gender,* and *H₂O and the Waters of Forgetfulness*. The essay reprinted here first appeared in *The New York Review of Books* in November 1969. It presents a generally unexpected point of view about aid given to the Third World. Illich asserts that exporting the kinds of health care, educational programs, and transportation facilities common in industrialized nations may cause harm.

It is now common to demand that the rich nations convert their war machine into a program for the development of the Third World. The poorer four-fifths of humanity multiply unchecked while their per capita consumption actually declines. This population expansion and decrease of consumption threaten the industrialized nations, who may still, as a result, convert their defense budgets to the economic pacification of poor nations. And this in turn could produce irreversible despair, because the plows of the rich can do as much harm as their swords. U.S. trucks can do more lasting damage than U.S. tanks. It is easier to create mass demand for the former than for the latter. Only a minority needs heavy weapons, while a majority can become dependent on unrealistic levels of supply for such productive machines as modern trucks. Once the Third World has become a mass market for the goods, products, and processes which are designed by the rich for themselves, the discrepancy between demand for these Western artifacts and the supply will increase indefinitely. The family car cannot drive the poor into the jet age, nor can a school system provide the

349

poor with education, nor can the family icebox insure healthy food for them.

It is evident that only one man in a thousand in Latin America can 2 afford a Cadillac, a heart operation, or a Ph.D. This restriction on the goals of development does not make us despair of the fate of the Third World, and the reason is simple. We have not yet come to conceive of a Cadillac as necessary for good transportation, or of a heart operation as normal healthy care, or of a Ph.D. as the prerequisite of an acceptable education. In fact, we recognize at once that the importation of Cadillacs should be heavily taxed in Peru, that an organ transplant clinic is a scandalous plaything to justify the concentration of more doctors in Bogotá, and that a Betatron is beyond the teaching facilities of the University of São Paolo.

Unfortunately, it is not held to be universally evident that the 3 majority of Latin Americans — not only of our generation, but also of the next and the next again — cannot afford any kind of automobile, or any kind of hospitalization, or for that matter an elementary school education. We suppress our consciousness of this obvious reality because we hate to recognize the corner into which our imagination has been pushed. So persuasive is the power of the institutions we have created that they shape not only our preferences, but actually our sense of possibilities. We have forgotten how to speak about modern transportation that does not rely on automobiles and airplanes. Our conceptions of modern health care emphasize our ability to prolong the lives of the desperately ill. We have become unable to think of better education except in terms of more complex schools and of teachers trained for ever longer periods. Huge institutions producing costly services dominate the horizons of our inventiveness.

We have embodied our world view into our institutions and are 4 now their prisoners. Factories, news media, hospitals, governments, and schools produce goods and services packaged to contain our view of the world. We — the rich — conceive of progress as the expansion of these establishments. We conceive of heightened mobility as luxury and safety packaged by General Motors or Boeing. We conceive of improving the general well-being as increasing the supply of doctors and hospitals, which package health along with protracted suffering. We have come to identify our need for further learning with the demand for ever longer confinement to classrooms. In other words, we have packaged education with custodial care, certification for jobs, and the right to vote, and wrapped them all together with indoctrination in the Christian, liberal or communist virtues.

In less than a hundred years industrial society has molded patent 5 solutions to basic human needs and converted us to the belief that man's needs were shaped by the Creator as demands for the products we have invented. This is as true for Russia and Japan as for the North Atlantic community. The consumer is trained for obsolescence, which means continuing loyalty toward the same producers who will give him the same basic packages in different quality or new wrappings.

Industrialized societies can provide such packages for personal   6
consumption for most of their citizens, but this is no proof that these societies are sane, or economical, or that they promote life. The contrary is true. The more the citizen is trained in the consumption of packaged goods and services, the less effective he seems to become in shaping his environment. His energies and finances are consumed in procuring ever new models of his staples, and the environment becomes a by-product of his own consumption habits.

The design of the "package deals" of which I speak is the main   7
cause of the high cost of satisfying basic needs. So long as every man "needs" his car, our cities must endure longer traffic jams and absurdly expensive remedies to relieve them. So long as health means maximum length of survival, our sick will get ever more extraordinary surgical interventions and the drugs required to deaden their consequent pain. So long as we want to use school to get children out of their parents' hair or to keep them off the street and out of the labor force, our young will be retained in endless schooling and will need ever-increasing incentives to endure the ordeal.

Rich nations now benevolently impose a straightjacket of traffic   8
jams, hospital confinements, and classrooms on the poor nations, and by international agreement call this "development." The rich and schooled and old of the world try to share their dubious blessings by foisting their pre-packaged solutions on to the Third World. Traffic jams develop in São Paolo, while almost a million northeastern Brazilians flee the drought by walking 500 miles. Latin American doctors get training at the New York Hospital for Special Surgery, which they apply to only a few, while amoebic dysentery remains endemic in slums where 90 percent of the population live. A tiny minority gets advanced education in basic science in North America — not infrequently paid for by their own governments. If they return at all to Bolivia, they become second-rate teachers of pretentious subjects at La Paz or Cochibamba. The rich export outdated versions of their standard models.

Each car which Brazil puts on the road denies fifty people good   9
transportation by bus. Each merchandised refrigerator reduces the chance of building a community freezer. Every dollar spent in Latin America on doctors and hospitals costs a hundred lives, to adopt a phrase of Jorge de Ahumada, the brilliant Chilean economist. Had each

dollar been spent on providing safe drinking water, a hundred lives could have been saved. Each dollar spent on schooling means more privileges for the few at the cost of the many; at best it increases the number of those who, before dropping out, have been taught that those who stay longer have earned the right to more power, wealth, and prestige. What such schooling does is to teach the schooled the superiority of the better schooled.

All Latin American countries are frantically intent on expanding   10 their school systems. No country now spends less than the equivalent of 18 percent of tax-derived public income on education — which means schooling — and many countries spend almost double that. But even with these huge investments, no country yet succeeds in giving five full years of education to more than one third of its population; supply and demand for schooling grow geometrically apart. And what is true about schooling is equally true about the products of most institutions in the process of modernization in the Third World.

Continued technological refinements of products which are al-   11 ready established on the market frequently benefit the producer far more than the consumer. The more complex production processes tend to enable only the largest producer to continually replace out-moded models, and to focus the demand of the consumer on the marginal improvement of what he buys, no matter what the concomi-tant side effects: higher prices, diminished life span, less general usefulness, higher cost of repairs. Think of the multiple uses for a simple can opener, whereas an electric one, if it works at all, opens only some kinds of cans, and costs one hundred times as much.

This is equally true for a piece of agricultural machinery and for   12 an academic degree. The midwestern farmer can become convinced of his need for a four-axle vehicle which can go 70 m.p.h. on the high-ways, has an electric windshield wiper and upholstered seats, and can be turned in for a new one within a year or two. Most of the world's farmers don't need such speed, nor have they ever met with such comfort, nor are they interested in obsolescence. They need low-priced transport, in a world where time is not money, where manual wipers suffice, and where a piece of heavy equipment should outlast a generation. Such a mechanical donkey requires entirely different engi-neering and design than one produced for the U.S. market. This vehi-cle is not in production.

Most of South America needs paramedical workers who can func-   13 tion for indefinite periods without the supervision of an MD. Instead of establishing a process to train midwives and visiting healers who know how to use a very limited arsenal of medicines while working inde-pendently, Latin American universities establish every year a new school of specialized nursing or nursing administration to prepare professionals who can function only in a hospital, and pharmacists who know how to sell increasingly more dangerous drugs.

Some years ago I watched workmen putting up a sixty-foot Coca-Cola sign on a desert plain in the Mexquital. A serious drought and famine had just swept over the Mexican highland. My host, a poor Indian in Ixmiquilpan, had just offered his visitors a tiny tequila glass of the costly black sugar-water. When I recall this scene I still feel anger; but I feel much more incensed when I remember UNESCO meetings at which well-meaning and well-paid bureaucrats seriously discussed Latin American school curricula, and when I think of the speeches of enthusiastic liberals advocating the need for more schools.   14

The fraud perpetrated by the salesmen of schools is less obvious but much more fundamental than the self-satisfied salesmanship of the Coca-Cola or Ford representative, because the schoolman hooks his people on a much more demanding drug. Elementary school attendance is not a harmless luxury, but more like the coca chewing of the Andean Indian, which harnesses the worker to the boss.   15

The higher the dose of schooling an individual has received, the more depressing his experience of withdrawal. The seventh-grade dropout feels his inferiority much more acutely than the dropout from the third grade. The schools of the Third World administer their opium with much more effect that the churches of other epochs. As the mind of a society is progressively schooled, step by step its individuals lose their sense that it might be possible to live without being inferior to others. As the majority shifts from the land into the city, the heridinary inferiority of the peon is replaced by the inferiority of the school dropout who is held personally responsible for his failure. Schools rationalize the divine origin of social stratification with much more rigor than churches have ever done.   16

Until this day no Latin American country has declared youthful underconsumers of Coca-Cola or cars as lawbreakers, while all Latin American countries have passed laws which define the early dropout as a citizen who has not fulfilled his legal obligations. The Brazilian government recently almost doubled the number of years during which schooling is legally compulsory and free. From now on any Brazilian dropout under the age of sixteen will be faced during this lifetime with the reproach that he did not take advantage of a legally obligatory privilege. This law was passed in a country where not even the most optimistic could foresee the day when such levels of schooling would be provided for only 25 percent of the young. The adoption of international standards of schooling forever condemns most Latin Americans to marginality or exclusion from social life — in a word, underdevelopment.   17

EXERCISES

Words to Know

Third World (paragraph 1), per capita (1), pacification (1), discrepancy (1), artifacts (1), prerequisite (2), embodied (4), mobility (4), protracted (4), indoctrination (4), patent solutions (5), obsolescence (5), staples (6), confinements (8), dubious (8), foisting (8), geometrically (10), marginal (11), concomitant (11), paramedical (13), midwives (13), arsenal (13), drought (14), UNESCO (14), peon (16), rationalize (16), social stratification (16), compulsory (17), obligatory (17), underdevelopment (17).

Some of the Issues

1. In paragraph 1 Illich's comment "the plows of the rich can do as much harm as their swords" refers to a passage in the Bible (Isaiah II,4): "They shall beat their swords into plowshares. . . ." What does Illich mean?
2. In paragraph 3 Illich says: "So persuasive is the power of the institutions we have created that they shape not only our preferences, but actually our sense of possibilities." Explain his meaning, referring to the examples with which he supports his assertion.
3. In paragraphs 4 through 6 Illich describes us as "prisoners" of our institutions. What does he mean by this, and how does he support his assertion?
4. What is the meaning of Illich's statement, "the rich export outdated versions of their standard models" (paragraph 8)?
5. In paragraph 9, after discussing the increase in money spent on public education, Illich says, "What such schooling does is to teach the schooled the superiority of the better schooled." What point is Illich trying to make?
6. In paragraph 10 Illich appears to make a distinction between education and schooling. What might that distinction be?
7. What accounts for Illich's anger at seeing the Coca-Cola sign in the Mexican desert, and for his greater anger toward UNESCO officials and "enthusiastic liberals" (paragraph 14)?
8. Illich deals with several different aspects of development: medical care, transportation, and education in particular. In what respects is his argument the same in discussing all three? In what respects is it different?
9. What does Illich say about dropouts (paragraphs 16 and 17)? What, in his opinion, causes the dropout "problem"?

10. Illich tells the reader what kind of transportation, education, and health care services he disapproves of. What might be the components of a system he might look on more favorably?

The Way We Are Told

11. Illich's method is to state or imply the commonly accepted view and then contradict it. Give several examples of this method of argument.
12. At times Illich uses a specific example or event or product to stand for a large category of items. How effective is this part-for-the-whole technique of argument? Cite examples.
13. Note the repetitive use of "we" in paragraph 4 and of "each" or "every" in paragraph 9. What effect is created?

Some Subjects for Essays

14. Illich talks about the effect of "development" on the Third World, but perhaps his argument might apply to the United States as well. Some critics of United States health care have deplored the availability of very risky major surgery and the presence of expensive but seldom used equipment in hospitals, when preventive health care and clinics are underfunded. Support or oppose this view.
15. Examine the advertisements in one or two issues of a popular magazine designed for a general audience. In your opinion which of the advertised objects are really useful to people? What are the appeals made to the consumer? Are these appeals made on the basis of the products' usefulness or on other factors?
16. The views that Illich expresses about education in poor countries are perhaps the most controversial parts of his article. In an essay, summarize his views and then comment on them.
17. Illich claims that the consumer is trained for obsolescence. Agree or disagree, focusing on the marketing of one product, such as automobiles, appliances, or clothing.
* 18. The photograph on page 326 of Singapore, an independent city state at the southernmost point of the Asian mainland, symbolizes the contrast between old and new. Imagine that you were the developer of that modern highrise; what arguments would you have used to justify its construction? What do you think Illich would have said in response?

LIFE ON THE GLOBAL ASSEMBLY LINE

Barbara Ehrenreich
and Annette Fuentes

Barbara Ehrenreich, born in 1941, is a journalist writing for *The New York Times*, among other publications. She is the coauthor of *For Her Own Good: 150 Years of the Experts Advice to Women* (1979), *The American Health Empire* (1970), and *Witches, Midwives and Nurses: A History of Women Healers* (1972), and the author of *Re-Making Love: The Feminization of Sex* (1986). Ehrenreich's latest book is *Fear of Falling* (1989), a discussion of the professional middle class in America, its rise to affluence and move to conservatism.

Annette Fuentes, also a journalist, is the editor of *Sisterhood Is Global*.

This selection, which first appeared in *Ms* magazine in January 1981, traces the consequences of large corporations shifting their production to Third World countries to take advantage of cheaper labor. Many of their new employees are women, lured by a promise of higher salaries and relative independence. The reality of these jobs for most Third World women is different from the promise. They perform tedious, often health-destroying tasks, at wages too low to accumulate savings. If the company moves, or a woman has exhausted her health, she is unlikely to find another job and is often unable to reintegrate herself into the traditional society she had left.

In Ciudad Juárez, Mexico, Anna M. rises at 5 A.M. to feed her son 1 *before starting on the two-hour bus trip to the maquiladora (factory). He will spend the day along with four other children in a neighbor's one-room home. Anna's husband, frustrated by being unable to find work for himself, left for the United States six months ago. She wonders, as she carefully applies her new lip gloss, whether she ought to consider herself still married. It might be good to take a night course, become a secretary. But she seldom gets home before eight at night, and the factory, where she stitches brassieres that will be sold in the United States through J.C. Penney, pays only $48 a week.*

356

In Penang, Malaysia, Julie K. is up before the three other   2
young women with whom she shares a room, and starts heating the
leftover rice from last night's supper. She looks good in the com-
pany's green-trimmed uniform, and she's proud to work in a mod-
ern, American-owned factory. Only not quite so proud as when she
started working three years ago — she thinks as she squints out the
door at a passing group of women. Her job involves peering all day
through a microscope, bonding hair-thin gold wires to a silicon
chip destined to end up inside a pocket calculator, and at 21, she is
afraid she can no longer see very clearly.

Every morning, between four and seven, thousands of women   3
like Anna and Julie head out for the day shift. In Ciudad Juárez, they
crowd into *ruteras* (run-down vans) for the trip from the slum neighborhoods to the industrial parks on the outskirts of the city. In Penang
they squeeze, 60 or more at a time, into buses for the trip from the
village to the low, modern factory buildings of the Bayan Lepas free
trade zone. In Taiwan, they walk from the dormitories — where the
night shift is already asleep in the still-warm beds — through the
checkpoints in the high fence surrounding the factory zone.

This is the world's new industrial proletariat: young, female,   4
Third World. Viewed from the "first world," they are still faceless,
genderless "cheap labor," signaling their existence only through a
label or tiny imprint — "made in Hong Kong," or Taiwan, Korea, the
Dominican Republic, Mexico, the Philippines. But they may be one of
the most strategic blocs of womanpower in the world of the 1980s.
Conservatively, there are 2 million Third World female industrial
workers employed now, millions more looking for work, and their
numbers are rising every year. Anyone whose image of Third World
women features picturesque peasants with babies slung on their backs
should be prepared to update it. Just in the last decade, Third World
women have become a critical element in the global economy and a
key "resource" for expanding multinational corporations.

It doesn't take more than second-grade arithmetic to understand   5
what's happening. In the United States, an assembly-line worker is
likely to earn, depending on her length of employment, between
$3.10 and $5 an hour. In many Third World countries, a woman doing
the same work will earn $3 to $5 a *day*. According to the magazine
Business Asia, in 1976 the average hourly wage for unskilled work
(male or female) was 55 cents in Hong Kong, 52 cents in South Korea,
32 cents in the Philippines, and 17 cents in Indonesia. The logic of the
situation is compelling: why pay someone in Massachusetts $5 an hour
to do what someone in Manila will do for $2.50 a day? Or, as a
corollary, why pay a male worker anywhere to do what a female
worker will do for 40 to 60 percent less?

And so, almost everything that can be packed up is being moved   6
out to the Third World; not heavy industry, but just about anything
light enough to travel — garment manufacture, textiles, toys, foot-
wear, pharmaceuticals, wigs, appliance parts, tape decks, computer
components, plastic goods. In some industries, like garment and textile, American jobs are lost in the process, and the biggest losers are
women, often black and Hispanic. But what's going on is much more
than a matter of runaway shops. Economists are talking about a "new
international division of labor," in which the process of production is
broken down and the fragments are dispersed to different parts of the
world. In general, the low-skilled jobs are farmed out to the Third
World, where labor costs are minuscule, while control over the overall
process and technology remains safely at company headquarters in
"first world" countries like the United States and Japan.

The American electronics industry provides a classic example: 7
circuits are printed on silicon wafers and tested in California; then the
wafers are shipped to Asia for the labor-intensive process by which
they are cut into tiny chips and bonded to circuit boards; final assembly into products such as calculators or military equipment usually
takes place in the United States. Garment manufacture too is often
broken into geographically separated steps, with the most repetitive,
labor-intensive jobs going to the poor countries of the southern hemisphere. Most Third World countries welcome whatever jobs come
their way in the new division of labor, and the major international
development agencies — like the World Bank and the United States
Agency for International Development (AID) — encourage them to
take what they can get.

So much any economist could tell you. What is less often noted is   8
the *gender* breakdown of the emerging international division of labor.
Eighty to 90 percent of the low-skilled assembly jobs that go to the
Third World are performed by women — in a remarkable switch from
earlier patterns of foreign-dominated industrialization. Until now,
"development" under the aegis of foreign corporations has usually
meant more jobs for men and — compared to traditional agricultural
society — a diminished economic status for women. But multinational
corporations and Third World governments alike consider assembly-
line work — whether the product is Barbie dolls or missile parts — to
be "women's work."

One reason is that women can, in many countries, still be legally   9
paid less than men. But the sheer tedium of the jobs adds to the
multinationals' preference for women workers — a preference made
clear, for example, by this ad from a Mexican newspaper: *We need
female workers; older than 17, younger than 30; single and without
children: minimum education primary school, maximum educa-*

tion one year of preparatory school (high school): available for all shifts.

It's an article of faith with management that only women can do, or will do, the monotonous, painstaking work that American business is exporting to the Third World. Bill Mitchell, whose job is to attract United States businesses to the Bermudez Industrial Park in Ciudad Juárez told us with a certain macho pride: "A man just won't stay in this tedious kind of work. He'd walk out in a couple of hours." The personnel manager of a light assembly plant in Taiwan told anthropologist Linda Gail Arrigo: "Young male workers are too restless and impatient to do monotonous work with no career value. If displeased, they sabotage the machines and even threaten the foreman. But girls? At most, they cry a little." 10

In fact, the American businessmen we talked to claimed that Third World women genuinely enjoy doing the very things that would drive a man to assault and sabotage. "You should watch these kids going into work," Bill Mitchell told us. "You don't have any sullenness here. They smile." A top-level management consultant who specializes in advising American companies on where to relocate their factories gave us this global generalization: "The [factory] girls genuinely enjoy themselves. They're away from their families. They have spending money. They can buy motorbikes, whatever. Of course it's a regulated experience too — with dormitories to live in — so it's a healthful experience." 11

What is the real experience of the women in the emerging Third World industrial work force? The conventional Western stereotypes leap to mind: You can't really compare, the standards are so different. . . . Everything's easier in warm countries. . . . They really don't have any alternatives. . . . Commenting on the low wages his company pays its women workers in Singapore, a Hewlett-Packard vice-president said, "They live much differently here than we do. . . ." But the differences are ultimately very simple. To start with, they have less money. 12

The great majority of the women in the new Third World work force live at or near the subsistence level for one person, whether they work for a multinational corporation or a locally owned factory. In the Philippines, for example, starting wages in U.S.-owned electronics plants are between $34 to $46 a month, compared to a cost of living of $37 a month; in Indonesia the starting wages are actually about $7 a month less than the cost of living. "Living," in these cases, should be interpreted minimally: a diet of rice, dried fish, and water — a Coke might cost a half-day's wages — lodging in a room occupied by four or more other people. Rachael Grossman, a researcher with the Southeast Asia Resource Center, found women employees of U.S. multinational 13 firms in Malaysia and the Philippines living four to eight in a room in boardinghouses, or squeezing into tiny extensions built onto squatter huts near the factory. Where companies do provide dormitories for their employees, they are not of the "healthful," collegiate variety implied by our corporate informant. Staff from the American Friends Service Committee report that dormitory space is "likely to be crowded, with bed rotation paralleling shift rotation—while one shift works, another sleeps, as many as twenty to a room." In one case in Thailand, they found the dormitory "filthy," with workers forced to find their own place to sleep among "splintered floorboards, rusting sheets of metal, and scraps of dirty cloth."

Wages do increase with seniority, but the money does not go to   14
pay for studio apartments or, very likely, motorbikes. A 1970 study of young women factory workers in Hong Kong found that 88 percent of them were turning more than half their earnings over to their parents. In areas that are still largely agricultural (such as parts of the Philippines and Malaysia), or places where male unemployment runs high (such as northern Mexico), a woman factory worker may be the sole source of cash income for an entire extended family.

But wages on a par with what an 11-year-old American could earn   15
on a paper route, and living conditions resembling what Engels found in 19th-century Manchester are only part of the story. The rest begins at the factory gate. The work that multinational corporations export to the Third World is not only the most tedious, but often the most hazardous part of the production process. The countries they go to are, for the most part, those that will guarantee no interference from health and safety inspectors, trade unions, or even free-lance reformers. As a result, most Third World factory women work under conditions that already have broken or will break their health—or their nerves— within a few years, and often before they've worked long enough to earn any more than a subsistence wage.

Consider first the electronics industry, which is generally   16
thought to be the safest and cleanest of the exported industries. The factory buildings are low and modern, like those one might find in a suburban American industrial park. Inside, rows of young women, neatly dressed in the company uniform or T-shirt, work quietly at their stations. There is air conditioning (not for the women's comfort, but to protect the delicate semiconductor parts they work with), and high-volume piped-in Bee Gees hits (not so much for entertainment, as to prevent talking).

For many Third World women, electronics is a prestige occupa-   17
tion, at least compared to other kinds of factory work. They are un-likely to know that in the United States the National Institute on Occupational Safety and Health (NIOSH) has placed electronics on its

select list of "high health-risk industries using the greatest number of toxic substances." If electronics assembly work is risky here, it is doubly so in countries where there is no equivalent of NIOSH to even issue warnings. In many plants toxic chemicals and solvents sit in open containers, filling the work area with fumes that can literally knock you out. "We have been told of cases where ten to twelve women passed out at once," an AFSC field worker in northern Mexico told us, "and the newspapers report this as 'mass hysteria.'"

In one stage of the electronics assembly process, the workers have to dip the circuits into open vats of acid. According to Irene Johnson and Carol Bragg, who toured the National Semiconductor plant in Penang, Malaysia, the women who do the dipping "wear rubber gloves and boots, but these sometimes leak, and burns are common." Occasionally, whole fingers are lost. More commonly, what electronics workers lose is the 20/20 vision they are required to have when they are hired. Most electronics workers spend seven to nine hours a day peering through microscopes, straining to meet their quotas.

One study in South Korea found that most electronics assembly workers developed severe eye problems after only one year of employment; 88 percent had chronic conjunctivitis; 44 percent became nearsighted, and 19 percent developed astigmatism. A manager for Hewlett-Packard's Malaysia plant, in an interview with Rachael Grossman, denied that there were any eye problems. "These girls are used to working with scopes. We've found no eye problems. But it sure makes me dizzy to look through those things."

Electronics, recall, is the "cleanest" of the exported industries. Conditions in the garment and textile industry rival those of any 19th-century (or 20th—see below) sweatshop. The firms, generally local subcontractors to large American chains such as J.C. Penney and Sears, as well as smaller manufacturers, are usually even more indifferent to the health of their employees than the multinationals. Some of the worst conditions have been documented in South Korea, where the garment and textile industries have helped spark that country's "economic miracle." Workers are packed into poorly lit rooms, where summer temperatures rise above 100 degrees. Textile dust, which can cause permanent lung damage, fills the air. When there are rush orders, management may require forced overtime of as much as 48 hours at a stretch, and if that seems to go beyond the limits of human endurance, pep pills and amphetamine injections are thoughtfully provided. In her diary (originally published in a magazine now banned by the South Korean government) Min Chong Suk, 30, a sewing-machine operator, wrote of working from 7 A.M. to 11:30 P.M. in a garment factory. "When [the apprentices] shake the waste threads from the clothes, the whole room fills with dust, and it is hard to breathe. Since we've been working in such dusty air, there have been increasing numbers of people getting tuberculosis, bronchitis, and eye diseases. Since we are women, it makes us so sad when we have pale, unhealthy, wrinkled faces like dried-up spinach. . . . It seems to me that no one knows our blood dissolves into the threads and seams, with sighs and sorrow.''

In all the exported industries, the most invidious, inescapable   21
health hazard is stress. On their home ground United States corporations are not likely to sacrifice productivity for human comfort. On someone else's home ground, however, anything goes. Lunch breaks may be barely long enough for a woman to stand in line at the canteen or hawkers' stalls. Visits to the bathroom are treated as privilege; in some cases, workers must raise their hands for permission to use the toilet, and waits up to a half hour are common. Rotating shifts—the day shift one week, the night shift the next—wreak havoc with sleep patterns. Because inaccuracies or failure to meet production quotas can mean substantial pay losses, the pressures are quickly internalized; stomach ailments and nervous problems are not unusual in the multinationals' Third World female work force. In some situations, good work is as likely to be punished as slow or shoddy work. Correspondent Michael Flannery, writing for the AFL-CIO's *American Federationist*, tells the story of 23-year-old Basilia Altagracia, a seamstress who stitched collars onto ladies' blouses in the La Romana (Dominican Republic) free trade zone (a heavily guarded industrial zone owned by Gulf & Western Industries, Inc.):

"A nimble veteran seamstress, Miss Altagracia eventually began to   22
earn as much as $5.75 a day. . . . 'I was exceeding my piecework quota by a lot. . . . But then, Altagracia said, her plant supervisor, a Cuban emigré, called her into his office. 'He said I was doing a fine job, but that I and some other of the women were making too much money, and he was being forced to lower what we earned for each piece we sewed.' On the best days, she now can clear barely $3, she said. 'I was earning less, so I started working six and seven days a week. But I was tired and I could not work as fast as before.'" Within a few months, she was too ill to work at all.

As if poor health and the stress of factory life weren't enough to   23
drive women into early retirement, management actually encourages a high turnover in many industries. "As you know, when seniority rises, wages rise,'' the management consultant to U.S. multinationals told us. He explained that it's cheaper to train a fresh supply of teenagers than to pay experienced women higher wages. "Older women, aged 23 or 24, are likely to be laid off and not rehired.

We estimate, based on fragmentary data from several sources, that   24 the multinational corporations may already have used up (cast off) as many as 6 million Third World workers — women who are too ill, too old (30 is over the hill in most industries), or too exhausted to be useful any more. Few "retire" with any transferable skills or savings. The lucky ones find husbands.

The unlucky ones find themselves at the margins of society — as   25 bar girls, "hostesses," or prostitutes.

At 21, Julie's greatest fear is that she will never be able to find   26 *a husband. She knows that just being a "factory girl" is enough to give anyone a bad reputation. When she first started working at the electronics company, her father refused to speak to her for three months. Now, every time she leaves Penang to go back to visit her home village she has to put up with a lecture on morality from her older brother — not to mention a barrage of lewd remarks from men outside her family. If they knew that she had actually gone out on a few dates, that she had been to a discotheque, that she had once kissed a young man who said he was a student. . . . Julie's stomach tightens as she imagines her family's reaction. She tries to concentrate on the kind of man she would like to marry: an engineer or technician of some sort, someone who had been to California, where the company headquarters are located and where even the grandmothers wear tight pants and lipstick — someone who had a good attitude about women. But if she ends up having to wear glasses, like her cousin who worked three years at the "scopes," she might as well forget about finding anyone to marry her.*

One of the most serious occupational hazards that Julie and   27 millions of women like her may face is the lifelong stigma of having been a "factory girl." Most of the cultures favored by multinational corporations in their search for cheap labor are patriarchal in the grand old style: any young woman who is not under the wing of a father, husband, or older brother must be "loose." High levels of unemployment among men, as in Mexico, contribute to male resentment of working women. (Ironically, in some places the multinationals have increased male unemployment — for example, by paving over fishing and farming villages to make way for industrial parks.) Add to all this the fact that certain companies — American electronics firms are in the lead — actively promote Western-style sexual objectification as a means of insuring employee loyalty: there are company-sponsored cosmetics classes, "guess whose legs these are" contests, and swimsuit-style beauty contests where the prize might be a free night *for two* in a fancy hotel. Corporate-promoted Westernization only heightens the hostility many men feel toward any independent working women —having a job is bad enough, wearing jeans and mascara to work is going too far.

Anthropologist Patricia Fernandez, who has worked in a *maquiladora* herself, believes that the stigmatization of working women serves, indirectly, to keep them in line. "You have to think of the kind of socialization that girls experience in a very Catholic—or, for that matter, Muslim—society. The fear of having a 'reputation' is enough to make a lot of women bend over backward to be 'respectable' and ladylike, which is just what management wants." She points out that in northern Mexico, the tabloids delight in playing up stories of alleged vice in the *maquiladoras*—indiscriminate sex on the job, epidemics of venereal disease, fetuses found in factory rest rooms. "I worry about this because there are those who treat you differently as soon as they know you have a job at a *maquiladora*," one woman told Fernandez, "Maybe they think that if you have to work, there is a chance you're a whore." 28

And there is always a chance you'll wind up as one. Probably only a small minority of Third World factory workers turn to prostitution when their working days come to an end. But it is, as for women everywhere, the employment of last resort, the only thing to do when the factories don't need you and traditional society won't—or, for economic reasons, can't—take you back. In the Philippines, the brothel business is expanding as fast as the factory system. If they can't use you one way, they can use you another. 29

EXERCISES

Terms to Know

proletariat (paragraph 4), Third World (4), genderless (4), imprint (4), picturesque (4), multinational (4), compelling (5), corollary (5), pharmaceuticals (6), farmed-out (6), minuscule (6), silicon wafers (7), labor-intensive (7), emerging (8), under the aegis of (8), tedium (9), article of faith (10), painstaking (10), macho (10), sabotage (10), sullenness (11), stereotypes (12), subsistence (13), collegiate (13), seniority (14), sole (14), extended family (14), tedious (15), toxic (17), solvents (17), chronic (19), astigmatism (19), sweatshop (20), amphetamine (20), tuberculosis (20), bronchitis (20), invidious (21), inescapable (21), wreak havoc (21), hawker (21), internalized (21), emigré (22), lewd (26), stigma (27), patriarchal (27), ironically (27), objectification (27), Westernization (27), hostility (27), stigmatization (28), socialization (28), tabloids (28), alleged (28), indiscriminate (28).

Some of the Issues

1. In paragraph 5, the authors discuss the wage differential between the First and Third World. What are its consequences? Who loses jobs as a result (paragraph 6)?
2. What do economists mean when they speak of a "new international division of labor"? How does this concept differ from the traditional meaning of the term "division of labor"?
3. How does the American electronics industry exemplify both that new division of labor and the consequences of wage differentials (paragraph 7)?
4. In paragraph 8 the authors begin to discuss in detail the "gender breakdown" of the new division of labor. What do they refer to? What are the reasons for the fact that 80–90 percent of the assembly line jobs go to women?
5. What do the authors believe are the contradictions between the "conventional Western stereotypes" (paragraph 12) and the realities of women's work (paragraphs 13–14)?
6. In paragraphs 16–19 the authors describe the differences between appearance and reality in the electronics industry. What are the various hazards workers risk?
7. On what grounds do the authors assert that the garment industry is even worse than the electronics industry (paragraphs 20–22)?
8. What additional risks do women run when they rise in seniority?
9. Describe the conflicts that may arise in traditional societies between the young women who work in factories and their families.
10. What is "the employment of last resort" (paragraph 29) and how are women driven to it?

The Way We Are Told

11. Three paragraphs of this essay (1, 2, and 26) are set in italics. What do you think is the reason?
12. The authors base the essay on different kinds of research. Cite examples of each kind and evaluate their effectiveness.
13. In a number of instances (paragraphs 11 and 12, for example) the authors cite what people in the First World assume to be the case, and compare that view to reality. Cite some other instances and examine the effectiveness of the comparison.
* 14. Read Ivan Illich's "Effects of Development." Both articles have in

common an attack on Third World practices. Both contradict conventional assumptions held in many developed countries. Compare not the subjects of the attacks, which differ of course, but the ways the respective authors build their cases and substantiate their arguments.

Some Subjects for Essays

15. If you have any work experience, describe it. How did its reality differ from your expectations before starting?
16. Ehrenreich and Fuentes describe the hardships of women workers in the Third World. Compare and contrast the situations the authors describe with the situation of women workers in industrialized societies. Give supporting evidence gained from library research.
17. Write an essay documenting discrimination in the workplace against one of the following groups: women, a racial or religious minority, the handicapped, the young worker, the older worker, or any other group of workers you believe is treated unjustly. Support your argument with evidence gained from library research.

A MODEST PROPOSAL

Jonathan Swift

Jonathan Swift (1667–1745) is the author of *Gulliver's Travels* (1726). Born in Dublin of a Protestant family in a Catholic country, he was educated at Trinity College, Dublin, and Oxford University. He took orders in the Anglican Church and eventually became Dean of St. Patrick's Cathedral in Dublin. One of the great satirists of English literature, he attacked religious as well as social and educational corruption in his books *A Tale of a Tub* and *Gulliver's Travels*. In his "Modest Proposal" Swift addresses himself to the English absentee rulers of Ireland.

"This great town" in the first paragraph refers to Dublin. The last sentence of paragraph 1 refers to the practice of poor people committing themselves, usually for a fixed number of years, to service in a military enterprise or in a colony (including the American colonies).

A MODEST PROPOSAL

*For Preventing the Children of Poor People in Ireland
from Being a Burden to Their Parents or Country,
and for Making Them Beneficial to the Public*

It is a melancholy object to those who walk through this great town or 1
travel in the country, when they see the streets, the roads, and cabin doors, crowded with beggars of the female sex, followed by three, four, or six children, all in rags and importuning every passenger for an alms. These mothers, instead of being able to work for their honest livelihood, are forced to employ all their time in strolling to beg sustenance for their helpless infants, who, as they grow up, either turn thieves for want of work, or leave their dear native country to fight for the Pretender in Spain, or sell themselves to the Barbadoes.

I think it is agreed by all parties that this prodigious number of 2
children in the arms, or on the backs, or at the heels of their mothers, and frequently of their fathers, is in the present deplorable state of the kingdom a very great additional grievance; and therefore whoever could find out a fair, cheap, and easy method of making these children sound, useful members of the commonwealth would deserve so well of the public as to have his statue set up for a preserver of the nation.

367

But my intention is very far from being confined to provide only   3
for the children of professed beggars; it is of a much greater extent,
and shall take in the whole number of infants at a certain age who are
born of parents in effect as little able to support them as those who
demand our charity in the streets.

As to my own part, having turned my thoughts for many years   4
upon this important subject, and maturely weighed the several
schemes of other projectors, I have always found them grossly mistaken in their computation. It is true, a child just dropped from its dam
may be supported by her milk for a solar year, with little other nourishment; at most not above the value of two shillings, which the
mother may certainly get, or the value in scraps, by her lawful occupation of begging; and it is exactly at one year old that I propose to
provide for them in such a manner as instead of being a charge upon
their parents or the parish, or wanting food and raiment for the rest of
their lives, they shall on the contrary contribute to the feeding, and
partly to the clothing, of many thousands.

There is likewise another great advantage in my scheme, that it   5
will prevent those voluntary abortions, and that horrid practice of
women murdering their bastard children, alas, too frequent among us,
sacrificing the poor innocent babes, I doubt, more to avoid the expense than the shame, which would move tears and pity in the most
savage and inhuman breast.

The number of souls in this kingdom being usually reckoned one   6
million and a half, of these I calculate there may be about two hundred
thousand couples whose wives are breeders; from which number I
subtract thirty thousand couples who are able to maintain their own
children, although I apprehend there cannot be so many under the
present distress of the kingdom; but this being granted, there will
remain an hundred and seventy thousand breeders. I again subtract
fifty thousand for those women who miscarry, or whose children die
by accident or disease within the year. There only remain an hundred
and twenty thousand children of poor parents annually born. The
question therefore is, how this number shall be reared and provided
for, which, as I have already said, under the present situation of affairs,
is utterly impossible by all the methods hitherto proposed. For we can
neither employ them in handicraft nor agriculture; we neither build
houses (I mean in the country) nor cultivate land. They can very
seldom pick up a livelihood by stealing till they arrive at six years old,
except where they are of towardly parts; although I confess they learn
the rudiments much earlier, during which time they can however be
looked upon only as probationers, as I have been informed by a
principal gentleman in the country of Cavan, who protested to me that
he never knew above one or two instances under the age of six, even in

a part of the kingdom so renowned for the quickest proficiency in that art.

I am assured by our merchants that a boy or a girl before twelve years old is no salable commodity; and even when they come to this age, they will not yield above three pounds, or three pounds and half a crown at most on the Exchange; which cannot turn to account either to the parents or the kingdom, the charge of nutriment and rags having been at least four times that value. 7

I shall now therefore humbly propose my own thoughts, which I hope will not be liable to the least objection. 8

I have been assured by a very knowing American of my acquaintance in London, that a young healthy child well nursed is at a year old a most delicious, nourishing, and wholesome food, whether stewed, roasted, baked, or boiled; and I make not doubt that it will equally serve in a fricassee or a ragout. 9

I do therefore humbly offer it to public consideration that of the hundred and twenty thousand children, already computed, twenty thousand may be reserved for breed, whereof only one fourth part to be males, which is more than we allow to sheep, black cattle, or swine; and my reason is that these children are seldom the fruits of marriage, a circumstance not much regarded by our savages, therefore one male will be sufficient to serve four females. That the remaining hundred thousand may at a year old be offered in sale to the persons of quality and fortune through the kingdom, always advising the mother to let them suck plentifully in the last month, so as to render them plump and fat for a good table. A child will make two dishes at an entertainment for friends; and when the family dines alone, the fore or hind quarter will make a reasonable dish, and seasoned with a little pepper or salt will be very good boiled on the fourth day, especially in winter. 10

I have reckoned upon a medium that a child just born will weigh twelve pounds, and in a solar year if tolerably nursed increaseth to twenty-eight pounds. 11

I grant this food will be somewhat dear, and therefore very proper for landlords, who, as they have already devoured most of the parents, seem to have the best title to the children. 12

Infant's flesh will be in season throughout the year, but more plentiful in March, and a little before and after. For we are told by a grave author, an eminent French physician, that fish being a prolific diet, there are more children born in Roman Catholic countries about nine months after Lent, than at any other season; therefore, reckoning a year after Lent, the markets will be more glutted than usual, because the number of popish infants is at least three to one in this kingdom; and therefore it will have one other collateral advantage, by lessening the number of Papists among us. 13

I have already computed the charge of nursing a beggar's child   14
(in which list I reckon all cottagers, laborers, and four fifths of the
farmers) to be about two shillings per annum, rags included; and I
believe no gentleman would repine to give ten shillings for the carcass
of a good fat child, which, as I have said, will make four dishes of
excellent nutritive meat, when he hath only some particular friend or
his own family to dine with him. Thus the squire will learn to be a
good landlord, and grow popular among the tenants; the mother will
have eight shillings net profit, and be fit for work till she produces
another child.

Those who are more thrifty (as I must confess the times require)   15
may flay the carcass; the skin of which artificially dressed will make
admirable gloves for ladies, and summer boots for fine gentlemen.

As to our city of Dublin, shambles may be appointed for this   16
purpose in the most convenient parts of it, and butchers we may be
assured will not be wanting; although I rather recommend buying the
children alive, and dressing them hot from the knife as we do roasting
pigs.

A very worthy person, a true lover of this country, and whose   17
virtues I highly esteem, was lately pleased in discoursing on this
matter to offer a refinement upon my scheme. He said that many
gentlemen of his kingdom, having of late destroyed their deer, he
conceived that the want of venison might be well supplied by the
bodies of young lads and maidens, not exceeding fourteen years of age
nor under twelve, so great a number of both sexes in every county
being now ready to starve for want of work and service; and these to be
disposed of by their parents, if alive, or otherwise by their nearest
relations. But with due deference to so excellent a friend and so
deserving a patriot, I cannot be altogether in his sentiments; for as to
the males, my American acquaintance assured me from frequent experience that their flesh was generally tough and lean, like that of our
schoolboys, by continual exercise, and their taste disagreeable; and to
fatten them would not answer the charge. Then as to the females, it
would, I think with humble submission, be a loss to the public,
because they soon would become breeders themselves; and besides, it
is not improbable that some scrupulous people might be apt to censure such a practice (although indeed very unjustly) as a little bordering upon cruelty; which, I confess, hath always been with me the
strongest objection against any project, how well soever intended.

But in order to justify my friend, he confessed that this expedient   18
was put into his head by the famous Psalmanazar, a native of the island
Formosa, who came from thence to London above twenty years ago,
and in conversation told my friend that in his country when any young
person happened to be put to death, the executioner sold the carcass

to the persons of quality as a prime dainty; and that in his time the body of a plump girl of fifteen, who was crucified for an attempt to poison the emperor, was sold to his Imperial Majesty's prime minister of state, and other great mandarins of the court, in joints from the gibbet, at four hundred crowns. Neither indeed can I deny that if the same use were made of several plump young girls in this town, who without one single groat to their fortunes cannot stir abroad without a chair, and appear at the playhouse and assemblies in foreign fineries which they never will pay for, the kingdom would not be the worse.

Some persons of a desponding spirit are in great concern about   19
that vast number of poor people who are aged, diseased, or maimed, and I have been desired to employ my thoughts what course may be taken to ease the nation of so grievous an encumbrance. But I am not in the least pain upon that matter, because it is very well known that they are every day dying and rotting by cold and famine, and filth and vermin, as fast as can be reasonably expected. And as to the younger laborers, they are now in almost as hopeful a condition. They cannot get work, and consequently pine away for want of nourishment to a degree that if any time they are accidentally hired to common labor, they have not strength to perform it; and thus the country and themselves are happily delivered from the evils to come.

I have too long digressed, and therefore shall return to my sub-   20
ject. I think the advantages by the proposal which I have made are obvious and many, as well as of the highest importance.

For first, as I have already observed, it would greatly lessen the   21
number of Papists, with whom we are yearly overrun, being the principal breeders of the nation as well as our most dangerous enemies; and who stay at home on purpose to deliver the kingdom to the Pretender, hoping to take their advantage by the absence of so many good Protestants, who have chosen rather to leave their country than to stay at home and pay tithes against their conscience to an Episcopal curate.

Secondly, the poorer tenants will have something valuable of   22
their own, which by law may be made liable to distress, and help to pay their landlord's rent, their corn and cattle being already seized and money a thing unknown.

Thirdly, whereas the maintenance of an hundred thousand chil-   23
dren, from two years old and upwards, cannot be computed at less than ten shillings a piece per annum, the nation's stock will be thereby increased fifty thousand pounds per annum, besides the profit of a new dish introduced to the tables of all gentlemen of fortune in the kingdom who have any refinement in taste. And the money will circulate among ourselves, the goods being entirely of our own growth and manufacture.

Fourthly, the constant breeders, besides the gain of eight shillings sterling per annum by the sale of their children, will be rid of the charge for maintaining them after the first year.   24

Fifthly, this food would likewise bring great custom to taverns, where the vintners will certainly be so prudent as to procure the best receipts for dressing it to perfection, and consequently have their houses frequented by all the fine gentlemen, who justly value themselves upon their knowledge in good eating; and a skillful cook, who understands how to oblige his guests, will contrive to make it as expensive as they please.   25

Sixthly, this would be a great inducement to marriage, which all wise nations have either encouraged by rewards or enforced by laws and penalties. It would increase the care and tenderness of mothers toward their children, when they were sure of a settlement for life to the poor babes, provided in some sort by the public, to their annual profit instead of expense. We should see an honest emulation among the married women, which of them could bring the fattest child to the market. Men would become as fond of their wives during the time of their pregnancy as they are now of their mares in foal, their cows in calf, or sows when they are ready to farrow; nor offer to beat or kick them (as is too frequent a practice) for fear of a miscarriage.   26

Many other advantages might be enumerated. For instance, the addition of some thousand carcasses in our exportation of barreled beef, the propagation of swine's flesh, and improvements in the art of making good bacon, so much wanted among us by the great destruction of pigs, too frequent at our tables, which are no way comparable in taste or magnificence to a well-grown, fat, yearling child, which roasted whole will make a considerable figure at a lord mayor's feast or any other public entertainment. But this and many others I omit, being studious of brevity.   27

Supposing that one thousand families in this city would be constant customers for infants' flesh, besides others who might have it at merry meetings, particularly weddings and christenings, I compute that Dublin would take off annually about twenty thousand carcasses, and the rest of the kingdom (where probably they will be sold somewhat cheaper) the remaining eighty thousand.   28

I can think of no one objection that will possibly be raised against this proposal, unless it should be urged that the number of people will be thereby much lessened in the kingdom. This I freely own, and it was indeed one principal design in offering it to the world. I desire the reader will observe, and I calculate my remedy for this one individual kingdom of Ireland and for no other that ever was, is, or I think ever can be upon earth. Therefore, let no man talk to me of other expedients: of taxing our absentees at five shillings a pound: of using neither   29 clothes nor household furniture except what is of our own growth and manufacture: of utterly rejecting the materials and instruments that promote foreign luxury: of curing the expensiveness of pride, vanity, idleness, and gaming in our women: of introducing a vein of parsimony, prudence, and temperance: of learning to love our country, in the want of which we differ even from Laplanders and the inhabitants of Topinamboo: of quitting our animosities and factions, nor acting any longer like the Jews, who were murdering one another at the very moment their city was taken: of being a little cautious not to sell our country and conscience for nothing: of teaching landlords to have at least one degree of mercy toward their tenants: lastly, of putting a spirit of honesty, industry, and skill into our shopkeepers; who, if a resolution could not be taken to buy only our native goods, would immediately unite to cheat and exact upon us in the price, the measure, and the goodness, nor could ever yet be brought to make one fair proposal of just dealing, though often and earnestly invited to it.

Therefore, I repeat, let no man talk to me of these and the like expedients, til he hath at least some glimpse of hope that there will ever be some hearty and sincere attempt to put them in practice. 30

But as to myself, having been wearied out for many years with offering vain, idle, visionary thoughts, and at length utterly despairing of success, I fortunately fell upon this proposal, which, as it is wholly new, so it hath something solid and real, of no expense and little trouble, full in our own power, and whereby we can incur no danger in disobliging England. For this kind of commodity will not bear exportation, the flesh being of too tender a consistence to admit a long continuance in salt, although perhaps I could name a country which would be glad to eat up our whole nation without it. 31

After all, I am not so violently bent upon my own opinion as to reject any offer proposed by wise men, which shall be found equally innocent, cheap, easy, and effectual. But before something of that kind shall be advanced in contradiction to my scheme, and offering a better, I desire the author or authors will be pleased maturely to consider two points. First, as things now stand, how they will be able to find food and raiment for an hundred thousand useless mouths and backs. And secondly, there being a round million of creatures in human figure throughout this kingdom, whose sole subsistence put into a common stock would leave them in debt two millions of pounds sterling, adding those who are beggars by profession to the bulk of farmers, cottagers, and laborers, with their wives and children who are beggars in effect; I desire those politicians who dislike my overture, and may perhaps be so bold to attempt an answer, that they will first ask the parents of these mortals whether they would not at this day think it a great happiness to have been sold for food at a year old in this manner I 32

prescribe, and thereby have avoided such a perpetual scene of misfor- 33
tunes as they have since gone through by the oppression of landlords,
the impossibility of paying rent without money or trade, the want of
common sustenance, with neither house nor clothes to cover them
from the inclemencies of the weather, and the most inevitable prospect of entailing the like or greater miseries upon their breed forever.

I profess, in the sincerity of my heart, that I have not the least
personal interest in endeavoring to promote this necessary work, having no other motive than the public good of my country, by advancing
our trade, providing for infants, relieving the poor, and giving some
pleasure to the rich. I have no children by which I can propose to get a
single penny; the youngest being nine years old, and my wife past
childbearing.

EXERCISES

Words to Know

object (paragraph 1), importuning (1), alms (1), sustenance (1),
Pretender (1), prodigious (2), dam (4), raiment (4), towardly parts
(6), rudiments (6), probationer (6), commodity (7), nutriment (7),
fricassee (9), ragout (9), quality (10), fortune (10), popish (13),
collateral (13), Papist (13), repine (14), shambles (16), deference
(17), scrupulous (17), censure (17), expedient (18), gibbet (18),
groat (18), assemblies (18) desponding (19), maimed (19), encumbrance (19), vermin (19), digressed (20), prudent (25), receipts
(25), propagation (27), gaming (29), parsimony (29), inclemencies
(32).

Some of the Issues

1. Paragraphs 1 through 6 are an introduction. What is the main
   point the author wants to make?
2. Paragraph 7 is a transition. Before you have read the rest, what
   might it foretell?
3. The short paragraph 8 is the beginning of the real proposal; and
   paragraph 9, its central idea. Explain that idea.
4. Paragraph 10 expands the proposal in 9. It relates in particular to
   paragraph 6. Why are all these statistical calculations important?
   What do they contribute to the impact of the essay?
5. Look back to paragraph 5. What hints of the idea to come do you
   now find in it?

6. Paragraphs 15 through 17 offer refinements on the main theme. What are they?
7. Examine the logic of each of the advantages of the proposal, as listed in paragraphs 21 through 26. Why is the lessening of the number of Papists a particular advantage?
8. In paragraph 29, when the essay turns to possible objections, which are the ones that are omitted completely? Why? Why does the narrator so vehemently concentrate on Ireland in this paragraph?
9. In paragraph 29 other remedies are also proposed for solving the plight of Ireland. What distinguishes them from the one the narrator is advocating?

The Way We Are Told

10. Readers of this essay will for a time take Swift's observations at face value. At what point in the essay are they likely to change their minds?
11. Swift creates a narrator whose modest proposal this is. Try to imagine him: what kind of person might he be? What might be his profession? Consider some of the phrases he uses, his obsession with statistics and the financial aspects of the problem, and his attention to detail.
12. In paragraph 4, in the narrator's choice of words, you find the first hint of what is to come. Locate it. Do you find an echo in paragraph 6?
13. Having made his proposal boldly in paragraph 9, the narrator develops it in paragraphs 10 through 14. Paragraphs 15 through 17 heighten the effect. Consider the choice of images in these paragraphs.

Some Subject for Essays

14. Do you have any modest proposals as to what to do with teachers, younger brothers or sisters, former boyfriends or girlfriends, or anyone else?

PART NINE

Communicating

How do we communicate? The first answer that is likely to come to most people's minds is through language: we speak, we listen, we read, we write. When we think further, we become increasingly aware that we also communicate in nonverbal ways, through gestures and body movements. The signals given by our "body language" are often more revealing than the words we use. Most of us will have had the experience of someone saying something to us — making a flattering remark, for instance — that we felt was insincere. Why did we feel that? Maybe it was the tone in which it was said, or something in the person's movement or eye contact with us.

When we turn to communication processes across cultures, the complexities and complications multiply. Language is again the most obvious example. If you speak only English and the person you try to talk to speaks only Japanese, communication will be limited — though you will, if you both really try, be able to understand each other to some extent by means of gestures. Even with speakers of the same language, problems may be the result of intracultural differences, that is, distinctions between subgroups within a culture. Gloria Naylor, in the first selection, alerts the reader to one such problem. It concerns the use of the word "nigger" in the black as distinguished from the white American community.

Naylor's essay is about ethnic roles, or more accurately an

ethnic put-down. The next two essays are about gender, or rather about the way language or linguistic customs allow a put-down of women. William Hines cites the case of doctors who address women patients they have never met before by their first names while expecting to be addressed by their proper titles. Robin Lakoff in her essay "You Are What You Say" demonstrates that English usage provides ample opportunity to make women unequal.

The four essays that follow give some indication of the scope of the different ways in which we communicate. Myrna Knepler exemplifies the emotional as distinct from the informational impact of language in a cross-cultural setting. American advertisers use French words to enhance the appeal of their products, just as French advertisers use English for the same purpose. Edward T. Hall's essay on "Private Space" reminds us that communication is by no means confined to language. He discusses the meaning of the different ways Germans and Americans look upon the use of physical space. Peter Farb in "How to Talk About the World" shows how we use language to classify our experience and to organize our impression of the world around us. The authors of "World Language: English" demonstrates that English has become a world language, in fact the first real world language, and analyze some of the consequences of that development.

The final three selections are concerned with issues involved in speaking, or being educated in, more than one language. Richard Rodriguez ("Public and Private Language") and James Fallows ("Bilingual Education") hold opposite views as to the value of bilingual education. Rodriguez argues against it, whereas Fallows supports the principle on which it rests. Lastly, Ngugi wa Thiong'o, a Kenyan writer who grew up speaking two East African languages but had most of his education in English, draws attention to the problem of many authors in his position: Should he write in his native language and thereby restrict his audience, or in English, which will in the end never be fully his language?

THE MEANING OF A WORD

Gloria Naylor

Gloria Naylor, a native of New York City, was born in 1950 and educated at Brooklyn College and Yale. She has taught at George Washington, New York, and Boston universities. Her first novel, *The Women of Brewster Place* (1982), won an American Book Award. Since then she has written *Linden Hills* (1985) and *Mama Day* (1988). The essay included here appeared in the *New York Times* on February 20, 1986.

The word whose meaning Naylor learned was "nigger." She explains that she had heard it used quite comfortably by friends and relatives, but the way it was uttered to her by a white child in school was so different that she at first did not realize that it was the same word.

Language is the subject. It is the written form with which I've managed to keep the wolf away from the door and, in diaries, to keep my sanity. In spite of this, I consider the written word inferior to the spoken, and much of the frustration experienced by novelists is the awareness that whatever we manage to capture in even the most transcendent passages falls far short of the richness of life. Dialogue achieves its power in the dynamics of a fleeting moment of sight, sound, smell and touch.

I'm not going to enter the debate here about whether it is language that shapes reality or vice versa. That battle is doomed to be waged whenever we seek intermittent reprieve from the chicken and egg dispute. I will simply take the position that the spoken word, like the written word, amounts to a nonsensical arrangement of sounds or letters without a consensus that assigns "meaning." And building from the meanings of what we hear, we order reality. Words themselves are innocuous; it is the consensus that gives them true power.

I remember the first time I heard the word nigger. In my third-grade class, our math tests were being passed down the rows, and as I handed the papers to a little boy in back of me, I remarked that once again he had received a much lower mark than I did. He snatched his test from me and spit out that word. Had he called me a nymphomaniac or a necrophiliac, I couldn't have been more puzzled. I didn't know what a nigger was, but I knew that whatever it meant, it was something he shouldn't have called me. This was verified when I raised my hand, and in a loud voice repeated what he had said and watched the teacher scold him for using a "bad" word. I was later to go home and ask the inevitable question that every black parent must face — "Mommy, what does 'nigger' mean?"

And what exactly did it mean? Thinking back, I realize that this could not have been the first time the word was used in my presence. I was part of a large extended family that had migrated from the rural South after World War II and formed a close-knit network that gravitated around my maternal grandparents. Their ground-floor apartment in one of the buildings they owned in Harlem was a weekend mecca for my immediate family, along with countless aunts, uncles and cousins who brought along assorted friends. It was a bustling and open house with assorted neighbors and tenants popping in and out to exchange bits of gossip, pick up an old quarrel or referee the ongoing checkers game in which my grandmother cheated shamelessly. They were all there to let down their hair and put up their feet after a week of labor in the factories, laundries and shipyards of New York.   4

Amid the clamor, which could reach deafening proportions — two or three conversations going on simultaneously, punctuated by the sound of a baby's crying somewhere in the back rooms or out on the street — there was still a rigid set of rules about what was said and how. Older children were sent out of the living room when it was time to get into the juicy details about "you-know-who" up on the third floor who had gone and gotten herself "p-r-e-g-n-a-n-t!" But my parents, knowing that I could spell well beyond my years, always demanded that I follow the others out to play. Beyond sexual misconduct and death, everything else was considered harmless for our young ears. And so among the anecdotes of the triumphs and disappointments in the various workings of their lives, the word nigger was used in my presence, but it was set within contexts and inflections that caused it to register in my mind as something else.   5

In the singular, the word was always applied to a man who had distinguished himself in some situation that brought their approval for his strength, intelligence or drive: 6

"Did Johnny *really* do that?"   7

"I'm telling you, that nigger pulled in $6,000 of overtime last year. Said he got enough for a down payment on a house."   8

When used with a possessive adjective by a woman — "my nigger" — it became a term of endearment for husband or boyfriend. But it could be more than just a term applied to a man. In their mouths it became the pure essence of manhood — a disembodied force that channeled their past history of struggle and present survival against the   9 odds into a victorious statement of being: "Yeah, that old foreman found out quick enough—you don't mess with a nigger."

In the plural, it became a description of some group within the community that have overstepped the bounds of decency as my family defined it: Parents who neglected their children, a drunken couple who fought in public, people who simply refused to look for work, those with excessively dirty mouths or unkempt households were all "trifling niggers." This particular circle could forgive hard times, unemployment, the occasional bout of depression—they had gone through all of that themselves—but the unforgivable sin was a lack of self-respect.   10

A woman could never be a "nigger" in the singular, with its connotation of confirming worth. The noun girl was its closest equivalent in that sense, but only when used in direct address and regardless of the gender doing the addressing. "Girl" was a token of respect for a woman. The one-syllable word was drawn out to sound like three in recognition of the extra ounce of wit, nerve or daring that the woman had shown in the situation under discussion.   11

"G-i-r-l, stop. You mean you said that to his face?"   12

But if the word was used in a third-person reference or shortened so that it almost snapped out of the mouth, it always involved some element of communal disapproval. And age became an important factor in these exchanges. It was only between individuals of the same generation, or from an older person to a younger (but never the other way around), that "girl" would be considered a compliment.   13

I don't agree with the argument that use of the word nigger at this social stratum of the black community was an internalization of racism. The dynamics were the exact opposite: the people in my grandmother's living room took a word that whites used to signify worthlessness or degradation and rendered it impotent. Gathering there together, they transformed "nigger" to signify the varied and complex human beings they knew themselves to be. If the word was to disappear totally from the mouths of even the most liberal of white society, no one in that room was naïve enough to believe it would disappear from white minds. Meeting the word head-on, they proved it had absolutely nothing to do with the way they were determined to live their lives.   14

So there must have been dozens of times that the "nigger" was spoken in front of me before I reached the third grade. But I didn't "hear" it until it was said by a small pair of lips that had already learned it could be a way to humiliate me. That was the word I went home and asked my mother about. And since she knew that I had to grow up in America, she took me in her lap and explained.   15

EXERCISES

Words to Know

transcendent (paragraph 1), intermittent (2), reprieve (2), consensus
(2), innocuous (2), nymphomaniac (3), necrophiliac (3), extended
family (4), gravitated (4), mecca (4), possessive (9), essence (9),
disembodied (9), unkempt (10), trifling (10), connotation (11),
communal (13), social stratum (14), internalization (14), degradation (14), naïve (14).

Some of the Issues

1. What reasons does Naylor give for considering the spoken word
   superior to the written?
2. Reread paragraph 2. What, according to Naylor, gives meaning to
   words?
3. In paragraph 3 the author tells a story from her experience as a
   child. How does it relate to the general statement on language
   that she made in the first two paragraphs? What is it that made
   Naylor think that she had been called by a "bad" word?
4. At the end of paragraph 5 and in the examples that follow Naylor
   demonstrates that she had heard the word "nigger" before the
   boy in her class used it. Why did the previous uses register with
   her as something different?

The Way We Are Told

5. Naylor starts with a general statement — "language is the
   subject" — which she then expands on in paragraphs 1 and 2.
   What focus does this beginning give her essay? How would the
   focus differ if she started with the anecdote in paragraph 3?
6. Naylor asserts that "the written word is inferior to the spoken."
   What devices does she use to help the reader *hear* the dialogue?
7. The essay consists of three parts: paragraphs 1 and 2, 3 to 13, and
   14 – 15. The first is a general statement and the second an anecdote followed by records of conversations. How does the third
   part relate to the preceding?

Some Subjects for Essays

8. Many words differ in their meaning depending on the circumstances in which they are used. Write a brief essay on the different words applied to a particular nationality or ethnic group and
   explain their impact.

9. "Sticks and stones may break my bones but words can never hurt me." Do you have any experiences that would either confirm or deny the truth of that saying?

* 10. Read Countee Cullen's poem "Incident." The subject is the same as Naylor's, but the way we are told is of course different. Try to analyze the difference in two respects: as a poem compared to a prose essay, and as to the actual circumstances of the two events they describe.

HELLO, JUDY. I'M DR. SMITH

William Hines

William Hines is a reporter for the *Chicago Sun-Times*, in which
this article appeared on June 2, 1983. Here he concerns himself
with a habit that reflects the attitudes of medical practitioners,
usually male, toward women: at first meeting they often address
female patients by their first names while, of course, expecting to
be respectfully addressed by their titles and last names.

If feminine reaction to one aspect of the doctor-patient relationship is 1
any indication, it's high time for some consciousness-raising in the
medical profession.

Many women, not solely of the feminist persuasion, object to 2
being first-named by a physician they hardly know — especially when
the man in the white coat makes it clear that he, in turn, expects to be
addressed as "Doctor."

The opening bell for another round in this battle of the sexes 3
sounded early this year when Elizabeth Babbott Conant of Buffalo,
N.Y., wrote the New England Journal of Medicine laying out her objections to doctors addressing patients by their first names.

"It is a bogus, unearned familiarity," said Conant, who sports a 4
doctor's degree of her own, in biology, which she teaches at Canisius
College. It causes "a loss of confidence, of dignity and of one's sense
of individuality," she added.

More than just demeaning to a person who doesn't like familiarity 5
from every Tom, Dick and Harry, Conant contended that the practice
also may defeat the purpose of treatment.

"The physician's role includes the task of enlisting the patient's 6
own healing powers," Conant wrote. "Any procedure that increases
confidence and inner energy will be important; any procedure that
disempowers or diminishes the sense of self may impede the patient's
progress.

"An insidious effect of the automatic use of the first name is to 7
make the patient a child again. By reinforcing dependency and passivity, you" — directly addressing the Journal's medical readership —
"have stolen power from your potential ally."

Conant's letter evoked a reply published in the most recent issue   8
of the Journal. Dr. Marc E. Heller of the Mary Imogene Bassett Hospital
at Copperstown, N.Y., said a survey of obstetrics-gynecology patients
there disclosed that "78 percent wished to be called by their first
name" and only 2 percent specifically objected.

This drew a hearty snort the other day from a leading feminist   9
with A-1 scientific credentials and medical connections.

"Very interesting," said Professor Estelle Ramey, a physiologist at   10
the Georgetown University school of medicine here. "Ob-Gyn people
did it. That questionnaire would never be done by anyone who dealt
with a practice that included men. Men would be absolutely astonished even to be asked such a thing."

The 78 percent who endorsed first-name use, Ramey opined,   11
"were answering what they thought the doctor wanted them to
answer."

Ramey reserved most of her feminists corn for specialists in   12
childbirth and women's diseases, but in point of fact it was not Ob-
Gyns at all that prompted Conant's letter; it was radiologists. Not only
the doctors, but also technicians first-named the patients at this clinic,
she said.

Doctors in general seem to treat their female patients with more   13
familiarity and what is taken as condescension than they exhibit in
dealing with male patients. Belita Cowan, head of the Washington-
based National Women's Health Network, said the medical literature
contains evidence of this.

Cowan cited a study reported in the New England Journal in   14
1973 showing that when men and women go to a doctor complaining
of identical symptoms the doctor is far more likely to ascribe the
problem to psychological factors when the patient is female.

The authors of the study, physicians Jean and John Lennane, said   15
the tendency to brush off women's complaints as psychogenic leads to
"inadequate and even derisive treatments for patients."

Many women who said they detest first-naming by doctors they   16
don't really know are reluctant to object. "He's like God," one normally hard-bitten Washington career woman said.

Ellen Warren, a member of the Sun-Times Washington bureau,   17
said she gets "livid" when her male gynecologist calls her "Ellen."
She is diffident about calling him "Don" and is "damned if I'll call
him Doctor," so the upshot is that Warren calls her physician nothing.

Ramey acknowledged that it's difficult to brace a doctor about   18
first-naming. She said it's "like that terrible TV ad where the woman in
the dental chair says, 'Oh, by the way, you've got bad breath.'

"If you did that you'd have to have rocks in your head," Ramey   19
said. "He'd put the drill right through the top of your skull."

How do doctors feel about this? Official doctrine is that the   20
patient's dignity should be preserved at all times. Formal discourse
between patient and physician is to be preferred, both the American
College of Obstetricians and Gynecologists and the Association of
American Medical Colleges say. But when the doctor is out there in
private practice, it's dealer's choice.

Dr. Vicki Seltzer, director of Ob-Gyn at Queens Hospital Center,   21
said she prefers to be on a "Mrs. So-and-so — Dr. Seltzer" basis with
her patient until she really knows them well, after which mutual
first-naming is appropriate.

A patient who objects to being first-named should say so, Seltzer   22
said, "not hostilely but factually: 'I'd prefer it if you'd call me Mrs.
Whatever.'" If she basically doesn't like the doctor's style, Seltzer
added, she should get a new one.

Dr. August Swanson, director of academic affairs for AAMC, a   23
national association representing more than 100 U.S. medical schools,
blames the way doctors are trained for some of the traits that come
through as insensitivity toward patients. The association is reviewing
medical curricula, and human relations is one of the areas under study,
he said.

The old rule still applies, however: A gentleman never uninten-   24
tionally offends — and on this score many a female patient thinks her
physician is no gentleman.

EXERCISES

Words to Know

consciousness-raising (paragraph 1), bogus (4), demeaning (5), dis-
empower (6), impede (6), insidious (7), dependency (7), passivity
(7), potential (7), obstetrics-gynecology (Ob-Gyn) (8), snort (9),
physiologist (10), endorsed (11), radiologists (12), condescension
(13), psychogenic (15), derisive (15), reluctant (16), livid (17),
diffident (17), brace (18), doctrine (20), formal discourse (20),
dealer's choice (20).

Some of the Issues

1. In paragraphs 5 through 7 Hines cites an argument against the
   causal use of first names. What is it?
2. What is the argument in favor of using first names in paragraph 8,
   and how is it countered in paragraphs 9 and 10?

3. In paragraph 10 Hines cites a study; how do the results of that study relate to the overall topic of the essay?
4. Why are women who do not like doctors to call them by their first names hesitant to object?
5. Does the article propose any solutions to the problem? What are they? Are they likely to be effective?

The Way We Are Told

6. In paragraph 3 Hines uses the term "opening bell"; what does he refer to?
7. Hines quotes a number of people throughout the article. What is their claim to authority?
8. As a feature article in a daily newspaper, the selection is designed to draw and hold the casual reader's attention. How well does the author succeed in doing this?

Some Subjects for Essays

9. The essay presents an argument; it raises objections to a current practice and proposes changes. Write an essay carefully explaining what Hines argues for, and how he supports his argument.
10. Choose a subject for which you are able to collect evidence from friends or acquaintances as authorities. For example, if you have friends who are parents of young children, interview them on their opinions on child rearing; or if you have friends interested in music, interview them about their tastes and attitudes. Write an essay quoting your authorities and generalizing on what you have found out.

YOU ARE WHAT YOU SAY

Robin Lakoff

Robin Lakoff (1942–) is a professor of linguistics at the University of California, Berkeley. She was educated at Radcliffe, the University of Indiana, and Harvard, and is the author of *Language and Women's Place* (1975) and co-author of *Face Value: The Politics of Beauty* (1984). In the following essay (*Ms* magazine, July 1974) Lakoff discusses language used by, about, and toward women. She demonstrates in detail how the English language contributes extensively to put-downs of the "weaker sex."

"Women's language" is that pleasant (dainty?), euphemistic, never-aggressive way of talking we learned as little girls. Cultural bias was built into the language we were allowed to speak, the subjects we were allowed to speak about, and the ways we were spoken of. Having learned our linguistic lesson well, we go out in the world, only to discover that we are communicative cripples — damned if we do, and damned if we don't.

If we refuse to talk "like a lady," we are ridiculed and criticized for being unfeminine. ("She thinks like a man" is, at best, a left-handed compliment.) If we do learn all the fuzzy-headed, unassertive language of our sex, we are ridiculed for being unable to think clearly, unable to take part in a serious discussion, and therefore unfit to hold a position of power.

It doesn't take much of this for a woman to begin feeling she deserves such treatment because of inadequacies in her own intelligence and education.

"Women's language" shows up in all levels of English. For example, women are encouraged and allowed to make far more precise discriminations in naming colors than men do. Words like *mauve*, *beige*, *ecru*, *aquamarine*, *lavender*, and so on, are unremarkable in a woman's active vocabulary, but largely absent from that of most men. I know of no evidence suggesting that women actually *see* a wider range of colors than men do. It is simply that fine discriminations of this sort are relevant to women's vocabularies, but not to men's; to men, who control most of the interesting affairs of the world, such distinctions are trivial — irrelevant.

388

In the area of syntax, we find similar gender-related peculiarities [5]
of speech. There is one construction, in particular, that women use
conversationally far more than men: the tag-question. A tag is midway
between an outright statement and a yes-no question; it is less assertive
than the former, but more confident than the later.

A *flat statement* indicates confidence in the speaker's knowledge [6]
and is fairly certain to be believed; a *question* indicates a lack of
knowledge on some point and implies that the gap in the speaker's
knowledge can and will be remedied by an answer. For example, if, at
a Little League game, I have had my glasses off, I can legitimately ask
someone else: "Was the player out at third?" A *tag question*, being
intermediate between statement and question, is used when the
speaker is stating a claim, but lacks full confidence in the truth of that
claim. So if I say, "Is Joan here?" I will probably not be surprised if my
respondent answers "no"; but if I say, "Joan is here, isn't she?" instead, chances are I am already biased in favor of a positive answer,
wanting only confirmation. I still want a response, but I have enough
knowledge (or think I have) to predict that response. A tag question,
then, might be thought of as a statement that doesn't demand to be
believed by anyone but the speaker, a way of giving leeway, of not
forcing the addressee to go along with the views of the speaker.

Another common use of the tag question is in small talk when the [7]
speaker is trying to elicit conversation: "Sure is hot here, isn't it?"

But in discussing personal feelings or opinions, only the speaker [8]
normally has any way of knowing the correct answer. Sentences such
as "I have a headache, don't I?" are clearly ridiculous. But there are
other examples where it is the speaker's opinions, rather than perceptions, for which corroboration is sought, as in "The situation in Southeast Asia is terrible, isn't it?"

While there are, of course, other possible interpretations of a [9]
sentence like this, one possibility is that the speaker has a particular
answer in mind — "yes" or "no" — but is reluctant to state it baldly.
This sort of tag question is much more apt to be used by women than
by men in conversation. Why is this the case?

The tag question allows a speaker to avoid commitment, and [10]
thereby avoid conflict with the addressee. The problem is that, by so
doing, speakers may also give the impression of not really being sure of
themselves, or looking to the addressee for confirmation of their
views. This uncertainty is reinforced in more subliminal ways, too.
There is a peculiar sentence intonation-pattern, used almost exclusively by women, as far as I know, which changes a declarative answer
into a question. The effect of using the rising inflection typical of a
yes-no question is to imply that the speaker is seeking confirmation,
even though the speaker is clearly the only one who has the requisite

information, which is why the question was put to her in the first place:

> (Q) When will dinner be ready?
> (A) Oh . . . around six o'clock . . .?

It is as though the second speaker were saying, "Six o'clock — if that's okay with you, if you agree." The person being addressed is put in the position of having to provide confirmation. One likely consequence of this sort of speech-pattern in a woman is that, often unbeknownst to herself, the speaker builds a reputation of tentativeness, and others will refrain from taking her seriously or trusting her with any real responsibilities, since she "can't make up her mind," and "isn't sure of herself."

Such idiosyncrasies may explain why women's language sounds 11 much more "polite" than men's. It is polite to leave a decision open, not impose your mind, or views, or claims, on anyone else. So a tag question is a kind of polite statement, in that it does not force agreement or belief on the addressee. In the same way a request is a polite command, in that it does not force obedience on the addressee, but rather suggests something be done as a favor to the speaker. A clearly stated order implies a threat of certain consequences if it is not followed, and — even more impolite — implies that the speaker is in a superior position and able to enforce the order. By couching wishes in the form of a request, on the other hand, a speaker implies that if the request is not carried out, only the speaker will suffer; noncompliance cannot harm the addressee. So the decision is really left up to addressee. The distinction becomes clear in these examples:

> Close the door.
> Please close the door.
> Will you close the door?
> Will you please close the door?
> Won't you close the door?

In the same ways as words and speech patterns used *by* women 12 undermine her image, those used *to describe* women make matters even worse. Often a word may be used of both men and women (and perhaps of things as well); but when it is applied to women, it assumes a special meaning that, by implication rather than outright assertion, is derogatory to women as a group.

The use of euphemisms has this effect. A euphemism is a substitute for a word that has acquired a bad connotation by association with 13 something unpleasant or embarrassing. But almost as soon as the new word comes into common usage, it takes on the same old bad connotations, since feelings about the things or people referred to are not altered by a change of name; thus new euphemisms must be constantly found.

There is one euphemism for *woman* still very much alive. The   14
word, of course, is *lady*. *Lady* has a masculine counterpart, namely *gentleman*, occasionally shortened to *gent*. But for some reason *lady* is very much commoner than *gent (leman)*.

The decision to use *lady* rather than *woman*, or vice versa, may   15
considerably alter the sense of a sentence, as the following examples show:

> (a) A woman (lady) I know is a dean at Berkeley.
> (b) A woman (lady) I know makes amazing things out of shoelaces and old boxes.

The use of *lady* in (a) imparts a frivolous, or nonserious, tone to   16
the sentence: the matter under discussion is not one of great moment. Similarly, in (b), using *lady* here would suggest that the speaker considered the "amazing things" not to be serious art, but merely a hobby or an aberration. If *woman* is used, she might be a serious sculptor. To say *lady doctor* is very condescending, since no one ever says *gentleman doctor* or even *man doctor*. For example, mention in the San Francisco *Chronicle* of January 31, 1972, of Madalyn Murray O'Hair as the *lady atheist* reduces her position to that of scatterbrained eccentric. Even *woman atheist* is scarcely defensible: sex is irrelevant to her philosophical position.

Many women argue that, on the other hand, *lady* carries with it   17
overtones recalling the age of chivalry: conferring exalted stature on the person so referred to. This makes the term seem polite at first, but we must also remember that these implications are perilous: they suggest that a "lady" is helpless, and cannot do things by herself.

Lady can also be used to infer frivolousnss, as in titles of organi-   18
zations. Those that have a serious purpose (not merely that of enabling "the ladies" to spend time with one another) cannot use the word *lady* in their titles, but less serious ones may. Compare the *Ladies' Auxiliary* of a men's group, or the *Thursday Evening Ladies' Browning and Garden Society* with *Ladies' Liberation* or *Ladies' Strike for Peace*.

What is curious about this split is that *lady* is in origin a   19
euphemism — a substitute that puts a better face on something people find uncomfortable — for *woman*. What kind of euphemism is it that

subtly denigrates the people to whom it refers? Perhaps *lady* functions as a euphemism for *woman* because it does not contain the sexual implications present in *woman:* it is not "embarrassing" in that way. If this is so, we may expect that, in the future, *lady* will replace woman as the primary word for the human female, since *woman* will have become too blatantly sexual. That this distinction is already made in some contexts at least is shown in the following examples, where you can try replacing *woman* with *lady*:

(a) She's only twelve, but she's already a woman.
(b) After ten years in jail, Harry wanted to find a woman.
(c) She's my woman, see, so don't mess around with her.

Another common substitute for *woman* is *girl*. One seldom hears [20] a man past the age of adolescence referred to as a boy, save in expressions like "going out with the boys," which are meant to suggest an air of adolescent frivolity and irresponsibility. But women of all ages are "girls": one can have a man — not a boy — Friday, but only a girl — never a woman or even a lady — Friday; women have girlfriends, but men do not — in a nonsexual sense — have boyfriends. It may be that this use of *girl* is euphemistic in the same way the use of *lady* is: in stressing the idea of immaturity, it removes the sexual connotations lurking in *woman*. *Girl* brings to mind irresponsibility: you don't send a girl to do a woman's errand (or even, for that matter, a boy's errand). She is a person who is both too immature and too far from real life to be entrusted with responsibilities or with decisions of any serious or important nature.

Now let's take a pair of words which, in terns of the possible [21] relationships in an earlier society, were simple male-female equivalents, analogous to *bull: cow*. Suppose we find that, for independent reasons, society has changed in such a way that the original meanings now are irrelevant. Yet the words have not been discarded, but have acquired new meanings, metaphorically related to their original senses. But suppose these new metaphorical uses are no longer parallel to each other. By seeing where the parallelism breaks down, we discover something about the different roles played by men and women in this culture. One good example of such a divergence through time is found in the pair, *master: mistress*. Once used with reference to one's power over servants, these words have become unusable today in their original master-servant sense as the relationship has become less prevalent in our society. But the words are still common.

Unless used with reference to animals, *master* now generally [22] refers to a man who has acquired consummate ability in some field, normally nonsexual. But its feminine counterpart cannot be used this way. It is practically restricted to its sexual sense of "paramour." We start out with two terms, both roughly paraphrasable as "one who has power over another." But the masculine form, once one person is no longer able to have absolute power over another, becomes usable metaphorically in the sense of "having power over *something*." *Master* requires as its object only the name of some activity, something inanimate and abstract. But *mistress* requires a masculine noun in the possessive to precede it. One cannot say: "Rhonda is a mistress." One must be *someone's* mistress. A man is defined by what he does, a woman by her sexuality, that is, in terms of one particular aspect of her relationship to men. It is one thing to be an *old master* like Hans Holbein, and another to be an *old mistress*.

The same is true of the words *spinster* and *bachelor*—gender   23
words for "one who is not married." The resemblance ends with the definition. While *bachelor* is a neuter term, often used as a compliment, *spinster* normally is used pejoratively, with connotations of prissiness, fussiness, and so on. To be a bachelor implies that one has the choice of marrying or not, and this is what makes the idea of a bachelor existence attractive in the popular literature. He has been pursued and has successfully eluded his pursuers. But a spinster is one who has not been pursued, or at last not seriously. She is old, unwanted goods. The metaphorical connotations of *bachelor* generally suggests sexual freedom; of *spinster*, puritanism or celibacy.

These examples could be multiplied. It is generally considered a   24
faux pas, in society, to congratulate a woman on her engagement, while it is correct to congratulate her fiancé. Why is this? The reason seems to be that it is impolite to remind people of things that may be uncomfortable to them. To congratulate a woman on her engagement is really to say, "Thank goodness! You had a close call!" For the man, on the other hand, there was no such danger. His choosing to marry is viewed as a good thing, but not something essential.

The linguistic double standard holds throughout the life of the   25
relationship. After marriage, bachelor and spinster become man and wife, not man and woman. The woman whose husband dies remains "John's widow"; John, however, is never "Mary's widower."

Finally, why is it that salesclerks and others are so quick to call   26
women customers "dear," "honey," and other terms of endearment they really have no business using? A male customer would never put up with it. But women, like children, are supposed to enjoy these endearments, rather than being offended by them.

In more ways than one, it's time to speak up.   27

EXERCISES

Words to Know

euphemistic (paragraph 1), bias (1), linguistic (1), left-handed compliment (2), unassertive (2), syntax (5), gender-related (5), confirmation (6), leeway (6), small talk (7), elicit (7), corroboration (8), baldly (9), subliminal (10), intonation pattern (10), declarative (10), inflection (10), requisite (10), idiosyncrasies (11), couching (11), noncompliance (11), implication (12), derogatory (12), frivolous (16), moment (16), aberration (16), condescending (16), atheist (16), overtones (17), chivalry (17), exalted (17), perilous (17), denigrates (19), blatantly (19), connotations (20), lurking (20), analogous (21), metaphorically (21), consummate (22), paramour (22), paraphrasable (22), neuter (23), pejoratively (23), eluded (23), puritanism (23), celibacy (23), *faux pas* — misstep (24), double standard (25).

Some of the Issues

1. In paragraph 1 Lakoff says, "we are damned if we do, and damned if we don't." What does she refer to?
2. In paragraph 2 Lakoff refers to a "left-handed compliment." Why "left-handed"? What is implied in this phrase?
3. Paragraph 5 through 10 are devoted to tag questions. Why, according to Lakoff, are such questions characteristic of women's speech?
4. What does Lakoff mean in paragraph 11 when she says that women's language is more "polite" than men's language? Is politeness considered a virtue here?
5. Paragraphs 1 through 11 deal with the way women talk and paragraphs 12 through 15 with the way women are talked about. Sum up the major parts of the argument in each of these sections.
6. In paragraphs 21 through 23 Lakoff discusses pairs of male-female terms. Can you add further examples to that list?
7. Cite examples of the ways, in recent times, we have tried to avoid male-female stereotyping, for example, by replacing "mailman" with "letter carrier."

The Way We Are Told

8. Examine the first two paragraphs and show how Lakoff uses words with strong connotations (emotional impact) to reinforce her argument.

9. Who is Lakoff's audience? Is it one that needs convincing or one that looks for reinforcement? Cite reasons for your answer.
10. Who is the "we" in the first two paragraphs?

Some Subjects for Essays

11. Search for examples of language used by groups other than women: minorities, certain occupations. Select one such group and write an essay describing what you have found.
12. Keep a notebook for two weeks in which you record examples of women's language and men's language. At the end of that period look over your notes, try to classify them, and write an analytical paper about the results.

SOLD AT FINE STORES EVERYWHERE, NATURELLEMENT

Myrna Knepler

Myrna Knepler, born in 1934, is a professor of linguistics at North-eastern Illinois University and the author of textbooks in English as a second language. The following selection is reprinted from the February 1978 issue of *Verbatim*, a magazine about language. It describes a particular gambit in the language of advertising — the use of the snob appeal French has for some Americans, as well as the opposite, the use of English to enhance the sales appeal of some products to the French.

Why is it that a high priced condominium is advertised in American 1
newspapers as a *de luxe* apartment while French magazines try to sell their more affluent readers *appartements de grand standing*? Madison Avenue, when constructing ads for high priced non-necessary items, may use French phrases to suggest to readers that they are identified as super-sophisticated, subtly sexy, and privy to the secrets of old world charm and tradition. In recent years French magazines aimed at an increasingly affluent public have made equally canny use of borrowed English words to sell their wares.

The advertising pages of the *New Yorker* and the more elegant 2
fashion and home decorating magazines often depend on blatant flattery of the reader's sense of exclusiveness. Time and time again the reader is told "only *you* are elegant, sophisticated, discriminating and rich enough to use this product." Of course the "you" must encompass a large enough group to insure adequate sales. Foreign words, particularly prestigious French words, may be used to reinforce this selling message.

French magazines often use English words in their advertising to 3
suggest to potential consumers a slightly different but equally flattering self-image. The reader is pictured as someone in touch with new ideas from home and abroad who has not forgotten the traditional French arts of living, but is modern enough to approach them in a completely up-to-date and casual manner.

Of course, each language has borrowed words from the other   4
which have, over the course of time, been completely assimilated. It is
not these that the advertiser exploits but rather words that are foreign
enough to evoke appealing images of an exotic culture. When the
French reader is urged to try "Schweppes, le 'drink' des gens raffinés"
or an American consumer is told that a certain manufacturer has "the
savoir faire to design *la crème de la crème* of luxurious silky knits,"
the foreign words do not say anything that could not be as easily said
by native ones. What they do convey is something else. They invite the
reader to share in the prestige of the foreign language and the power of
the images associated with that language's country of origin.

In each country a knowledge of the other's language is an impor-   5
tant sign of cultivation. Today, English is the language studied by an
overwhelming majority of French students, and the ability to speak it
well is increasingly valued as a symbol of prestige as well as a market-
able skill. Despite the decrease in foreign language study in the United
States, French has maintained its reputation as a language people ought
to know. Adding a few obvious foreign words from the prestige language not only increases the prestige of the product itself but also
flatters the reader by reminding him that he has enough linguistic
talent to understand what is being said. As in the "only-*you*-are-
elegant,-sophisticated,-discriminating-and-rich enough" appeal, the
advertiser must be careful not to exclude too many potential customers, and the foreign expressions are usually transparent cognates or
easily understood words. A French reader may be urged to buy cigarettes by being told that "partout dans le monde c'est YES á Benson and
Hedges" while the *New Yorker* reader can consider a vacation on "an
island [off the cost of South Carolina] where change hasn't meant
commercialism, and tranquility still comes *au naturelle*."

Even monolinguals are not excluded from this flattery. The word   6
can be given in the foreign language and then translated; the reader is
still in on the secret: " 'goût' is the French word for taste and Christofle
is the universal word for taste in vases."

The prestige of a foreign term and its possible ambiguity for the   7
reader may serve to disguise a negative fact about the product. A
necklace of *Perle de Mer* advertised in an American magazine is not
composed of real pearls made by nature in the seas but of simulated
pearls produced by a large American manufacturer. By the same token,
when a French advertisement for a packaged tour offers "aller et retour
en classe coach" the prestige of the English word *coach* disguises the
fact that it is the less luxurious form of airline transportation that is
being offered.

But the most important function of borrowed words in advertis-   8
ing is to project an image of their country of origin in order to create

for the reader the illusion that the product, and by implication its user, will share in the good things suggested by that image. French names like *Grand Prix*, *Coupe De Ville*, and *Monte Carlo* attached to American car models help the advertiser to get across the message that the car is luxurious, sophisticated, and elegantly appointed and that driving such an automobile reflects positively on the taste of its potential owner. In almost all cases French names are reserved for the more expensive models while American words are favored for small meat-and-potatoes cars like *Charger*, *Maverick*, *Pinto* and *Bronco*. Similarly, the French reader is likely to encounter a large number of American technical terms in ads for appliances, radio and television equipment, cameras, and "gadgets de luxe," since the manufacturer benefits by associating American mechanical skills with his products. An advertisement for French-made hi-fi equipment appearing in a French magazine spoke of the product's "push-pull ultra linéaire, 6 haut-parleurs, 2 elliptiques et 4 tweeters . . . montés sur baffle."

Images, which are used again and again, are often based on myths   9
of the other country's culture. Words like *tomahawk* and *trading posts* are used in French advertisements to evoke images of a western-movie America of naturalness, freedom, and adventure in order to sell products like "Chemise de 'cow girl,'" "bottes Far West," and vests in the style of "Arizona Bill," irrespective of the real West that is or was. The name *Monte Carlo* attached to an American-made car trades on the American consumer's image of a once-exclusive vacation spot, now available as part of low-cost travel packages. Thus the name *Monte Carlo* can convey to an automobile a prestige that the real trip to Monte Carlo has long since lost.

These images that are not completely mythic are usually gross   10
stereotypes of the other country's culture. Few Americans would recognize the image of American life presented in French advertising — a new world filled with eternally youthful, glamorously casual, up-to-date men and women devoted to consuming the products of their advanced technology. Similarly, few French men and women would recognize the nation of elegant and knowing consumers of food, wine, and sophisticated sex pictured in American ads.

The image of France as a nation of lovers, bold yet unusually   11
subtle in their relations with the opposite sex, is often called upon to sell perfume and cosmetics, sometimes of French origin but packaged and advertised specifically for the American market. An ad which appeared several years ago in the *New Yorker* showed a bottle of perfume labeled "voulez-vous" implanted next to a closeup of a sexy and elegant woman, her face shadowed by a male hand lighting her cigarette. The text: "The spark that starts the fire. Voulez-vous a new perfume." *Audace*, *Robe d'un Soir*, and *Je Reviens* are other perfumes

advertised in American magazines with pictures and copy that reinforce the sexual suggestiveness of the prominently featured French
name on the label.

It may be surprising for Americans to learn that English names are   12
given to perfumes sold in France to enhance their romantic image. *My
Love, Partner, and Shocking* are some examples. Advertisements for
French-made men's cosmetics in French magazines may refer to products such as *l'after-shave* and *le pre-shave*. Givenchy's *Gentleman* is
advertised to Frenchmen as an eau de toilette for the man who dares to
appear at business lunches in a turtleneck sweater and has the courage
to treat love in a casual manner.

The recent swelling of the list of Americanisms used in French   13
advertising and in French speech has pained many Frenchmen and has
even caused the government to take action. For a number of years the
leader in this "war against anglicisms" has been René Etiemble, a
professor at the Sorbonne. Etiemble, through magazine articles, radio
and television appearances and his widely read book, *Parlez-vous
franglais?*, struggles vehemently against what he most often refers to
as an "invasion" of American terms. He does little to disguise his
strong anti-American sentiments. American words are rejected as
agents of a vulgar American culture and both are seen as threats to the
French way of life. According to Etiemble "[the]" heritage of words [is
the] heritage of ideas: with *le twist* and *la ségrégation, la civilisation
cocolcoolique*, the American manner of not living will disturb and
contaminate all that remains of your cuisine, wines, love and free
thought." It would be difficult to find a stronger believer in the power
of words than Etiemble.

In response to the concerns of Etiemble and others, a series of   14
committees composed of highly placed French scientists and language
experts were charged with the task of finding Gallic equivalents for
such popular terms as *le meeting, le marketing, le management*, and
le know-how. The recommended replacements are: *la réunion, la
commercialisation, la direction*, and, of course, *le savoir faire*. The
replacements do not seem to have taken root.

At the end of 1975 a more radical step was taken. The French   15
National Assembly passed a law banning the use of all foreign words in
advertising in those cases in which a native alternative has been officially suggested, and instituting a fine against violators.

Both Etiemble and the government purists rely strongly on the   16
"logical" argument that most loan words are not needed because there
already exists a native equivalent with exactly the same meaning. Yet a
look at the advertising pages of French and American magazines will
show that borrowed words are used again and again when there are
obvious native equivalents. Certainly the English words in "c'est YES á

Benson and Hedges" and "Le 'drink' des gens raffinés" could be translated without loss of literal meaning—but they are not.

It is precisely because of the connotations associated with the culture of its country of origin, not its denotations, that advertisers find the borrowed word attractive. 17

EXERCISES

Words to Know

affluent (paragraph 1), Madison Avenue (1), privy (1), blatant (2), potential (3), assimilated (4), exploits (4), *raffinés*—refined (4), *savoir faire*—sophistication, liteally know-how (4), *crème de la crème*—the very best (4), discriminating (5), cognates (5), *partout dans le monde*—throughout the whole world (5), monolinguals (6), ambiguity (7), *Perle de Mer*—"Pearls of the Sea" (7), *aller et retour*—round trip (7), elegantly appointed (8), *haut-parleurs*—loudspeakers (8), *montés sur*—mounted on (8), *chemise*—shirt (9), *bottes*—boots (9), mythic (10), *Voulez-vous*—Are you willing? (11), *Audace*—Boldness (11), *Robe d'un Soir*—Evening wrap (11), *Je Reviens*—I will return (11), anglicisms (13), *Parlez-vous franglais?*—Do you speak franglais? (13), vehemently (13), Gallic (14), connotations (17), denotations (17).

Some of the Issues

1. According to Knepler, what classes of people are addressed through the use of French words in American advertising, and vice versa? How do her examples substantiate her argument?
2. Advertisers use foreign words to provide a sense of exclusivity for the reader; at the same time, they want to make sure their message comes across. How is this done? Cite some examples.
3. What kinds of products are likely to be sold in America with the use of French words? What kinds of products will use English to enhance sales appeal in France?
4. Paragraph 7 presents cases in which the foreign language disguises negative information. Explains the examples.
5. What kind of stereotype of America does French advertising play upon?

The Way We Are Told

6. Consider the first three paragraphs. Why does paragraph 1 begin

with a question? Is it answered? How do paragraphs 2 and 3 relate to the first paragraph?

7. In paragraphs 9 through 11 Knepler discusses the myths the Americans and the French believe about each other's culture. What means does Knepler use to make the reader believe in the unreality of these respective views?

Some Subjects for Essays

8. Examine several magazine advertisements for a particular kind of product, for example, automobiles, clothes, liquor. What flattering images of the potential consumer are used to sell the product? Explain the effect in detail.

9. Write an essay comparing and contrasting the reality of a specific place, type of person, or institution you know with the myth or stereotype about it.

* 10. Read Michael Arlen's "Ring Around the Collar!" Write an essay in which you analyze one particular magazine advertisement in a manner similar to Arlen's. You need to describe what the ad conveys, how it does it, and its social and cultural implications.

PRIVATE SPACE

Edward T. Hall

Edward T. Hall (1914–) served as professor of anthropology at
Northwestern University, has taught at several other institutions,
and has been in government service in Washington. His research
has been concerned with cross-cultural issues related to body
language (kinesics). In particular, he did pioneering work in
proxemics: the investigation of the relative distances by which
people of different cultures separate themselves from each other
as, for example, in conversation. In his widely read books he
successfully addresses both general and specialized audiences:
The Silent Language (1954), *The Hidden Dimension* (1966),
Beyond Culture (1976), and *The Dance of Life* (1983). The
following selection comes from *The Hidden Dimension*. Hall
discusses a particular element of nonverbal communication. He
describes and analyzes the differences between German and American feelings about privacy, and the misunderstandings they may
cause.

I shall never forget my first experience with German proxemic pat-   1
terns, which occurred when I was an undergraduate. My manners, my
status, and my ego were attacked and crushed by a German in an
instance where thirty years' residence in this country and an excellent
command of English had not attenuated German definitions of what
constitutes an intrusion. In order to understand the various issues that
were at stake, it is necessary to refer back to two basic American
patterns that are taken for granted in this country and which Americans
therefore tend to treat as universal.

First, in the United States there is a commonly accepted, invisible   2
boundary around any two or three people in conversation which sepa-
rates them from others. Distance alone serves to isolate any such group
and to endow it with a protective wall of privacy. Normally, voices are
kept low to avoid intruding on others and if voices are heard, people
will act as though they had not heard. In this way, privacy is granted
whether it is actually present or not. The second pattern is somewhat
more subtle and has to do with the exact point at which a person is
experienced as actually having crossed a boundary and entered a room.
Talking through a screen door while standing outside a house is not
considered by most Americans as being inside the house or room in any

sense of the word. If one is standing on the threshold holding the door open and talking to someone inside, it is still defined informally and experienced as being *outside*. If one is in an office building and just "pokes his head in the door" of an office he's still outside the office. Just holding on to the doorjamb when one's body is inside the room still means a person has one foot "on base" as it were so that he is not quite inside the other fellow's territory. None of these American spatial definitions is valid in northern Germany. In every instance where the American would consider himself *outside* he has already entered the German's territory and by definition would become involved with him. The following experience brought the conflict between these two patterns into focus.

It was a warm spring day of the type one finds only in the high,   3
clean, clear air of Colorado, the kind of day that makes you glad you are alive. I was standing on the doorstep of a converted carriage house talking to a young woman who lived in an apartment upstairs. The first floor had been made into an artist's studio. The arrangement, however, was peculiar because the same entrance served both tenants. The occupants of the apartment used a small entryway and walked along one wall of the studio to reach the stairs to the apartment. You might say that they had an "easement" through the artist's territory. As I stood talking on the doorstep, I glanced to the left and noticed that some fifty to sixty feet away, inside the studio, the Prussian artist and two of his friends were also in conversation. He was facing so that if he glanced to one side he could just see me. I had noted his presence, but not wanting to appear presumptuous or to interrupt his conversation, I unconsciously applied the American rule and assumed that the two activities—my quiet conversation and his conversation—were not involved with each other. As I was soon to learn, this was a mistake, because in less time than it takes to tell, the artist had detached himself from his friends, crossed the intervening space, pushed my friend aside, and with eyes flashing, started shouting at me. By what right had I entered his studio without greeting him? Who had given me permission?

I felt bullied and humiliated, and even after almost thirty years, I   4
can still feel my anger. Later study has given me greater understanding of the German pattern and I have learned that in the German's eyes I really had been intolerably rude. I was already "inside" the building and I intruded when I could *see* inside. For the German, there is no such thing as being inside he room without being inside the zone of intrusion, particularly if one looks as the other party, no matter how far away.

Recently, I obtained an independent check on how Germans feel   5
about visual intrusion while investigating what people look at when

they are in intimate, personal, social, and public situations. In the course of my research, I instructed subjects to photograph separately both a man and a women in each of the above contexts. One of my assistants, who also happened to be German, photographed his subjects out of focus at public distance because, as he said, "You are not really supposed to look at other people at public distances *because it's intruding.*" This may explain the informal custom behind the German laws against photographing strangers in public without their permission.

Germans sense their own space as an extension of the ego. One 6 sees a clue to this feeling in the term "Lebensraum," which is impossible to translate because it summarizes so much. Hitler used it as an effective psychological lever to move the Germans to conquest.

In contrast to the Arab, the German's ego is extraordinarily exposed, and he will go to almost any length to preserve his "private sphere." This was observed during World War II when American soldiers were offered opportunities to observe German prisoners under a variety of circumstances. In one instance in the Midwest, German P.W.s were housed four to a small hut. As soon as materials were available, each prisoner built a partition so that he could have *his own space*. In a less favorable setting in Germany when the *Wehrmacht* was collapsing, it was necessary to use open stockades because German prisoners were arriving faster than they could be accommodated. In this situation each soldier who could find the materials built his own tiny dwelling unit, sometimes no larger than a foxhole. It puzzled the Americans that the Germans did not pool their efforts and their scarce materials to create a larger, more efficient space, particularly in view of the very cold spring nights. Since that time I have observed frequent instances of the use of architectural extensions of this need to screen the ego. German houses with balconies are arranged so that there is visual privacy. Yards tend to be well fenced; but fenced or not, they are sacred.

The American view that space should be shared is particularly 8 troublesome to the German. I cannot document the account of the early days of World War II occupation when Berlin was in ruins but the following situation was reported by an observer and it has the nightmarish quality that is often associated with inadvertent cross-cultural blunders. In Berlin at that time the housing shortage was indescribably acute. To provide relief, occupation authorities in the American zone ordered those Berliners who still had kitchens and baths intact to share them with their neighbors. The order finally had to be rescinded when the already overstressed Germans started killing each other over the shared facilities.

Public and private buildings in Germany often have double doors 9 for soundproofing, as do many hotel rooms. In addition, the door is taken very seriously by Germans. Those Germans who come to America feel that our doors are flimsy and light. The meanings of the open door and the closed door are quite different in the two countries. In offices, Americans keep doors open; Germans keep doors closed. In Germany, the closed door does not mean that the man behind it wants to be alone or undisturbed, or that he is doing something he doesn't want someone else to see. It's simply that Germans think that open doors are sloppy and disorderly. To close the door preserves the integrity of the room and provides a protective boundary between people. Otherwise, they get too involved with each other. One of my German subjects commented, "If our family hadn't had doors, we would have had to change our way of life. Without doors we would have had many, many more fights . . . When you can't talk, you retreat behind a door. . . . If there hadn't been doors, I would always have been within reach of my mother."

Whenever a German warms up to the subject of American enclosed space, he can be counted on to comment on the noise that is transmitted through walls and doors. To many Germans, our doors epitomize American life. They are thin and cheap; they seldom fit; and they lack the substantial quality of German doors. When they close they don't sound and feel solid. The click of the lock is indistinct, it rattles and indeed it may even be absent.   10

The open-door policy of American business and the closed-door patterns of German business culture cause clashes in the branches and subsidiaries of American firms in Germany. The point seems to be quite simple, yet failure to grasp it has caused considerable friction and misunderstanding between American and German managers overseas. I was once called in to advise a firm that has operations all over the world. One of the first questions asked was, "How do you get the Germans to keep their doors open?" In this company the open doors were making the Germans feel exposed and gave the whole operation an unusually relaxed and unbusinesslike air. Closed doors, on the other hand, gave the Americans the feeling that there was a conspiratorial air about the place and that they were being left out. The point is that whether the door is open or shut, it is not going to mean the same thing in the two countries.   11

The orderliness and hierarchical quality of German culture are communicated in their handling of space. Germans want to know where they stand and object strenuously to people crashing queues or people who "get out of line" or who do not obey signs such as "Keep out," "Authorized personnel only," and the like. Some of the German attitudes toward ourselves are traceable to our informal attitudes toward boundaries and to authority in general.   12

However, German anxiety due to American violations of order is   13
nothing compared to that engendered in Germans by the Poles, who
see no harm in a little disorder. To them lines and queues stand for
regimentation and blind authority. I once saw a Pole crash a cafeteria
line just "to stir up those sheep."

Germans get very technical about intrusion distance, as I men-   14
tioned earlier. When I once asked my students to describe the distance
at which a third party would intrude on two people who were talking,
there were no answers from the Americans. Each student knew that he
could tell when he was being intruded on but he couldn't define
intrusion or tell how he knew when it had occurred. However, a
German and an Italian who had worked in Germany were both members of my class and they answered without any hesitation. Both stated
that a third party would intrude on two people if he came within seven
feet!

Many Americans feel that Germans are overly rigid in their behav-   15
ior, unbending and formal. Some of this impression is created by
differences in the handling of chairs while seated. The American
doesn't seem to mind if people hitch their chairs up to adjust the
distance to the situation — those that do mind would not think of
saying anything, for to comment on the manners of others would be
impolite. In Germany, however, it is a violation of the mores to change
the position of your chair. An added deterrent for those who don't
know better is the weight of most German furniture. Even the great
architect Mies van der Rohe, who often rebelled against German tradition in his buildings, made his handsome chairs so heavy that anyone
but a strong man would have difficulty in adjusting his seating position. To a German, light furniture is anathema, not only because it
seems flimsy but because people move it and thereby destroy the order
of things, including intrusions on the "private sphere." In one instance reported to me, a German newspaper editor who had moved to
the United States had his visitor's chair bolted to the floor "at the
proper distance" because he couldn't tolerate the American habit of
adjusting the chair to the situation.

EXERCISES

Words to Know

proxemic (see headnote) (paragraph 1), attenuated (1), spatial (2),
presumptuous (3), *Wehrmacht*—the German Army (7), inadvertent
(8), rescinded (8), integrity (9), epitomize (10), conspiratorial (11),

hierarchical (12), queues (12), regimentation (13), deterrent (15), anathema (15).

Some of the Issues

1. What are the "two basic American patterns" Hall refers to in paragraphs 1 and 2?
2. Describe the basic differences between the German and the American concepts of private space.
3. In what way do Germans protect and reinforce their concept of private space?

The Way We Are Told

4. Hall begins with a reference to a personal experience (paragraph 1), but does not return to it until paragraph 3. What is the function of paragraph 2? Is this way of telling his experience effective, or should he have omitted the personal reference in paragraph 1, cut off as it is from the rest of the story?
5. Why does Hall refer (paragraph 3) to the weather, to Colorado, to the young woman as he tells the story? What does this information contribute?
6. In paragraph 5 and then again in paragraphs 6 through 8 Hall moves on to other examples. Do you see any order in this progression?

Some Subjects for Essays

7. Hall explains that concepts of space can differ widely from culture to culture. They may also differ among individuals. Have you ever offended someone, or been offended, because you intruded in some way on the other person's space? If so, describe the event.
8. Another concept that can differ from culture to culture is time: punctuality, being late or early. In America, for example, being more than five minutes late for an appointment may require an apology. On the other hand, arriving at a party at eight o'clock on the nose is likely to make you early, even if you were invited for eight. Write an essay about what it means to be "on time" in different circumstances in your culture.

HOW TO TALK
ABOUT THE WORLD

Peter Farb

Peter Farb (1929–1980) was trained as a linguist and developed wide-ranging interests in the role language plays in human behavior. He also took a particular interest in American Indians. His books include *Man's Rise to Civilization as Shown by the Indians of North America*. He is coauthor of *Consuming Passions: The Anthropology of Eating* (1980). The selection included here comes from *Word Play: What Happens When People Talk* (1974).

Farb explains that words are far more than labels we attach to specific objects, ideas, and so forth. They also help us to classify experience, to group elements into categories. These categories may differ from culture to culture. Trying to communicate with people of a different culture will show that they may be "linguistically deaf" to categories that we consider natural just as we may fail to understand their ways of sorting out experience. Classification is therefore culturally conditioned.

If human beings paid attention to all sights, sounds, and smells that [1]
besiege them, their ability to codify and recall information would be swamped. Instead, they simplify the information by grouping it into broad verbal categories. For example, human eyes have the extraordinary power to discriminate some ten million colors, but the English language reduces these to no more than four thousand color words, of which only eleven basic terms are commonly used. That is why a driver stops at all traffic lights whose color he categorizes as *red*, even though the lights vary slightly from one to another in their hues of redness. Categorization allows people to respond to their environment in a way that has great survival value. If they hear a high-pitched sound, they do not enumerate the long list of possible causes of such sounds: a human cry of fear, a scream for help, a policeman's whistle, and so on. Instead they become alert because they have categorized high-pitched sounds as indicators of possible danger.

Words, therefore, are more than simply labels for specific objects; [2]
they are also parts of sets of related principles. To a very young child, the word *chair* may at first refer only to his highchair. Soon

408

afterward, he learns that the four-legged object on which his parents sit at mealtimes is also called a *chair*. So is the thing with only three legs, referred to by his parents as a *broken chair*, and so is the upholstered piece of furniture in the living room. These objects form a category, *chair*, which is set apart from all other categories by a unique combination of features. A *chair* must possess a seat, legs, and back; it may also, but not necessarily, have arms; it must accommodate only one person. An object that possesses these features with but a single exception — it accommodates three people — does not belong to the category *chair* but rather to the category *couch*, and that category in turn in described by a set of unique features.

Furthermore, Americans think of *chairs* and *couches* as being   3
related to each other because they both belong to a category known in English as *household furniture*. But such a relationship between the category *chair* and the category *couch* is entirely arbitrary on the part of English and some other speech communities. Nothing in the external world decrees that a language must place these two categories together. In some African speech communities, for example, the category *chair* would most likely be thought of in relation to the category *spear*, since both are emblems of ruler's authority.

The analysis of words by their categories for the purpose of   4
determining what they mean to speakers of a particular language — that is, what the native speaker, and not some visiting linguist, feels are the distinguishing features or components of that word — is known as "componential analysis" or "formal semantic analysis." The aim, in brief, is to determine the components or features that native speakers use to distinguish similar terms from one another so that more exact meanings can be achieved.

Anyone who visits an exotic culture quickly learns that the peo-   5
ple are linguistically deaf to categories he considers obvious, yet they are extraordinarily perceptive in talking about things he has no easy way to describe. An English-speaking anthropologist studying the Koyas of India, for example, soon discovers that their language does not distinguish between dew, fog, and snow. When questioned about these natural phenomena, the Koyas can find a way to describe them, but normally their language attaches no significance to making such distinctions and provides no highly codable words for the purpose. On the other hand, a Koya has the linguistic resources to speak easily about seven different kinds of bamboo — resources that the visiting anthropologist utterly lacks in his own language. More important than the significance, or the lack of it, that a language places on objects and ideas is the way that language categorizes the information it does find significant. A *pig*, for example, can be categorized in several ways: a mammal with cloven hoofs and bristly hairs and adapted for digging

with its snout; a mold in which metal is cast; a British sixpence coin. The Koyas categorize the pig in none of these ways; they simply place it in the category of animals that are edible. Their neighbors, Muslims, think of it in a different way by placing it in the category of defiled animals.

Everyone, whether he realizes it or not, classifies the items he   6
finds in his environment. Most speakers of English recognize a category that they call *livestock*, which is made up of other categories known as *cattle, horses, sheep,* and *swine* of different ages and sexes. An English speaker who is knowledgeable about farm life categorizes a barnyardful of these animals in a way that establishes relationships based on distinguishing features. For example, he feels that a *cow* and a *mare*, even though they belong to different species, are somehow in a relationship to each other. And of course they are, because they both belong to the category of Female Animal under the general category of Livestock. The speaker of English unconsciously groups certain animals into various sub-categories that exclude other animals:

	LIVESTOCK			
	Cattle	*Horses*	*Sheep*	*Swine*
Female	cow	mare	ewe	sow
Intact Male	bull	stallion	ram	boar
Castrated Male	steer	gelding	wether	barrow
Immature	heifer	colt/filly	lamb	shoat/gilt
Newborn	calf	foal	yearling	piglet

A table such as this shows that speakers of English are intuitively   7
aware of certain contrasts. They regard a *bull* and a *steer* as different —which they are, because one belongs to a category of Intact Males and the other to a category of Castrated Males. In addition to discriminations made on the basis of livestock's sex, speakers of English also contrast mature and immature animals. A *foal* is a newborn horse and a *stallion* is a mature male horse.

The conceptual labels by which English-speaking peoples talk   8
about barnyard animals can now be understood. The animal is defined by the point at which two distinctive features intersect: sex (male, female, or castrated) and maturity (mature, immature, or newborn). A *stallion* belongs to a category of horse that is both intact male and mature; a *filly* belongs to a category of horse that is both female and immature. Nothing in external reality dictates that barnyard animals should be talked about in this way; it is strictly a convention of English and some other languages.

In contrast, imagine that an Amazonian Indian is brought to the   9
United States so that linguists can intensively study his language. When

the Indian returns to his native forests, his friends and relatives listen in disbelief as he tells about all the fantastic things he saw. He summarizes his impressions of America in terms of the familiar categories his language has accustomed him to. He relates that at first he was bewildered by the strange animals he saw on an American farm because each animal not only looked different but also seemed to represent a unique concept to the natives of the North American tribe. But after considerable observation of the curious folkways of these peculiar people, at last he understood American barnyard animals. He figured out that some animals are good for work and that some are good for food. Using these two components — rather than the Americans' features of sex and maturity — his classification of livestock is considerably different. He categorized *stallion*, *mare*, and *gelding* as belonging to both the Inedible and Work (Riding) categories. The *bull* also belonged to the Inedible category but it was used for a different kind of Work as a draught animal. He further placed a large number of animals —*cow*, *ewe*, *lamb*, *sow*, and so on — in the category of Edible but Useless for Work. Since his method of categorizing the barnyard failed to take into account the breeding process, which depends upon the categories of sex and maturity, he no doubt found it inexplicable that some animals — *ram*, *colt*, *boar*, and so on — were raised even though they could not be eaten or used for work.

To an American, the Amazonian Indian's classification of barn- 10
yard animals appears quite foolish, yet it is no more foolish than the American's system of classification by the features of sex and maturity. Speakers of each language have the right to recognize whatever features they care to. And they have a similar right to then organize these features according to the rules of their own speech communities. No one system is better than another in making sense out of the world in terms that can be talked about; the systems are simply different. A speaker of English who defines a *stallion* as a mature, male horse is no wiser than the Amazonian who claims it is inedible and used for riding. Both the speaker of English and the speaker of the Amazonian language have brought order out of the multitudes of things in the environment —and, in the process, both have shown something about how their languages and their minds work.

EXERCISES

Words to Know

codify (paragraph 1), categorizes (1), enumerate (1), semantic (4), linguistically (5), perceptive (5), anthropologist (5), phenomena (5), conceptual (8), convention (8).

Some of the Issues

1. Why, according to Farb, do we categorize information?
2. What does Farb mean (paragraph 5) when he says that a visitor may find the natives of a given culture are "linguistically deaf" to categories he considers obvious? How does he support that assertion?
3. Try to think of a classification for livestock that differs both from the one Farb gives in paragraph 6 and the one his imaginary Amazonian Indian develops in paragraph 9. Under what circumstances would your category be used?
4. What is Farb's overall purpose in writing this essay?
*5. Read Lakoff's "You Are What You Say." Like Farb, she talks about words referring to color near the start of her essay. Why do both use the same example? How do their purposes differ?

The Way We Are Told

6. Farb's first example concerns colors, his second chairs, and his most extended one, livestock. Can you justify both the choices and the order in which they are given?
7. In paragraph 3, Farb briefly refers to a possible re-categorization of chairs in an African culture. Why does he do so at that point?

Some Subjects for Essays

8. Develop a classification for some group of things with which you are familiar: college courses, video games, shoes. Describe your method, explaining the criteria on which it is based and its possible uses.
9. Politicians in America are generally classified as Democrats or Republicans, omitting the smaller parties. In what other ways could you classify politicians, and what purposes would each of the different classifications serve? Develop your ideas in an essay.

WORLD LANGUAGE: ENGLISH

Robert McCrum, William Cran, and Robert MacNeil

In 1988 Public Television produced a nine-part series "The Story of English," which described the development of English from its beginnings to its present position as the world's most widely spoken language. The selection included here is taken from the opening chapter of the volume that accompanied the series. Of the authors the best known is Robert MacNeil, coanchor of the "MacNeil-Lehrer News Hour" on PBS. MacNeil was born in Montreal in 1931 and received a B.A. from Carleton University. He worked for the British and the Canadian Broadcasting corporations before coming to Public Broadcasting in the United States. He holds honorary degrees from a number of universities, including George Washington and Brown, and has received several broadcasting awards.

In this selection the authors demonstrate that English has developed, in the course of a few centuries, from the language of a small island on the periphery of Europe to become the dominant world language of our time. They show the extent of that domination and the impact it has had on the lives of millions whose first language is not English.

The rise of English is a remarkable success story. When Julius Caesar landed in Britian nearly two thousand years ago, English did not exist. Five hundred years later, *Englisc*, incomprehensible to modern ears, was probably spoken by about as few people as currently speak Cherokee — and with about as little influence. Nearly a thousand years later, at the end of the sixteenth century, when William Shakespeare was in his prime, English was the native speech of between five and seven million Englishmen and it was, in the words of a contemporary, "of small reatch, it stretcheth no further than this iland of ours, naie not there over all." 1

Four hundred years later, the contrast is extraordinary. Between 1600 and the present, in armies, navies, companies and expeditions, 2

413

the speakers of English — including Scots, Irish, Welsh, American and many more — travelled into every corner of the globe, carrying their language and culture with them. Today, English is used by at least 750 million people, and barely half of those speak it as a mother tongue. Some estimates have put that figure closer to one billion. Whatever the total, English at the end of the twentieth century is more widely scattered, more widely spoken and written, than any other language has ever been. It has become *the* language of the planet, the first truly global language.

The statistics of English are astonishing. Of all the world's languages (which now number some 2700), it is arguably the richest in vocabulary. The compendious *Oxford English Dictionary* lists about 500,000 words; and a further half million technical and scientific terms remain uncatalogued. According to traditional estimates, neighbouring German has a vocabulary of about 185,000 words and French fewer than 100,000, including such Franglais as *le snacque-barre* and *le hit-parade*. About 350 million people use the English vocabulary as a mother tongue: about one-tenth of the world's population, scattered across every continent and surpassed, in numbers, though not in distribution, only by the speakers of the many varieties of Chinese. Three-quarters of the world's mail, and its telexes and cables, are in English. So are more than half the world's technical and scientific periodicals: it is the language of technology from Silicon Valley to Shanghai. English is the medium for 80 per cent of the information stored in the world's computers. Nearly half of all business deals in Europe are conducted in English. It is the language of sports and glamour: the official language of the Olympics and the Miss Universe competition. English is the official voice of the air, of the sea, and of Christianity: it is the ecumenical language of the World Council of Churches. Five of the largest broadcasting companies in the world (CBS, NBC, ABC, BBC, CBC) transmit in English to audiences that regularly exceed one hundred million.

English has a few rivals, but no equals. Neither Spanish nor Arabic, both international languages, have this global sway. Another rival, Russian, has the political and economic under-pinning of a world language, but far from spreading its influence outside the Soviet empire, it, too, is becoming mildly colonized by new works known as *Russlish*, for example *seksapil* (sex appeal) and *noh-khau* (know-how). Germany and Japan have, in matching the commercial and industrial vigour of the United States, achieved the commercial precondition of language-power, but their languages have also been invaded by English, in the shape of *Deutchlish* and *Japlish*.

The first level of the global sway of English is to be found in those countries, formerly British colonies, in which English as a second language has become accepted as a fact of cultural life that cannot be wished away. In Nigeria, it is an official language; in Zambia, it is recognized as one of the state languages; in Singapore, it is the major language of government, the legal system and education; and in India, the Constitution of 1947 recognizes English as an "associate" official language. In the heady early days of independence, the first prime minister, Nehru, declared that "within one generation" English would no longer be used in India. By the 1980s, most Indians would admit that, like it or not, English was as much a national language of India as Hindi.

The power of English in Indian life also extends to fundamentals   6 like choosing a wife. In the Institute of Home Economics, in Delhi, one of the girls remarked that 95 per cent of Indian men "do definitely consider English as a prerequisite for brides . . . We are still very much influenced by what the British left us . . . English represents class."

The students even distinguish between British and American En-   7 glish. In class, for formal writing, and to impress their parents, they will use British English. Colloquially, they use American English. "We're getting to use American English more these days. That's because of the influence of movies . . . The books you read are mostly published in America and written by American authors . . . One has a tendency to pick up that kind of speech, any slang that they use."

At a second, equally important, level global English has become   8 the one foreign language that much of the world wants to learn. While this appears to be a nearly universal aspiration, some countries (Singapore, Japan, China, Indonesia and the Philippines) exhibit it more than others. One basic force is an international need and desire to communicate. The more English-speaking the world becomes the more desirable the language becomes to all societies. English is the language of the "media" industries — news-journalism, radio, film and television. Almost any international press conference held to disseminate information about an internationally significant event will be conducted in English. The roll-call of contemporary world figures who speak to the press in English includes the Chancellor of West Germany, Helmut Kohl; the Libyan leader and Islamic fundamentalist, Colonel Qadhafi; the President of Pakistan, General Zia; and former President Marcos of the Philippines; in the recent past, moreover, it was well known that the leaders of France and Germany, Valéry Giscard d'Estaing and Helmut Schmidt, used to speak to each other in English.

The demands of modernization, technological change and inter-   9 national bank funding, still largely controlled by Anglo-American corporations, provide the main reason for global English, the language of the multinational corporations. Of the leading countries in world trade, eight are countries in which English either is an official language or was an official language in colonial times: Australia, Canada, India, Malaya, New Zealand, South Africa, the United Kingdom, and the United States. These countries accounted for more than 25 per cent of the world's imports in 1974. By contrast, the leading French-speaking countries (Belgium, Canada, France and Switzerland) accounted for only 15 per cent, the second highest figure for a language bloc.

Many multinational Japanese companies (like Nissan) write inter-   10
national memoranda in English. The Chase Manhattan Bank gives English instructions to staff members on three continents. Aramco — a big oil multinational — teaches English to more than 10,000 workers in Saudi Arabia. In Kuwait, the university's language centre teaches predominantly English, much of it highly specialized. "The engineering faculty has its own English language, geared to its own profession," the director, Dr Rasha Al-Sabah, reports, "so we provide a course in engineering English." The pressure to learn English in this environment is strictly commercial. A businessman who doesn't know English and who has to run to his bilingual secretary is at a serious competitive disadvantage. The "necessity of English" has created some interesting business enterprises, perhaps the most famous being the IVECO heavy truck company. Based in Turin, financed by French, German and Italian money, staffed by Europeans for whom English is only an alternative language, it none the less conducts *all* its business in English. Giorgio Bertoldi describes a monthly board meeting in which "the vast majority of the people attending are Italian, or French, or German. But the common language is English. Everybody talks English and the minutes of these meetings are written in English." Peter Raahauge, a Dane, commented that "you wouldn't get a job at a certain level in IVECO if you didn't speak good English." Company executives take courses to improve their proficiency. Jean Pierre Neveu, an IVECO product planner, points out that, for successful trading in the international truck market, the advantage of communicating with the outside world in English is that the company gets its answers in English. "This gives two advantages. One is first to have a language which is easier for everyone to understand, and second, it does without any translation."

What is true of individuals and companies applies, writ large, to   11
countries. If the people do not know English they cannot benefit from multinational development programs. The classic case is China's. For centuries, China preserved a lofty isolation from the outside world. After the Revolution of 1949 it sustained a Marxist contempt for Anglo-American culture. Briefly, in the 1960s, there was a Russian-learning phase. Then, in the late 1970s and 1980s, the decision to develop China's industrial and technological base by encouraging

Western investment and Western expertise has led to a crash-program of English teaching. Chinese television began to transmit several English-language classes each week, with titles like *Yingying Learns English* and *Mary Goes to Peking*. The most popular was a BBC-produced series, *Follow Me*, which achieved an audience of more than fifty million and transformed the presenter of the program, Kathy Flower, into a media celebrity. Kathy Flower describes the contemporary craze for English in China: "You go into a shop and find two 60-year-olds practising the dialogue from *Follow Me* the night before." The passion for English drives people to make extraordinary sacrifices. A young man whose monthly wages are 36 yuan spends one third of his total income on English classes, dictionaries, cassettes, novels.

For a developing country like China, Singapore or Indonesia, English is vital. As well as being the language of international trade and finance, it is the language of technology, especially computers, of medicine, of the international aid bodies like Oxfam and Save The Children, and of virtually all international, quasi-diplomatic exchanges from UNESCO, to the World Health Organization, to the UN, to Miss World, to the Olympic Committee, to world summits. The textbook case in the new Pacific prosperity sphere is Singapore. Now the most prosperous Far East Asian society after Japan, Singapore is a multi-ethnic society which has been rigorously educated in English by its long-time prime minister, Lee Kuan Yew, who was not above lecturing his ministers and civil servants on the necessity of good grammar. Until the mid-1980s, the English First policy was seen as integral to the island's success. Now, with a falling growth rate, and the first stirrings of real opposition to the ruling People's Action Party, the future of Singapore English is perhaps less certain.

The power of English is not confined to the invention and manufacture of new technology. All major corporations advertise and market their products in English. Nowhere is this more dramatically apparent than in present-day Japan. Of all the things that Japan has imported from the West (to which Tokyo advertising bears witness), few have had as great an impact as English words. The Japanese have always borrowed words, first from the Portuguese and Dutch who landed in trading ships in the sixteenth and eighteenth centuries, but since the end of the Second World War so many new words have been added to the Japanese vocabulary—more than 20,000 by some estimates—that some fear the language will lose its identity. Special dictionaries have been produced to explain the meaning of, for example, *inflight*, *infield*, *input* and *influenza*. Better than these straight imports there is Japlish (or Janglish): fascinating new formations like *man-shon* (mansion), Japanese for an apartment/condominium, or *aisu-kurimu* (ice-cream). Ownership is important. If you don't live in a *man-shon* you live in a *mai-homu* (my home). The Japanese now have *mai-kaa*, *mai-town*, and *mai-com* (my compuyter). Television has embraced Japlish with enthusiasm. One nightly baseball program is called *Eku-saito Naita* (Excite Niter). Another popular program of songs is called *Reffsu Go Yangu* (Let's Go Young). It was inevitable that when a new weekly glossy magazine was launched in Tokyo in 1985, it bore the name *Friday*. Even the hit songs in the Tokyo top twenty have English titles.

English as the language of international pop music and mass entertainment is a worldwide phenomenon. In 1982, a Spanish punk rock group, called Asfalto (Asphalt), released a disc about learning English, which became a hit. The Swedish group Abba records all its numbers in English. Michael Luszynski is a Polish singer who performs almost entirely in English. There is no Polish translation for words like "Baby-baby" and "Yeah-yeah-yeah." Luszynski notes wryly that a phrase like "Slysze warkot pociągu nadjedzie na torze" does not roll as smoothly in a lyric as "I hear the train a-coming, it's rolling down the line . . ." This will sound better to a Pole, or, on the other side of the world, to a Japanese simply because they grew up listening to English and American lyrics. With a few exceptions, the culture of popular entertainment and mass consumerism is an Anglo-American one, expressing itself in a variety of English. 14

Perhaps the most scientific study of the invasion of a language by English comes from Sweden. Professor Magnus Ljung of Stockholm University, investigating "Swinglish," the English hybrids in the Swedish language, questioned some two thousand Swedes. Sixty per cent claimed that their Swedish was being "corrupted" by watching English television programs. Twenty-six per cent blamed English books, newspapers and magazines for the same process. Fourteen per cent admitted that their Swedish was changing but could not attribute the change to any particular cause. More than half confessed to using the English plural *s* instead of the Swedish *or, ar, er*. A characteristic piece of Swinglish is *baj baj* (bye bye), or *tajt jeans* (*tight jeans*). The difficulty about such language surveys is that people tend to blame changes in language for changes in society. The Swede who deplores English television is probably venting his anxieties about the development of Swedish society. Complaints about language are as old as complaints about the weather. 15

Inventions like *baj baj* are natural in English-invaded countries throughout the world. In Hong Kong, a discotheque becomes a *dixie-go*. To be a "swinger" in Ecuador is *travoltarse* (from John Travolta). In Germany, teenagers wear *die Jeans* and listen to *die Soundtrack*. 16

The French have probably now abandoned the fight against *le week-end*, *le drugstore*, *le playboy* and *le bifteck* (though not against some other imports). In Russia, a Muscovite can drink a *viskey* or a *dzhin-in-tonik* and go to a *dzhazz-saission*. Even Spain's prestigious dictionary of Castilian, *The Dictionary of the Royal Academy*, the virtually "official" voice of Castilian Spanish, now admits *whiskey*, together with several English technical terms (*escaner* for *scanner*) in the latest edition.

The global influence of English can be measured by the opposition of its old rival, French, "the most meagre and inharmonious of all languages" according to Horace Walpole. For centuries, French was the international language *par excellence*, as the phrase goes. The French have cherished their language through the Académie Française, but it was not until the mid-1970s that successive Presidents became sufficiently concerned to come officially to the defence of the French language. "We must not let the idea take hold that English is the only possible instrument for industrial, economic and scientific communication," said President Pompidou. He, and his successor Giscard d'Estaing and, later, President Mitterrand's Socialists, took a series of government-sponsored initiatives to check the spread of *la langue du Coca-Cola*, abolishing borrowed words where possible and inventing suitable French alternatives. *Hot money* became *capitaux fébriles*, *jumbo jet* became *gros porteur* and *fast food* turned into *prêt-à-manger*. Despite these efforts, it is estimated that, in a newspaper like *Le Monde*, one word in 166 will be English. Another calculation claims that about one-twentieth of day-to-day French vocabulary is composed of *anglicismes*.

17

The darker, aggressive side of the spread of global English is the elimination of regional language variety, the attack on deep cultural roots. Perhaps the most dramatic example of the power of English can be found in Canada, which shares a 3000-mile border with the USA. Canadian English has been colonized by American English, especially in the mass media, and the French-speaking third of the community, living mainly in Quebec, has felt threatened to breaking point. Formerly the "two solitudes," living an uneasy co-existence, Canada since 1945 has had a powerful Quebec separatist movement, sustained as much by opposition to that northward glacier, the American language and culture, as by historic resentment of English-speaking Canada. It developed enough political steam to elect a provincial government in 1976 which, the next year, enacted the notorious "charter of the French language"—better known as Loi 101. English billboards, posters and storefronts were banned. Students were not allowed to attend English-language Quebec schools unless one of the parents had been educated in English at a Quebec elementary school. Many other

18

minorities, Greek, Italian, and Chinese, protested. One result is that there are now more than a thousand unregistered students in Montreal Catholic schools illegally studying English. "We decided to have a fairly high-profile campaign offering instruction in English to all comers," the Secretary General of the provincial association of Catholic schoolteachers is reported as saying. "It was a flagrant defiance of the law. We had to have special classes. We 'borrowed' school board property." Teachers for these special classes — in some cases accounting for one sixth of all pupils — were hired unofficially and paid under the table. The explanation is simple. Parents want their children's education to be useful to them. As one businessman commented: "I don't mind having to Francicize my business. Here we do everything in French. [Only about 15 per cent of Quebec province's six million inhabitants consider English to be their first language.] But when it comes to my family, I'm going to fight like a tiger."

Legislation like Loi 101 shows the desperate measures necessary   19
to stem the tide of English. The campaign has changed the English Canadian perception of their French neighbours, and the official policy of bilingualism means that French is safe for a few more generations. But all the legislation in the world cannot disguise the fact that even in the French-speaking parts of Canada the reality of the English-speaking world is inescapable. French-speaking air-traffic controllers have to use English in Canadian airspace. The banks of Quebec have to deal in English outside the province. Even Canadian English is under attack. American textbooks, especially American dictionaries, predominate in schools.

EXERCISES

Words to Know

incomprehensible (paragaph 1), Cherokee (1), in his prime (1), arguable (3), compendious (3), Silicon valley (3), ecumenical (3), global sway (4), heady (5), prerequisite (6), aspiration (8), disseminate (8), multinational corporations (9), memoranda (9), predominantly (10), bilingual (10), competitive (10), proficiency (10), Marxist (11), media (11), quasi-diplomatic (12), prosperity sphere (12), multi-ethnic (12), integral (12), phenomenon (14), hybrids (15), colonized (18), separatist (18), glacier (18), notorious (18), flagrant (18), defiance (18).

Some of the Issues

1. The basic argument of the essay is that English has become "the first truly global language." How do the authors support that argument in paragraphs 1 – 4? What particular areas of activity do they cite?
2. According to the authors, what kinds of development in the world favor the further spread of English (paragraphs 8 – 10)? How do they substantiate their assertion?
3. Why is English particularly important to Third World countries (paragraphs 11 – 12)?
4. How does the consumption of goods and services contribute to the global spread of English? How does it affect popular entertainment?

The Way We Are Told

5. The authors' essay argues that English is "the first truly global language." Why do they place a brief history of the language ahead of the information intended to support their argument?
6. The authors support their basic argument mainly through the selective use of statistics and a variety of specific examples and brief case histories. However, on a few occasions they also use words or phrases that have a more subjective appeal. Find some examples.

Some Subjects for Essays

* 7. Read Ngugi wa Thiong'o's "The Politics of Language." What insight does it give regarding the spread of English in former British colonies (first referred to in paragraph 5)? How does it exemplify what the authors of "World Language: English" call "the darker, aggressive side of [its] spread" (paragraph 18)?
8. In a week's normal television watching and newspaper and magazine reading, what evidence can you find of the "global sway" of English?

PUBLIC AND
PRIVATE LANGUAGE

Richard Rodriguez

Richard Rodriguez was born in California in 1944, attended Stanford and Columbia universities, and received his doctorate in English literature from the University of California, Berkeley. In addition to a number of articles, he has written his autobiography, *Hunger of Memory* (1982), from which the following selection was taken.

Bilingual education continues to be a subject of controversy. Its advocates believe that children entering school with little or no English will progress better if they are taught most subjects in their own language while learning English. In most bilingual programs the use of the first language is diminished or discontinued when children have mastered English.

Richard Rodriguez, whose first language was Spanish, uses his own experience to argue against bilingual education. To him Spanish remains his private language, the one he used at home, and English the public language he had to master in school in order to make his way in life. He believes that this distinction has helped him and would have been blurred if he had been taught in Spanish.

1   I remember to start with that day in Sacramento — a California now nearly thirty years past — when I first entered a classroom, able to understand some fifty stray English words.

2   The third of four children, I had been preceded to a neighborhood Roman Catholic school by an older brother and sister. But neither of them had revealed very much about their classroom experiences. Each afternoon they returned, as they left in the morning, always together, speaking in Spanish as they climbed the five steps of the porch. And their mysterious books, wrapped in shopping-bag paper, remained on the table next to the door, closed firmly behind them.

3   An accident of geography sent me to a school where all my classmates were white, many the children of doctors and lawyers and business executives. All my classmates certainly must have been uneasy on that first day of school — as most children are uneasy — to find themselves apart from their families in the first institution of their lives. But I was astonished.

The nun said, in a friendly but oddly impersonal voice, 'Boys and   4
girls, this is Richard Rodriguez.' (I heard her sound out: *Rich-heard
Road-ree-guess*.) It was the first time I had heard anyone name me in
English. 'Richard,' the nun repeated more slowly, writing my name
down in her black leather book. Quickly I turned to see my mothers's
face dissolve in a watery blur behind the pebbled glass door.

Many years later there is something called bilingual education —   5
a scheme proposed in the late 1960s by Hispanic-American social
activists, later endorsed by a congressional vote. It is a program that
seeks to permit non-English-speaking children, many from lower-class
homes, to use their family language as the language of school. (Such is
the goal its supporters announce.) I heard them and am forced to say
no: It is not possible for a child — any child — ever to use his family's
language in school. Not to understand this is to misunderstand the
public uses of schooling and to trivialize the nature of intimate life —
a family's 'language.'

Memory teaches me what I know of these matters; the boy re-   6
minds the adult. I was a bilingual child, a certain kind — socially
disadvantaged — the son of working-class parents, both Mexican
immigrants.

In the early years of my boyhood, my parents coped very well in   7
America. My father had steady work. My mother managed at home.
They were nobody's victims. Optimism and ambition led them to a
house (our home) many blocks from the Mexican south side of town.
We lived among *gringos* and only a block from the biggest, whitest
houses. It never occurred to my parents that they couldn't live wherever they chose. Nor was the Sacramento of the fifties bent on teaching
them a contrary lesson. My mother and father were more annoyed than
intimidated by those two or three neighbors who tried initially to make
us unwelcome. ('Keep your brats away from my sidewalk!') But despite all they achieved, perhaps because they had so much to achieve,
any deep feeling of ease, the confidence of 'belonging' in public was
withheld from them both. They regarded the people at work, the faces
in crowds, as very distant from us. They were the others, *los gringos*.
That term was interchangeable in their speech with another, even
more telling, *los americanos*.

I grew up in a house where the only regular guests were my   8
relations. For one day, enormous families of relatives would visit and
there would be so many people that the noise and the bodies would
spill out to the backyard and front porch. Then, for weeks, no one
came by. (It was usually a salesman who rang the doorbell.) Our house
stood apart. A gaudy yellow in a row of white bungalows. We were the
people with the noisy dog. The people who raised pigeons and
chickens. We were the foreigners on the block. A few neighbors smiled

and waved. We waved back. But no one in the family knew the names of the old couple who lived next door; until I was seven years old, I did not know the names of the kids who lived across the street.

In public, my father and mother spoke a hesitant, accented, not   9
always grammatical English. And they would have to strain — their bodies tense — to catch the sense of what was rapidly said by *los gringos*. At home they spoke Spanish. The language of their Mexican past sounded in counterpoint to the English of public society. The words would come quickly, with ease. Conveyed through those sounds was the pleasing, soothing, consoling reminder of being at home.

During those years when I was first conscious of hearing, my   10
mother and father addressed me only in Spanish; in Spanish I learned to reply. By contrast, English (*inglés*), rarely heard in the house, was the language I came to associate with *gringos*. I learned my first words of English overhearing my parents speak to strangers. At five years of age, I knew just enough English for my mother to trust me on errands to stores one block away. No more.

I was a listening child, careful to hear the very different sounds of   11
Spanish and English. Wide-eyed with hearing, I'd listen to sounds more than words. First, there were English (*gingro*) sounds. So many words were still unknown that when the butcher or the lady at the drugstore said something to me, exotic polysyllabic sounds would bloom in the midst of their sentences. Often, the speech of people in public seemed to me very loud, booming with confidence. The man behind the counter would literally ask, 'What can I do for you?' But by being so firm and so clear, the sound of his voice said that he was a *gringo*; he belonged in public society.

I would also hear then the high nasal notes of middle-class Ameri-   12
can speech. The air stirred with sound. Sometimes, even now, when I have been traveling abroad for several weeks, I will hear what I heard as a boy. In hotel lobbies or airports, in Turkey or Brazil, some Americans will pass, and suddenly I will hear it again — the high sound of American voices. For a few seconds I will hear it with pleasure, for it is now the sound of *my* society — a reminder of home. But inevitably — already on the flight headed for home — the sound fades with repetition. I will be unable to hear it anymore.

When I was a boy, things were different. The accent of *los*   13
gringos was never pleasing nor was it hard to hear. Crowds at Safeway or at bus stops would be noisy with sound. And I would be forced to edge away from the chirping chatter above me.

I was unable to hear my own sounds, but I knew very well that I   14
spoke English poorly. My words could not stretch far enough to form complete thoughts. And the words I did speak I didn't know well

enough to make into distinct sounds. (Listeners would usually lower their heads, better to hear what I was trying to say.) But it was one thing for *me* to speak English with difficulty. It was more troubling for me to hear my parents speak in public: their high-whining vowels and guttural consonants; their sentences that got stuck with 'ch' and 'ah' sounds; the confused syntax; the hesitant rhythm of sounds so different from the way *gringos* spoke. I'd notice, moreover, that my parents' voices were softer than those of *gringos* we'd meet.

I am tempted now to say that none of this mattered. In adulthood   15
I am embarrassed by childhood fears. And, in a way, it didn't matter very much that my parents could not speak English with ease. Their linguistic difficulties had no serious consequences. My mother and father made themselves understood at the county hospital clinic and at government offices. And yet, in another way, it mattered very much — it was unsettling to hear my parents struggle with English. Hearing them, I'd grow nervous, my clutching trust in their protection and power weakened.

There were many times like the night at a brightly lit gasoline   16
station (a blaring white memory) when I stood uneasily, hearing my father. He was talking to a teenaged attendant. I do not recall what they were saying, but I cannot forget the sounds my father made as he spoke. At one point his words slid together to form one word — sounds as confused as the threads of blue and green oil in the puddle next to my shoes. His voice rushed through what he had left to say. And, toward the end, reached falsetto notes, appealing to his listener's understanding. I looked away to the lights of passing automobiles. I tried not to hear anymore. But I heard only too well the calm, easy tones in the attendant's reply. Shortly afterward, walking toward home with my father, I shivered when he put his hand on my shoulder. The very first chance that I got, I evaded his grasp and ran on ahead into the dark, skipping with feigned boyish exuberance.

But then there was Spanish. *Español:* my family's language.   17
Español: the language that seemed to me a private language. I'd hear strangers on the radio and in the Mexican Catholic church across town speaking in Spanish, but I couldn't really believe that Spanish was a public language, like English. Spanish speakers, rather, seemed related to me, for I sensed that we shared — through our language — the experience of feeling apart from *los gringos*. It was thus a ghetto Spanish that I heard and I spoke. Like those whose lives are bound by a barrio, I was reminded by Spanish of my separateness from *los otros*, *los gringos* in power. But more intensely than for most barrio children — because I did not live in a barrio — Spanish seemed to me the language of home. (Most days it was only at home that I'd hear it.) It became the language of joyful return.

A family member would say something to me and I would feel   18
myself specially recognized. My parents would say something to me
and I would feel embraced by the sounds of their words. Those sounds
said: *I am speaking with ease in Spanish. I am addressing you in
words I never use with* los gringos. *I recognize you as someone
special, close, like no one outside. You belong with us. In the
family.*

(*Ricardo.*)   19

At the age of five, six, well past the time when most other   20
children no longer easily notice the difference between sounds uttered
at home and words spoken in public, I had a different experience. I
lived in a world magically compounded of sounds. I remained a child
longer than most; I lingered too long, poised at the edge of language
—often frightened by the sounds of *los gringos*, delighted by the
sounds of Spanish at home. I shared with my family a language that was
startlingly different from that used in the great city around us.

For me there were none of the gradations between public and   21
private society so normal to a maturing child. Outside the house was
public society; inside the house was private. Just opening or closing
the screen door behind me was an important experience. I'd rarely
leave home all alone or without reluctance. Walking down the sidewalk, under the canopy of tall trees, I'd warily notice the — suddenly
—silent neighborhood kids who stood warily watching me. Nervously,
I'd arrive at the grocery store to hear there the sounds of the *gringo* —
foreign to me — reminding me that in this world so big, I was a
foreigner. But then I'd return. Walking back toward our house, climbing the steps from the sidewalk, when the front door was open in
summer, I'd hear voices beyond the screen door talking in Spanish. For
a second or two, I'd stay, linger there, listening. Smiling, I'd hear my
mother call out, saying in Spanish (words): 'Is that you, Richard?' All
the while her sounds would assure me: *You are home now; come
closer; inside. With us.*

'*Si*,' I'd reply.   22

Once more inside the house I would resume (assume) my place   23
in the family. The sounds would dim, grow harder to hear. Once more
at home, I would grow less aware of that fact. It required, however, no
more than the blurt of the doorbell to alert me to listen to sounds all
over again. The house would turn instantly still while my mother went
to the door. I'd hear her hard English sounds. I'd wait to hear her voice
return to soft-sounding Spanish, which assured me, as surely as did the
clicking tongue of the lock on the door, that the stranger was gone.

Plainly, it is not healthy to hear such sounds so often. It is not   24
healthy to distinguish public words from private sounds so easily. I
remained cloistered by sounds, timid and shy in public, too dependent

on voices at home. And yet it needs to be emphasized: I was an extremely happy child at home. I remember many nights when my father would come back from work, and I'd hear him call out to my mother in Spanish, sounding relieved. In Spanish, he'd sound light and free notes he never could manage in English. Some nights I'd jump up just at hearing his voice. With *mis hermanos* I would come running into the room where he was with my mother. Our laughing (so deep was the pleasure!) became screaming. Like others who know the pain of public alienation, we transformed the knowledge of our public separateness and made it consoling — the reminder of intimacy. *We are speaking now the way we never speak out in public. We are alone — together*, voices sounded, surrounded to tell me. Some nights, no one seemed willing to loosen the hold sounds had on us. At dinner, we invented new words. (Ours sounded Spanish, but made sense only to us.) We pieced together new words by taking, say, an English verb and giving it Spanish endings. My mother's instructions at bedtime would be lacquered with mock-urgent tones. Or a word like *si* would become, in several notes, able to convey added measures of feeling. Tongues explored the edges of words, especially the fat vowels. And we happily sounded that military drum roll, the twirling roar of the Spanish *r*. Family language: my family's sounds. The voices of my parents and sisters and brother. Their voices insisting: *You belong here. We are family members. Related. Special to one another. Listen!* Voices singing and sighing, rising, straining, then surging, teeming with pleasure that burst syllables into fragments of laughter. At times it seemed there was steady quiet only when, from another room, the rustling whispers of my parents faded and I moved closer to sleep.

Supporters of bilingual education today imply that students like   25
me miss a great deal by not being taught in their family's language. What they seem not to recognize is that, as a socially disadvantaged child, I considered Spanish to be a private language. What I needed to learn in school was that I had the right — and the obligation — to speak the public language of *los gringos*. The odd truth is that my first-grade classmates could have become bilingual, in the conventional sense of that word, more easily than I. Had they been taught (as upper-middle-class children are often taught early) a second language like Spanish or French, they could have regarded it simply as that: another public language. In my case such bilingualism could not have been so quickly achieved. What I did not believe was that I could speak a single public language.

Without question, it would have pleased me to hear my teachers   26
address me in Spanish when I entered the classroom. I would have felt much less afraid. I would have trusted them and responded with ease.

But I would have delayed — for how long postponed? — having to learn the language of public society. I would have evaded — and for how long could I have afforded to delay? — learning the great lesson of school, that I had a public identity.

Fortunately my teachers were unsentimental about their responsibility. What they understood was that I needed to speak a public language. So their voices would search me out, asking me questions. Each time I'd hear them, I'd look up in surprise to see a nun's face frowning at me. I'd mumble, not really meaning to answer. The nun would persist, 'Richard, stand up. Don't look at the floor. Speak up. Speak to the entire class, not just to me!' But I couldn't believe that the English language was mine to use. (In part, I did not want to believe it.) I continued to mumble. I resisted the teacher's demands. (Did I somehow suspect that once I learned the public language my pleasing family life would be changed?) Silent, waiting for the bell to sound, I remained dazed, diffident, afraid.   27

Because I wrongly imagined that English was intrinsically a public language and Spanish an intrinsically private one, I easily noted the difference between classroom language and the language of home. At school, words were directed to a general audience of listeners. ('Boys and girls.') Words were meaningfully ordered. And the point was not self-expression alone but to make oneself understood by many others. The teacher quizzed: 'Boys and girls, why do we use that word in this sentence? Could we think of a better word to use there? Would the sentence change its meaning if the words were differently arranged? And wasn't there a better way of saying much the same thing?' (I couldn't say. I wouldn't try to say.)   28

Three months. Five. Half a year passed. Unsmiling, ever watchful, my teachers noted my silence. They began to connect my behavior with the difficult progress my older sister and brother were making. Until one Saturday morning three nuns arrived at the house to talk to our parents. Stiffly, they sat on the blue living room sofa. From the doorway of another room, spying the visitors, I noted the incongruity — the clash of two worlds, the faces and the voices of school intruding upon the familiar setting of home. I overheard one voice gently wondering, 'Do your children speak only Spanish at home, Mrs. Rodriguez?' While another voice added, 'That Richard especially seems so timid and shy.'   29

That Rich-heard!   30

With great tact the visitors continued, 'Is it possible for you and your husband to encourage your children to practice their English when they are home?' Of course, my parents complied. What would they not do for their children's well-being? And how could they have questioned the Church's authority which those women represented? In an instant, they agreed to give up the language (the sounds) that had   31 revealed and accentuated our family's closeness. The moment after the visitors left, the change was observed, '*Ahora*, speak to us *en inglés*,' my father and mother united to tell us.

At first, it seemed a kind of game. After dinner each night, the   32
family gathered to practice 'our' English. (It was still then *inglés*, a language foreign to us, so we felt drawn as strangers to it.) Laughing, we would try to define words we could not pronounce. We played with strange English sounds, often overanglicizing our pronunciations. And we filled the smiling gaps of our sentences with familiar Spanish sounds. But that was cheating, somebody shouted. Everyone laughed. In school, meanwhile, like my brother and sister, I was required to attend a daily tutoring session. I needed a full year of special attention. I also needed my teachers to keep my attention from straying in class by calling out, *Rich-heard* — their English voices slowly prying loose my ties to my other name, its three notes, *Ri-car-do*. Most of all I needed to hear my mother and father speak to me in a moment of seriousness in broken — suddenly heartbreaking — English. The scene was inevitable: One Saturday morning I entered the kitchen where my parents were talking in Spanish. I did not realize that they were talking in Spanish however until, at the moment they saw me, I heard their voices change to speak English. Those *gringo* sounds they uttered startled me. Pushed me away. In that moment of trivial misunderstanding and profound insight, I felt my throat twisted by unsounded grief. I turned quickly and left the room. But I had no place to escape to with Spanish. (The spell was broken.) My brother and sisters were speaking English in another part of the house.

Again and again in the days following, increasingly angry, I was   33
obliged to hear my mother and father: 'Speak to us *en inglés*. (*Speak.*) Only then did I determine to learn classroom English. Weeks after, it happened: One day in school I raised my hand to volunteer an answer. I spoke out in a loud voice. And I did not think it remarkable when the entire class understood. That day, I moved very far from the disadvantaged child I had been only days earlier. The belief, the calming assurance that I belonged in public, had at last taken hold.

Shortly after, I stopped hearing the high and low sounds of *los*   34
gringos. A more and more confident speaker of English, I didn't trouble to listen to *how* strangers sounded, speaking to me. And there simply were too many English-speaking people in my day for me to hear American accents anymore. Conversations quickened. Listening to persons who sounded eccentrically pitched voices, I usually noted their sounds for an initial few seconds before I concentrated on *what* they were saying. Conversations became content-full. Transparent. Hearing someone's *tone* of voice — angry or questioning or sarcastic or happy or sad — I didn't distinguish it from the words it expressed. Sound and word were thus tightly wedded. At the end of a day, I was

often bemused, always relieved to realize how 'silent,' though crowded with words, my day in public had been. (This public silence measured and quickened the change in my life.)

At last, seven years old, I came to believe what had been techni- 35 cally true since my birth: I was an American citizen.

But the special feeling of closeness at home was diminished by 36 then. Gone was the desperate, urgent, intense feeling of being at home; rare was the experience of feeling myself individualized by family intimates. We remained a loving family, but one greatly changed. No longer so close; no longer bound tight by the pleasing and troubling knowledge of our public separateness. Neither my older brother nor sister rushed home after school anymore. Nor did I. When I arrived home there would often be neighborhood kids in the house. Or the house would be empty of sounds.

The silence at home, however, was finally more than a literal 37 silence. Fewer words passed between parent and child, but more profound was the silence that resulted from my inattention to sounds. At about the time I no longer bothered to listen with care to the sounds of English in public, I grew careless about listening to the sounds family members made when they spoke. Most of the time I heard someone speaking at home and didn't distinguish his sounds from the words people uttered in public. I didn't even pay much attention to my parents' accented and ungrammatical speech. At least not at home. Only when I was with them in public would I grow alert to their accents. Though, even then, their sounds caused me less and less concern. For I was increasingly confident of my own public identity.

I would have been happier about my public success had I not 38 sometimes recalled what it had been like earlier, when my family had conveyed its intimacy through a set of conveniently private sounds. Sometimes in public, hearing a stranger, I'd hark back to my past. A Mexican farmworker approached me downtown to ask directions to somewhere. '¿Hijito . . .?' he said. And his voice summoned deep longing. Another time, standing beside my mother in the visiting room of a Carmelite convent, before the dense screen which rendered the nuns shadowy figures, I heard several Spanish-speaking nuns — their busy, singsong overlapping voices — assure us that yes, yes, we were remembered, all our family was remembered in their prayers. (Their voices echoed faraway family sounds.) Another day, a dark-faced old woman — her hand light on my shoulder — steadied herself against me as she boarded a bus. She murmured something I couldn't quite comprehend. Her Spanish voice came near, like the face of a never-before-seen relative in the instant before I was kissed. Her voice, like so many of the Spanish voices I'd heard in public, recalled the golden age of my youth. Hearing Spanish then, I continued to be a careful, if sad, listener to sounds. Hearing a Spanish-speaking family walking behind me, I turned to look. I smiled for an instant, before my glance found the Hispanic-looking faces of strangers in the crowd going by.

Today I hear bilingual educators say that children lose a degree of 'individuality' by becoming assimilated into public society. (Bilingual schooling was popularized in the seventies, that decade when middle-class ethnics began to resist the process of assimilation — the American melting pot.) But the bilingualists simplistically scorn the value and necessity of assimilation. They do not seem to realize that there are *two* ways a person is individualized. So they do not realize that while one suffers a diminished sense of *private* individuality by becoming assimilated into public society, such assimilation makes possible the achievement of *public* individuality. 39

The bilingualists insist that a student should be reminded of his difference from others in mass society, his heritage. But they equate mere separateness with individuality. The fact is that only in private —with intimates — is separateness from the crowd a prerequisite for individuality. (An intimate draws me apart, tells me that I am unique, unlike all others.) In public, by contrast, full individuality is achieved, paradoxically, by those who are able to consider themselves members of the crowd. Thus it happened for me: Only when I was able to think of myself as an American, no longer an alien in *gringo* society, could I seek the rights and opportunities necessary for full public individuality. The social and political advantages I enjoy as a man result from the day that I came to believe that my name, indeed, is *Rich-heard Road-ree-guess*. It is true that my public society today is often impersonal. (My public society is usually mass society.) Yet despite the anonymity of the crowd and despite the fact that the individuality I achieve in public is often tenuous — because it depends on my being one in a crowd — I celebrate the day I acquired my new name. Those middle-class ethnics who scorn assimilation seem to me filled with decadent self-pity, obsessed by the burden of public life. Dangerously, they romanticize public separateness and they trivialize the dilemma of the socially disadvantaged. 40

EXERCISES

Words to Know

bilingual education (paragraph 5), trivialize (5), disadvantaged (6), *gringos* (7), counterpoint (9), exotic (11), polysyllabic (11), nasal (12), chirping (13), guttural (14), syntax (14), linguistic (15), falsetto (16), evaded (16), feigned (16), exuberance (16), ghetto (17), barrio (17), *los otros*—the others (17), lingered (20), poised (20), gradations (21), canopy (21), warily (21), cloistered (24), *mis hermanos*—my brothers (24), alienation (24), lacquered (24), mock-urgent (24), evaded (26), diffident (27), intrinsically (28), incongruity (29), tact (31), *ahora*—now (31), over-anglicizing (32), inevitable (32), uttered (32), profound (32), insight (32), eccentrically (34), bemused (34), *hijito*—my boy (38), assimilated (39), popularized (39), ethnics (39), simplistically (39), prerequisite (40), unique (40), paradoxically (40), anonymity (40), tenuous (40), decadent (40), obsessed (40), romanticize (40), dilemma (40).

Some of the Issues

1. In paragraph 3 Rodriquez claims that on his first day of school most other children were uneasy but he was astonished. What accounts for his astonishment?
2. In paragraph 5 Rodriguez first states the theme of his essay—the distinction between family language and public language. What does he say about each?
3. Rodriguez describes his mother and father as being in many ways set off from American life and in some ways part of it. How did Rodriguez's family life differ from that of his neighbors?
4. In paragraph 11 Rodriguez describes himself as "a listening child." To what aspects of language is he particularly sensitive, and why?
5. In paragraph 20 he says he remained a child longer than most children. What reason does he give?
6. In paragraph 25 he asserts that English-speaking children in his school could have become bilingual more easily than he. What evidence does he give? Do you believe he is right?
7. In paragraphs 27 and 28 he says that he would have been happy as a child if his teachers had spoken to him in Spanish but now believes it is fortunate that they did not. Why does he believe that?
8. What does Rodriguez mean in paragraph 28 when he says he was wrong in imagining that English was intrinsically a public language and Spanish an intrinsically private one?
9. What is the turning point reported in paragraphs 35 and 36? Judging from these final two paragraphs and the rest of the essay, what has Rodriguez lost? What has he gained?

The Way We Are Told

10. Rodriguez waits until paragraph 5 to state his thesis, after devoting the first four paragraphs to the experience of his first day at

school. It would have been more conventional to begin with the thesis. What does he gain by putting his personal experience first?

11. How does Rodriguez show us his awareness of the sounds of English and Spanish?

12. At several points Rodriguez uses short paragraphs, including one consisting of a single word. What is the effect?

13. Rodriguez uses some Spanish words. When does he? What is the effect he wants to achieve?

14. Rodriguez interrupts his personal recollections in several places to speak more impersonally about public policy. Examine how these sections differ in style and yet relate to the memories that precede and follow them.

Some Subjects for Essays

15. If you grew up with two languages, compare and contrast your experience with the one Rodriguez presents.

16. Throughout the essay Rodriguez asserts that it is the role of schools and other public institutions to help children adjust to the norms of the society. Examine his argument and agree or disagree with it.

17. What is the nature of the evidence Rodriguez uses to support his argument against bilingual education? In an essay examine and evaluate that evidence. Is it sufficient?

* 18. Rodriguez argues against bilingual education from his experience as a bilingual child. Read James Fallows's "Bilingual Education"; Gloria Ramirez, one of the teachers whom Fallows interviewed, grew up in similar circumstances but supports bilingual education. In an essay compare and evaluate their respective arguments.

* 19. Read Grace Paley's short story "The Loudest Voice." Do you find evidence in it that argues against Rodriguez's assertion that schools have a responsibility to adjust children to mainstream or "public" culture?

* 20. Read Ngugi wa Thiong'o's "The Politics of Language." In speaking of Gikuyu, his first language, and English, which displaced it in his later education, Ngugi can be said to refer to a concept of a private and a public language similar to Rodriguez's. Describe Ngugi's and Rodriguez's concepts, noting in particular the differences in the points of view of the two writers.

BILINGUAL
EDUCATION

James Fallows

James Fallows is the Washington editor of *The Atlantic Monthly*.
Born in 1949, he received his A.B. degree from Harvard and continued his studies at Oxford as a Rhodes scholar. In the 1980s he
spent several years in Asia, particularly in Japan. In his most recent
book, *More Like Us: Making America Great Again* (1989), he
reflects on American society and on the consequences to the
United States of the rise of Japanese economic power.

The selection included here is part of an extensive survey,
"Immigration: How It's Affecting Us," which he published in *The
Atlantic Monthly* in November 1983.

In this essay Fallows examines bilingual education. He describes how he gradually changed his view from one of suspicion
of bilingual education to a recognition that, well executed, it had
definite advantages for the education of children for whom English was a second language. (For another view of bilingual education see Richard Rodriguez's "Public and Private Language.")

A national culture is held together by official rules and informal sig-   1
nals. Through their language, dress, taste, and habits of life, immigrants
initially violate the rules and confuse the signals. The United States has
prided itself on building a nation out of diverse parts. *E Pluribus
Unum* originally referred to the act of political union in which separate colonies became one sovereign state. It now seems more fitting as
a token of the cultural adjustments through which immigrant strangers
have become Americans. Can the assimilative forces still prevail?

The question arises because most of today's immigrants share one   2
trait: their native language is Spanish.

From 1970 to 1978, the three leading sources of legal immi-   3
grants to the U.S. were Mexico, the Philippines, and Cuba. About 42
percent of legal immigration during the seventies was from Latin
America. It is thought that about half of all illegal immigrants come
from Mexico, and 10 to 15 percent more from elsewhere in Latin
America. Including illegal immigrants makes all figures imprecise, but
it seems reasonable to conclude that more than half the people who
now come to the United States speak Spanish. This is a greater concen-

434

tration of immigrants in one non-English language group than ever before.

Is it a threat? The conventional wisdom about immigrants and   4
their languages is that the Spanish-speakers are asking for treatment different from that which has been accorded to everybody else. In the old days, it is said, immigrants were eager to assimilate as quickly as possible. They were placed, sink or swim, in English-language classrooms, and they swam. But now the Latin Americans seem to be insisting on bilingual classrooms and ballots. "The Hispanics demand that the United States become a bilingual country, with all children entitled to be taught in the language of their heritage, at public expense," Theodore White has written. Down this road lie the linguistic cleavages that have brought grief to other nations.

This is the way many people think, and this is the way I myself   5
thought as I began this project.

The historical parallel closest to today's concentration of Span-   6
ish-speaking immigrants is the German immigration of the nineteenth century. From 1830 to 1890, 4.5 million Germans emigrated to the United States, making up one third of the immigrant total. The Germans recognized that command of English would finally ensure for them, and especially for their children, a place in the mainstream of American society. But like the Swedes, Dutch, and French before them, they tried hard to retain the language in which they had been raised.

The midwestern states, where Germans were concentrated, es-   7
tablished bilingual schools, in which children could receive instruction in German. In Ohio, German-English public schools were in operation by 1840; in 1837, the Pennsylvania legislature ordered that German-language public schools be established on an equal basis with English-language schools. Minnesota, Maryland, and Indiana also operated public schools in which German was used, either by itself or in addition to English. In *Life with Two Languages*, his study of bilingualism, François Grosjean says, "What is particularly striking about German Americans in the nineteenth century is their constant efforts to maintain their language, culture, and heritage."

Yet despite everything the Germans could do, their language   8
began to die out. The progression was slow and fraught with pain. For the immigrant, language was the main source of certainty and connection to the past. As the children broke from the Old World culture and tried out their snappy English slang on their parents, the pride the parents felt at such achievements was no doubt mixed with the bittersweet awareness that they were losing control.

At first the children would act as interpreters for their parents: 9
then they would demand the independence appropriate to that role; then they would yearn to escape the coarse ways of immigrant life. And

in the end, they would be Americans. It was hard on the families, but it built an assimilated English-language culture.

The pattern of assimilation is familiar from countless novels, as well as from the experience of many people now living. Why, then, is the currently fashionable history of assimilation so different? Why is it assumed, in so many discussions of bilingual education, that in the old days immigrants switched quickly and enthusiastically to English?   10

One reason is that the experience of Jewish immigrants in the early twentieth century was different from this pattern. German Jews, successful and thoroughly assimilated here in the nineteenth century, oversaw an effort to bring Eastern European Jews into the American mainstream as quickly as possible. In New York City, the Lower East Side's Hebrew Institute, later known as the Educational Alliance, defined its goal as teaching the newcomers "the privileges and duties of American citizenship." Although many Jewish immigrants preserved their Yiddish, Jews generally learned English faster than any other group.   11

Another reason that nineteenth-century linguistic history is so little remembered lies in the political experience of the early twentieth century. As an endless stream of New Immigrants arrived from Eastern Europe, the United States was awash in theories about the threats the newcomers posed to American economic, sanitary, and racial standards, and the "100 percent Americanism" movement arose. By the late 1880s, school districts in the Midwest had already begun reversing their early encouragement of bilingual education. Competence in English was made a requirement for naturalized citizens in 1906. Pro-English-language leagues sprang up to help initiate the New Immigrants. California's Commission on Immigration and Housing, for example, endorsed a campaign of "Americanization propaganda," in light of "the necessity for all to learn English — the language of America." With the coming of World War I, all German-language activities were suddenly cast in a different light. Eventually, as a result, Americans came to believe that previous immigrants had speedily switched to English, and to view the Hispanics' attachment to Spanish as a troubling aberration.   12

The bilingual system is accused of supporting a cadre of educational consultants while actually retarding the students' progress into the English-speaking mainstream. In this view, bilingual education could even be laying the foundation for a separate Hispanic culture, by extending the students' Spanish-language world from their homes to their schools.   13

Before I traveled to some of the schools in which bilingual education was applied, I shared the skeptics' view. What good could come of a system that encouraged, to whatever degree, a language   14 other than the national tongue? But after visiting elementary, junior high, and high schools in Miami, Houston, San Antonio, Austin, several parts of Los Angeles, and San Diego, I found little connection between the political debate over bilingual education and what was going on in these schools.

To begin with, one central fact about bilingual education goes   15
largely unreported. It is a *temporary* program. The time a typical student stays in the program varies from place to place — often two years in Miami, three years in Los Angeles — but when that time has passed, the student will normally leave. Why, then, do bilingual programs run through high school? Those classes are usually for students who are new to the district — usually because their parents are new to the country.

There is another fact about bilingual education, more difficult to   16
prove but impressive to me, a hostile observer. Most of the children I saw were unmistakably learning to speak English.

In the elementary schools, where the children have come straight   17
out of all-Spanish environments, the background babble seems to be entirely in Spanish. The kindergarten and first- to third-grade classrooms I saw were festooned with the usual squares and circles cut from colored construction paper, plus posters featuring Big Bird and charts about the weather and the seasons. Most of the schools seemed to keep a rough balance between English and Spanish in the lettering around the room; the most Spanish environment I saw was in one school in East Los Angeles, where about a third of the signs were in English.

The elementary school teachers were mostly Mexican-American   18
women. They prompted the children with a mixture of English and Spanish during the day. While books in both languages are available in the classrooms, most of the first-grade reading drills I saw were in Spanish. In theory, children will learn the phonetic principle of reading more quickly if they are not trying to learn a new language at the same time. Once comfortable as readers, they will theoretically be able to transfer their ability to English.

In a junior high school in Houston, I saw a number of Mexican   19
and Salvadoran students in their "bilingual" biology and math classes. They were drilled entirely in Spanish on the parts of amoeba and on the difference between a parallelogram and a rhombus. When students enter bilingual programs at this level, the goal is to keep them current with the standard curriculum while introducing them to English. I found my fears of linguistic separatism rekindled by the sight of fourteen-year-olds lectured to in Spanish. I reminded myself that many of the students I was seeing had six months earlier lived in another country.

The usual next stop for students whose time in bilingual educa- 20
tion is up is a class in intensive English, lasting one to three hours a
day. These students are divided into two or three proficiency levels,
from those who speak no English to those nearly ready to forgo special
help. In Houston, a teacher drilled two-dozen high-school-age Cambodians, Indians, Cubans, and Mexicans on the crucial difference between the voiced *th* sound of "this" and the voiceless *th* of "thing." In
Miami, a class of high school sophomores included youths from Cuba,
El Salvador, and Honduras. They listened as their teacher read a Rock-
wellesque essay about a student with a crush on his teacher, and then
set to work writing an essay of their own, working in words like
"garrulous" and "sentimentalize."

One of the students in Miami, a sixteen-year-old from Honduras, 21
said that his twelve-year-old brother had already moved into mainstream classes. Linguists say this is the standard pattern for immigrant
children. The oldest children hold on to their first language longest,
while their younger sisters and brothers swim quickly into the new
language culture.

The more I saw of the classes, the more convinced I became that 22
most of the students were learning English. Therefore, I started to
wonder what it is about bilingual education that has made it the focus
of such bitter disagreement.

For one thing, most immigrant groups other than Hispanics take a 23
comparatively dim view of bilingual education. Haitians, Vietnamese,
and Cambodians are eligible for bilingual education, but in general
they are unenthusiastic. In Miami, Haitian boys and girls may learn to
read in Creole rather than English. Still, their parents push to keep
them moving into English. "A large number of [Haitian] parents come
to the PTA meetings, and they don't want interpreters," said the principal of Miami's Edison Park Elementary School last spring. "They
want to learn English. They don't want notices coming home in three
languages. When they come here, unless there is total noncommunica-
tion, they will try to get through to us in their broken English. The
students learn the language *very* quickly."

Bilingual education is inflammatory in large part because of what 24
it symbolizes, not because of the nuts and bolts of its daily operation.
In reality, bilingual programs move students into English with greater
or lesser success; in reality, most Spanish-speaking parents understand
that mastery of English will be their children's key to mobility. But in
the political arena, bilingual education presents a different face. To
the Hispanic ideologue, it is a symbol of cultural pride and political
power. And once it has been presented that way, with full rhetorical

flourish, it naturally strikes other Americans as a threat to the operating rules that have bound the country together.

Once during the months I spoke with and about immigrants I felt   25
utterly exasperated. It was while listening to two Chicano activist lawyers in Houston who demanded to know why their people should be required to learn English at all. "It is unrealistic to think people can learn it that quickly," one lawyer said about the law that requires naturalized citizens to pass a test in English. "*Especially when they used to own this part of the country*, and when Spanish was the *historic language* of this region."

There is a historic claim for Spanish — but by the same logic   26
there is a stronger claim for, say, Navajo as the historic language of the Southwest. The truth is that for more than a century the territory has been American and its national language has been English.

I felt the same irritation welling up when I talked with many   27
bilingual instructors and policy-makers. Their arguments boiled down to: What's so special about English? They talked about the richness of the bilingual experience, the importance of maintaining the children's abilities in Spanish — even though when I watched the instructors in the classroom I could see that they were teaching principally English.

In my exasperation, I started to think that if such symbols of the   28
dignity of language were so provocative to me, a comfortable member of the least-aggrieved ethnic group, it might be worth reflecting on the comparable sensitivities that lie behind the sentiments of the Spanish-speaking.

Consider the cases of Gloria Ramirez and Armandina Flores, who   29
taught last year in the bilingual program at the Guerra Elementary School, in the Edgewood Independent School District, west of San Antonio.

San Antonio has evaded questions about the balance between rich   30
and poor in its school system by carving the city up into independent school districts. Alamo Heights is the winner under this approach, and Edgewood is the loser. The Edgewood School District is perennially ranked as one of the poorest in the state. The residents are almost all Mexican-Americans or Mexicans. It is a settled community, without much to attract immigrants, but many stop there briefly on their way somewhere else, enough to give Edgewood a sizable illegal-immigrant enrollment.

In the middle of a bleak, sunbaked stretch of fields abutting a   31
commercial vegetable farm, and within earshot of Kelly Air Force Base, sits Edgewood's Guerra School. It is an ordinary-looking but well-kept one-story structure that was built during the Johnson Administration. Nearly all the students are Mexican or Mexican-American.

Gloria Ramirez, who teaches first grade, is a compact, attractive   32
woman of thirty-three, a no-nonsense veteran of the activist movements of the 1960s. Armandina Flores, a twenty-seven-year-old kindergarten teacher, is a beauty with dark eyes and long hair. During
classroom hours, they deliver "Now, children" explanations of what is
about to happen in both Spanish and English, although when the
message really must get across, it comes in Spanish.

Both are remarkable teachers. They have that spark often thought   33
to be missing in the public schools. There is no hint that for them this
is just a job, perhaps because it symbolizes something very different
from the worlds in which they were raised.

Gloria Ramirez was born in Austin, in 1950. Both of her parents   34
are native Texans, as were two of her grandparents, but her family, like
many other Mexican-American families, "spoke only Spanish when I
was growing up," she says. None of her grandparents went to school at
all. Her parents did not go past the third grade. Her father works as an
auto-body mechanic; her mother raised the six children, and recently
went to work at Austin State Hospital as a cleaner.

Ramirez began learning English when she started school; but the   35
school, on Austin's east side, was overwhelmingly Mexican-American,
part of the same culture she'd always known. The big change came
when she was eleven. Her family moved to a working-class Anglo area
in South Austin. She and her brother were virtually the only Mexican-
Americans at the school. There was no more Spanish on the playground, or even at home. "My parents requested that we speak more
English to them from then on,"she says. "Both of them could speak it,
but neither was comfortable."

"Before then, I didn't realize I had an accent. I didn't know until   36
a teacher at the new school pointed it out in a ridiculing manner. I
began learning English out of revenge." For six years, she took speech
classes. "I worked hard so I could sound — like this," she says in
standard American. She went to the University of Texas, where she
studied history and philosophy and became involved in the Mexican-
American political movements of the 1970s. She taught bilingual-edu-
cation classes in Boston briefly before coming home to Texas.

Armandina Flores was born in Ciudad Acuña, Mexico, across the   37
river from Del Rio, Texas. Her mother, who was born in Houston, was
an American citizen, but *her* parents had returned to Mexico a few
months after her birth, and she had never learned English. Flores's
father was a Mexican citizen. When she reached school age, she began
commuting across the river to a small Catholic school in Del Rio,
where all the other students were Chicano. When she was twelve and
about to begin the sixth grade, her family moved to Del Rio and she
entered an American public school.

At that time, the sixth grade was divided into tracks, which ran   38
from 6-1 at the bottom to 6-12. Most of the Anglos were at the top;
Armandina Flores was initially placed in 6-4. She showed an aptitude
for English and was moved up to 6-8. Meanwhile, her older sister,
already held back once, was in 6-2. Her parents were proud of Armandina's progress; they began to depend on her English in the family's
dealings in the Anglo world. She finished high school in Del Rio, went
to Our Lady of the Lake College in San Antonio, and came to Edgewood
as an aide in 1978, when she was twenty-two.

Considered one way, these two stories might seem to confirm   39
every charge made by the opponents of bilingual education. Through
the trauma of being plucked from her parents' comfortable Spanish-
language culture and plunged into the realm of public language,
Gloria Ramirez was strengthened, made a cosmopolitan and accomplished person. Her passage recalls the one Richard Rodriguez describes in *Hunger of Memory*, an autobiography that has become the
most eloquent text for opponents of bilingual programs.

"Without question, it would have pleased me to hear my teachers   40
address me in Spanish when I entered the classroom," Rodriguez
wrote. "I would have felt much less afraid. . . . But I would have
delayed — for how long postponed? — having to learn the language of
public society."

Gloria Ramirez concedes that the pain of confused ethnicity and   41
lost loyalties among Mexican-Americans is probably very similar to
what every other immigrant group has endured. She even admits that
she was drawn to bilingual education for political as well as educational reasons. As for Armandina Flores, hers is a calmer story of
successful assimilation, accomplished without the crutch of bilingual
education.

Yet both of these women insist, with an edge to their voices, that   42
their students are fortunate not to have the same passage awaiting
them.

It was a very wasteful process, they say. They swam; many others   43
sank. "You hear about the people who make it, but not about all the
others who dropped out, who never really learned," Ramirez says.
According to the Mexican-American Legal Defense and Education
Fund, 40 percent of Hispanic students drop out before they finish high
school, three times as many as among Anglo students.

"Many people around here don't feel comfortable with them-   44
selves in either language," Ramirez says. Flores's older sister never
became confident in English; "she feels like a lower person for it." She
has just had a baby and is anxious that he succeed in English. Ram-
mirez's older brother learned most of his English in the Marines. He is
married to a Mexican immigrant and thinks that it is very important

that their children learn English. And that is more likely to happen, the teacher says, if they have a transitional moment in Spanish.

Otherwise, "a child must make choices that concern his sur-   45
vival," Ramirez says. "He can choose to learn certain words, only to survive; but it can kill his desire to learn, period. Eventually he may be able to deal in the language, but he won't be educated." If the natural-immersion approach worked, why, they ask, would generation after generation of Chicanos, American citizens living throughout the Southwest, have lived and died without ever fully moving into the English-language mainstream?

These two teachers, and a dozen others with parallel experience,   46
might be wrong in their interpretation of how bilingual education works. If so, they are making the same error as German, Polish, and Italian immigrants. According to the historians hired by the Select Commission, "Immigrants argued, when given the opportunity, that the security provided them by their cultures eased rather than hindered the transition." Still, there is room for reasonable disagreement about the most effective techniques for bringing children into English. A former teacher named Robert Rossier, for example, argues from his experience teaching immigrants that intensive courses in English are more effective than a bilingual transition. Others line up on the other side.

But is this not a question for factual resolution rather than for   47
battles about linguistic and ethnic pride? Perhaps one approach will succeed for certain students in certain situations and the other will be best for others. The choice between bilingual programs and intensive-English courses, then, should be a choice between methods, not ideologies. The wars over bilingual education have had a bitter, symbolic quality. Each side has invested the issue with a meaning the other can barely comprehend. To most Mexican-American parents and children, bilingual education is merely a way of learning English; to Hispanic activists, it is a symbol that they are at last taking their place in the sun. But to many other Americans, it sounds like a threat not to assimilate.

EXERCISES

Words to Know

e pluribus unum—out of many, one (paragraph 1), sovereign (1), assimilative (1), conventional wisdom (4), linguistic (4), cleavages (4), mainstream (6), bittersweet (8), assimilated (9), awash (12), aberration (12), cadre (13), skeptics (14), hostile (16), babble (17), festooned (17), phonetic (18), amoeba (19), parallelogram (19), rhombus (19), rekindled (19), intensive English (20), proficiency (20), garrulous (20), eligible (23), inflammatory (24), symbolizes (24), ideologue (24), rhetorical (24), flourish (24), exasperated (25), Chicano (25), naturalized citizens (25), provocative (28), least-aggrieved (28), sensitivities (28), evaded (30), perennially (30), Anglo (35), aptitude (38), trauma (39), ethnicity (41), natural-immersion (45), ideologies (47).

Some of the Issues

1. The first paragraph describes what, in the author's view, holds a national culture together. What is it? Why do immigrants "initially violate the rules"? Try to give specific answers to both questions.
2. What, according to "conventional wisdom," distinguishes Spanish-speakers from other immigrants? (Paragraph 4)
3. Fallows finds several parallels between today's Spanish-speaking immigrants and the German-speaking immigrants of the nineteenth century. What are the parallels?
4. What reasons does Fallows cite in paragraphs 11 and 12 for the disappearance of the nineteenth-century attitudes that produced the earlier system of bilingual education?
5. Paragraph 13 summarizes some of the arguments against bilingual education. What are they? Why does Fallows gradually turn away from them?
6. What differences does Fallows see between the attitudes of Spanish-speaking immigrants and those from other backgrounds? (Paragraph 23)
7. Consider paragraphs 24 through 28: Why has bilingual education become an inflammatory issue according to Fallows?
8. In paragraphs 32 through 45 Fallows tells the personal histories of two bilingual teachers. In what ways do these histories shed light on the controversies about bilingual education?
9. In paragraphs 45 and 46 Fallows, in his conclusion, proposes to shift the argument about the linguistic education of students whose native language is not English to a "factual resolution." What does he propose?

The Way We Are Told

10. Several times throughout the essay Fallows uses the device of asking a question and then proceeding to answer it. Although such questions might seem artificial, they are often used by writers. What advantage might this kind of rhetorical question have for the writer?

11. Paragraphs 2, 5, and 42 consists of single sentences that precede and follow longer, more fully developed paragraphs. Are these single-sentence paragraphs effective? Why or why not?

12. In paragraphs 4 and 5 Fallows states what he used to believe about bilingual education, and then goes to tell what he now believes. A similar statement about former and present beliefs is made in paragraphs 13 and 14. What advantage does Fallows gain by putting things this way?

13. Fallows' report is devoted to making a fair and objective evaluation of the controversy about bilingual education. He does, however, at times indicate his own strong personal feelings, as in paragraph 25 for example. Does this help or hinder your belief in his ultimate objectivity?

14. Fallows identifies himself as a member of the "least-aggrieved ethnic group" (paragraph 28). What does he mean, and why is it important for him to identify himself?

15. Who is Fallows' audience? Do you think they share his original views on bilingual education?

Some Subjects for Essays

16. If you grew up speaking a language other than English at home, trace your own encounters with learning English in and out of school, and comment on your experience.

17. Is there an issue on which you at first held one opinion and later, through experience, came either to modify or reverse your ideas? In an essay, first state your original opinion and then trace the experiences that led you to change your minds.

18. Fallows uses the device of a rhetorical question—a question to which the author already knows the answer and will proceed to give it. Experiment with writing paragraphs which begin with rhetorical questions. Develop the best one into a short assay.

* 19. Gloria Ramirez, one of the bilingual teachers Fallows interviewed, tells a story much like that of Richard Rodriguez in "Public and Private Language." Ramirez and Rodriguez come to different conclusions about the meaning of their experience. Read Rodriguez and compare and contrast the two views and experiences in an essay.

* 20. The photograph on page 376 shows a bilingual classroom in Arlington, Virginia. Write two separate paragraphs describing it. One paragraph should be written from the point of view of a believer in bilingual education, the other from the point of view of an opponent.

THE POLITICS
OF LANGUAGE

Ngugi wa Thiong'o

Ngugi wa Thiong'o was born in Limuru, Kenya, in 1938. He is considered one of Africa's most important contemporary writers. He was educated at Makerere University in Uganda and taught briefly in the United States. From 1972 until his detention in 1978 he served as head of the English Department at the University of Nairobi in Kenya. Since his release he has devoted himself to his writing. His earlier works were written in English and include the novels *Weep Not, Child, The River Between*, and *Petals of Blood*, as well as the plays *The Black Hermit* and *The Trial of Dedan Kimathi*.

Decolonizing the Mind, from which this selection is taken, was originally given as a series of lectures at Auckland University in New Zealand. In an introductory statement, Ngugi says: "This book . . . is my farewell to English as a vehicle of any of my writings. From now on it is Gĩkũyũ and Kiswahili all the way."

What language to write in — for writers in many cultures that is a serious and thorny question. It is a particularly difficult one for African writers. Until the 1960s almost all of Africa was ruled as colonies by European powers, most notably and extensively by Britain and France. Education beyond the elementary level was largely provided only for a select few, and in the language of the ruling power, so much so that one usually referred to various countries as Anglophone or Francophone respectively, depending on whether they had been British or French (or Belgian) colonies before independence. Major African authors Chinua Achebe and Wole Soyinka, who both are Nigerians, write in English; and Leopold Senghor and Ousmane Sembene, both Senegalese, write in French.

In his essay Ngugi first describes his own experience: how, working in the fields during the day, and around the fireside in the evening, stories were told; how such stories, well told, had power beyond the meaning of the words; how, "through images and symbols, [language] gave us a view of the world." Then he relates how "this harmony was broken" when his education shifted to the language of the colonizers, English, and relates the pressures on the children to abandon their native language. Ngugi then turns to a more general consideration of language, which he sees as consisting of two major divisions: language as communication and

445

language as a carrier of culture. The imposition of a colonial language and its literature, he says, produces a sense of alienation from his environment for the African child and may diminish his feeling of self-worth.

You may want to relate Ngugi's ideas to Robert McCrum, William Cran, and Robert McNeil's "World Language: English," as well as to Richard Rodriguez's "Public and Private Language."

I was born into a large peasant family: father, four wives and about   1
twenty-eight children. I also belonged, as we all did in those days, to a wider extended family and to the community as a whole.

We spoke Gĩkũyũ as we worked in the fields. We spoke Gĩkũyũ in   2
and outside the home. I can vividly recall those evenings of story-telling around the fireside. It was mostly the grown-ups telling the children but everybody was interested and involved. We children would re-tell the stories the following day to other children who worked in the fields picking the pyrethrum flowers, tea-leaves or coffee beans of our European and African landlords.

The stories, with mostly animals as the main characters, were all   3
told in Gĩkũyũ. Hare, being small, weak but full of innovative wit and cunning, was our hero. We identified with him as he struggled against the brutes of prey like lion, leopard, hyena. His victories were our victories and we learnt that the apparently weak can outwit the strong. We followed the animals in their struggle against hostile nature — drought, rain, sun, wind — a confrontation often forcing them to search for forms of co-operation. But we were also interested in their struggles amongst themselves, and particularly between the beasts and the victims of prey. These twin struggles, against nature and other animals, reflected real-life struggles in the human world.

Not that we neglected stories with human beings as the main   4
characters. There were two types of characters in such human-centered narratives: the species of truly human beings with qualities of courage, kindness, mercy, hatred of evil, concern for others; and a man-eat-man two-mouthed species with qualities of greed, selfishness, individualism and hatred of what was good for the larger co-operative community. Co-operation as the ultimate good in a community was a constant theme. It could unite human beings with animals against ogres and beasts of prey, as in the story of how dove, after being fed with castor-oil seeds, was sent to fetch a smith working far away from home and whose pregnant wife was being threatened by these man-eating two-mouthed ogres.

There were good and bad story-tellers. A good one could tell the   5
same story over and over again, and it would always be fresh to us, the listeners. He or she could tell a story told by someone else and make it

more alive and dramatic. The differences really were in the use of words and images and the inflexion of voices to effect different tones.

We therefore learnt to value words for their meaning and 6
nuances. Language was not a mere string of words. It had a suggestive power well beyond the immediate and lexical meaning. Our appreciation of the suggestive magical power of language was reinforced by the games we played with words through riddles, proverbs, transpositions of syllables, or through nonsensical but musically arranged words. So we learnt the music of our language on top of the content. The language, through images and symbols, gave us a view of the world, but it had a beauty of its own. The home and the field were then our pre-primary school but what is important, for this discussion, is that the language of our evening teach-ins, and the language of our immediate and wider community, and the language of our work in the fields were one.

And then I went to school, a colonial school, and this harmony 7
was broken. The language of my education was no longer the language of my culture. I first went to Kamaandura, missionary run, and then to another called Maanguuũ run by nationalists grouped around the Gĩkũyũ Independent and Karinga Schools Association. Our language of education was still Gĩkũyũ. The very first time I was ever given an ovation for my writing was over a composition in Gĩkũyũ. So for my first four years there was still harmony between the language of my formal education and that of the Limuru peasant community.

It was after the declaration of a state of emergency over Kenya in 8
1952 that all the schools run by patriotic nationalists were taken over by the colonial regime and were placed under District Education Boards chaired by Englishmen. English became the language of my formal education. In Kenya, English became more than a language: it was *the* language, and all the others had to bow before it in deference.

Thus one of the most humiliating experiences was to be caught 9
speaking Gĩkũyũ in the vicinity of the school. The culprit was given corporal punishment — three to five strokes of the cane on bare buttocks — or was made to carry a metal plate around the neck with inscriptions such as I AM STUPID or I AM A DONKEY. Sometimes the culprits were fined money they could hardly afford. And how did the teachers catch the culprits? A button was initially given to one pupil who was supposed to hand it over to whoever was caught speaking his mother tongue. Whoever had the button a the end of the day would sing who had given it to him and the ensuing process would bring out all the culprits of the day. Thus children were turned into witch-hunters and in the process were being taught the lucrative value of being a traitor to one's immediate community.

The attitude to English was the exact opposite: any achievement 10 in spoken or written English was highly rewarded; prizes, prestige, applause; the ticket to higher realms. English became the measure of intelligence and ability in the arts, the sciences, and all the other branches of learning. English became *the* main determinant of a child's progress up the ladder of formal education.

As you may know, the colonial system of education in addition to   11
its apartheid racial demarcation had the structure of a pyramid: a broad primary base, a narrowing secondary middle, and an even narrower university apex. Selections from primary into secondary were through an examination, in my time called Kenya African Preliminary Examination, in which one had to pass six subjects ranging from Maths to Nature Study and Kiswahili. All the papers were written in English. Nobody could pass the exam who failed the English language paper no matter how brilliantly he had done in the other subjects. I remember one boy in my class of 1954 who had distinctions in all subjects except English, which he had failed. He was made to fail the entire exam. He went on to become a turn boy in a bus company. I who had only passes but a credit in English got a place at the Alliance High School, one of the most elitist institutions for Africans in colonial Kenya. The requirements for a place at the University, Makerere University College, were broadly the same: nobody could go on to wear the undergraduate red gown, no matter how brilliantly they had performed in all the other subjects unless they had a credit — not even a simple pass! — in English. Thus the most coveted place in the pyramid and in the system was only available to the holder of an English language credit card. English was the official vehicle and the magic formula to colonial elitedom.

Literary education was now determined by the dominant lan-   12
guage while also reinforcing that dominance. Orature (oral literature) in Kenyan languages stopped. In primary school I now read simplified Dickens and Stevenson alongside Rider Haggard. Jim Hawkins, Oliver Twist, Tom Brown — not Hare, Leopard and Lion — were now my daily companions in the world of imagination. In secondary school, Scott and G. B. Shaw vied with more Rider Haggard, John Buchan, Alan Paton, Captain W. E. Johns. At Makerere I read English: from Chaucer to T. S. Eliot with a touch of Graham Greene.

Thus language and literature were taking us further and further   13
from ourselves to other selves, from our world to other worlds.

What was the colonial system doing to us Kenyan children? What   14
were the consequences of, on the other hand, this systematic suppression of our languages and the literature they carried, and on the other the elevation of English and the literature it carried? To answer those questions, let me first examine the relationship of language to human experience, human culture, and the human perception of reality.

*   *   *

Language, any language, has a dual character: it is both a means of   15
communication and a carrier of culture. Take English. It is spoken in
Britain and in Sweden and Denmark. But for Swedish and Danish
people English is only a means of communication with non-Scandina-
vians. It is not a carrier of their culture. For the British, and particularly
the English, it is additionally, and inseparably from its use as a tool of
communication, a carrier of their culture and history. Or take Swahili
in East and Central Africa. It is widely used as a means of communication across many nationalities. But it is not the carrier of a culture and
history of many of those nationalities. However in parts of Kenya and
Tanzania, and particularly in Zanzibar, Swahili is inseparably both a
means of communication and a carrier of the culture of those people
to whom it is a mother-tongue.

Language as communication has three aspects or elements. There   16
is first what Karl Marx once called the language of real life, the
element basic to the whole notion of language, its origins and development: that is, the relations people enter into with one another in the
labour process, the links they necessarily establish among themselves
in the act of a people, a community of human beings, producing
wealth or means of life like food, clothing, houses. A human community really starts its historical being as a community of co-operation in
production through the division of labour; the simplest is between
man, woman and child within a household; the more complex divisions are between branches of production such as those who are sole
hunters, sole gatherers of fruits or sole workers in metal. Then there
are the most complex divisions such as those in modern factories
where a single product, say a shirt or a shoe, is the result of many hands
and minds. Production is co-operation, is communication, is language,
is expression of a relaxation between human beings and it is specifically human.

The second aspect of language as communication is speech and it   17
imitates the language of real life, that is communication in production.
The verbal signposts both reflect and aid communication or the relations established between human beings in the production of their
means of life. Language as a system of verbal signposts makes that
production possible. The spoken word is to relations between human
beings what the hand is to the relations between human beings
and nature. The hand through tools mediates between human
beings and nature and forms the language of real life: spoken
words mediate between human beings and form the language of
speech.

The third aspect is the written signs. The written word imitates   18
the spoken. Where the first two aspects of language as communication
through the hand and the spoken word historically evolved more or
less simultaneously, the written aspect is a much later historical devel-

opment. Writing is representation of sounds with visual symbols, from the simplest knot among shepherds to tell the number in a herd or the hieroglyphics among the Agĩkũyũ gicaandi singers and poets of Kenya, to the most complicated and different letter and picture writing systems of the world today.

In most societies the written and the spoken languages are the   19
same, in that they represent each other: what is on paper can be read to another person and be received as that language which the recipient has grown up speaking. In such a society there is broad harmony for a child between the three aspects of language as communication. His interaction with nature and with other men is expressed in written and spoken symbols or signs which are both a result of that double interaction and a reflection of it. The association of the child's sensibility is with the language of his experience of life.

But there is more to it: communication between human beings is   20
also the basis and process of evolving culture. In doing similar kinds of things and actions over and over again under similar circumstances, similar even in their mutability, certain patterns, moves, rhythms, habits, attitudes, experiences and knowledge emerge. Those experiences are handed over to the next generation and become the inherited basis for their further actions on nature and on themselves. There is a gradual accumulation of values which in time become almost self-evident truths governing their conception of what is right and wrong, good and bad, beautiful and ugly, courageous and cowardly, generous and mean in their internal and external relations. Over a time this becomes a way of life distinguishable from other ways of life. They develop a distinctive culture and history. Culture embodies those moral, ethical and aesthetic values, the set of spiritual eyeglasses, through which they come to view themselves and their place in the universe. Values are the basis of a people's identity, their sense of particularity as members of the human race. All this is carried by language. Language as culture is the collective memory bank of a people's experience in history. Culture is almost indistinguishable from the language that makes possible its genesis, growth, banking, articulation and indeed its transmission from one generation to the next.

Language as culture also has three important aspects. Culture is a   21
product of the history which it in turn reflects. Culture in other words is a product and a reflection of human beings communicating with one another in the very struggle to create wealth and to control it. But culture does not merely reflect that history, or rather it does so by actually forming images or pictures of the world of nature and nurture. Thus the second aspect of language as culture is as an image-forming

agent in the mind of a child. Our whole conception of ourselves as a people, individually and collectively, is based on those pictures and images which may or may not correctly correspond to the actual reality of the struggles with nature and nurture which produced them in the first place. But our capacity to confront the world creatively is dependent on how those images correspond or not to that reality, how they distort or clarify the reality of our struggles. Language as culture is thus mediating between me and my own self; between my own self and other selves; between me and nature. Language is mediating in my very being. And this brings us to the third aspect of language as culture. Culture transmits or imparts those images of the world and reality through the spoken and the written language, that is through a specific language. In other words, the capacity to speak, the capacity to order sounds in a manner that makes for mutual comprehension between human beings is universal. This is the universality of language, a quality specific to human beings. It corresponds to the universality of the struggle against nature and that between human beings. But the particularity of the sounds, the words, the word order into phrases and sentences, and the specific manner, or laws, of their ordering is what distinguishes one language from another. Thus a specific culture is not transmitted through language in its universality but in its particularity as the language of a specific community with a specific history. Written literature and orature are the main means by which a particular language transmits the images of the world contained in the culture it carries.

22 Language as communication and as culture are then products of each other. Communication creates culture: culture is a means of communication. Language carries culture, and culture carries, particularly through orature and literature, the entire body of values by which we come to perceive ourselves and our place in the world. How people perceive themselves affects how they look at their culture, at their politics and at the social production of wealth, at their entire relationship to nature and to other beings. Language is thus inseparable from ourselves as a community of human beings with a specific form and character, a specific history, a specific relationship to the world.

23 So what was the colonialist imposition of a foreign language doing to us children?

24 The real aim of colonialism was to control the people's wealth: what they produced, how they produced it, and how it was distributed; to control, in other words, the entire realm of the language of real life. Colonialism imposed its control of the social production of

wealth through military conquest and subsequent political dictatorship. But its most important area of domination was the mental universe of the colonised, the control, through culture, of how people
perceived themselves and their relationship to the world. Economic
and political control can never be complete or effective without mental control. To control a people's culture is to control their tools of
self-definition in relationship to others.

For colonialism this involved two aspects of the same process: 25
the destruction or the deliberate undervaluing of a people's culture,
their art, dances, religions, history, geography, education, orature and
literature, and the conscious elevation of the language of the coloniser. The domination of a people's language by the languages of the
colonising nations was crucial to the domination of the mental universe of the colonised.

Take language as communication. Imposing a foreign language,   26
and suppressing the native languages as spoken and written, were
already breaking the harmony previously existing between the African
child and the three aspects of language. Since the new language as a
means of communication was a product of and was reflecting the 'real
language of life' elsewhere, it could never as spoken or written prop-
erly reflect or imitate the real life of that community. This may in part
explain why technology always appears to us as slightly external, *their*
product and not *ours*. The word 'missile' used to hold an alien faraway sound until I recently learnt its equivalent in Gĩkũyũ, *nguru-
kuhi*, and it made me apprehend it differently. Learning, for a colonial
child, became a cerebral activity and not an emotionally felt experience.

But since the new, imposed languages could never completely   27
break the native languages as spoken, their most effective area of
domination was the third aspect of language as communication, the
written. The language of an African child's formal education was foreign. The language of the books he read was foreign. The language of
his conceptualisation was foreign. Thought, in him, took the visible
form of a foreign language. So the written language of a child's upbringing in the school (even his spoken language within the school
compound) became divorced from his spoken language at home.
There was often not the slightest relationship between the child's
written world, which was also the language of his schooling, and the
world of his immediate environment in the family and the community.
For a colonial child, the harmony existing between the three aspects of
language as communication was irrevocably broken. This resulted in
the disassociation of the sensibility of that child from his natural and
social environment, what we might call colonial alienation. The alien-

ation became reinforced in the teaching of history, geography, music, where bourgeois Europe was always the centre of the universe.

This disassociation, divorce, or alienation from the immediate environment becomes clearer when you look at colonial language as a carrier of culture.   28

Since culture is a product of the history of a people which it in turn reflects, the child was now being exposed exclusively to a culture that was a product of a world external to himself. He was being made to stand outside himself to look at himself.   29

Since culture does not just reflect the world in images but actually, through those very images, conditions a child to see that world in a certain way, the colonial child was made to see the world and where he stands in it as seen and defined by or reflected in the culture of the language of imposition.   30

And since those images are mostly passed on through orature and literature it meant the child would now only see the world as seen in the literature of his language of adoption. From the point of view of alienation, that is of seeing oneself from outside oneself as if one was another self, it does not matter that the imported literature carried the great humanist tradition of the best in Shakespeare, Goethe, Balzac, Tolstoy, Gorky, Brecht, Sholokhov, Dickens. The location of this great mirror of imagination was necessarily Europe and its history and culture and the rest of the universe was seen from that centre.   31

But obviously it was worse when the colonial child was exposed to images of his world as mirrored in the written languages of his coloniser. Where his own native languages were associated in his impressionable mind with low status, humiliation, corporal punishment, slow-footed intelligence and ability or downright stupidity, non-intelligibility and barbarism, this was reinforced by the world he met in the works of such geniuses of racism as a Rider Haggard or a Nicholas Monsarrat; not to mention the pronouncement of some of the giants of western intellectual and political establishment, such as Hume ('. . . the negro is naturally inferior to the whites . . .'), Thomas Jefferson ('. . . the blacks . . . are inferior to the whites on the endowments of both body and mind . . .'), or Hegel with his Africa comparable to a land of childhood still enveloped in the dark mantle of the night as far as the development of self-conscious history was concerned. Hegel's statement that there was nothing harmonious with humanity to be found in the African character is representative of the racist images of Africans and Africa such a colonial child was bound to encounter in the literature of the colonial languages. The results could be disastrous.   32

EXERCISES

Words to Know

extended family (paragraph 1), innovative (3), cunning (3), prey (3), outwit (3), hostile (3), drought (3), ogres (4), inflection (5), nuances (6), lexical (6), deference (8), corporal punishment (9), lucrative (9), apartheid (11), demarcation (11), apex (11), elitist (11), coveted (11), orature (12), vied (12), Karl Marx (16), sole (16), hieroglyphics (18), sensibility (19), evolving (20), mutability (20), man (20), embodies (20), aesthetic (20), particularity (20), collective memory bank (20), genesis (20), nurture (21), mediating (21), universality (21), cerebral (26), conceptualization (27), irrevocably (27), disassociation (27), alienation (27), bourgeois (27), imposition (30), impressionable (32), non-intelligibility (32), barbarism (32).

Some of the Issues

1. Examine the animal stories Ngugi tells about in paragraph 3. With whom do the storytellers and their listeners identify? What are the lessons the listeners are likely to learn?
2. Do you know any similar animal stories or fairytales? Do they differ in their message from the Gĩkũyũ stories?
3. What are the themes of the stories about humans that Ngugi describes in paragraph 4?
4. In paragraph 6 Ngugi repeatedly refers to the "suggestive magical power" of language. What is the place of language in his early life?
5. How was the use of English enforced in the school sytem?
6. What is the "dual character" of language (paragraph 15)? For whom is it merely a means of communication? For whom also a carrier of culture?
7. Among the "three aspects or elements" of language as communication that Ngugi cites in paragraph 16, the first he calls, after Karl Marx, "the language of real life." What does that phrase mean? Does it mean something we ordinarily would call language?
8. How does Ngugi define culture and cultural values in paragraph 20? How are they related to language and communication?
9. How does Ngugi sum up the reciprocal relationship of language as culture and as communication?
10. What according to Ngugi was "the real aim of colonialism" (paragraph 24)?
11. What role did the colonizer's language play in establishing control (paragraphs 24 – 26)?

* 12. Read Robert McCrum, William Cran, and Robert MacNeil's "World Language: English." It presents a different view of the role of English as a second language. What are the arguments for the use of English developed in that essay? How do they relate to Ngugi's view?

The Way We Are Told

13. Ngugi's essay is concerned with language. Yet the first paragraph does not introduce that topic but speaks of family and community. Why is that relevant?
14. In the essay two paragraphs — 13 and 23 — stand out because each of them consists of only one short sentence. What is the function of each?

Some Subjects for Essays

15. In a statement prefacing his book *Decolonizing the Mind*, Ngugi says that it will be his last work in English and that his future writing will be in Gĩkũyũ and Kiswahili. Examine the advantages and disadvantages in this step he intends to take.
* 16. Read Richard Rodriguez's "Public and Private Language." Ngugi, in discussing the divorce between the language of home and school (paragraph 27), makes the same distinction as Rodriguez. However, each of them comes to a different conclusion as to the meaning of that split. In an essay present their respective conclusions and explain how and why they reach them.

ACKNOWLEDGMENTS

Agueros, Jack. "Halfway to Dick and Jane" by Jack Agueros, copyright © 1971 by Doubleday, a division of Bantam Doubleday Dell Publishing Group, Inc. From *The Immigrant Experience* by Thomas Wheeler. Used by permission of the publisher.

Angelou, Maya. "Graduation" from *I Know Why the Caged Bird Sings* by Maya Angelou. Copyright © 1969 by Maya Angelou. Reprinted by permission of Random House Inc.

Arlen, Michael J. Excerpt from "Three Views of Women" from *The View from Highway 1* by Michael J. Arlen. Copyright © 1974, 1975, 1976 by Michael J. Arlen. Originally appeared in *The New Yorker*. Reprinted by permission of Farrar, Straus and Giroux, Inc.

Atwood, Margaret. "Canadians: What Do They Want?" by Margaret Atwood. Reprinted with permission from *Mother Jones* magazine. Copyright © 1982, Foundation for National Progress.

Bellah, Robert N. et al. "American Individualism" from *Habits of the Heart* by Robert N. Bellah, Richard Madsen, William M. Sullivan, Ann Swidler, and Steven M. Tipton. Copyright © 1985 by The Regents of the University of California. Reprinted by permission of the University of California Press.

Bohannon, Laura. "Shakespeare in the Bush" from *Natural History*, August/September, 1966, Vol. 75, No. 7, by Dr. Laura Bohannon. Reprinted by permission of the author.

Brooks, Gwendolyn. "We Real Cool" by Gwendolyn Brooks. Taken from *Blacks*, copyright 1987. Published by The David Co., Chicago. Reprinted by permission of the author.

Bruchac, Joseph. "Ellis Island" by Joseph Bruchac. Reprinted by permission of the author.

Buruma, Ian. "Work as a Form of Beauty" by Ian Buruma. Excerpt from *Tokyo: Form and Spirit* by Ian Buruma. Reprinted by permission of the author.

Campa, Arthur L. "Anglo vs. Chicano: Why?" in *Western Review*, 1972. Copyright © 1972. Reprinted by permission of Mrs. Arthur L. Campa.

Claiborne, Robert. "A Wasp Stings Back." Copyright © 1974 by Robert Claiborne. All rights reserved. Reprinted by permission.

Cooke, Alistair. "The Huddled Masses." From *Alistair Cooke's America* by Alistair Cooke. Copyright © 1973 by Alistair Cooke. Reprinted by permission of Alfred A. Knopf, Inc.

Cross, Donna Woolfolk. "Sin, Suffer and Repent." Reprinted by permission of the Putnam Publishing Group from *Media Speak: How Television Makes Up Your Mind* by Donna Woolfolk Cross. Copyright © 1983 by Donna Woolfolk Cross.

Cullen, Countee. "Incident," from the book *On These I Stand* by Countee Cullen. Reprinted by permission of GRM Associates, Inc., agents for the Estate of Ida M. Cullen. Copyright © 1925 by Harper & Brothers; copyright renewed 1953 by Ida M. Cullen.

de Jesus, Carolina Maria. "Diary," by Carolina Maria de Jesus. From *Child of the Dark* by Carolina Maria de Jesus. Copyright © 1962. Reprinted by permission of the publisher, Dutton, an imprint of New American Library, a division of Penguin Books USA, Inc.

Deloria, Vine, Jr. *Custer Died for Your Sins*. Reprinted with permission of Macmillan Publishing Company from *Custer Died for Your Sins* by Vine Deloria, Jr. Copyright © 1969 Vine Deloria, Jr.

Dorris, Michael. *For the Indians, No Thanksgiving*. Copyright © Michael Dorris 1989. From the *Chicago Tribune*, November 24, 1988. Reprinted with permission.

Ehrenreich, Barbara and Annette Fuentes. "Life on the Global Assembly Line." Reprinted from *Ms* magazine, June, 1981. Barbara Ehrenreich is a freelance writer based in New York.

Fallows, James. "Immigration: How It's Affecting Us," by James Fallows. Reprinted from *The Atlantic* magazine, November, 1983. Reprinted with the author's permission.

Farb, Peter. "How to Talk About the World." From *Word Play: What Happens When People Talk* by Peter Farb. Copyright © 1973 by Peter Farb. Reprinted by permission of Alfred A. Knopf, Inc.

Giovanni, Nikki. "They Clapped." From *My House* by Nikki Giovanni. Copyright © 1972 by Nikki Giovanni. Reprinted by permission of William Morrow & Co.

Hall, Edward T. "Private Space." Excerpts from *The Hidden Dimension* by Edward T. Hall, copyright © 1966 by Edward T. Hall. Used by permission of Doubleday, a division of Bantam, Doubleday, Dell Publishing Group, Inc.

Harrington, Michael. "The Invisible Poor." Reprinted with permission of Macmillan Publishing Company from *The Other America* by Michael Harrington. Copyright © 1962 by Michael Harrington.

Hines, William. "Hello, Judy. I'm Dr. Smith." Reprinted with permission from *Chicago Sun Times*/1990.

Houston, Jeanne Wakatsuki and James D. Houston. "Shikata Ga Nai" from *Farewell to Manazar* by Jeanne Wakatsuki Houston and James D. Houston. Copyright © 1973 by James D. Houston. Reprinted by permission of Houghton Mifflin Company.

Howard, Jane. "Families," by Jane Howard. Copyright © 1978 by Jane Howard. Reprinted by permission of Simon & Schuster, Inc.

Illich, Ivan. "Effects of Development." Reprinted with permission from *The New York Review of Books*. Copyright © 1969 Nyrev, Inc.

Johnson, James Weldon. "Lift Ev'ry Voice and Sing," song in Maya Angelou, *I Know Why the Caged Birds Sing*. Used by permission.

Kazin, Alfred. Excerpt from "The Kitchen" in *A Walker in the City*, copyright 1951 and renewed 1979 by Alfred Kazin, reprinted by permission of Harcourt Brace Jovanovich, Inc.

Kingston, Maxine Hong. "Girlhood Among Ghosts." From *The Woman Warrior: Memoirs of a Girlhood Among Ghosts* by Maxine Hong Kingston. Copyright © 1975, 1976 by Maxine Hong Kingston. Reprinted by permission of Alfred A. Knopf, Inc.

Kluckhohn, Clyde. "Customs," by Clyde Kluckhohn from *Mirror for Man*. Reprinted with permission.

Knepler, Myrna. "Sold at Fine Stores, Naturellement," in *Verbatim*, February, 1978. Copyright © 1978 by *Verbatim*, Vol. 4, No. 4. Permission granted by the publisher.

Kottak, Conrad Phillip. "Swimming in Cross-Cultural Currents." Used with permission from *Natural History*, May, 1985; copyright the American Museum of Natural History, 1985.

Lakoff, Robin. "You Are What You Say." From *Ms* magazine, July, 1974. Reprinted by permission.

Mabry, Marcus. "Living in Two Worlds." From *Newsweek on Campus* April, 1988. Copyright © 1988, Newsweek, Inc. All rights reserved. Reprinted by permission.

Malcolm X. "Hair." From *The Autobiography of Malcolm X* by Malcolm X, with the assistance of Alex Haley. Copyright © 1964 by Alex Haley and Malcolm X. Copyright © 1965 by Alex Haley and Betty Shabazz. Reprinted by permission of Random House, Inc.

McCrum, Robert, William Cran, Robert MacNeil. "World Language: English." From *The Story of English* by Robert McCrum, William Cran, and Robert MacNeil. Copyright © Robert McCrum, William Cran, and Robert MacNeil, 1986. All rights reserved. Reprinted by permission of Viking Penguin, a division of Penguin Books USA, Inc.

Miner, Horace. "Body Ritual Among the Nacirema." Reproduced by permission of the American Anthropological Association from *American Anthropologist* 58:3, 1956. Not for further reproduction.

Montagu, Ashley. "American Men Don't Cry," by Ashley Montagu. Reprinted by permission of the *New York Times* and the author.

Morley, John David. "Living in a Japanese Home." From the book, *Pictures*

AUTHOR/TITLE INDEX